Cognitive psychology

International Library of Psychology

General editor: Max Coltheart
Professor of Psychology, University of London

Cognitive psychology
New directions

Edited by

Guy Claxton

Routledge & Kegan Paul
London, Boston and Henley

First published in 1980
by Routledge & Kegan Paul Ltd
39 Store Street, London WC1E 7DD,
9 Park Street, Boston, Mass. 02108, USA and
Broadway House, Newtown Road,
Henley-on-Thames, Oxon RG9 1EN

Set in 10 on 12 Baskerville
and printed in Great Britain by
Lowe & Brydone Printers Ltd, Thetford, Norfolk

British Library Cataloguing in Publication Data

Cognitive psychology.

(International library of psychology).
1. Cognition
I. Claxton, Guy II. Series
153.4   BF311   79-41758

ISBN 0 7100 0485 0
ISBN 0 7100 0486 9 Pbk

For the teachers who provoked me
Michael Shayer
Colin Blakemore
Alan Watson
and Anne Treisman

Contents

1 Cognitive psychology: a suitable case for what sort of treatment?
  Guy Claxton   1

2 Patterns and actions: cognitive mechanisms are content-specific
  D. Alan Allport   26

3 Actions: the mechanisms of motor control
  Nigel Harvey and Kerry Greer   65

4 Attention and performance
  D. Alan Allport   112

5 Developing the concept of working memory
  Graham J. Hitch   154

6 Remembering and understanding
  Guy Claxton   197

7 Psycholinguistics: cognitive aspects of human communication
  David W. Green   236

8 Thinking: experiential and information processing approaches
  Jonathan St B. T. Evans   275

9 Cross-cultural perspectives on cognition
  H. Valerie Curran   300

  Index   335

The authors and the publishers are grateful to Holt, Rinehart & Winston, Inc., C . V. Mosby, Co., the Academic Press and the editor of the *Psychological Review* for permission to reproduce diagrams.

Contributors

D. Alan Allport
Department of Psychology, University of Reading

Guy L. Claxton
Centre for Science Education, Chelsea College, University of London

H. Valerie Curran
Department of Child Development and Educational Psychology, University of London Institute of Education

Jonathan St B. T. Evans
School of Behavioural and Social Science, Plymouth Polytechnic

Kerry Greer
Department of Physiology, University College London

David W. Green
Department of Psychology, University College London

Nigel Harvey
Department of Psychology, University College London

Graham J. Hitch
Department of Psychology, University of Manchester

There are good reasons to expect, in the coming decades, a return to a concreteness of basic ideas, to simpler fundamentals easily understood, to principles that will bring exact science closer to the human person.

Lancelot Law Whyte

The motor individual is driven from two sources. The world around it and its own lesser world within. It can be regarded as a system which in virtue of its arrangement does a number of things and is so constructed that the world outside touches triggers for their doing. But its own internal condition has a say as to which of those things, within limits, it will do, and how it will do them.

Sir Charles Sherrington

Only to the degree that there is (a) detailed, working model of general memory and its use can language behaviour and most other cognitive processing ever be understood by psychologists.

Quillian

Scientia difficultatem facit
(The theory creates the difficulties)

Quintilian

1 Cognitive psychology: a suitable case for what sort of treatment?

Guy Claxton

> I saw a man clothed with rags, standing in a certain place,
> with his face from his own house, a book in his hand, and a
> great burden on his back. I looked, and saw him open the
> book and read therein; and as he read he wept and trembled:
> and not being able longer to contain, he broke out with a
> lamentable cry, saying: 'What shall I *do*?'.
>
> John Bunyan, *The Pilgrim's Progress*

Imagine a student – perhaps yourself – approaching 'cognitive psychology'. Probably you have some expectations: it's quite new and exciting – fast moving, full of experiments and theories; it doesn't have much to do with feelings or needs — but that doesn't matter because they're covered somewhere else in the course; whatever it is it's a lot better than boring old S-R psychology, because it talks about things that are of interest to you in a language that makes a lot more sense than old-fashioned, simplistic ideas like 'stimulus', 'response', 'reinforcement', and 'association'; perhaps it's something to do with how the mind works, how the human nervous system comes to represent the world and its events so that it can respond easily and effectively to demands made on it. You might reasonably expect cognitive psychology to be about the intellectual processes of normal adults; and you're a normal adult, with better intellectual processes than most people of the same age; so it ought to have something meaningful to tell you. Oughtn't it?

What do you actually find when you enter the library armed with your (probably) enormous reading list? Let's have a look at one particular paper. It describes an experiment by Allan Collins and

1

Ross Quillian and is called 'Retrieval time from semantic memory', published in the *Journal of Verbal Learning and Verbal Behavior* in 1969. This is the authors' abstract for the paper:

To ascertain the truth of a sentence such as 'A canary can fly', people utilize long-term memory. Consider two possible organizations of this memory. First, people might store with each kind of bird that flies (e.g. canary) the fact that it can fly. Then they could retrieve this fact directly to decide the sentence is true. An alternative organization would be to store only the generalization that *birds* can fly, and to infer that 'A canary can fly' from the stored information that a canary is a bird and birds can fly. The latter organization is much more economical in terms of storage space but should require longer retrieval times when such inferences are necessary. The results of a true-false reaction-time task were found to support the latter hypotheses about memory organization.

If this economical model of memory is true, people should be able to answer questions like 'Is a canary yellow?' more quickly than 'Can canaries fly?', and 'Can canaries fly?' more quickly than 'Do canaries have skin?' – the latter requiring the further inference that birds are animals, and animals have skin. This is essentially what Collins and Quillian found.

After going through the paper – and a few others, with titles like 'Processing time as influenced by the number of elements in a visual display', 'Inter-aural attention shifting as response', 'Short-term retention of individual verbal items' and 'Unlearning, spontaneous recovery, and the partial-reinforcement effect in paired-associate learning' – you may already have become so immersed in the detail and its unfamiliar language that your own cognitive state is one of confusion and your affective state tinged with a vague disappointment that you have not seen yourself reflected from the pages of the journals as you had half dared to hope. I remember my own feelings of being overwhelmed by detail when first meeting cognitive psychology: I felt as if driven into the middle of a large wood blindfold, and left to make sense of it. The intention behind this book is not just to dump you there, but to drop you in by parachute in daylight, so that, on the way down, you have a brief opportunity to survey the whole wood and to orient yourself in it. This has meant digging out of cognitive psychology as many of the implicit attitudes and constraints as we could, and exposing them to you, so that you have an idea of the paradigms – the 'rules of the game' – that determine the public face of cognitive psychology.

One of these rules concerns the disparity between the public and private aspects—between the contents of the journals and the agonizing that goes on over coffee. I think it is fair to say that most researchers are aware of the presuppositions that I shall mention, and their attendant problems, but feel that if one were to become too introspective, no research would be done at all, and that, however flawed the current approach, it is a great deal more valuable than doing nothing. This attitude was expressed in a heated riposte to the first draft of this Introduction by a friend of mine, Stephen Monsell, that provides a somewhat cynical echo of Christian's despairing cry with which I started. 'A leisured adolescent', he wrote, 'observing a group of adults going about their tedious and difficult everyday tasks, diligently and conscientiously, but afflicted with the normal human failings, suddenly shouts: "My God, you're all so *stupid*, so *uptight*, so *competitive*, so *silly*. Why can't you let it all hang out and really *live*, really get behind some *experiencing?*". To which the weary answer as they pause momentarily (but only momentarily) in their tasks, comes: "OK, kid, show us".'

To start with, this look at cognitive psychology *is* somewhat critical, but this is a necessarily negative prelude to the more important and constructive business of suggesting improvement. We shall all have a shot at 'showing you'.

Of course, the fact that the cognitive psychological journals are full of detail is not in itself a bad thing. Any healthy science thrives on a diet of detail. The difference lies in the purpose of the detail: to what use is the data put? In the day-to-day research in physics, for example, details are collected to settle points of detail. The proto-typical study is not another, Millikan oil-drop experiment, or a Michelson-Morley; the 'big' issues which these helped to resolve eighty years ago are taken as read. Authors may disagree about what the picture of the sub-atomic world implicit in the mathematics of quantum mechanics or in the special theory of relativity means 'in words', but about the tools there is, for the moment, a wide consensus. Not so in psychology, where the majority of studies try to infer grand conceptions from minutiae. Newell (1973) for example, says: 'Far from providing the rungs of a ladder by which psychology gradually climbs to clarity, this form of conceptual structure (i.e. predominantly phenomenon-driven and dichotomy-testing) leads rather to an ever-increasing pile of issues, which we weary of, or become diverted from, but never really settle.' Instead of a healthy organism feeding and growing on this diet of research, psychology sometimes seems to be suffocating in a mountain of food.

Many researchers, as I say, are aware of many of the problems this book raises. Similar doubts have been aired recently by Allan Newell in the paper from which I have just quoted, 'You can't play Twenty Questions with Nature and win' (1973), by Ulric Neisser in *Cognition and Reality* (1976), and others. But it is, I think, a mistake to ignore these issues in the hope that they will go away. If taken to heart they lead, as Alan Allport and I try to show in this and the next chapter, to a different way of doing cognitive psychology that is as clear as, and more productive than, the *modus operandi* that the current public face assumes. There is a growing world of private uncertainty that lies behind the predominantly sleek assurance of the journals. It is that uncertainty which this and the following chapter investigate. The way I shall do this is to scrutinize just one paper – the one by Collins and Quillian – to see what it tells us about the state of cognitive psychology.

First, let us look at its methodology. Collins and Quillian's paper is about retrieval time: measuring reaction times is now one of the most popular activities of cognitive psychologists. Before cognitive psychology was really born, results were mostly in terms of success, rather than speed. The difficulty of tasks was varied, how well subjects did was measured, and inferences were made about the size of hypothetical memory stores, or the limits of perceptual acuity. The rationale of many studies from this period was to infer the nature of cognition by testing its limits, as Wittgenstein tried to infer the nature of language by looking at what could and what could not be said. But limits started to go out of style, technology improved, and it became easy and fashionable to take speed, rather than errors as the variable of prime interest. Thus at present we have the major chronometric traditions of Posner (1969), for example, in pattern recognition, of Sternberg (1969a) in short-term memory, of Collins and Quillian themselves, and their imitators, in long-term memory, and so on.

There is, of course, a relationship between speed and accuracy (itself well-researched by authors such as Rabbitt, 1966), but the increased emphasis on latency seems a healthy one. If you push people's performance far enough in any direction, you will find limits;

but the way that performance is controlled, the processses that are important, may be quite different from those that are operating in *unstressed* situations. Deprived of air for long enough people will die. You can measure the effect of drug A versus drug B on breathing by administering them to people and seeing, if you deprive them of air, who dies first. But this only tells you about the relative effects of the two drugs on asphyxiating people: it need tell you nothing about the control of breathing in those lucky enough to have an adequate supply of oxygen. Likewise, to demonstrate that people's ability to rehearse things under their breath is limited, and to show that the limit depends on whether the things they are required to remember are letters or words, or presented visually or auditorily, does *not* establish the existence of a 'short-term memory store', 'primary memory', or whatever, which must be written in to all subsequent models of mental processing. The fact that there are limits to short-term retention in some circumstances does not mean that a model accounting for those limits must be invoked in *all* circumstances. That is as mistaken a piece of logic as saying that I must know how long people can go without air before I can begin to explain how they read. On rare occasions these limits are relevant; on most they are absolutely not. Furthermore, in order to watch how people work at their limits requires them to make mistakes, and the occurrence of errors may itself alter the way they perform a task. The correction of an error, for example, or the performance that immediately follows a detected mistake may well be qualitatively different from error-free performance. Allport has suggested (in his chapter on attention) that while two concurrent tasks may not interfere with each other when both are running smoothly, they may compete for a *common* mechanism of error-detection and correction, and thus appear to conflict when both are working near the limit.

On the face of it, measuring time rather than errors avoids this pitfall. However, it is not quite so simple, for in most latency experiments subjects are requested 'to respond as quickly as you can without making any mistakes'. For example Collins and Quillian say 'The subject was instructed to press one button if the sentence was generally true, and the other button if it was generally false, and he was told to do so as accurately and as quickly as possible.' The rationale for this is clear enough: it gives neater data. If people are trying to be as quick and accurate as possible, their performance will be more consistent, they won't allow themselves to be distracted by the experimenter's legs or the thought of dinner, the variance of their response times will be smaller, and the likelihood of achieving the Statistically Significant Effect required for publication is greater. The subject's major task becomes coping with this demand, rather than processing the 'stimuli' in a 'normal' way. If you have ever been a subject in one of these experiments you will know the truth of this: one's mental processes are highly task-specific, like trying to guess the next question, having bets with oneself about how many more questions there are, trying to work out what the point of the experiment is, getting cross with oneself for making a mistake, worrying about whether one is doing as well as other people, or trying to keep one's eyes open.

There is, let me emphasize, a perfectly legitimate place for a cognitive psychology of how people operate near their limits: as Stephen Monsell pointed out, this kind of performance is required of all kinds of people from typists to welders, tennis stars to dentists. But it is not the only, or even the most common kind of performance. Even Chris Evert Lloyd and Oscar Peterson spend most of their time doing things where their perception, attention and understanding are *not* accompanied by any feelings of intention, effort or haste. And there is a vacancy for a psychology of *relaxed* cognition.

A common argument is that special strategies will somehow 'even out' over subjects, but this isn't so. For any experimental task there is a strategy that most people tend to arrive at (there may be two or three perhaps), that supplements, or even overlies, the particular structural feature or processing habit that the experimenter is out to investigate. The semantic memory studies sparked off by Collins and Quillian are a good case in point. In 1969 they presented a nice clear issue. 'We propose,' they said, 'that semantic memory is organized as a hierarchy of concepts, with only those features being attached to each concept which distinguish it from its superordinate class. If this is so, then these predictions follow.' And sure enough the predictions were confirmed. What followed, in fact, was a succession of papers demonstrating that their results said nothing directly about 'the structure of semantic memory' but were highly specific to both the particular task (e.g., Meyer, 1970), and the particular material (Wilkins, 1971; Conrad, 1972; Rips *et al.*, 1973) they had originally selected. It is little exaggeration to say that we are no more able to identify either general structural features, or general processing habits in 1979 than we were in 1969.

One other practical feature is connected with measuring reaction time: researchers do not always attempt to say how the time is spent. What matters is the Statistically Significant Difference between the times taken to process A and B. The absolute magnitudes of the times – they range from 100 milliseconds or less up to several seconds – and size of the difference, are often not discussed. While we are a long way from relating the temporal characteristics of the nervous system to decision times in cognitive tasks, I believe there are some bridges being built that might allow some speculative interpretations of total reaction time data.

There are some models around – the ACT system of John Anderson, for example, that I discuss in Chapter 6 – that attempts to make quantitative predictions about reaction time. But these are usually based on mathematical calculations that predict some aspects of the data of a given experiment from other values that have been obtained in the same, or very similar experiments. Cognitive psychology still lacks a general rationale for estimating the magnitude, or even the order of magnitude of task durations. Collins and Quillian's sentence verification task takes between one and one-and-a-half seconds: nowhere in their paper is there any indication of where that time goes, apart from the critical seventy-five millisecond difference between conditions. Yet it ought to be possible to pool results from studies of word recognition and of syntactic processing with those of sentence comprehension and verification to build up an overall picture of how the hypothetical sub-processes are integrated within a particular overall task. That this usually doesn't happen is symptomatic of a general worry about cognitive psychology to which we will return in more detail later: by and large researchers are extremely parochial in their attitudes to other related areas within the study of cognition, and even to other theoretical and methodological approaches within the same specific problem field.

The quality and quantity of subjects used in cognitive psychological experiments are worth noting: Collins and Quillian used employees of Bolt, Beranek and Newman; Bell Labs. use high-school students; Oxford and Cambridge (England) mostly use housewives. But it is probably still true that the majority of subjects are undergraduates. And the majority of those – one estimate in 98 per cent – are psychology students. While this should be remarked on, I am less ready to condemn it than some other critics seem to be. I am partly persuaded by the argument that undergraduates are (presumably) good at the kinds of things that cognitive psychologists study, and they are therefore the natural population to test. If I were interested in football, I would study footballers, not civil servants. As I am interested in intellectual skills, I study students, not sheet-metal workers, dockers, or dinner ladies. However, if I wish my hypotheses, based on students, to be applicable to the human race, I must, eventually, try them out on some different samples of people. When this has been done, the perspective it has provided has been most instructive, and sometimes surprising. The chapter on cross-cultural cognition, by Valerie Curran, I take to be one of the most important in this book, from the point of view of the title, ' Cognitive Psychology: New Directions'. It demonstrates just how culturally relative many of the basic assumptions of current cognitive psychology are. (The special problem with testing *psychology* students is the fact that they know, or can guess something about what's going on in an experiment, and this may influence their performance.)

Incidentally, the numbers of subjects used are typically rather small. Eight to twelve is common, though in one of the three experiments that Collins and Quillian report only three subjects produced usable data. I know that the statistics are supposed to take account of this, but still three Americans (of unspecified age and experience) seems a mite inadequate as a sample from which to draw conclusions about humanity.

These nineteen subjects (two lots of eight and one of three) were not, apparently, given any practice. Usually in reaction-time studies subjects are given a lot of practice, and the data from this is discarded. So not only are the subjects drawn from a small section of the population, they are given plenty of time to select that way of performing the task that most successfully meets its particular demands. This is another good reason for believing that laboratory results may not correspond at all closely to the different ways of operating that people have evolved in their everyday lives. On the other hand, if, like Collins and Quillian's subjects, people's performance is tested without any practice, the data shows them in a transitional state: they are learning how best to do the task. Sometimes this learning may be quick, with tasks that are familiar, or with experienced 'professional' subjects. At other times it may be very gradual. Allport suggests in his chapter on attention, for instance, that the requirement to do two things at once may be met by slowly altering the set of processes involved in each so that any individual processes for which the two tasks compete can be dropped. Practice in this case is similar to what happens when a proficient squash player takes up tennis: he has to learn what can usefully be transferred from one to the other, and what can not. And this may take months.

In general, cognitive psychology has been surprisingly little concerned with *learning* that changes process and capacity, focussing instead on the demonstration of processes and structures that are supposed to remain unaltered by the experiment, or on learning in the sense of acquiring new knowledge that changes content (you 'know' more) but not process (you cannot 'do' more).

A further methodological characteristic of the field, not ubiquitous but far too prevalent, is the rather casual way in which people treat their own data. Aspects may be ignored, or presented with some *post hoc* excuse, if they happen not to fit their author's expectations. Collins and Quillian provide us with relatively mild examples of each. 'Error rates were on the average about 8% and tended to increase where RT increased', is stated without any comment on the correlation of speed and accuracy. Sometimes people get worse as they get faster: here they got worse as they got slower. The fact that there are all sorts of reasons, some of them quite plausible, why, *in this task,* speed and accuracy should correlate positively doesn't excuse the authors' failure to discuss them. Had they thought about this, apparently minor, feature of their data they might well have learnt something about how subjects approached their task. Special pleading is invoked to account for one data point that isn't where it ought to be. Sentences like 'A canary is a canary' are faster to verify than expected – presumably (as Collins and Quillian suggest) because you can just match the two words visually, and avoid a search of semantic memory completely. In this case, the let out, albeit a *post hoc* one, is acceptable. In many cases this sort of exercise amounts to the most blatant distortion and trickery: Alan Allport's (1975) review documents some lovely examples.

Let us turn from the practical details of Collins and Quillian's experiment to identify some more conceptual features that are characteristic of cognitive psychology as a whole. There is a concern with the discovery of *general principles*. In their case, the question is: 'Is semantic memory organized this way or that way?' A small sample of materials and of subjects is assumed to be sufficient to provide a definitive answer to this question. Yet, as we have already seen, this is very simple-minded. The more realistic, and ultimately more fruitful, question is not 'whether' things are like this or like that, but 'when' are they one or the other. In what circumstances does memory, or attention, or language processing, appear thus? In what circumstances does it not? And why the difference? The illogical jump from performance in one small study to the existence of some basic procedure or structure leads to the waste of much time and journal space arguing whether such-and-such a result is or isn't 'real'. Such issues are resolved by a grudging recognition of 'procedural differences', or are simply forgotten. No real progress in understanding is made. Whereas, if people realized that 'circumstances alter cases', they would be eager to try different conditions to see if their result still obtained, rather than, as at present, reluctant, in case it didn't.

It is worth following this issue a little further, for it brings us face to face with several central features of current cognitive psychology, all of which can be called into question. The assumption is that human beings possess general cognitive abilities, skills and structures that sit around inside the head waiting to be called; that any task, in any context, in any form that 'logically' requires those abilities, will make them manifest; and that when they do so their properties will shine through the background haze of extraneous factors clearly and un-ambiguously. All experiments that are conducted in laboratories using 'simple' tasks and 'simple' materials rely on this rationale. (No one would want to say that such experiments *only* tell you about how undergraduates make decisions in darkened rooms: we are more ambitious than that.)

This assumption ignores, in particular, three important aspects of an experimental task, which are important aspects of any and every task that an organism undertakes. One is the specific *content* of the material which is to be dealt with. The second is the rest of the perceptual *context* (the 'ground', in Gestalt terms) in which the 'figure' is located. The third is the *purpose* for which it is being processed. We can illustrate these in turn from the Collins and Quillian experiment. First, it is assumed that what matters about the material is not the particular words chosen, but the logical relationships and constraints that are hypothesized to hold between them. It won't make any difference, says this assumption, whether we ask subjects 'Is a canary yellow?' or 'Does a piano have keys?' or 'Is a newspaper printed?' or 'Do things have a mass?' Provided we balance out all the nuisance factors like reading time and familiarity, and use the correct statistics (see Clark, 1973), the specific content of the question does not directly determine the processes that are called to deal with it. The most obvious use of this assumption is in research on remembering, especially short-term remembering, where there is a mythical beast called an 'item' which you give people to remember, and which can appear disguised as a letter, a digit, a nonsense syllable or a word: it doesn't matter, according to this rationale, because people immediately see through the disguise to the essential 'item-ness' underneath, and say 'Ah! Ha! You can't fool me: you're just another item!'

But my life outside the laboratory is not full of 'items'; it is full of sequences of things and events that bear a meaningful relationship to each other (like words in a sentence, or frames in a film) and which have individual and variable significance to me. I react to them in terms of what they are and what they mean to me, not as if they were dull, anonymous lodgers to be temporarily boarded inside my head. Valerie Curran's chapter elaborates on this point.

The second assumption that needs questioning is that the whole event in which the particular material of interest is presented does not affect the way that material is construed and processed. To go back to the terminology of the Gestalt psychologists, this is assuming that the ground does not affect the perception of the figure, an assumption that was clearly refuted more than forty years ago by the same Gestalt school of researchers. There are some famous examples of this: a grey blob on a black background appears much lighter than the same blob on a white background. One's perception of the blob is heavily influenced by its context. But it is not just in a few, relatively trivial situations that this effect occurs. Rather, these situations highlight an effect that is ubiquitous but often unnoticed. My understanding of a sentence depends on how I am feeling, who its author is, what has just been said, how much I know about the topic, *et cetera, et cetera*. The same quip may make me laugh or cry depending on whether it is told from a music-hall stage or a hospital bed. More to the point, the same sentence will be treated differently if it occurs in casual discourse or flashed on a computer-controlled cathode-ray display. If someone asks me 'Can canaries fly?' in the pub I will suspect either that he is an idiot or that he is about to tell me a joke. How I react will be a function of the entire circumstances, as I perceive them. And a laboratory does not provide an absence of such a context. It cannot be neutral: it is different.

One particular aspect of this problem is the issue of tacit and focal processing. In everyday life, the purpose of cognition is to help me to *do* things. The processes of perceiving, remembering, thinking and the rest are called into play as a means to an end, not an end in themselves. If I were to ask whether canaries can fly it would be because I want to know if I need a cage for the wounded bird I have just found. If I were to ask whether lemons have legs, it would be because I wanted to make you laugh ('Do lemons have legs?' 'No.' 'Oh, I must have squeezed the canary into my drink.'). The operation of cognitive processes is always under the control of a higher purpose, and they proceed without conscious awareness—to use Polanyi's (1967) word, *tacitly*. As a rule, these processes are not of interest in themselves, so conscious (*focal*) involvement is not required.

There are two related points here. The first is the general one that the way a sentence, let us say, is processed depends, possibly heavily, on when, where and for what it is being processed. The conditions of the psychological laboratory provide a special set of 'when', 'where' and 'what for' considerations, different from most everyday contexts and purposes. We must expect, therefore, that the results of experiments will not reveal the pure workings of these processes, any more than the behaviour of a rat in a box, or blood cells in a test-tube, will tell us everything there is to know about the behaviour of rats or blood cells in their natural environments. They tell us something, certainly; but the point is that any behaviour reflects the action of many parts of the cognitive system working in concert, not of any single part of the system that we can hypothetically isolate. This is true of blood cells, and infinitely more so of the 'cells' of mental activity.

Second, there is particularly good reason to doubt the relevance of laboratory cognition to everyday cognition. Not only is the laboratory situation a somewhat stressful one, as we have already seen, but also it makes *ends* out of processes that usually function as *means*. This is a serious problem not just for memory studies, like Collins and Quillian's, but for the whole of cognitive psychology, from perception right through to problem-solving and language comprehension. (There is a sprinkling of studies that look at processing that is incidental to some other focal task, and they do seem to be increasing; but as yet they are themselves incidental to the main stream of research.) The problem, let me stress again, is not that researchers don't know about the importance of these things, but that their way of doing research often doesn't seem to acknowledge it. There is a curious dislocation in long-term memory research (see Chapter 6) at the moment, for example, between the *content* of the experiments, many of which are designed precisely to show the influence of content, context and purpose, and the *form*, which denies these influences. Likewise, most short-term memory researchers know that the span for digits and words is different, yet fail to account for the difference in terms of the different *specific* processes that are called by the two types of stimulus, preferring instead to maintain the fiction of the 'item'.

Much of our hypothetical student's puzzlement and disappointment with cognitive psychology as he finds it stems from the fact that it does not, after all, deal with whole people, but with a very special and bizarre – almost Frankensteinian – preparation, which consists of a brain attached to two eyes, two ears, and two index fingers. This preparation is only to be found inside small, gloomy cubicles, outside which red lights burn to warn ordinary people away. It stares fixedly at a small screen, and its fingers rest lightly and expectantly on two small squares of black plastic – microswitches. It does not feel hungry or tired or inquisitive; it does not think extraneous thoughts or try to understand what is going on. It simply *processes information*. It is, in short, a computer, made in the image of the larger electronic organism that sends it stimuli and records its responses. ('The sentences were displayed one at a time on the cathode-ray tube (CRT) of a DEC PDP-1 computer. The timing and recording of responses were under program control' (Collins and Quillian).) Indeed, so important is the computer now, as a source of both ideas about cognition and technology for investigating it, that it is surprising that it is not credited with joint authorship: 'Collins, Quillian and DEC PDP-1 (1969)'. There is, in fact, a footnote in their paper explaining that DEC PDP-1 has moved from Bolt, Beranek and Newman, Inc., Cambridge, Massachusetts (where the experiment was carried out) to the University of Massachusetts at Amhurst, a conventional piece of information that is usually only provided for human members of the collaborative team. (This is, of course – of course? – a joke: but a telling one.)

Lest I be accused of sentimentality, I should stress that I have nothing against computers *per se*. It does not strike me that comparing a human being to a computer is intrinsically demeaning or dehumanizing. I am not affronted by the suggestion: it is simply (as I try to show in Chapter 6) a bad metaphor, for it leaves out much about human beings that cannot be left out if a sensible approach to explaining how they work is to be taken.

Much of this concern with the discovery of general principles takes the form of the search for functionally and structurally separable components of the cognitive system. We find it constantly analysed into all sorts of sub-systems, ranging from the 'Pattern Recognition System' and 'Response Executive' to a bewildering variety of memories: Precategorical Acoustic Storage, Sensory Register, Iconic Memory, Primary Memory, Working Memory, Semantic Memory, Episodic Memory, Response Buffer, and a host of others. This analytical approach gives rise to the familiar string of labelled boxes with arrows between them. There is no doubt that this taxonomic activity is an important component of any science. Sternberg (1969b) in particular has demonstrated the suitability of cognitive psychology's methods for detecting processes that are functionally independent of each other in certain situations. But there is a danger of forcing the facts to fit the method, and of trying to squeeze evidence for separate components out of a system that works, most of the time, as a *system*, in which the behaviour of each hypothetical component is influenced by its active colleagues and by the overall purpose of the processing. If one only ever heard a trumpet in an orchestra, one's assessment of its capacities and characteristics would depend on the other instruments playing, on the conductor and on the composition, as well as on the specific trumpeter and his instrument. Winograd (1977) has argued the desirability of a similar orchestral approach to cognition. And not only may components *appear* to be different in different contexts, they may actually be different. A more appropriate analogy than the trumpet might be a chameleon. Thus, while we are free to look for processes that do not affect each other, and whose properties are relatively constant over different materials and tasks, we must acknowledge that the view implicit in this search fails to capture the synthetic and interactional nature of cognition, and that the analytical methodology is not well suited to the investigation of these interactive and context-dependent properties.

These arguments bring us to the central issue of *fragmentation*. Alan Allport concludes, in his review of the state of the art in 1975, that the field is characterized by

> an uncritical, or selective or frankly cavalier attitude to experi-
> mental data: a pervasive atmosphere of special pleading; a curious
> parochialism in acknowledging even the existence of other workers,
> and other approaches, to the phenomena under discussion; inter-
> pretations of data relying on multiple, arbitrary choice-points;

and underlying all else the near vacuum of theoretical structure within which to interrelate different sets of experimental results, or to direct the search for significant new phenomena.

This means that much research falls into one of the three categories that David Bakan (1967) has labelled 'Bandwagon', 'No Stone Unturned', and 'Fancy That!' There is a distinct lack of any guiding framework that can provide a glue to stick the different areas of cognitive psychology together. We are like the inhabitants of thousands of little islands, all in the same part of the ocean, yet totally out of touch with each other. Each has evolved a different culture, different ways of doing things, different languages to talk about what they do. Occasionally inhabitants of one island may spot their neighbours jumping up and down and issuing strange cries; but it makes no sense, so they ignore it.

The most glaring example of this isolationism is seen at the very heart of cognitive psychology, in the study of conceptualization: what are concepts? how are they represented? how are they formed and used? We have the Cell-Assemblians (headed by D. O. Hebb), the Stored-Contingencies-of-Reinforcementists (led by Skinner), the Cambridge Logo-geneticists (under Chief John Morton), the Semantic-Networkers (like Collins and Quillian), the extinct but revered Old Schematicians (Bartlett), the Swiss Schematicians (Piaget), New Schematicians (Neisser) and a thousand others – all grappling with the same central problem. And all chatting away in their own lingo, happily re-inventing and rediscovering each other's work, often without even knowing it!

What cognition needs is a common language; a lingua franca that contains a repertoire of concepts rich enough to enable the formulation of interesting and testable propositions in a wide variety of particular areas, but which spring from the same underlying cognitive view, and are therefore mutually compatible, mutually supportive, and mutually informative. All other sciences possess such a central mythology, for without it research cannot be cumulative. At present cognitive psychology often looks like a dressed-up version of the childish ''Tis!'' 'Tisn't!', ''Tis!', ''Tisn't!', or possibly 'Mine's better (bigger, newer, more parsimonious) than yours!' 'Oh no, it isn't. Mine's better than yours!' The New Directions in cognitive psychology will not be significantly different from the Old Directions unless people are prepared to bury their egos along with their hatchets and start agreeing on a Metaphor for Mind. It doesn't have to be very sophisticated, any more than the atomic solar system Metaphor for Matter was: but we need something to fill the hole in the heart of cognitive psychology, so that its practitioners may see themselves as collaborators rather than individual beavers, gnawing away at their own problems and ignoring everyone else's.

The proliferation of languages and models means that cognitive psychology is full of specialist terminology ('jargon' is perhaps too pejorative a word). Much of it, only a few years old, seems already obsolete: psychologists generate and discard new models at a rate that the motor trade would envy. Researchers, being the manufacturers, tend to be less confused by this than consumers, the students. Trying to write an essay that 'compares and contrasts' models of visual pattern recognition, or short-term memory, or computer simulations of language comprehension, is an awful job, and one whose value, other than as a training of the critical faculties, is open to question.

Another aspect of the Collins and Quillian study that applied to much of cognitive psychology is its focus on verbal material and linguistic performance. There are traditions that use non-verbal stimuli, like the work of Shepard (Cooper and Shepard, 1972) on the mental rotation of shapes; memory for pictures, and chess-playing; or postulate non-verbal processes, like the work of Paivio (1971) and others on imagery. But the bulk of the journal space is concerned with the processing and retention of linguistic/symbolic information of one sort or another. A quick scan of two recent numbers of the cognitive section of the *Journal of Experimental Psychology*, for example, revealed that all but two of the papers used language stimuli. It is sufficient to point out here how this becomes counter-productive when it prevents people seeing that all verbal memory must be grounded in an *experiential* memory – one that contains the expectancies and correlations that we have been inducing from our experience almost from the moment of conception. Some of what we learn for ourselves conforms to the network of linguistic concepts that a culture overlays on its experience. Much of it does not. Both kinds of concept are primarily represented not as 'memories' but as functional changes in the nervous system that guide and subserve appropriate action. It seems to me very likely, though surprisingly untested as yet, that knowledge I have learned through experience ('Cats purr', say) will have some different properties from knowledge that is only parasitic on my linguistic categories (such as 'Beavers gnaw'). To suppose that all such statements are evaluated in terms of a network of linguistic (or proto-linguistic) propositions, or worse, to suppose that all knowledge is of this form, as many current models do, is at best unjustified and very likely daft. A propositional memory without an experiential base would be exactly as much use to me as a definition of light to a blind man.

It is interesting to see how much the western personality intrudes into cognitive psychology. The preoccupation of the former with the rational, the verbal, the conscious, the intentional, the individualistic and the competitive, are all present in the latter. Most of all there is a central, unrecognized conflict between our intuitive view of ourselves as an agent – deciding, choosing, acting, in some non-deterministic way – and cognitive psychology, one aim of which is (as I see it, at least) to provide an explicit, non-mystical, formal account of exactly how those decisions, choices and actions came about. As 'people' we are committed to preserving the 'mystery of self', while as 'scientists' we are committed to dispelling it. Thus the literature is peppered with bits of double-speak, like 'people could retrieve this fact directly' or 'the person need only start at the node canary and retrieve the properties stored there . . .' (Collins and Quillian), as if 'the person' were some agency separate from the cognitive system under discussion. Atkinson and Shiffrin (1968) provide a prime example: 'The term control processes refers to those processes that are not permanent features of memory, but are instead transient phenomena *under the control of the subject*' (my italics). So the control processes that are supposed to control memory have themselves to be controlled by an elusive ghost-in-the-machine, 'the subject'.

The emphasis on the deliberate processing of symbolic matter tends to divorce cognition from other branches of psychology to which, one day, it will have to be re-wedded. Action, and its integration with perception and cognition, has been left in the shade as the experimental spotlight has been trained on perceiving and understanding rather than purposeful doing. The chapter by Nigel Harvey and Kerry Greer describes the re-emergence of the cognitive study of action. Along with its ignorance of action, cognition has also not concerned itself with motivation – the internal needs and purposes that, together with perception of the outside world, guide and select what we are to do; and emotion – the affective tinges that colour our awareness of *all* cognition. To point out these missing areas is not to make the impossible demand that all experiments must study everything at once: it is only to insist that the conceptual framework within which we work must be *capable* of incorporating these influences and interactions. Instead of being a smooth rectangle our cognitive psychology must be like a piece of a jigsaw puzzle, with cavities and knobs for hooking other areas on to.

While I do not buy the argument that a critic has to provide answers to his own questions before he can be taken seriously, it is only fair that I should have a shot at spelling out the new directions that are implicit in what I have said. In fact the first question is: is there a future at all? If cognition has to be seen as reflecting a system of concurrently active and mutually modifying components acting in concert, the orchestration of which is heavily dependent on the precise nature of the content, context and purpose of processing; if we cannot ignore the specific strategies, procedures and expectations which a subject brings to experiments with him, and which are heavily dependent on the idiosyncrasies of that person's own auto-biography; if we can no longer asssume that performance at the limit has the same quality as unstressed performance, or that a failure to perform can be taken as *prima facie* evidence for an inability to per-form; if all these points are true, how can we proceed?

From a few basic changes in stance there will, I hope, emerge a viable science of cognition. First, we need to replace the central image of man-as-philosopher, concerned with reflection and judgement, with something like George Kelly's man-as-scientist, engaged in the active and urgent business of developing and testing a theory about the world that will reliably predict the outcome of action, and thereby enable desirable consequences to be obtained. The focus shifts from the processing of information to the initiation and control of action. This has immediate implications for the questions that one asks about cognition. Instead of looking solely for basic mechanisms – *what* skills and structures the cognitive system consists of – we shall have to be as concerned with eliciting circumstances – the questions of *when* and *what for*. Under what conditions do people of a certain kind manifest a particular cognitive skill or style? We shall have to be concerned with the way in which skills are 'called' by situations. This is central to the *production system* approach to cognition that Alan Allport explains in the next chapter, which postulates that *all* mental operations ('actions') are stored with a specification of the type of situation in which it is appropriate to use that operation (called the 'condition', or the 'calling-pattern'). With this view we can go on to ask what controls the *range* of situations that trigger an action. Why and how do differences in age, culture or history influence the calling-pattern that mediates the use of a procedure in a current situation? Why, for example, is the ability to make transitive inferences restricted in a four-year-old to situations where he can use himself as an 'anchor' (John is taller than you, and Bill is shorter than you. Who's the tallest?), while three years later the scope of the calling-pattern has widened and dropped this restriction (Harris, 1975)?

The circumstances that elicit action are not only those of the external world: they include the person's internal state – emotional, cognitive and motivational–as well. This orientation would therefore allow cognitive psychology to study the internal priorities, feelings and moods that attend and select certain courses of action. We know that coins look bigger to hungry children: there is much left to investigate about how the intelligence of cognition is affected by anxiety or by an overpowering need, for example.

The concern with the elicitation of ability might also generate an *ethology* of cognition, which would be interesting in its own right, and a useful counterbalance to the rather cramped picture that issues from the laboratory. What cognitive skills do people display in their everyday lives, with what fluency, and in what contexts? This is an attitude that is beginning to emerge, as Valerie Curran shows, in cross-cultural psychology; but it is clearly valuable to have an impression of our subjects' cognitive style, whether they are African or English, three years old or twenty-three, brain-damaged or gifted, students or housewives. At the very least such knowledge would prevent us making hasty statements about what people can't do that they do in fact do in their normal (extra-experimental) lives. And very likely it would stimulate new and significant areas of research as we watch and puzzle over cognition in its natural habitat.

In general, I think, there might be a swing towards the study of real-world activities. The current appeal for 'ecological validity' is not a sentimental one: it is a call for better science. As we have seen, the psychology of limits is all too often premised on the faulty logic that 'doesn't' implies 'can't'. The reverse reasoning, however, that 'does' implies 'can', is perfectly valid, and an orientation towards what people do do is likely to lead to an increased concern with what they usually, or normally, do. That this does not mean that we will all be doing problem-oriented 'applied research' is attested to by the theoretical output of the Medical Research Council's Applied Psychology Research Units. As Neisser has said in *Cognition and Reality,*

A psychology that cannot interpret ordinary experience is ignoring almost the whole range of its natural subject matter. It may hope to emerge from the laboratory some day with a new array of important ideas, but that outcome is unlikely unless it is already working with principles whose applicability to natural situations can be foreseen.

One straightforward methodological implication emerges. Before making any generalization whatsoever, even within a circumscribed population, we shall have to sample a range of materials and contexts, all of which instantiate the hypothetical process we are trying to track down. As Cole and Scribner (1974) put it,

> Our insistence on a variety of approaches to studying a particular kind of cognitive performance is neither a caprice nor an effort to garner a large number of publications. It is an absolute requirement, dictated by our conception of the origin and organization of cognitive processes.

If this were to be taken seriously, it would prevent the proliferation of models generated by research with a single paradigm and a single type of material.

These considerations throw up some new content areas of psychology as well as some new methodologies. Particularly the study of what 'metaphors' people base their actions on becomes important, as does the question of the 'decontextualization of knowledge', and what are the important influences on it. Do calling-patterns lose their specificity simply by the forgetting of details, and if so, when? Do they lose it through use, i.e. by being called in an ever-widening range of situations? Do they lose it through the application of language? (One of the accepted functions of language is, after all, to assist the freeing of our thought from the immediate and the concrete.) What effects do different learning or educational methods have on the decontextualization of what is learned? Scribner and Cole (1973), for instance, have argued that informal education (roughly, 'learning on the job') leads, on the whole, to a more context-limited kind of learning than formal education. Is decontextualization always a good thing? Are there circumstances under which we over-extend our programmes – in prejudice, for example, or in a failure to solve a problem through an incautious assumption about what kind of problem it is? How can we enhance, or prevent, decontextualization? And so on.

I hope that these examples give at least the flavour of a science of cognition that is somewhat different from the currently dominant one: 'somewhat' rather than 'radically', because, of course, the seeds of any New Directions must be present within the Old, and because we ourselves – the authors – are products of our own psychological upbringing. Nor can there be complete agreement: we have not produced a manifesto. My critique, although not completely idiosyncratic, is a personal one, and one from which all the contributors, at some point or other, would want to depart. We have tried to reach as much common ground as possible, but their orientations are to an extent different. Perhaps I can introduce them with some of my own reactions.

Alan Allport is the most closely sympathetic; in fact his first chapter, 'Patterns and actions: cognitive mechanisms are content-specific' is complementary in many respects to the present one. Whereas I have concentrated on analysing the current state of the art in some detail, and made a few suggestions about implications of the analysis for the future, Alan provides a quick historical introduction to the present scene and then expounds at greater length a framework for cognitive theory, that of Production Systems, that meets most of my desiderata. Central to his concern, as they are to mine, are the content-specific and distributed nature of cognitive processes; the interaction of cognition with motivation, emotion and, most importantly, action; the fuzziness of our knowledge and the consequent shift towards a language of 'cognitive physiology' and away from that of computer hardware; and the tacit, unobservable operation of much of our cognition. This chapter is a superb piece of work, and deserves to be studied by all psychologists, not just those concerned with cognition. The shift from seeing 'perception' as before everything else, to seeing it as *part* of all processing, is a profound one.

Action, when it is treated at all in cognitive terms, tends to get tacked on at the end. In recognition of its emerging importance, Nigel Harvey and Kerry Greer's chapter is placed next to Allport's. As they point out, his discussion of 'action demons' leads directly into their account of how the demonic activation is transformed into actual, physical activity. Their paper helps us to focus on the micro-logic of the conceptual nervous system: a logic that seems to cut right across the traditional separation of perception and action.

Alan Allport's second chapter, 'Attention and performance', provides ample illustration of, and justification for, the ideas expounded in Chapter 2. He launches a concerted attack on the ill-conceived notion of a 'general-purpose limited-capacity central processor', showing that there is in fact no compelling evidence at all for it, and reinterpreting much of the data on 'attention' in terms of content- and task-*specific* mechanisms. In doing so he also shows that one of the major tasks for cognitive psychology is to identify the calling-patterns of processes and groups of processes (what Valerie Curran will be calling 'functional systems') by looking at what behaviours do or do not conflict with each other. Instead of assuming that we can map the functional faults in cognition on the basis of single, 'critical' experiments, we shall have to *discover* where the breaks are in a more painstaking, but ultimately much more fruitful and cumulative, a fashion. His treatment of the effects of practice on the performance of simultaneous tasks is also important, for it instantiates the approach to *learning* that I mentioned earlier. One central aspect of learning is the way in which the calling-patterns of processes change with experience, the way those processes are de- or re-contextualized. Alan suggests that when concurrent tasks interfere because they call the same process, their calling-patterns change so that the offending process is dropped, or assigned exclusively to *one* task, and they then become functionally more independent.

In 'Developing the concept of working memory' Graham Hitch fights back on behalf of general purposes, limited capacities and central processors everywhere. It is my impression that even his more sophisticated, modular view of short-term memory, and especially its 'central executive', remain open to the kinds of criticism that Alan Allport and I have made; but in fairness the reader must judge that for himself. In one respect, though, Graham's paper is exemplary, and that is in his concern to look at working memory at work, across a range of tasks that bridge the gap between laboratory and classroom, common room or drawing-room.

The following two chapters, my 'Remembering and understanding' and David Green's 'Psycholinguistics: cognitive aspects of human communication', form another complementary pair. In the former I concentrate on the micro-modelling of memory structure and function. I argue that to understand the way word-meanings are stored and integrated we need to see them as embedded within two parallel systems of organization: a verbal one and an experiential one. And that while associative models of the former may be satisfactory, comprehension within the latter must be seen at a 'higher power magnification', under which concepts emerge as ill-defined and labile, and as being integrated and modified rather than simply associated. David Green pursues the story up through the level of sentences to texts, and discusses some of the additional syntactic and semantic factors that become important. His emphasis on the crucial role of the purpose for which a text is being read or heard, and the use of a production systems analysis echo the arguments of the opening chapters. And his discussion of theories of metaphor also, it seems to me, signals a healthy concern with the constructive and creative nature of comprehension.

The next chapter, 'Thinking; experiential and information-processing approaches' by Jonathan Evans, takes a close and critical look at the re-emergence of introspection as a tool in problem-solving. The significant conclusion is that one's conscious experience of one's behaviour, and reported reasons for it, are generated by processes that may be substantially different from those that generated the behaviour itself. Reports are thus seen not as acceptable explanations for action, but as themselves in need of explanation. As I have argued in this chapter, such insights may have radical repercussions for cognitive psychology as a whole. Finally, Valerie Curran's survey of cross-cultural cognition demonstrates just how seriously we have to take the content, context and task-specific nature of cognitive mechanisms.

The authors have each made their own statements about where they would like their particular fields to go. The main questions upon which each discussion is centred are: What are the background to and major influences on the current state of play? What are the principle issues at stake at the moment: what sorts of question are being asked? What are the most important answers around to these questions? What are some of the critical experiments and their implications? What methods are available? What is the place of each particular field within the whole of cognitive psychology: how do they fit together? What are the main deficiencies and limitations of current research? And finally where is the field going, and where *ought* it to be going? The two things we have *not* tried to provide, deliberately, are detailed historical surveys of the literature, or comprehensive reviews of the present scene. This book is meant to be a guidebook to organizing one's thoughts, and a life-raft to cling on to when in danger of drowning in the sea of detail.

Third, the style is important. I have criticized cognitive psychology for being at times jargon-laden, and virtually incomprehensible. We have tried to write in a way that is clear and easy to read, and, up to a point, entertaining. It has proved difficult, and sometimes impossible. But I certainly have found the effort worth while, if only because the attempt to simplify and communicate technical issues has often made me see them in perspective, and ask whether they are really as important, as difficult, or as novel, as their proponents insist. In his autobiography Erwin Schrödinger wrote: 'It is the duty of a teacher of science to impart to his listeners knowledge that will prove useful in their professions, but it should also be his intense desire to do it in such a way as to cause them pleasure.' If this is true for physics, how much more so for the science of human beings?

References

Allport, D. A. (1975), 'The state of cognitive psychology': a critical notice of W. G. Chase (ed.) *Visual Information Processing*, in *Quarterly Journal of Experimental Psychology, 27,* pp. 141-52.

Atkinson, R. C. and Shiffrin, R. H. (1968), 'Human memory: a proposed system and its control processes', in K. W. Spence and J. T. Spence (eds), *The Psychology of Learning and Motivation*, vol. 2, Academic Press: New York.

Bakan, D. (1967), *On Method,* Jossey-Bass: San Francisco.

Clark, H. H. (1973), 'The language-as-fixed-effect fallacy: a critique of language statistics in psychological research', *Journal of Verbal Learning and Verbal Behavior, 12,* pp. 335-59.

Cole, M., Gay, J., Glick, J. and Sharp D. W. (1971), *The Cultural Context of Learning and Thinking*, Basic Books: New York.

Cole, M. and Scribner, S. (1974), *Culture and Cognition: A Psychological Introduction*, Wiley: London.

Collins, A. M. and Quillian, M. R. (1969), 'Retrieval time for semantic memory', *Journal of Verbal Learning and Verbal Behavior, 8,* pp. 240-7.

Conrad, C. (1972), 'Cognitive economy in semantic memory', *Journal of Experimental Psychology, 92,* pp. 149-54.

Cooper, L. A. and Shepard, R. N. (1972), 'Chronometric studies of the rotation of mental images' in W. G. Chase (ed.), *Visual Information Processing*, Academic Press: New York.

Harris, P. (1975), 'Transitive inferences by four-year-old children'. Paper presented at SRCD, Denver, April.

Meyer, D. (1970), 'On the representation and retrieval of stored semantic information', *Cognitive Psychology, 1,* pp. 242-300.

Neisser, U. (1976), *Cognition and Reality,* Freeman: San Francisco.

Newell, A. (1973), 'You can't play Twenty Questions with Nature and win', in W. G. Chase (ed.), *Visual Information Processing*, Academic Press: New York.

Paivio, A. (1971), *Imagery and Verbal Processes*, Holt, Rinehart & Winston: New York.

Polanyi, M. (1967), *The Tacit Dimension*, Routledge & Kegan Paul: London.

Posner, M. I. (1969), 'Abstraction and the process of recognition', in G. H. Bower and J. T. Spence (eds.), *The Psychology of Learning and Motivation*, Academic Press: New York.

Rabbitt, P. M. A. (1966), 'Error and error correction in choice-response tasks', *Journal of Experimental Psychology, 71*, pp. 264-72.

Rips, L. J., Shoben, E. J. and Smith, E. E. (1973), 'Semantic distance and the verification of semantic relations', *Journal of Verbal Learning and Verbal Behavior, 12*, pp. 1-10.

Scribner, S. and Cole, M. (1973), 'Cognitive consequences of formal and informal education', *Science, 182*, pp. 553-9.

Sternberg, S. (1969a), 'Memory scanning: mental processes revealed by reaction time', *American Scientist, 57*, pp. 421-7.

Sternberg, S. (1969b), 'The discovery of processing stages: extensions of Donders' method', in W. G. Doster (ed.), *Attention and Performance, 2*, North Holland: Amsterdam.

Wilkins, A. J. (1971), 'Conjoint frequency, category size and categorization time', *Journal of Verbal Learning and Verbal Behavior, 10*, pp. 382-5.

Winograd, T. (1977), 'On some contested suppositions of generative linguistics about the scientific study of language', *Cognition, 5*, pp. 151-79.

2 Patterns and actions: cognitive mechanisms are content-specific

D. Alan Allport

Old directions

A pocket history

The 'information-processing' approach to the study of human cognition, which is still dominant, is a phenomenon broadly of the second half of the twentieth century. Some of its roots, however, reach back across the forty wilderness years of Radical Behaviourism to the academic psychology of the late nineteenth century, to the time of Wundt and of William James. For Wundt and his followers, in particular, psychological investigation depended on the painstaking commentary, by trained 'observers', on their own conscious experience. A prototypical research question of this period concerned the 'span of apprehension': the question of how much could be 'perceived' (in practice, reported) from a momentary configuration of events. The tachiscope was invented.

This Wundtian tradition persists both in the predominance of perception (rather than action) as the focus of information-processing research, and in many of the experimental paradigms that shaped the new approach in the 1950s and 1960s: tachistoscopic reports, a concern with the 'spans' of conscious memory recall, the capacity for division of consciousness (or of retrospective report) between concurrent linguistic or other events, and so on.

Under the behaviourist critique the methods of introspection had fallen into profound disrepute. For forty years research on human cognition was simply abandoned. The conceptual apparatus of Radical Behaviourism did not permit any view of what might be called the architecture of cognition. Indeed it did not permit any considerations of internal (or psychological) structure or mechanism at all, except the unordered associative bonds between highly intuitive, pseudo-observable entities called 'stimuli' and 'responses'.

This scientifically sterile refusal to contemplate cognitive processes, or structure, as a proper subject for psychological study, would doubtless have continued, but for two developments of the late 1940s onwards, that provided for these topics a new theoretical notation, a language in which to represent them, and thence a renewed intellectual respectability. These developments were: (a) the mathematical theory of communication ('information theory'), and (b), most importantly, the beginnings of computer science. Information theory appeared to offer a content-independent measure of psychological capacity and of mental work, in bits-per-second, and there were numerous early attempts to determine the maximum transmission rate that the human 'operator', seen as a simple transducer, could achieve. (Quastler, 1956, is a vintage example.)

Still more important, the obvious analogy between the processes performed in a digital computer and mental 'computation' began to suggest a whole new range of metaphors for cognitive processing. But the ideas that were assimilated early on, and that became the stock-in-trade of 'information-processing' psychology, tended to be those derived from the basic design of the sequential, general-purpose digital computer itself, rather than from the potential computational processes that might be implemented on it. These ideas included, first, the separation of active processor and passive storage; second, the localization of processing operations, of all different kinds, in one central processor of fixed capacity; and third, storage, regardless of content, of both data and programme at arbitrary locations in a memory as 'general purpose', or content-independent as the processor. It is not difficult to see each of these elementary characteristics of computer hardware reappearing either implicitly or explicitly in the models of human information processing of the 1950s and 1960s.

A classic example is the enduring belief in a system called STM (short-term memory) as responsible not only for the repetition span for lists of spoken words but also – quite gratuitously – as the 'central processor' through which all inputs and outputs to and from an individual's knowledge base (or LTM) must pass. Other examples can be found in those models that seek to represent a person's knowledge ('semantic memory') as a passive network that must be 'searched' by the same, limited-capacity central processor, if information is to be 'retrieved' (Chapter 6). Indeed, the numerous attempts to account for the limitations of human performance, in terms of a limited supply of *general-purpose* processing capacity, directly or indirectly reflect these same origins: the analogy with the content-independent hardware of the programmable computer. Moray (1967) is a connoisseur's example. Chapter 4 seeks to show (among other things) why this analogy has not been scientifically fruitful.

A distinct tradition, but one that has also had a formative influence on information-processing theories in psychology, derives from neurophysiology. Interestingly, one of its key ideas originates from a proposal in 1956 (and 1959) by a computer scientist, Oliver Selfridge, for a system of pattern-recognition and simple learning. He called it 'Pandemonium'. His scheme contained two simple but fundamental ideas. The first was that each type of recurrent pattern to be recognized (each written symbol, for example) should have its own special-purpose detector (its own, independent 'cognitive demon', to use Selfridge's Maxwellian terminology), whose only function was to collect evidence for the presence of that particular pattern, much like Hebb's 'cell assemblies' proposed a few years earlier (Hebb, 1949) or Konorski's 'gnostic units'. Second, the system was hierarchical: cognitive demons received their inputs from lower-level 'feature demons'.

Selfridge's proposals prompted Warren McCulloch and his colleagues to look for evidence of *neuronal* 'feature demons' in the frog's visual nervous system (Lettvin *et al.*, 1959). Since that pioneering study, overwhelming evidence has accumulated for the existence of specialized neurons, responding selectively to particular (often quite abstract) invariant properties of the sensory input, as a major design feature of the central nervous system in man and other animals. A somewhat similar hierarchical (or heterarchical) organization appears to be the rule in the control of action, with specialized neuronal structures ('demons') to represent each item in the organism's repertoire of actions, again at multiple levels of abstraction (Chapter 3).

Anne Treisman (1960) first suggested an extension of Selfridge's scheme to language. Her proposal was that even such complex and abstract patterns as spoken words each have their own autonomous recognition demons, which she called Dictionary Units. A Dictionary Unit could be excited summatively both by patterns of sensory input and by activity in other 'associated' Dictionary Units. Beyond a certain level of activity, the Dictionary Unit 'fired'.

There was no obvious reason, in her proposed system, why several Dictionary Units should not 'fire' simultaneously, given simultaneous inputs. Perhaps for this reason it was left unclear what was the relation between supra-threshold 'firing' of a Dictionary Unit and conscious perception of a word, or for that matter what was its relation to the control of overt or implicit speech. In a later formalization of Treisman's idea, Morton (1968, 1970) introduced two specific modifications: (a) Supra-threshold activity in Dictionary Units ('logogen' units, in Morton's terminology) could activate further (unspecified) structures in the 'semantic system' *in parallel,* whereas (b) for control of overt speech programmes the outputs of competing logogen units had to queue. However, still no mechanism was suggested for the assignment of priority between simultaneously competing logogen units.

For early information-processing theories, however, the property of Pandemonium that had even wider acceptance was the suggestion – certainly not unique to Pandemonium – that psychological processes could be broken down into a succession of stages, the results of one stage of processing forming the inputs to the next. The characteristic information-processing theory of this period is represented in the form of a flow-chart, in which there is a succession of boxes connected by arrows. What goes on in the boxes is often none too clearly defined. Neisser (1976) has aptly caricatured this sort of theory as:

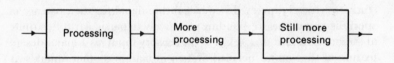

Still less clearly defined in such theories are the means by which the input of any one stage accesses the appropriate processes in the next. This too is a question to which we must return.

By the late 1960s computer science was beginning to exert a new and very different influence on theoretical development in cognitive psychology, in the form of artificial intelligence (AI). AI represents a methodology concerned with the design of *possible* mechanisms of intelligence: complex mechanisms whose properties could be investigated only by actually building them (usually in the form of computer programmes) and seeing how they performed. Its early influence can already be seen in Neisser's influential book, *Cognitive Psychology*, published in 1967. In contrast to the purely stimulus-driven character of Pandemonium, Neisser argued for the necessarily constructive, or synthesizing character of conscious perception and recall. However, although influenced by some of the early work in AI (for example, Minsky, 1961), Neisser explicitly rejected what he characterized as the 'computer simulation' approach. In fact, very few workers in AI see the goals of their research merely as the 'simulation' of already well-defined aspects of intelligent human performance. To the contrary, much of the difficulty of creating theories of human intelligence, both for psychology as well as for AI, lies in adequately describing what it is that we are trying to explain. The attempt to build mechanisms that will perform in any of the ill-defined domains of human skill – such as in the visual recognition of objects in visually guided manipulation, playing and planning ahead, making scientific hypotheses, recognizing speech, understanding stories or engaging in conversation – provides a method for confronting and articulating these problems.

It is ironical that, in 1967, Neisser's grounds for rejecting the 'computer-simulation' approach were that the contemporary efforts in this direction were, as yet, too simplistic and too task-specific to 'do justice to the complexity of human mental processes'. In what way, I wonder, did he find psychologists' theories less simplistic, or less paradigm-bound?

To my understanding, the only way that psychologists' theories (that is, theories expressed in words rather than in explicit processes: 'analysis-by-synthesis', for example) have succeeded in doing justice to the richness and complexity of human cognition is simply by being so general and underspecified, in process terms, as to mean almost anything. In particular the flow-chart conventions that have served as the principal theoretical notation for information-processing psychology make it only too easy to neglect the basic questions about *mechanism*. How does it work? What goes on in the boxes labelled 'unit formation', 'figural emphasis', and the like? The flow-chart notation tempts a similar indifference to questions of how the products of any hypothetical stage of processing are supposed to access the appropriate structures or processes in the next. It is not much of an overstatement to say that such questions are often magically disposed of by the convenient notational device of merely drawing an arrow between the adjacent boxes! The questions of access, of pattern recognition, of course, will not go away so easily, but they can be more comfortably neglected.

It can hardly be denied that, at the end of the 1970s, psychological research in cognition still has a fragmented, 'phenomenon-driven' character (Newell, 1973a). We still lack unifying theoretical principles. As Johnson-Laird commented, 'After twenty years, the experimental study of human information processing has not yielded them (unifying principles) and seems unlikely to do so. How should we proceed? (Johnson-Laird, 1978).

The responsibility for this chaotic state of cognitive psychology, I suggest, rests chiefly on the lack of an adequate theoretical notation in which to formulate questions about mental process. If we have no way of representing to ourselves serious candidate mechanisms, that is, mechanisms actually capable of realizing a given psychological function, our experimental tools on their own can achieve relatively little, except to pile up data. 'Experimental' research, on its own, becomes a business of perpetual preliminaries, a never-ending attempt to test out experimental tools for purposes that have not yet been properly formulated.

For this reason, I would claim, the advent of Artificial Intelligence is the single most important development in the history of psychology. (I shall have more to say about it in the next section.) Indeed, it seems to me not unreasonable to expect that Artificial Intelligence will ultimately come to play the role *vis à vis* the psychological and social sciences that mathematics, from the seventeenth century on, has done for the physical sciences. But that part of the story is still a long way in the future.

New directions

The first generation of theories in information-processing psychology was founded on the new process metaphors offered by the uni-processor, general-purpose computer. This dependence was perhaps most explicit in theories intended to account for what were seen as 'basic' limitations on human performance: limitations on maximum 'transmission rates', on short-term memory, on the division of attention, etc., seen as the expression of a limited, non-specific (i.e., general-purpose) processing capacity. (For a critique of this approach, see Chapter 4.) Let us now consider an alternative set of assumptions about cognitive mechanisms, in which 'capacity' is not a central concept at all; indeed, in which it is difficult to see how the concept of overall 'capacity' could have any well-defined meaning.

Distributed processing

First, suppose we forget all about the general-purpose digital computer. Forget about content-independent processors and stores. Let us start from the quite opposite assumption that in biological cognition everything is content-dependent – where 'content' here means pattern, configuration, context. What constrains the set of cognitive acts that can be made at any instant has nothing to do with the *quantity* of information to be processed. Let us suppose, as our initial assumption, that it depends solely on the presence of particular patterns, configurations of activity in the nervous system, and on the existence of previously established, specific neural structures which can 'resonate' to them; in other words, on the existence of corresponding, autonomous pattern detectors or 'cognitive demons'. Activity in particular demons can trigger 'resonant' activity in others, including of course action demons, which in turn can command a hierarchy of effector systems. The 'memory' of such a system – its means of representing knowledge – is thus defined by the patterns to which it can resonate, and is inseparable from its 'processing' capability.

Neuronally it is abundantly clear that the brain is capable of computing millions of quasi-independent functions concurrently, in parallel. However, 'until very recently', Nickerson (1977) wrote, commenting on information-processing models of memory, 'relatively little thought has been given to the possibility that memory and the processor are one and the same thing, . . . that computational capacity is distributed throughout the brain, that the same neural elements can be used for storing information and for processing it' (p. 716). The basic assumption throughout the remainder of this chapter is that processing- and memory-capacity is distributed throughout the nervous system over millions of special-purpose 'cognitive demons'.

There is strong support, from both neuroanatomy and neurophysiology, for a conception of the cerebral cortex as fundamentally modular in organization (see, for example, Eccles, 1977; Marr, 1976; Szentagothai and Arbib, 1974). In this view, the typical cortical 'integrative unit' consists of a narrow column, not more than half a millimetre in width, containing up to 10,000 neurons. Each such module contains input (afferent fibres) and output channels (principally, some hundreds of large pyramidal cells), and between them many hundreds of each of a great variety of other cell types, in an intricate but highly regular, lattice-like pattern of excitatory and inhibitory connections within the column, and with powerful inhibitory relations between adjacent columns (Szentagothai, 1975).* Some at least of the interneurons are tunable – they have 'memory' (see Uttley, 1976). Spinelli (1970) has suggested how such an arrangement might operate as a content-addressable memory system. We have little conception, as yet, of the computational capabilities of such almost unimaginably intricate circuitry, let alone of the way in which several million of these modules interact with and modulate one another's activity, and the activity of other, subcortical systems, in controlling and integrating behaviour. Nevertheless, the conception that emerges clearly is of a vast assemblage of *distributed* processing power, organized apparently in the form of resonant pattern-and-action units. As we shall see later on, the modular principle – of functionally separable sub-systems – appears to hold also at a molar level of analysis, with direct relevance to whole behavioural sub-systems of perception and action.

A secondary theme of this chapter is the relative neglect of *action*, and of the problems of environmental (sensory) and internal (non-sensory) control of appropriate action, in information-processing theories of psychology. In this emphasis on 'perception' at the expense of action the Wundtian traditions, I suspect, have played a part.

In this sense Morton's logogen model was a definite advance over Treisman's Dictionary Units, in that, in the logogen model the individual pattern detectors were explicitly coupled to mechanisms for specific actions. The actions that activation of a logogen unit 'made available', or provided access to, included both overt gestures, in the form of speech, and internal operations within the lexical-semantic system. The system was thus no longer left 'lost in thought', like Tolman's hypothetical rats.

---

*Marr (1970) had put forward a detailed and sophisticated theory of cortical memory, in which each module, or 'diagnostic unit', is based upon a *single* (pyramidal) output cell.

Patterns and actions

It is a commonplace of many areas of descriptive psychology that thoughts and actions are cued, or evoked, by particular situations. Such observations range from the sign stimuli or releasers described by ethologists to the everyday absent-minded errors that everyone makes. William James's example of someone going to his bedroom to change for dinner, undressing, and then getting into bed must be prototypical, and most people can recount numerous similar examples of their own (cf. Reason, 1976). Equally, when the appropriate cue is missing, one can fail to gain access to the appropriate act, the desired memory. In certain neurological patients this specificity of dependence on contextual cues for an action can become pathologically exaggerated. The patient is not able to enact 'drinking' from an empty glass, nor 'combing' his hair, unless a comb is in his hand.

In the old psychology, such linkages between a calling cue and a particular category of action were called 'habits'. The key idea of S-R psychology (one sometimes feels, the only idea) was that actions ('responses') are addressed or evoked by particular calling conditions ('stimuli'). If we undo the restriction that these $a \rightarrow b$ pairs must be directly observable events, and instead interpret the a's and b's as specific 'states of mind', providing in addition some relatively simple mechanisms for their interaction, then this simple associationistic conception can have surprising power. Its simplest and most direct application in information-processing terms can be seen in so-called 'Production Systems', first developed, for modelling psychological mechanisms, by Newell and Simon (1972).

In the basic form of Production System (PS), all of 'long-term memory' consists of modular *condition→action* rules, or Productions, as reflex-like units of know-how. The other principal component of a PS is a data base—or working memory—in which to represent the system's knowledge about the current state of the world, and through which (in a 'pure' PS) all communications between independent Production rules are channelled. A Production rule becomes active whenever its *condition* is satisfied by the data base; its associated *action* now becomes available for application, to add to, modify or otherwise manipulate the information already present in working memory.

In Newell's early PS models (Newell, 1973b) the entire working memory (STM) was restricted to a string of no more than seven independent symbols ('chunks'). His motive for this oddly self-denying ordinance—which was, in fact, crucial to the predictions of his PS models – was the curious but at that time still widespread belief to the effect that the span of immediate auditory-verbal repetition (the 'magical number 7' of the average subject) could be taken as a direct index of the total capacity of a hypothetical, unique input-output channel to long-term memory. It evidently did not occur to those who held this belief to subject it to simple test; for example, by requiring subjects to repeat telephone numbers of a length equal to their 'span', while at the same time engaging in other information-processing tasks (see Chapter 5). If this belief, embodied as a central postulate in Newell's PS models, were correct, the subject must presumably either forget the telephone number, or be quite unable to carry out the concurrent task. As it turns out, in a good many subjectively 'concentration-demanding' tasks, such as balancing a short dowel rod on one finger for example, concurrent digit-span recitation, if anything, enhances performance! In general, so long as the additional task does not also require (implicit) auditory-verbal memory, a digit-span 'load' certainly need not cause major disruption to its performance. I shall return to the subject of 'working memory' at the end of this chapter.

I need scarcely add that this sort of arbitrary restriction on the size of the data base is in no sense intrinsic to Production System design. Moreover, as we shall see, other, closely related systems may use varying degrees of direct communication between specific groups of Productions, as well as a great variety of special-purpose registers or monitors for keeping track of different variables, rather than channelling all internal messages through one globally accessible 'working memory'. Further reference to Production Systems can be found in Chapter 4. Some reasonably accessible, psychologically oriented introductions to PS ideas can be found in Fox (1978); Hunt and Poltrock (1974); Anderson (1976); and Young (1976, 1978); with reference respectively to perception; problem-solving and working memory; language and retrieval from LTM; and to cognitive development.

Undoubtedly the invariants that need to be detected by perceptual systems can be highly abstract. The variables within a 'condition' can themselves be complex structural relations, the critical values for which must also be adjustable to a rapidly shifting context, as in listening to different human voices. Moreover, many–if not all–the properties and relations important in human cognition appear to be inherently 'fuzzy', like family resemblances, rather than discrete (cf. Rosch and Lloyd, 1978). For the same reason, in modelling psychological processes it seems essential to have varying degrees of activation on individual Productions, according to the 'goodness' with which their required calling-patterns are satisfied in the current situation. Such activation must also be capable of summation over extended periods of time. These are all features that are readily incorporated in a PS.

Co-operating 'experts'

Production Systems have great computational power. Indeed, they can be shown to have formal equivalence to a Turing machine (Anderson, 1976). That is, in principle, a Production System can compute anything that is computable. In practice, too, workers in Artificial Intelligence have increasingly found that a Production System framework has advantages for the design of man-made 'intelligent' systems, especially where very large amounts of inherently fuzzy or informal knowledge is to be used, and where new pieces of knowledge are to be assimilated ('learned'?) piece-meal. These conditions clearly apply to systems that are to handle natural human language. A major Production-based system for the recognition of speech, called HEARSAY, has been described by Reddy (1975), Reddy and Newell (1974), and others; and psychologists interested in language understanding should be familiar with the work of Schank (1975) and of Wilks (1976). Production System principles have also provided the framework for some impressive Artificial Intelligence systems in other domains traditionally thought of as the sphere of characteristically *human* intelligence, such as scientific inference and hypothesis formation (Feigenbaum, 1977; Lenat, 1977) and medical diagnosis (Shortliffe, 1976).

The 'intelligence' of such systems depends on the possession of relatively large amounts of domain-specific knowledge – as it does in human experts – knowledge embodied in many individually incomplete, and partially overlapping fragments of procedural know-how. Such redundancy of knowledge-representation is important in enabling the system to maintain some sort of 'sensible' behaviour despite damage or modifications to, or error in other parts of the system. Conversely, the addition of partially redundant Production rules, one by one, can model remarkably effectively the stepwise acquisition of context-dependent 'strategies' in cognitive development (Young, 1978; see also Becker, 1973, and Anderson, 1976). In many other recent developments in Artificial Intelligence the most important common feature has been the use of modular, active knowledge units (schemata, ACTORS, frames, scripts . . .): essentially, structured bundles of Production rules, each bundle having its own calling pattern(s), its own statement of relevance, and which in turn, when activated, can set up further expectations (condition→ action rules) regarding other relevant contingencies. See, for example, Bobrow and Winograd (1977); Fahlman (1977); Hewitt (1977); Minsky (1975); Schank and Abelson (1977); Waterman and Hayes-Roth (1978).

Two ideas that are fundamental to all these approaches are that:

1 Procedures (or knowledge) in long-term memory are accessed via particular calling-patterns. *The basic mechanism of thought is seen as a process of pattern recognition.* As a direct consequence, too, such systems are highly 'distractible'. As in living organisms (and unlike conventional computer programmes), the arrival of new information can trigger an immediate and complete re-orientation of current activity by means of data interrupts (see below). This characteristic also is related to the important principle, enunciated by Bobrow and Norman (1975), that in a living brain 'all the input data must be accounted for'.

2 Their organization is highly modular. The performance of the whole system depends on the co-operating contributions of many independent, specialist sub-systems, none of which has a uniquely dominant or executive role. There is no one 'decision demon', no 'central executive', no homunculus. Control can be transferred between sub-systems as the result of something like a discussion among experts (cf. Smith and Davis, 1978), according to the principle of 'redundancy of potential command' advocated long ago by Warren McCulloch (1965). Whoever currently has access to the most important (or the best quality) data, or to other crucial resources, temporarily takes control. But every sub-part may have a power of veto over the equilibrium of the whole (see Ashby, 1960). For an excellent and highly readable introduction to some of these ideas of heterarchical organization, see Arbib (1972). I have recently

reviewed some of the potential implications of PS and related approaches for theories of human cognition (Allport 1979a).

System interactions: co-operation and competition

Plainly, in any such complex, heterarchical system, the control structure – the principles of organization that constrain what kinds of interaction can occur between individual sub-systems – will be crucial to its actual performance. The behaviour emerges from the interactions within a system of components, rather than as the property of the individual components themselves.

In Newell's simple PS models (Newell 1973b), an important assumption, as far as their psychological interpretation went, was that the time taken to evoke, and execute, a given Production (condition→action pair) was independent of the total number of Productions in the system. That is, Productions were supposedly accessed in an unlimited-capacity, or content-addressable manner. However, the Productions were then *executed* (i.e., their actions could be carried out) only one at a time, in fixed order of priority. Other PSs (for example: Anderson, 1976) in principle permit Productions to be executed in parallel. Obviously, for any distributed system, fundamental issues are raised by the demands of conflict resolution and of controlling undesirable interactions: of keeping separate processes separate. Such issues of system architecture are also of obvious and central importance for psychological theories.

In many large PSs, priority of execution between simultaneously evoked Production rules is decided by a variety of *meta-rules*, themselves also Production rules that can be activated, selectively if necessary, by different *goal* conditions (e.g., Hayes-Roth and Lesser 1977). For example, precedence may temporarily be given to certain types of calling-patterns ('stimulus set') or to particular categories of action ('response set'). Or priority may be assigned in terms of the frequency or recency with which any rule has been applied (e.g., Forgy and McDermott, 1977), the specificity or goodness of fit of the calling conditions that evoked it, or in terms of the confidence or other value attached to the individual rule.

One of the main difficulties of programming in Production Systems arises from what may be called 'data-specific limitations'. Process A leaves some products in working memory that trigger Productions relevant to some other process, or other task. A variety of defensive strategies have been developed to deal with this unintended cross-talk. Representations in working memory can be 'packed up', or chunked, to protect them from being interfered with by 'irrelevant' Productions, and then must be laboriously 'unpacked' again (e.g., Moran, 1973). Or particular regions of an otherwise globally accessible database may be temporarily frozen ('inhibited'?). Of course, this problem of *protection* of access by a given process to a given resource is an extremely general one in information-processing systems, whether biological or man-made. Kohout and Gaines (1976) and Kohout (1976), for example, illustrate (at a rather abstract level) the application of such automata-theory ideas to the biological organization of movement, and of language. In the chapter on attention (in this volume) I indicate how data-specific limitations, and related problems of protection, may apply also to our understanding of the 'division of attention', when people attempt to perform two or more tasks at the same time.

Motivation and action

A serious criticism of information-processing psychology is that it has largely by-passed questions of motivation. 'Cognition' is supposedly one subject, 'motivation' quite another. By contrast, and perhaps paradoxically so, in cybernetics and automata theory the conceptions of purposive or *goal-seeking* (therefore 'motivational') mechanisms, regulated by feedback and feedforward, have been right at the centre. In a control system, goals can be thought of, very naturally, as reference signals. 'Stimuli' (or 'problems'!) are disturbances that cause a mismatch with a reference signal. Ashby's superb book *Design for a Brain* (1960) provides perhaps the best of all introductions for psychologists. For a later reminder, see Powers (1978).

In Production Systems the concept of GOAL is crucial, also. Nearly all Production rules have as their calling-pattern not only an informational condition, but also a GOAL condition. The Production is evoked only if that GOAL is active. The action of some Productions will be to change the currently active goal; for example, by instating a new sub-goal or by re-establishing a previously unsatisfied goal that had been temporarily 'pushed down' on a special working register called a GOAL STACK. In this way, GOALs make possible the concept of sub-procedures, and provide the principal method by which control of an entire PS remains coherent.

Goals, and actions, can of course be represented at many different levels of abstraction. At one level we may think of the behaviour of organisms, their fundamental 'motivation', in terms simply of approach or avoidance of different environments. Perhaps more usefully, at least for higher organisms, we may seek to categorize behaviour in terms of a set of biologically basic, and more-or-less mutually exclusive 'modes' of activity: eating, sleeping, hunting, sex, grooming, excretion, alerting to possible danger, fight, flight, and so forth. (At this level of analysis, reading this chapter, perhaps—or writing it—and all the multifarious 'intellectual' activities of humans might be thought of as part of a rather special mode of activity: 'play'.)

Different basic modes (or goals) of behaviour are appropriate to, and so must be evoked by, different conditions of the internal or external environment. In so far as they are mutually incompatible, goals must compete with one another for dominance. One thing that is essential for survival is that such competition should not get dead-locked; the whole organism must be able to switch its commitment abruptly from one basic mode or goal to another. (Anyone who has watched human infants alternating between bouts of feeding, crying, 'cooing' and sleeping knows how sudden and dramatic these shifts can be. A beautiful analysis of alternating shifts, in relation to feeding behaviour, is given by David McFarland, 1974, 1978.)

H. A. Simon (1967) has offered a thought-provoking account of human emotions as information-processing interrupts, and Pribram (1971) argues for a somewhat similar position. This perspective, in turn, can be referred back to a common ancestry with Ashby's (1960) notion of veto regulation, exercised by each part of a dynamic system over the equilibrium of the whole, and to his conception of the 'ultrastable' system.

Several years ago, Kilmer *et al.* (1969) described (and simulated) a 'central command system', based on the anatomy and physiology of certain brain-stem structures, that could control the moment-by-moment dominance among competing, biologically basic modes of behaviour. Dominance was computed on the basis of currently available information, from many different sources, about the conditions of internal and external environment. Indisputably, 'motivational' mechanisms are also 'information-processing' ones.

Interestingly, their proposed system was itself made up of a number of relatively autonomous, distributed modules. The system as a whole cycled alternately between an isolationist and an interactive manner of decision-making among the separate modules.

In the case of higher mental functions, by contrast, some combinations of activities at least (i.e., some goals) are not mutually incompatible. In planful behaviour there will necessarily be a hierarchy of current goals and sub-goals. A sophisticated system should be able to divide its commitment between concurrent, non-conflicting goals. (See Chapter 4 and the problem of 'divided attention'.)

One further remark about 'eliciting conditions': In 'intelligent' behaviour one important category of situation→action rule will be *meta*-rules – sometimes called *strategies* – rules about when to apply other kinds of rules. Some such strategies will be specific to a narrow range of situations that can evoke them; others may have extremely wide application. Jon Baron (1978) has some interesting speculations about the role of three such meta-rules (stimulus analysis, relatedness search and checking) that he suggests have rather general application in what could be seen as 'problem' situations, and that, he conjectures, may contribute to variations in 'general intelligence'.

Action demons and the cueing of actions.

In understanding the control of skilled action, two basic ideas provide a starting point. The first of these is the idea of multi-level or hierarchical control. The higher levels direct the course of action typically over larger spans of time (and space), and at a more abstract level of specification, while remaining in 'executive ignorance' of the detailed adjustments made by the lower levels to the constraints of their 'local' context: to the starting position of the limb, the relative size, position or inertia of the objects to be acted upon, and so forth. (See the following chapter by Harvey and Greer.)

The second basic idea relates to the necessity for some kind of library, or 'thesaurus', of action-patterns (cf. Shallice, 1978). We should not fall into the trap of thinking of stored specifications for action, in biological systems, as separate from the mechanism that interprets or processes them. There is an obvious parallel between the idea of input-pattern-specific recognition demons and output-pattern-specific action demons: that is, content-specific mechanisms for the control of a particular class of action. I propose, as a fundamental assumption, that different categories of skilled action are controlled, at a relatively abstract level, by special-purpose (i.e., content-specific) mechanisms, here called 'action demons'.

We know little about the neuronal embodiment of action demons, (though Rosenbaum, 1977, has pioneered one promising behavioural approach to their exploration). In some species they may even take the form of individual 'command neurons', though action systems consisting of large groups of neurons seem more likely to be the rule (Kupferman and Weiss, 1978).

The question on which I wish to focus, however, is this: How are appropriate actions in an individual's repertoire called upon when needed? How are they indexed? The obvious requirement is that actions must be evoked by an intention, that is by a representation of some goal or intended result, together with the environmental conditions under which such a result can be effected by such an action. In Miller, Galanter and Pribram's (1960) elementary TOTE units (TEST-OPERATE-TEST-EXIT: see Chapter 3 and Pribram, 1971), each 'operate' procedure must be accessed via a test mechanism, that contains a specification of the operation's *intended result,* and against which the success of the operation can be evaluated.

Essentially the same idea was embodied in one of the earliest 'intelligent' programmes, the General Problem Solver (GPS) of Newell and Simon (1963). All of the specific (i.e., content-dependent) knowledge of GPS – its knowledge of 'means' and 'ends' – was organized in the form of a Table of Effects. A different Table of Effects was needed for each of the 'task environments' (logic, chess, etc.) in which GPS was intended to operate. (To give the general idea: if change-of-location is what is wanted, a relevant 'operator' might be 'walking'. But walking can only be done properly from a standing position. So long as you are lying down, trying the normal walking movements will not get you very far.)

To find a particular action (an 'operator') relevant to the current situation and the current goal was a simple look-up process. Production Systems (see above) are a generalization of just such a (content-addressing) look-up process. In Hewitt's ACTOR model too, as in the PLANNER formalism that preceded it (Hewitt, 1972, 1977) procedures are addressed by a specification of their characteristic GOAL. Biological action demons can similarly be thought of as

Production-like mechanisms, whose characteristic calling-patterns include a specification both of internal (GOAL) and external (CUE) conditions for their execution. Failure to maintain the specification for the originally intended goal is evidently one very common cause of 'absent-minded' errors, like the one recounted by William James, as well as for performance failures when attempting to do several things at once (Reason, 1976).

How a current goal might be represented in the central nervous system is open to conjecture. Consistent with the framework of this chapter we may think in terms of another category of gnostic units, or 'goal demons'. Activity in each of these functional units represents the current strength of that particular goal. Goals are, of course, evoked by conditions, just as actions are.

In many complex tasks the relation between environmental cues and overt responses may depend on successive transformations of the initial input, before the desired procedure can be accessed. Many of the difficulties of recalling information from long-term memory appear to be due to the insufficiency of the current retrieval cue to specify *uniquely* the further information that is being sought: the problem of 'cue overload' (Tulving 1974). Similarly, in certain types of pathological amnesia, the patients' inability to recall specific events has been attributed to an excess of irrelevant information evoked by the same retrieval cue (Warrington and Weiskrantz, 1973). Norman (1968) has sketched an account of remembering as an iterative process of generating, and refining, the appropriate retrieval cue to which the sought-for information quite abruptly 'springs to mind' – it becomes available to the rest of the system. And so it appears to be in many other problem-solving tasks (see Chapter 8). By contrast, in certain highly practised S-R or transcription skills, such as reading aloud, even though the sensory cues may require immensely complex transformations before they can gain potential command of an overt action, such as speech, they may come to do so in a series of unique, rather than one-to-many, condition-action steps (La Berge, 1975).

Notice that, even when access from a given sensory calling-pattern to a particular action is (or has become) relatively direct or 'compatible' (see below), this clearly does not mean that the action is triggered compulsively whenever that sensory pattern appears. An action demon requires as calling conditions both a CUE and a specification of a particular, currently active GOAL: for example, the goal of reading words aloud. When other goals are active, the same cue can command quite different actions: writing, typing, searching, comparing, etc. etc. Through learning, also, the same action demon (say, pronouncing a particular word) can come under potential command of many different calling cues, in conjunction with different current goals.

The relative directness with which stimuli can cue responses varies over an indefinitely wide range, from the immediacy of 'ideo-motor-compatible' mappings at one end (see below) to what are usually thought of as problem-solving relations at the other. In a crossword, for instance, a properly constructed clue uniquely determines its solution, yet access to the correct word may be mediated by very complex inferences.

As a convenient shorthand we can speak of the 'strength' of any cue as a calling-pattern for a particular action. Its strength might be expected to depend on many variables, including the current priority or 'focus' assigned to that part of the environment, the frequency and recency with which that condition→action link has been utilized, and the degree to which that link is temporarily enabled by the current goal state.

However, the actual effectiveness of a particular cue in evoking a given response will depend not only on its own current cue-strength with respect to the desired response, but also on the relative strengths (and distinctiveness) of all *other* cue-response links that are evoked either by the same stimulus event, or by other concurrently active external or internal conditions. That, obviously enough, is where a whole heap of questions about the limitations of 'attention' come in: about the ability to ignore, selectively, certain 'irrelevant' cues in the environment, or to engage concurrently in two or more independent activities. Some of these questions are discussed in Chapter 4.

Cue-response compatibility

The directness with which a given environmental event can evoke a specified action is sometimes known as the cue-response (or S-R) 'compatibility'.

Remember how, in the basic TOTE units of Miller, Galanter and Pribram (1960), control was passed to a given operator via a conditional test mechanism that evaluated the successful result of the operation. If, in biological systems, a given action demon is indeed directly accessed via a representation of its expected (or intended) result, then one category of stimulus must have a specially privileged status as a calling-cue for that action: namely, the pattern of feedback associated with its successful execution. For example: the motor programme needed to produce a particular speech sound should be peculiarly directly cued by the *auditory* pattern which that motor programme, if executed, would produce. When cued in this way the immediate effect of such an action will thus be to reproduce the stimulus pattern that evoked it. Such a relation between 'stimulus' and 'response' has been termed, following William James, 'ideo-motor (I-M) compatibility' (Greenwald, 1970).

I-M compatible relationships may be rather exceptional in everyday life. However, in many interactions with the physical environment (such as touching, grasping, or locomotion) there is a degree of built-in *spatial* correspondence between the cue evoking the action and the spatial directedness of the appropriate response. This includes actions effected on one's own body (e.g., scratching an itch). To a striking extent the brain preserves the spatial topology of events from sense organ to effector, and this spatial (or somatotopic) correspondence forms the basis of a second – and again powerful – form of cue-response compatibility. A beautiful example can be seen in the mechanisms that control the direction of gaze. Two 'maps', one representing the position of objects in the field of vision, the other representing target positions for saccadic movements of the eyes, are superimposed in the brainstem superior colliculus. This is a truly 'parallel' computational system, with no 'central executive'. Arbib (1972, ch. 7) gives an excellent introductory description of it.

At the other pole of cue-response incompatibility, certain types of mental operation can be entirely unable to command a given modality of action. Such functional disconnections between different processes may be only transitory (as when the revelant condition→ action link is temporarily inhibited by the current goal state); or they may be permanent (the relevant link simply does not exist). In many instances, we can obtain definite evidence that a given information-process occurs, through its effects, direct or indirect, on *one* channel of behaviour. Yet that process can remain quite unable to control *other* specified modalities of action. The section that follows, on 'unconscious' processing, documents some of the more radical instances of such process-to-process disconnection, or incompatibility. In particular it points to processes that cannot control that peculiar class of actions known as 'perceptual reports'.

'Unconscious' information-processing

A patient who has recently had a large section of his visual cortex surgically excised is sitting in front of a 'perimeter', a standard device for testing visual responsiveness across the visual field. The patient is asked to keep his eye on a central spot, and then to 'say when he sees a light' anywhere else in the perimeter. In one half of the visual field his responses are normal, but in much of the remainder, and in one quadrant in particular, he is completely blind. He has no experience of 'seeing' anything at all in this region of space.

Now the patient is asked to do a slightly different task. Each time a light comes on he is to reach out to touch it with his hand, still keeping fixation of the centre spot. A buzzer sounds to indicate when he is to do so, and, if unsure, he is asked to guess. In this task, except for the very smallest lights, his responses are virtually perfect, even in the totally 'blind' region, and even though he doggedly insists that, in that region, he is simply guessing. This is the phenomenon that Weiskrantz and his colleagues (Weiskrantz *et al.*,1974; Weiskrantz, 1977) have termed 'blindsight'. It appears that ambient (subcortical) visual mechanisms are able to control with great accuracy such discriminative actions as reaching, or the direction of gaze, and – in monkeys at least – can control locomotion and the avoidance of obstacles. But they cannot control 'perceptual reports'. They are not 'conscious'.

It is not only such biologically 'hard wired' (and spatially compatible) processes that can operate without gaining access to the mechanisms of 'conscious reports'. A formidable range of evidence has now accumulated to the effect that the discrimination of complex, learned patterns, such as written or spoken words and their meanings, can occur similarly without the results of this processing being able to control overt voluntary responses. Many of these demonstrations concern indirect effects, produced by a word of whose presence the subject may be wholly unaware, on the way in which another, semantically related word is responded to. Thus, in the visual modality, words presented non-centrally (e.g., Bradshaw, 1974;

Willows and McKinnon, 1973; Underwood, 1976 or in conditions of retinal rivalry (Somekh and Wilding, 1973), and which the
subject cannot explicitly report, can still bias the interpretation of
other, simultaneously presented words or pictures. The important
point is that the word need not be consciously perceived, need not be
available for explicit report, for it to exert effects on behaviour that
depend critically on the *meaning* of that word. Analogous results in the
auditory modality are described in Chapter 4. Of particular interest
here, 'unattended' words in the dichotic shadowing task can release
conditioned autonomic responses that have been previously associated, either to particular words or to an entire conceptual category
(Corteen and Wood, 1972; Corteen and Dunn, 1974; Von Wright *et
al.*, 1975; Forster and Govier, 1978). In Corteen's experiments the
subjects were not able to make voluntary (manual) responses, nor to
interrupt shadowing, as a means of indicating that they had detected
a word from the pre-specified conceptual category, if it occurred in the
non-shadowed ear. Retrospectively, also, they had no conscious
memory of the occurrence of those target words in the non-shadowed
input. Yet words in the target category still selectively evoked
autonomic responses (GSRs), of equal magnitude, regardless
of whether they occurred in the shadowed or in the unshadowed ear.
Apparently, in successfully preventing the speech in the not-to-be-
shadowed ear from capturing control of the shadowing task, this
information (although categorized semantically) was also selectively
isolated from some, but not all, other behavioural systems.

There are many other demonstrations of the 'unconscious' processing of word-meanings. Some striking examples of this kind have
been observed under conditions of visual pattern masking (Allport,
1977; Marcel and Patterson, 1978; Marcel, in press). In a rapid word→
mask sequence, the subject may be unable to judge, at better than chance
accuracy, whether or not *any* stimulus had preceded masking pattern, let
alone to report the word's identity. The remarkable thing is that, even
under these conditions, the *meaning* of the masked word can affect the
subject's response to other words (Marcel, in press). One way of thinking
about these results is that the complete recognize – act cycle of a
visual word-demon has been interrupted. Its *recognize* phase has been
initiated, but its *response* – of labelling (or 'verifying') the visual
pattern that evoked it in the data base with a particular word-
identity-hypothesis – is pre-empted by the fact that the relevant
word-pattern has by now been displaced from the data base by the

mask (Allport 1977, 1979b). Its identity is therefore not directly available to word-*naming* demons: it cannot be reported.

Incidentally, what this suggestion implies is that the forever-fleeting stream of perceptual awareness is in some way constituted by these momentary acts of perceptual verification. Consciousness is not a *container*, with 'contents', but an *activity*, a process of inter-communication between parts of a dynamic system.

Indeed, much the greater part of human information processing is undoubtedly 'unconscious'. We cannot arbitrarily couple its products at any given level to control particular action.* Still less can we report on, or introspect about, the processes themselves. Consider, for example, the immensely complex processes that must underlie the understanding of speech or of a coherent visual scene. 'Seeing' or 'understanding' is normally so successful, and so effortless, that one of the hardest problems in first coming to study psychology is to appreciate that there is anything there to explain. Certainly there is little in the way of conscious processes that we can 'report' about.

Functional anatomy and 'double dissociations' of function

So far, our discussion of distributed processing ('memory and pro-cessor are one and the same thing') has proceeded without explicit reference to the observable localization, or specialization, of functions in the nervous system. There is, in fact, a rich source of evidence in the behavioural effects of cerebral injury, indicating that the brain is organized at a relatively gross anatomical level into functionally isolable components, such that local injury can selectively destroy, or disconnect, one or two among an astonishing variety of specialized sub-systems.

Some of these represent very obviously distinct domains or modalities of processing. For example, the comprehension or produc-tion of language can be defective, or even abolished, while leaving such skills as musical performance, visual recognition, drawing and copying, or spatial and constructional reasoning essentially un-impaired. See, for example, Goodglass and Geschwind (1976), Luria (1966), Zangwill (1964). Conversely, spatial construction (Warring-

---

*This point has been well made by Henderson (1977). But it has been all too often overlooked in the design and interpretation of laboratory experiments.

ton, 1969), or musical understanding or performance (Gardner, 1975) may be shattered without accompanying signs of language disturbance. In the jargon of neuropsychology, such functions are said to be 'doubly dissociated'.

I referred earlier to the pathological inability on the part of certain patients to enact an object's use without the appropriate object in hand. By contrast, other patients have been described who, although able to mime actions to verbal command, nevertheless cannot make proper use of the actual objects (e.g., DeRenzi *et al.*, 1968). Both are examples of 'apraxias', the disorganization or destruction of once-skilled action programs. Rather similar disabilities can represent a selective disconnection: the patient is unable to evoke a given gesture or action on verbal command, although he can both demonstrate verbally that he has understood the instruction, and can execute the action flawlessly on imitation (Heilman, 1973). Conversely, disorders of object naming have been observed that are restricted to particular modalities of *input* (Lhermitte and Beauvois, 1973).

The dissociations that can be observed are by no means always intuitive. For example, Elizabeth Warrington (1975) has described a patient, a man previously of high intelligence, whose knowledge or recognition of common objects (acorn, needle, goose) *or* of their written or spoken names was grossly impaired, yet who could still use (and give fluent definitions of) complex *abstract* words or concepts (arbiter, pact, supplication). Patients can also be found whose knowledge of quite limited conceptual or linguistic domains – for example, of parts of the human body – appears to be selectively destroyed or disconnected from other sources of information (Caramazza and Berndt, 1978; Goodglass and Geschwind, 1976; Yamadori and Albert, 1973).

Some of the most striking and dramatic dissociations of function can be found *within* the numerous sub-systems of language: for example, between the mechanisms of syntax – responsible for the production (and comprehension) of grammatically formed phrases and inflections – and of word-meanings and the lexicon (Caramazza and Berndt, 1978; Marin *et al.*, 1976).

In reading, certain lesions leave the patient able to speak and to write fluently, yet unable to read a word of what he has written. Certain patients may succeed in naming a written word, but be unable to identify the letters of which it is composed (Shallice and Warrington, 1977), while others can read numerals, but not letters or

words (Hécaen and Kremin, 1976). Other lesions permit the patient
to comprehend, and to read aloud, words denoting concrete objects
from a vocabulary running into many thousands, including words
with relatively complex orthography ('chrysanthemum'), yet leave
him unable to read aloud words with abstract meaning, or with a
specialized syntactic function such as pronouns or conjunctions, and
unable to sound out even short written nonsense-syllables (Coltheart
et al., 1980; Saffran and Marin, 1977). Patients are also occasionally
seen with highly selective disorders of writing, or of written spelling,
in the absence of other obvious disorders either of oral language or of
reading (Dubois *et al.*, 1969; Kinsbourne and Rosenfeld, 1974). In
some cases these patients can form individual letters normally, yet
they make gross errors in the written spelling of words that they can
spell out, orally, without a mistake.

Lastly, in so-called conduction aphasia, the patient may appear
superficially to have more or less normal auditory and even written
comprehension, as well as normal, intelligent understanding of the
physical world; and normal ability to form new episodic memories. In
some cases, at least, his spontaneous speech also can be entirely fluent
(Shallice and Butterworth, 1977). Yet he is not able to repeat back,
word-for-word, arbitrary sequences of more than one or at most two
nonsense-words; nor can he repeat spoken sentences of more than a
few words, except in the form of a radical paraphrase, though he
remains unaware that this is what he is doing. However, only when
the sentences depart from the familiar subject-verb-object sequence
does he make any obvious errors in understanding them (Saffran and
Marin, 1975).

Here, then, is a dramatically selective disorder of auditory-verbal
short-term memory. The STM system that has been damaged (or
disconnected?), however, is manifestly not some universal input-
output device on long-term memory. Still less can it be identified with
a general-purpose 'limited-capacity central processor', as many
psychologists have suggested in the past. If it were, conduction
aphasics would obviously suffer all kinds of calamitous and general
intellectual deficits, which in fact they do not.

This whole range of results, and many others like them, provide
striking illustrations of the way in which intelligent human action
must depend on a very large number of functionally, and often
anatomically, separable modular sub-systems, with quite specific and
local paths of communication between the specialized modules.

Indeed, such data offer the strongest possible hints about the identity of, and the boundaries between, some of these sub-systems.

Summary of some 'New Directions' for cognitive psychology

I have tried to contrast two different directions for cognitive psychology. One direction could be characterized as the search for *basic* ('hardware') constraints on the human computer: the search for *generalized* information-processing limitations: limitations of processing rates, of capacity, of memory spans and memory persistence, of retrieval time, and so forth. A fundamental, but generally unexamined assumption of this kind of research is that the basic psychological processes it seeks to uncover are essentially independent of their particular information content. This direction of research is predisposed to ask questions such as 'For how long is an "item" held in "storage"?' rather than 'How can such information be represented at all?'

A different and contrasting orientation focusses directly on information *content*, and on *content-specific* (hence distributed) mechanisms for its representation and use. This latter orientation has emerged in three ways.

First, it has become clear that particular psychological procedures – mental or physical actions in the repertoire of the individual – must be cued by appropriate eliciting conditions. From this standpoint, therefore, one of the most central, and enormous, tasks for psychology, is to discover (and to develop appropriate notations for describing) the codes or patterns that act as effective calling-cues for particular cerebral processes. There is a striking convergence between this orientation and the approach of J. J. Gibson and his followers (Gibson, 1966; Johansson, 1979; Lee, in press), whose goal is to provide descriptions for the global patterns of (optical) information-flow that, they claim, directly signal the actions that they 'afford' – the surface-that-can-be-walked-on, and so forth – despite the fact that the Gibsonian approach has often been presented as antagonistic to both 'information-processing' and 'neo-associationistic' psychology. (The difference is that, in the orientation sketched here, the enterprise does not *end* with a description of the optic flow-field.) A similar shift of emphasis can be seen in the psychology of cognitive development. Margaret Donaldson (1978) gives some beautiful examples of the way in which supposedly content-independent (Piagetian) limitations in young children's reasoning powers can be radically altered by the particular content of the problems devised to test them, and by the form and context of their presentation. Valerie Curran (Chapter 9) illustrates the same theme in a cross-cultural perspective. As one further example, also in the realm of cognitive development, David Booth (1978) has shown how early language acquisition can be effectively described by the addition of Production-like, situation→action rules (cf. also Shatz, 1978).

The second, and perhaps the critically important, impetus towards a changed direction for cognitive psychology comes from Artificial Intelligence, in providing both a potentially rich theoretical notation and a radically different criterion for the sufficiency of a theory (Boden, 1977). The criterion that thrusts itself upon anyone attempting to build computational models of psychological processes is that the process should actually work. Just pretending that one has a theory of how one process is to access another, by drawing in an arrow between two boxes, butters no parsnips at all! This new concern with detail, with the contents of information-processing rather than the supposed 'amount' of it (bits-per-second) is just beginning to make contact with the empirical resources of laboratory psychology. (A notable example is the work on text understanding and reference, by Sanford and Garrod, 1979). This combination of theoretical and empirical psychology, I dare to hope, offers the makings at least of a true science of cognition, rather than, as previously, a going-through-the-motions of scientific activity, without substantive content to the 'theories' under investigation.

Third, the evidence of neuropsychology, as of neurophysiology, argues that cognitive organization is indeed highly distributed and content-specific: that the nervous system is built up of many functionally autonomous (though richly interacting) specialized subsystems. The major contribution of experimental neuropsychology lies in identifying where in the architecture of cognition these natural break-lines are to be found.

Implications for other topics in this book

There is space here to recapitulate only a few general points.

Perception and action: I have tried to emphasize the interdependence of these traditionally distinct areas of psychology. Harvey and Greer's discussion of a 'perceptual theory of motor control' based on an internal space-co-ordinate system (Chapter 3) takes up this theme directly. Among perceptual theories, David Marr's work on 'low level vision' (1976) is a superb illustration of the AI method. Here is a detailed theory, based on clear principles and on the known physiology of the mammalian visual system, that really works! The 'primal sketch' could clearly be thought of as one level of representation in the multi-layered data base, or 'working memory', of a large Production System. My one reservation about this work is that it should take as its starting point the problem of segmenting regions (or objects) in an isolated snapshot. For a mobile organism the visual input is a continuous flow-pattern, the transformations of which can specify in a peculiarly direct way which parts 'go together' (Clocksin, 1978). True, people in our society can readily make sense of still photographs, but we need to know more about the relationship of this ability to the processing of dynamic visual inputs in a moving animal, and about the relationship of *that* to the potential command of action.

A particularly interesting example of the interdependence of perception and action can be seen in our recognition of the gestures and facial expressions of other people, that 'elaborate and secret code that is written nowhere, known by none, and understood by all', as Edward Sapir described it, and in our ability to imitate. F. A. Hayek (1962) has a characteristically brilliant essay in which this and many other issues germane to this chapter are discussed. A young animal, surrounded every day by the species-characteristic actions of its elders and siblings, Hayek argues, must somehow recognize and *assimilate* these characteristic patterns, encoded from outside, to its own repertoire of gestures and intentions sensed internally. Indeed, anything that even approximately fits these species-specific schemata will tend to be assimilated to them. Hence, Hayek suggests, the phenomenal world will first be built up of those internalized action patterns characteristic of the individual's own species. These will form some of the earliest and most important categories in terms of which the animal perceives the world; and not only the animate world. A 'threatening cloud', a 'smiling landscape' need not be 'mere metaphors' but a true representation of how we encode events (See Chapter 7).

Memory and understanding: Perhaps the most central problem of memory, indeed of cognitive psychology in general, is that of *assimilation*. How does a sensory event, similar though not identical to a previously experienced event or category of events, gain selective access to knowledge already acquired about that category? To put it a little differently, how is *similarity* coded? More particularly, how are similarity relationships *selectively* computed, as in analogy, metaphor, and in probably all important forms of inference and problem-solving? Central as these questions undoubtedly are, in human memory research, they have remained for practical purposes virtually untouched.

In Artificial Intelligence a few relatively direct attacks have been made on possible processes of assimilation, of which Moore and Newel's (1974) work on ß-structures and Fahlman's (1977) hologram-like memory system are particularly interesting examples. In theoretical psychology and neurophysiology, respectively, recent papers by Ratcliff (1978) and by Cavanagh (1975) are also of interest.

Short-term memory and attention: Questions about 'the control structure' of cognitive processes, discussed in this chapter, have obvious relevance to those subject areas of psychology, traditionally labelled attention, performance, and short-term memory. Chapter 4 draws out some implications of the orientation presented here for our understanding of the phenomena of 'attention'.

In Chapter 5 Graham Hitch puts forward a conception of short-term memory with which I find points of agreement, although there is one issue on which, for the present, we agree to differ. We clearly have common cause in arguing that the phenomena conventionally attri-buted to STM reflect a number of distinct mechanisms. Following Baddeley and Hitch's (1974) classic demonstration of the independence of processes responsible, respectively, for transient 'recency' effects in free recall and for the auditory-verbal repetition span, in Chapter 5 Graham Hitch identifies *two* relatively specific sub-systems contributing to short-term verbal retention. These are, first, an auditory-verbal 'input register', important for some aspects of speech comprehension, and that Hitch has related to the recency phenomenon in immediate free recall; and second, an articulatory 'output buffer' necessary for the fluent production of speech, and which contributes to a variety of laboratory tasks that benefit from sub-vocal rehearsal.

Furthermore, besides these two auditory-vocal sub-systems there are numerous indications of other functionally dissociable components of temporary representation, specific both to the domain of representation (e.g., lexical identity *v.* speech prosody, melodic contour *v.* pitch) as well as to the modality of input or output (visual, tactile, kinaesthetic, manual). Such functional dissociations are attested both in the neuropsychological literature (e.g., Milner, 1971; Gardner, 1975; Hécaen and Albert, 1978), in the capabilities of normal subjects in concurrent tasks (Chapter 4), and in the selectivity of forgetting or interference (e.g., Aldridge, 1978; Dowling 1978; Proctor, 1978, among many others). That is to say, along with the specialist sub-systems identified by Graham Hitch, we evidently have to do with a great variety of different content- and modality-specific forms of representation that can contribute to temporary memory.

Hitch also postulates, as a component of 'the short-term memory system', a *general-purpose limited-capacity central processor* (GPLCCP), sometimes referred to as a 'central executive': a content and modality-independent device for 'initiating . . . and monitoring' mental processes. It is here that, for the present, we must agree to differ. To be sure, such is our ignorance of cerebral organization, we should by no means rule out the possibility of some such general-purpose device, initiating and monitoring all cerebral processes. Well, perhaps not *all* cerebral processes. But if not all, then *which* processes? Should we perhaps look for separate 'mini-executives', specialized for initiating or monitoring different types, or different combinations of activities? (For one recent discussion of some related ideas see Schwartz, 1978). In the split-brain patient, should we suppose the existence anyway of two different GPLCCPs?)

My objection to the hypothesis of a GPLCCP is twofold. First, I am not convinced that the behavioural evidence at present available demands this hypothesis, certainly not in connection with the repetition span. Second, I am far from clear what such a device is actually supposed to do.

The evidence on 'divided attention' would take us too far away from STM, and it is more appropriately considered in Chapter 4. Very briefly, however, I should point out that, in a distributed system, competition for a common 'processor' is not the only potential source of interference between concurrent tasks. Data-specific limitations (discussed in Chapter 4) can also be a major constraint on dual task performance.

With respect to the mechanisms involved in immediate verbal repetition ('span') tasks and STM, discussed in Chapter 5, I must confine myself to four short points:

1   Granted that the articulatory buffer is not the only memory component contributing to repetition span, as Badddeley *el al.* have convincingly shown, this in itself is no particular reason for supposing that the other component (or *an* other component) must be a GPLCCP-demanding tasks at the same time. We need experiments the behavioural 'span' appears not to be held in a phonological code.

2   If this other information were indeed held in the GPLCCP, as Graham Hitch has proposed, its occupation of this limited-capacity device might be expected to conflict with the execution of any *other* GLCCP-demanding tasks at the same time. We need experiments that test for this possibility. Some tasks, at least, that Baddeley and Hitch conjecture must make demands on the GPLCCP, are unaffected by concurrent retention of a six-letter 'span'. A good example is the verbal reasoning (sentence verification) task used by Baddeley and Hitch (1974), in which subjects have to decide 'true' or 'false', as quickly as possible, in respect of sentences like '*A is not preceded by B*' – *AB*. They have clearly shown that successful, simultaneous retention of a six-letter span causes absolutely no loss of speed or accuracy in this sentence verification task (Hitch and Baddeley, 1976, Experiment II: see Figure 4, the bottom left panel).

3   So there is a dilemma. If the sentence verification task does make substantial demands on the GPLCCP, and if Hitch is correct in supposing that the 'other' component in memory span retention, besides the articulatory buffer, is the *same* GPLCCP, this result should surely be impossible. On the other hand, if the sentence verification task does not make demands on the GPLCCP, then experiments involving this task are irrelevant to the question at issue.

4   Of course, the finding that overt span *rehearsal* does significantly increase concurrent sentence verification time, though it does not affect its accuracy (Hitch and Baddeley, 1976, Experiment III), is consistent with the view that it is the difficulty of concurrent *retrieval* processes that causes conflict with the verification task. It would be interesting to know whether verification time is also delayed by simultaneous free recall from *long-term* memory. If it were, this would be further indication that, whatever the source of conflict here, it is not specific to the short-term memory system.

I return to wondering what the hypothetical general-purpose

central processor is required to *do*. One answer, I suppose, is that it is the literal equivalent of the central processing unit in a conventional digital computer. This literal computer metaphor is discussed, at some length, in Chapter 4. If we can put this metaphor aside (and with it some more shadowy homunculi), what might a GPLCCP be needed for in a system that is *not* a uni-processing general-purpose computer? In particular it may be useful to put this question into Production System terms.

The distinguishing feature of a 'pure' Production System is the possession of a centralized message centre, or 'working memory', on which messages left by any one process can be 'read' by any other. An excellent example is provided by the HEARSAY speech recognition system (Reddy and Newell, 1974), whose message centre (called the 'blackboard') contains both the current speech input and competing hypotheses, at many different levels, about its interpretation. Even here, in fact, different groups of productions ('knowledge sources') are specialized to read and write only in particular regions (or 'levels') of the blackboard. Moreover, if the HEARSAY structure were to be extended, *mirabile dictu*, to include, say, a visual system, this would plainly involve the differentiation of further, specialized regions of the common blackboard. Indeed, in so far as human cognition can be envisaged in Production System terms, as I have already argued, the great diversity and selectivity of 'disconnection syndromes' seen following cerebral injury must point to highly specialized channels of communication between different sub-systems. But, this aside, even supposing a highly centralized blackboard as the working memory of a Production-based cognitive system, this would still not turn into a 'central executive', or a GPLCCP. In a Production System (as distinct from the mechanisms needed to implement one on a sequential computer) there is no 'central executive'. The blackboard is merely a passive data-structure.

'Control processes', in a Production System, are primarily effected by those condition→action rules that have as their action the activation of a new goal; but they are executed like any other Production rule.

It may be that, as we come to understand more about content-addressing, distributed computation in biological systems, some role for a GPLCCP will yet be found. I would certainly welcome any such demonstration. But the idea, so far, lacks definition. Perhaps I can provoke those who believe in a 'central executive' into proving me wrong by the rude assertion that, in biological cognition, a GPLCCP (if such a thing were provided) would simply have nothing to do. And that consequently – Nature being lavish but never wasteful with her gifts – no such thing exists.

References

Aldridge, J. W. (1978), 'Levels of processing in speech perception', *Journal of Experimental Psychology: Human Perception and Performance, 4*, pp. 164-77.

Allport, D. A. (1977), 'On knowing the meaning of words we are unable to report: the effects of visual masking', in S. Dornic (ed.), *Attention and Performance, 6*, Lawrence Erlbaum: Hillsdale, N. J.

Allport, D. A. (1979a), 'Conscious and unconscious cognition: a computational metaphor for the mechanism of attention and integration', in L. G. Nilsson (ed.), *Perspectives in Memory Research*, Lawrence Erlbaum: Hillsdale, N. J.

Allport, D. A. (1979b), 'Word recognition in reading', in P. A. Kolers, M. E. Wrolstad and H. Bouma (eds), *Processing of Visible Language, 1*, Plenum: New York.

Anderson, J. R. (1976), *Language, Memory and Thought*, Lawrence Erlbaum: Hillsdale, N. J.

Arbib, M. A. (1972), *The Metaphorical Brain*, Wiley-Interscience: New York.

Ashby, W. R. (1960), *Design for a Brain*, 2nd edn, Chapman & Hall: London.

Baddeley, A. D. and Hitch, G. J. (1974), 'Working memory', in G. Bower (ed.), *The Psychology of Learning and Motivation*, vol. 8, Academic Press: New York.

Baron, J. (1978), 'Intelligence and general strategies', in G. Underwood (ed.), *Strategies of Information Processing*, Academic Press: London.

Becker, J. D. (1973), 'A model for the encoding of experiential information', in R. C. Schank, and K. M. Colby (eds), *Computer Models of Thought and Language*, Freeman: San Francisco.

Bobrow, D. G. and Norman, D. A. (1975), 'Some principles of memory schemata', in D. G. Bobrow and A. Collins (eds), *Representation and Understanding*, Academic Press: New York.

Bobrow, D. G. and Winograd, T. (1977), 'An overview of KRL, a knowledge representation language', *Cognitive Science, 1*.

Boden, M. A. (1977), *Artificial Intelligence and Natural Man*, Harvester Press: Hassocks, England.

Booth, D. A. (1978), 'Language acquisition as the addition of verbal routines', in R. Campbell and P. T. Smith (eds), *Recent Advances in the Psychology of Language*, Plenum: New York.

Bradshaw, J. L. (1974), 'Peripherally presented and unreported words may bias the perceived meaning of a centrally fixated homograph', *Journal of Experimental Psychology, 103*, pp. 1200-2.

Caramazza, A. and Berndt, R. S. (1978), 'Semantic and syntactic processes in aphasia: a review of the literature', *Psychological Bulletin, 85*, pp. 898-918.

Cavanagh, J. P. (1975), 'Two classes of holographic processes realizable in the neural realm', *Lecture Notes in Computer Science, 22*, pp. 14-40.

Charniak, E. and Wilks, Y. (1979), *Computational Semantics*, North Holland: Amsterdam.

Clocksin, W. (1978), 'A.I. theories of vision', *AISB Quarterly, 31*, pp. 23-7.

Coltheart, M., Patterson, K. E. and Marshall, J. C. (eds) (1980), *Deep Dyslexia*, Routledge & Kegan Paul: London.

Corteen, R. S. and Dunn, D. (1974), 'Shock-associated words in a non-attended message: a test for momentary awareness', *Journal of Experimental Psychology, 102*, pp. 1143-4.

Corteen, R. S. and Wood, B. (1972), 'Autonomic responses to shock-associated words in an unattended channel', *Journal of Experimental Psychology, 94*, pp. 308-13.

DeRenzie, E., Pieczulo, A. and Vignolo, L. (1968), 'Ideational apraxia: a quantitative study', *Neuropsychologia, 6*, pp. 41-52.

Donaldson, M. (1978), *Children's Minds*, Fontana/Collins: Glasgow.

Dowling, W. J. (1978), 'Scale and contour: two components of a theory of memory for melodies', *Psychological Review, 85*, pp. 341-54.

Dubois, J., Hécaen, H. and Marcie, P. (1969), 'L'agraphie "pure" ', *Neuropsychologia, 7*, pp. 271-86.

Eccles, J. C. (1977), 'The cerebral cortex', in K. R. Popper and J. C. Eccles, *The Self and its Brain*, Springer International: Berlin, London, New York.

Fahlman, S. (1977), 'A system for representing and using real-world knowledge', PhD thesis, MIT, Cambridge, Mass.

Feigenbaum, E. A. (1977), 'Themes and case studies of knowledge engineering', *Fifth International Joint Conference on Artificial Intelligence*, Cambridge, Mass.

Forgy, C. and McDermott, J. (1977), 'OPS, a domain-independent production system language', *Fifth International Joint Conference on Artificial Intelligence*, Cambridge, Mass., pp. 933-9.

Forster, P. M. and Govier, E. (1978), 'Discrimination without awareness?' *Quarterly Journal of Experimental Psychology, 30*, pp. 289-95.

Fox, J. (1978), 'Continuity, concealment and visual attention', in G. Underwood (ed.), *Strategies of Information Processing*, Academic Press: London.

Gardner, H. (1975), *The Shattered Mind*, Knopf: New York; Routledge & Kegan Paul: London, 1977.

Gibson, J. J. (1966), *The Senses Considered as Perceptual Systems*, Houghton Mifflin: Boston, Mass.

Goodglass, H. and Geschwind, N. (1976), 'Language disorders (aphasia)', in E. C. Carterette and M. Friedman (eds), *Handbook of Perception*, vol. 7, Academic Press: New York.

Greenwald, A. G. (1970), 'Sensory feedback mechanisms in performance control: with special reference to the ideo-motor mechanism', *Psychological Review, 77*, pp. 73-99.

Hayek, F. A. (1962), 'Rules, perception, and intelligibility', *Proceedings of the British Academy, 48*, pp. 321-44.

Hayes-Roth, F. and Lesser, V. R. (1977), 'Focus of attention in the

HEARSAY-II Speech understanding system', *Fifth International Joint Conference on Artificial Intelligence*, Cambridge, Mass.

Hebb, D. O. (1949), *The Organization of Behavior*, Wiley: New York.

Hécaen, H. and Albert, M. L. (1978), *Human Neuropsychology*, Wiley: New York.

Hécaen, H. and Kremin, H. (1976), 'Neurolinguistic research on reading disorders from left hemisphere lesions: aphasic and "pure" alexias', in H. Whitaker and H. A. Whitaker (eds), *Studies in Neurolinguistics*, vol. 2, Academic Press: New York.

Heilman, K. M. (1973),'Ideational apraxia – a redefinition', *Brain, 96,* pp. 861-4.

Henderson, L. (1977), 'Word recognition', in N. S. Sutherland (ed.), *Tutorial Essays in Psychology*, vol. 1, Lawrence Erlbaum: Potomac, Md.

Hewitt, C. (1972), 'Description and theoretical analysis (using schemata) of PLANNER: a language for proving theorems and manipulating models in a robot', Artificial Intelligence Technical Report, no. 258, MIT Press: Cambridge, Mass.

Hewitt, C. (1977), 'Viewing control structures as patterns of passing messages', *Artificial Intelligence, 8,* pp. 323-64.

Hitch, G. J. and Baddeley, A. D. (1976), 'Verbal reasoning and working memory', *Quarterly Journal of Experimental Psychology, 28,* pp. 603-21.

Hunt, E. B. and Poltrock, S. E. (1974), 'The mechanics of thought', in B. H. Kantowitz (ed.), *Human Information Processing: Tutorials in Performance and Cognition*, Wiley: New York.

Johansson, G. (1979), 'Memory functions in visual event perception', in L. G. Nilsson (ed.), *Perspective in Memory Research*, Erlbaum: Hillsdale, N.J.

Johnson-Laird, P. N. (1978), 'The correspondence and coherence theories of cognitive truth', *The Behavioural and Brain Sciences, 1,* pp. 108-9.

Kilmer, W. L., McCulloch, W. S. and Blum, J. (1969), 'A model of the vertebrate central command system', *International Journal of Man-machine Studies, 1,* pp. 279-309.

Kinsbourne, M. and Rosenfeld, D. (1974), 'Agraphia selective for written spelling', *Brain and Language, 1,* pp. 215-25.

Kohout, L. J. (1976), 'Representation of functional hierarchies of movement in the brain', *International Journal of Man-machine Studies, 8,* pp. 699-709.

Kohout, L. J. and Gaines, B. R. (1976), 'Protection as a general systems problem', *International Journal of General Systems, 3,* pp. 3-23.

Kupferman, I. and Weiss, K. R. (1978), 'The command neuron concept', *The Behavioural and Brain Sciences, 1,* pp. 3-39.

La Berge, D. (1975), 'Acquisition of automatic processing in perceptual and associative learning', in P. M. A. Rabbitt and S. Dornic (eds), *Attention and Performance*, 5, Academic Press: London.

Lee, D. N., 'The optic flow-field: the foundation of vision', *Proceedings of the Royal Society, B,* in press.

Lenat, D. B. (1977), 'AM: an artificial intelligence approach to discovery in mathematics as heuristic search', Stanford Univeristy, Department of Computer Science, Memo SAIL AIM-286.

Lettvin, J. Y., Maturana, H., McCulloch, W. S. and Pitts, W. H. (1959), 'What the frog's eye tells the frog's brain', *Proceedings of the Institute of Radio Engineers*, New York, *47*, pp. 1940-51.

Lhermitte, F. and Beauvois, M. F. (1973), 'A visual-speech disconnextion syndrome: Report of a case with optic aphasia, agnosia, alexia and colour agnosia', *Brain, 96*, pp. 695-714.

Luria, A. R. (1966), *Higher Cortical Functions in Man*, Basic Books: New York.

McCulloch, W. S. (1965), *Embodiments of Mind*, MIT Press: Cambridge, Mass.

McFarland, D. J. (1974), 'Time sharing as a behavioral phenomenon', in D. Lehrman, R. A. Hinde and E. Shaw (eds), *Advances in the Study of Behavior*, vol. 5, Academic Press: New York.

McFarland, D. J. (1978), 'Hunger in interaction with other aspects of motivation', in D. A. Booth (ed.), *Hunger Models: Computable Theory of Feeding Control*, Academic Press: London.

Marcel, A. J., 'Unconscious perception: the effects of visual masking on word processing', *Cognitive Psychology*, in press.

Marcel, A. J. and Patterson, K. (1978), 'Word recognition and production: reciprocity in clinical and normal studies', in J. Requin (ed.), *Attention and Performance, 7*, Lawrence Erlbaum: Hillsdale, N.J.

Marin, O. S. M., Saffran, E. M. and Schwartz, M. F. (1976), 'Dissociations of language in aphasia: implications for normal function', *Annals of the New York Academy of Sciences, 280*, pp. 868-84.

Marr, D. (1970), 'A theory of cerebral neocortex', *Proceedings of the Royal Society, B, 176*, pp. 161-234.

Marr, D. (1976), 'Early processing of visual information', *Philosophical Transactions of the Royal Society, B, 275*, pp. 483-534.

Miller, G. A., Galanter, E. and Pribram, K. H. (1960), *Plans and the Structure of Behavior*, Holt, Rinehart & Winston: New York.

Milner, B. (1971), 'Interhemispheric differences in the localization of psychological processes in man', *British Medical Bulletin, 27*, pp. 272-7.

Minsky, M. (1961), 'Steps toward artificial intelligence', *Proceedings of the Institute of Radio Engineers, 49*, pp. 8-30. Reprinted in E. A. Feigenbaum and J. Feldman (eds), *Computers and Thought* (1963), McGraw-Hill: New York.

Minsky, M. (1975), 'A framework for representing knowledge', in P. H. Winston (ed.), *The Psychology of Computer Vision*, McGraw-Hill: New York.

Moore, J. and Newell, A. (1974), 'How can Merlin understand?' in L. W. Gregg (ed.), *Knowledge and Cognition*, Lawence Erlbaum: Potomac, Md.

Moran, T. P. (1973), 'The symbolic imagery hypothesis: a production system model', unpublished doctoral dissertation, Carnegie-Mellon University, Pittsburgh, Pa.

Moray, N. (1967), 'Where is capacity limited? A survey and a model', *Acta Psychologica, 27*, pp. 84-92.

Morton, J. (1968), 'Consideration of grammar and computation in language behavior', in J. C. Catford (ed.), *Studies in Language and Language Behavior*, Progress Report VI, US Office of Education.

Morton, J. (1970), 'A functional model for memory', in D. A. Norman (ed.), *Models for Human Memory*, Academic Press: New York.

Neisser, U. (1967), *Cognitive Psychology*, Appleton-Century-Crofts: New York.

Neisser, U. (1976), *Cognition and Reality*, Freeman: San Francisco.

Newell, A. (1973a), 'You can't play Twenty Questions with Nature and win', in W. G. Chase (ed.), *Visual Information Processing*, Academic Press: New York.

Newell, A. (1973b), 'Production systems: models of control structures', in W. G. Chase (ed.), *Visual Information Processing*, Academic Press: New York.

Newell, A. and Simon, H. A. (1963), 'GPS, a program that simulates human thought', in E. A. Feigenbaum and J. Feldman (eds), *Computers and Thought*, McGraw-Hill: New York.

Newell, A. and Simon, H. A. (1972), *Human Problem Solving*, Prentice-Hall: Englewood Cliffs, N.J.

Nickerson, R. S. (1977), 'Crossword puzzles and lexical memory', in S. Dornic (ed.), *Attention and Performance, 6*, Lawrence Erlbaum: Hillsdale, N.J.

Norman D. A. (1968), 'Toward a theory of memory and attention', *Psychological Review, 75*, pp. 522–36.

Powers, W. T. (1978), 'Quantitative analysis of purposive systems', *Psychological Review, 85*, pp. 417–35.

Pribram, K. H. (1971), *Language of the Brain: Experimental Paradoxes and Principles in Neuropsychology*, Prentice-Hall: Englewood Cliffs, New Jersey.

Proctor, R. W. (1978), 'Attention and modality-specific interference in visual short-term memory', *Journal of Experimental Psychology: Human Learning and Memory', 4*, pp. 239-45.

Quastler, H. (1956), 'Studies of human channel capacity', in E. C. Cherry (ed.), *Information Theory: Proceedings of Third London Symposium*, Butterworth: London.

Ratcliff, R. (1978), 'A theory of memory retrieval', *Psychological Review, 85*, pp. 59–108.

Reason, J. (1976), 'Absent minds', *New Society*, 4 November, pp. 244–5.

Reddy, D. R. (1975), *Speech Recognition*, Wiley: New York.

Reddy, D. R. and Newell, A. (1974), 'Knowledge and its representation in a speech understanding system', in L. W. Gregg (ed.), *Knowledge and Cognition*, Lawrence Erlbaum: Potomac, Md.

Rosch, E. and Lloyd, B. (eds) (1978), *Cognition and Categorization*, Wiley: New York.

Rosenbaum, D. A. (1977), 'Selective adaptation of "command neurons" in the human motor system', *Neuropsychologia, 15*, pp. 81–91.

Saffran, E. M. and Marin, O.S.M. (1975), 'Immediate memory for word lists and sentences in a patient with deficient auditory short-term memory', *Brain and Language, 2*, pp. 420–33.

Saffran, E. M. and Marin, O. S. M. (1977), 'Reading without phonology: evidence from a aphasia', *Quarterly Journal of Experimental Psychology, 29*, pp. 515-25.

Sanford, A. and Garrod, S. (1979), 'Memory and attention in text comprehension: the problem of relevance', in R. S. Nickerson (ed.), *Attention and Performance, 8*, Lawrence Erlbaum, Hillsdale, N.J.

Schank, R. (1975), *Conceptual Information Processing*, North Holland: Amsterdam.

Schank, R. and Abelson, R. (1977), *Scripts, Plans, Goals, and Understanding*, Lawrence Erlbaum: Hillsdale, N.J.

Schwartz, J. (1978), 'Distributed synchronization of communicating sequential processes', University of Edinburgh, Department of Artificial Intelligence, Research Report no. 56.

Selfridge, O. G. (1956), 'Pattern recognition and learning', *Methodos, 8,* pp. 163-76.

Selfridge, O. G. (1959), 'Pandemonium: a paradigm for learning', in *The Mechanization of Thought Processes*, H.M. Stationery Office: London. Reprinted in L. Uhr (ed.), *Pattern Recognition*, Wiley: New York, 1966.

Shallice, T. (1978), 'The dominant action system: an information-processing approach to consciousness', in K. S. Pope and J. L. Singer (eds), *The Stream of Consciousness: Scientific Investigations into the Flow of Human Experience*, Plenum: New York.

Shallice, T. and Butterworth, B. (1977), 'Short-term memory impairment and spontaneous speech', *Neuropsychologia, 13,* pp. 729-36.

Shallice, T. and Warrington, E. K. (1977), 'The possible role of selective attention in acquired dyslexia', *Neuropsychologia, 15,* pp. 31-42.

Shatz, M. (1978), 'On the development of communicative understandings: an early strategy for interpreting and responding to messages', *Cognitive Psychology, 10,* pp. 271-301.

Shortliffe, E. (1976), *MYCIN: computer-based medical consultations*, American Elsevier: New York.

Simon, H. A. (1967), 'Motivational and emotional controls of cognition', *Psychological Review, 74,* pp. 29-39.

Smith, R. G. and Davis, R. (1978), 'Distributed problem solving: a contract-net approach', Stanford University Computer Science Department, Report no. STAN-CS-78-667.

Somekh, D. E. and Wilding, J. M. (1973), 'Perception without awareness in a dichoptic viewing situation', *British Journal of Psychology, 64,* pp. 339-49.

Spinelli, D. N., (1970), 'OCCAM: A content-addressable memory model for the brain', in K. H. Pribram and D. E. Broadbent (eds), *The Biology of Memory*, Academic Press: New York.

Szentagothai, J. (1975), 'The "module-concept" in cerebral cortex architecture', *Brain Research, 95,* pp. 475-96.

Szentagothai, J. and Arbib, M. A. (1974), 'Conceptual models of neural organization', *Neurosciences Research Program Bulletin, 12,* pp. 307-510.

Treisman, A. M. (1960), 'Contextual cues in selective listening', *Quarterly Journal of Experimental Psychology, 12,* pp. 242-8.

Tulving, E. (1974), 'Cue-dependent forgetting', *American Scientist, 62,* pp. 74-82.

Underwood, G. (1976), 'Semantic interference from unattended printed words', *British Journal of Psychology, 67,* pp. 327-38.

Uttley, A. M. (1976), 'Neurophysiological predictions of a two-pathway information theory of neural conditioning', *Brain Research, 102,* pp. 55-70.

Von Wright, J. M., Anderson, K. and Stenman, U. (1975), 'Generalization of conditioned GSRs in dichotic listening', in P. M. A. Rabbitt and S. Dornic (eds), *Attention and Performance, 5,* Academic Press: New York.

Warrington, E. K. (1969), 'Constructional apraxia', in P. Vincken and G. Bruyn (eds), *Handbook of Clinical Neurology*, North Holland: Amsterdam.

Warrington, E. K. (1975), 'The selective impairment of semantic memory', *Quarterly Journal of Experimental Psychology, 27*, pp. 635-58.

Warrington, E. K. and Weiskrantz, L. (1973), 'An analysis of short-term and long-term memory defects in man', in J. A. Deutsch (ed.), *The Physiological Basis of Memory*, Academic Press: New York.

Waterman, D. and Hayes-Roth, R. (eds) (1978), *Pattern Directed Inference Systems*, Academic Press: New York.

Weiskrantz, L. (1977), 'Trying to bridge some neuropsychological gaps between monkey and man', *British Journal of Psychology, 68*, pp. 431- 45.

Weiskrantz, L., Warrington, E. K., Sanders, M. D. and Marshall, J. C. (1974), 'Visual capacity in the hemianopic field following a restricted occipital ablation', *Brain, 97*, pp. 709-28.

Wilks, Y. (1976), 'Parsing English II', in E. Charniak and Y. Wilks (eds), *Computational Semantics*, North Holland: Amsterdam, pp. 155-84.

Wilks, Y. (1978), 'Making preferences more active', *Artificial Intelligence, 11*, pp. 197-223.

Willows, D. M. and McKinnon, G. E. (1973), 'Selective reading: attention to the "unattended" lines', *Canadian Journal of Psychology, 27*, pp. 292-304.

Yamadori, A. and Albert, M. L. (1973), 'Word category aphasia', *Cortex, 9*, pp. 83-9.

Young, R. M. (1976), *Seriation by Children: a Production-System Approach*, Birkhäuser, Basle.

Young, R. M. (1978), 'Strategies and the structure of a cognitive skill', in G. Underwood (ed.), *Strategies of Information Processing*, Academic Press: London.

Zangwill, O. L. (1964), 'Intelligence in aphasia', in A. V. S. de Reuck and M. O'Connor (eds), *Disorders of Language*, Churchill: London.

3 Action: the mechanisms of motor control

Nigel Harvey and Kerry Greer

Introduction

Motor control was one of the last areas of psychology to be left untouched by the 'cognitive revolution'. At first glance, this seems surprising. Arguably the vanguard of the revolution had been the publication in 1960 of Miller, Galanter and Pribram's book *Plans and the Structure of Behavior* (1960). Their very title suggests that the action was to provide the focal topic of their work. However, the subject was only really approached in their relatively short chapter on motor skills, and that did not noticeably inspire much new research. It was their contributions to problem-solving, memory and decision-making which fired the imagination of their fellow psychologists. Pre-revolutionary ideas appear to have been even more deeply entrenched in the study of action than elsewhere.

This may have been because the demands of the Second World War had a greater effect on that area than on any other. In the 1920s and 1930s, behaviourists (e.g., Watson, 1929) viewed the acquisition of a skill as the linking up of individual movements into a chain of behaviour. Suppose I have learned, say, to throw a grenade. Initially taking hold of it with one hand provides me with a stimulus to position it so that I can take out the pin. Feedback from ascertaining that position provides me with a further stimulus for actually removing the pin; and feedback from that removal, in turn, leaves me with yet another stimulus for projecting the grenade towards the target. This theoretical approach gave few clues as to how one should actually go about training people to throw grenades or to acquire considerably more complex weaponry skills. Unfortunately, it was exactly this knowledge which was required of psychologists during the Second

65

World War. Success in armed conflict depended on the use of new techniques and equipment. People had to be trained to use them in the shortest possible time. Theoretical behaviourism could provide no advice. As a result, trainers and applied psychologists adopted a strongly atheoretical task-oriented approach. Types of task were classified. Methods of training were classified. The best method of training for each type of task was discovered largely by trial and error. After the war, this type of approach became absorbed into ergonomics. The study of motor skills had been effectively excised from psychology. Of course, during the 1950s there was an area of psychology which was examined under the heading 'motor skills'. But it was largely the study of decision-making and its limitations as revealed by the use of information theory to interpret variations in the speed of responses to signals.

So, perhaps, the reason for Miller *et al.*'s failure to stimulate interest in the study of action was that it was the one area in which they had little to react against. The troops of the cognitive revolution had no opponents and could win no victories. In fact, it was not troops that were needed but spies willing to venture into neutral territory. For all the while that psychologists had shunned the study of action, it had been alive and well and living underground in physiology and, to some extent, in physical education. It was not until the 1970s that cognitive psychologists showed much sign of realizing this. As a result they had had to learn to appreciate and employ the concepts and techniques of neurophysiology to develop and test their own ideas. This has not been as difficult as it might have been. The motor control involved in action had always been one of the most cognitive areas of physiology. This is emphasized by use of terms such as 'sense of effort', by concern over whether information transmitted from some receptors but not others reaches consciousness and, of course, by the distinction between reflex and voluntary movement. Today, the control of action is an area of increasing interaction between the disciplines and so we must outline the underlying anatomical and physiological basis for movement. We will, however, keep this to an absolute minimum. Detail will be sacrificed for simplicity.

Motor behaviour in man can be broadly catagorized into reflex activity, such as withdrawal from a painful stimulus or the knee jerk, and voluntary movement, which consists of co-ordinated sequences of muscular contractions that are often performed at a subconscious level and acquired through practice. Voluntary behaviour has three important properties:

1   It is self controlled. (We decide what to do.)
2   It is adaptive. (We decide how and when to do it.)
3   Every movement is an answer to a motor problem. Environmental demands require solutions that take the form of motor activity.

These three aspects of skilled movement are paralleled in the operating systems studied by cyberneticians, and so it is not very surprising to find that motor theorists have utilized cybernetic concepts in their investigations and explanations of man's motor behaviour.

The fundamental unit in cybernetics is the feedback loop, a set of communication channels between effectors that operate on the environment, and controllers that control the effectors. Orders are sent by controllers to the effectors. Ensuing alterations caused by the activity of the effectors are fed back to the controller which thus receives information about the new state of the system. (See Figure 3.1)

Miller, Galanter and Pribram (1960) have conceptualized this type of feedback loop in terms of TOTE units, i.e. a sequence of operations: TEST-OPERATE-TEST-EXIT (Figure 3.2). The TEST represents a comparison between the plan to be executed by the effectors and the actual activity of the effectors. If the ongoing state of the effectors matches the planned state of the effectors (i.e. there is congruity), then the TOTE exits. Its job is complete. If there is incongruity, if there is a mismatch between the desired state and actual state of the effectors, then this 'error' is fed back into the system and the loop remains active until congruity is reached.

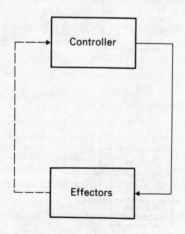

FIGURE 3.1   Schematic diagram of simple feedback loop

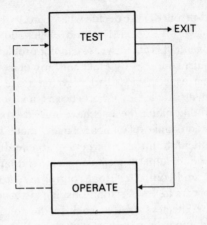

FIGURE 3.2 TOTE unit (after Miller, Galanter and Pribram, 1960)

Do such TOTE units exist in the human body? Are there physiological and anatomical correlates of feedback loops? The answer to these questions is emphatically affirmative. Miller, Galanter and Pribam's TOTE unit is an abstract version of Sherrington's (1906) 'final common path', the reflex loop. These loops are a series of simple

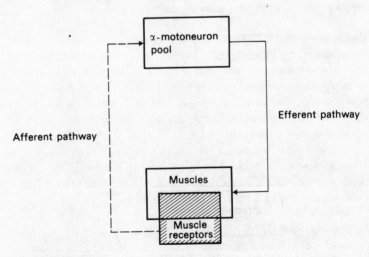

FIGURE 3.3   Schematic view of spinal reflex arc

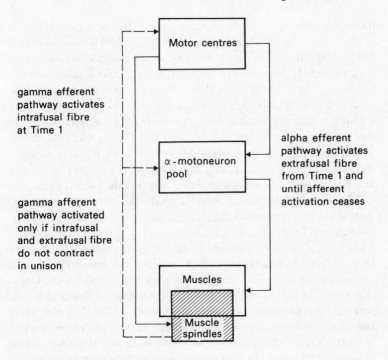

gamma efferent
pathway activates
intrafusal fibre
at Time 1

gamma afferent
pathway activated
only if intrafusal
and extrafusal fibre
do not contract
in unison

alpha efferent
pathway activates
extrafusal fibre
from Time 1 and
until afferent
activation ceases

FIGURE 3.4   Schematic view of alpha-gamma co-activation

circuits which connect each muscle with the spinal cord. The alpha-motoneurons situated in the spinal cord control the skeletal muscles. After receiving instructions from higher centres to produce a particular muscular contraction, they send OPERATE signals, in the form of electrical impuses, to the muscle. Receptors (called 'muscle spindles') located within the muscle TEST whether the contraction then produced matches what the higher centres have specified. If it does, if there is congruity, action stops. If it does not, if there is incongruity (say, because a higher than expected force opposed the action), signals are *fed back* via afferent nerves to the alpha-motoneurons, which then continue to send OPERATE signals to the muscle until the TEST is passed (Figure 3.3).

How are the receptors within the muscle able to TEST whether contraction has taken place to the extent specified by the higher centres? Inside the main (extrafusal) muscle is a smaller (intrafusal) muscle fibre. Contraction of the intrafusal fibre can take place independently via the gamma-motoneuron but it is insufficient to produce limb movement. However, if the extrafusal fibre is prevented from contracting because the force opposing movement was greater than expected, the intrafusal fibre can still contract inside the extrafusal one. Thus, after the higher centres have instructed both intrafusal and extrafusal fibres to contract, there will be a difference in the extent to which they both actually contract only if the extrafusal fibres meet resistance to movement which is different from that anticipated. The contraction of the extrafusal fibres represents actual movement, the contraction of the intrafusal fibre represents intended movement, and muscle spindles affectively TEST whether the two are the same.

The above description assumes that the extrafusal fibres are instructed to contract via the alpha-montoneurons at the same time as intrafusal fibres are instructed to contract via gamma-motoneurons. This way of using the system is called alpha-gamma co-activation (Figure 3.4). It is also possible to instruct the intrafusal fibres to contract prior to the extrafusal ones. This acts to feedforward a bias to the TEST phase of the TOTE unit. This bias is detected by the receptors in the muscle, and signals are sent via the afferent nerves to the alpha-motoneurons which then turn on 'the power' to cancel it out. This way of using the system has been likened to power steering (Merton, 1972) and is called follow-up servo (Figure 3.5).

The alpha-gamma loop discussed above needs a safety valve. Suppose I try to lift a chair. It is heavier than expected, hence a difference between the contraction of the extrafusal and intrafusal fibres is detected by the muscle spindles. They report back via the afferent nerves so that the alpha-motoneurons can instruct the extrafusal fibres to switch on more power. Now suppose that the reason the chair was heavier than expected was that it was screwed to the floor. The TEST between actual and intended movement will never be passed, and so continuing OPERATE signals will instruct the muscles to switch on ever more power. Eventually, the muscles and tendons (or perhaps the chair) would be damaged. To prevent this happening, other receptors, lying in the boundary region between muscles and tendons and called 'Golgi tendon organs', measure the overall tension in the muscle. When this tension gets too high, they can operate as a cut-out mechanism to switch off activity in the muscle-spindle TOTES. They may also be important for determining the extent to which a muscle contraction is isotonic (producing movement) or isometric (not producing movement).

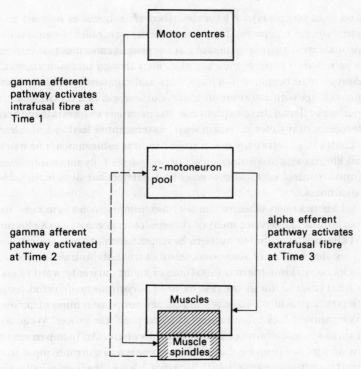

gamma efferent
pathway activates
intrafusal fibre at
Time 1

α - motoneuron
pool

gamma afferent
pathway activated
at Time 2

alpha efferent
pathway activates
extrafusal fibre
at Time 3

Muscles

Muscle
spindles

FIGURE 3.5   Schematic view of the follow-up servo

Golgi tendon organs will not provide the system with all the protection it needs. Continued muscle contraction in one part of the body may damage other parts of the body not involved in the contraction. I could hang from a beam just by keeping my finger joints flexed. However, doing it that way may, for instance, eventually damage my shoulder joints. Located inside the joints are *joint receptors*. They provide information about pressure on the joint (Mathews, 1977) and, according to Skoglund (1973), about its angle and the velocity and acceleration with which that angle changes. Some authors (Adams, 1977) think that joint receptors are important for providing us with information about limb position, but others (Greer and Harvey, 1978; Kelso, 1978; Mathews, 1977), aware that they tend to fire only at extremes of possible joint angles (Burgess and Clark, 1969; Millar, 1975), emphasize their protective role.

The three types of receptor (muscle spindles, Golgi tendon organs and joint receptors) we have described are sometimes referred to as kinaesthetic receptors. Together with the vestibular organs, which provide us with information about the position and movement of our whole body in space, they are also often termed proprioceptors. Of course, exteroceptors (our eyes, ears and cutaneous receptors) also provide us with information about our current behaviour, but it is perhaps relevant here to point out that exteroceptive and kinaesthetic feedback may differ in certain ways. Exteroceptive feedback is at least capable of penetrating consciousness but the same may not be true of all kinaesthetic information. We are usually totally unaware of such input: control of most movements is carried out at a level below awareness.

This question of consciousness has proved to be extremely important in the development of theories of motor control (Kelso and Wallace, 1978). Some authors have postulated that if information does not reach consciousness, then it cannot be used to control behaviour. Thus Merton (1964) argued that muscle spindles cannot subserve kinaesthesis because we are always unaware of the information they provide. To a psychologist, this proposal is quite surprising. Why should lack of awareness of input preclude its use? When one thinks about the work of Deutsch and Deutsch (1963) on perception, in which they propose that subjects receive and use more input from receptors than that of which they are aware, the apparent lack of consciousness of muscle afferent input becomes less impressive as an argument against its role in kinaesthesis. Dixon's (1971) work on subliminal stimuli clearly supports the view that conscious awareness is not a prerequisite for stimuli participating in the active process of perception – at least in the auditory and visual modalities. Greer (1977) demonstrated that subjects not only use the non-conscious spindle discharge to make positioning movements, but also learn to use it even though they are seemingly unaware of this input. Subjects were trained to make positioning movements of the top phalanx of the thumb in the absence of all but muscle spindle input. Their performance was comparable to that of subjects who had joint, cutaneous, and muscle receptor input. Furthermore, it was demonstrated that subjects could not, in a voluntary movement, learn to displace their thumb accurately just on the basis of sense of effort (similar to corollary discharge or efferent copy (see Section 3.5)). The studies provide *behavioural* evidence for the importance of muscle spindles in kinaesthesis.

The mechanisms we have discussed reflect just one aspect of the complexity of the motor system. Although the spinal centres do control the alpha-motoneurons, they also send information to higher centres which in turn can modify the activity of the motoneurons. The motor system can be envisaged as a series of interlocking feedback loops all of which converge on to the simple reflex circuits that connect each muscle with the spinal cord. You will notice from Figure 3.6 that the higher centres seem capable of influencing each other through efferent channels. Consider, for instance, the cerebellum's connections with the supraspinal structures. They provide another example of the cybernetic concept: feedforward. This is an essential component of any system which cannot for, say, reasons of 'time' use feedback control (i.e., when actions are more rapid than the feedback loop time). Essentially feedforward implies that corrections in motor movements can be entered before mistakes have been made. Perhaps an example might clarify this concept. Take a known 'reflex' activity such as walking. The motor loop performs the function of walking sequences. However, this basic pattern may need to be modified because of environmental changes (there's a big hole in the ground). We need to alter the reflex motor loop before any feedback from the muscles reaches the brain, otherwise we'll fall over. The cerebellum operates somewhat like this; it can act as a feedforward operator. 'Mistakes' in an ongoing programme are calculated and corrective instructions sent to lower levels, even though the actual movement errors may not physically occur.

Figure 3.6 fails to do justice to the complexity of the feedback and feedforward pathways that are physically present in the human body. It is even beyond the scope of this chapter to discuss the operation of the ones that are shown. However, we have included them in this schematized diagram to give you some idea of the interrelations between the brain and the musculature. Whether or not all these pathways are utilized in motor control (and some theorists think they are not), they nevertheless exist and one can only suppose that they exist for a purpose. We will discuss what sort of roles they may have in the following sections. In doing so we shall restrict ourselves to considering those which concern the cognitive processes involved in assessing and using information. Even within this area there will be certain factors (attention demands of movements, the role of vestibular feedback) which we shall ignore. We shall just consider those issues which are central to current theoretical developments.

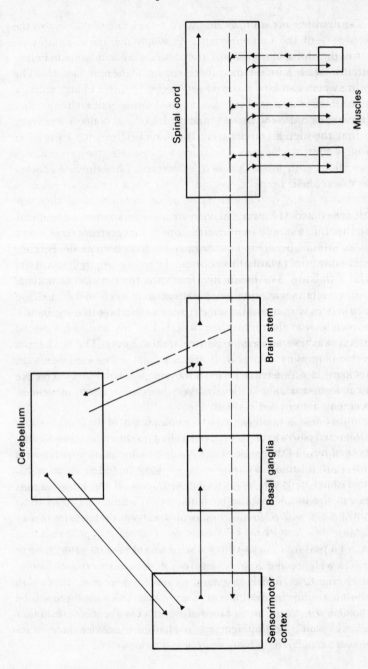

FIGURE 3.6   Schematic diagram of the motor system (after Henneman, 1974)

1   Controlling action

How does control of the overall action of 'throwing a grenade' relate to control of each individual movement within that action? How do the higher ('voluntary') and lower ('reflex') levels of the nervous system interact to carry out this control? Broadly speaking we can categorize theories of motor control into three classes: linear or chaining theories, hierarchical theories, and heterarchical theories.

1.1   Linear control

Both reflex and voluntary movement are mediated via the spinal reflex arc but, as we have seen, the reflex is an automatic response to sensory stimuli, whereas in voluntary movement there is centrally mediated control of both the motor *and* the sensory components of the spinal reflex arc. We mentioned that, according to behaviourists' theories, voluntary action is no more than a chain of reflexes (i.e., the motor system is a slave of the sensory system, where each response (R) occurs reflexly to a stimulus (S)).

S-R connections subserving particular movements could be chained together to produce an action in various ways. For Watson (1929) (see also Gagné, 1965), feedback from a movement was substituted for the sensory representation of the stimulus which would produce the next movement. Greenwald's (1970) ideo-motor hypothesis (see Section 3.7) represents an interesting development of this viewpoint (see also Chapter 2). Others have suggested that integration could take place by linking up successive movement commands or more centrally by connecting together separate sensori-motor mediators (Deutsch, 1960). Bindra (1976) has reviewed these theories and pointed out that none can account for how a particular movement can be attached to two quite different subsequent movements when it is part of different actions.

A cognitive solution to this problem would be similar to the one offered by Henry and Rogers (1960) in their 'memory drum' model, (see Section 2). In deciding how to reach some goal, a planner formulates action in advance. It may decide that some particular movement can form an appropriate part of quite different action plans to reach quite different goals. Hence the movement may be followed by different subsequent ones in different plans. For Henry and Rogers, a plan is still arranged as a linear chain of movements. However, it has been organized in such a way by a higher-level planner. So perhaps it is better to regard their model as viewing the control of action as a hierarchical process, albeit only a two-level one.

1.2   Hierarchical control

These theories are what we call 'top-down' explanations of motor control. Essentially they postulate the existence of a hierarchy of decision-makers. At the very top is the exeutive which formulates the total plan. The executive delegates parts of the plan to various autonomously functioning sub-control units, which in turn make the decision to pass certain 'jobs' to lower units, and so on till the bottom structure is reached (i.e., voluntary action dominates reflex action). There is no communication up from lower to higher motor centres, only down from higher to lower ones (i.e., those models propose rectified communication channels, they are unidirectional). Examples of this type of theory are those of Fitts (1964) and Paillard (1960).

1.3   Heterarchical control

Heterarchical control is somewhat like hierarchical control, but the communication channel within the various components is not rectified, it is multi-directional. This structure enables the individual components to contribute to the construction and differentiation of plans. Such a structure may exist in the motor systems of the body (see Figure 3.6). The cerebellum, for instance, receives input from all aspects of the motor system and could, in theory, act as co-ordinator for all motor and sensori-motor events. If control is heterarchical, the ascending pathways from spinal centres to the cerebellum would not carry information about muscle contraction (i.e. sensory feedback). Instead, they would provide information about how the spinal centres are dealing with even lower level structures (i.e. reflex loops). Similarly, descending pathways to spinal centres would not carry commands for muscles. They would carry instructions to the spinal centres. (In support of this, it is interesting to note that most descending fibres terminate in interneuronal pools rather than directly on motoneurons.) Spinal centres autonomously decide how to bias the reflex loops via the gamma-motoneurons on the basis of these instructions. Higher centres are not informed of the details of this tuning but only of how well the spinal centres have carried out the instructions they gave them. The instructions issued by the higher centres may be relatively abstract, and correspond to target positions in space (see Section 5.2). Successively lower centres work out the details of how to get to these positions. Heterarchical control models (Greene, 1971; Fowler and Turvey, 1978; Turvey 1977; Turvey *et al.*, 1978) suggest that voluntary movement relies on or exploits the reflex system rather than dominating or opposing it.

2 Planning action

When throwing a grenade, do we plan the whole sequence of movements in advance? According to the models devised by the behaviourists, we do not. Instead we just formulate the first one. Executing that provides the cue for the next one, and so on, as shown in Figure 3.7a.

Miller, Galanter and Pribram (1960) were not satisfied with this approach. For them, action is planned in advance (Figure 3.7b). At the time this appeared to be more of a statement of conviction than a theory based on experimental evidence. However, Henry and Rogers (1960) found that the time taken to initiate a sequence of movements increased with the number of movements in the sequence. It was difficult for the behaviourists' models to account for this finding. Henry and Rogers suggested that the whole sequence of movements is planned in advance but that, because of memory or other constraints, the resulting plan would not be loaded into the motor or output buffer until the starting signal was given. The effect they found occurred because longer plans take longer to load. (Their model differs from Miller *et al.*'s in two important ways. The plan is executed without taking feedback into account and it is linear rather than hierarchical.)

Recently there has been renewed interest in movement initiation time as a measure which reflects advance planning (Kerr, 1978) but the way it does so is still a matter of debate. For instance, Sternberg and colleagues (1978) discovered that it is not only the time taken to initiate a movement sequence that increases with the length of the sequence. The time interval between each item in the sequence does

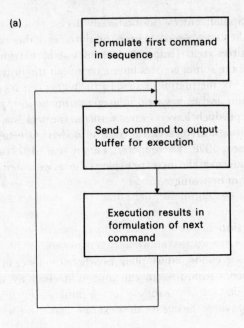

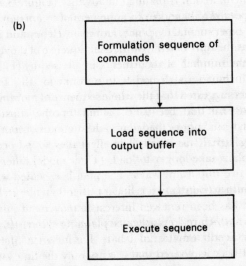

FIGURE 3.7   Mechanisms for (a) unplanned and (b) planned movement

so too. This additional effect is difficult for Henry and Rogers's model to account for. As they found that both initiation time and inter-item time increased *linearly* with the number of items in the sequence, they extended Sternberg's memory-scanning model to motor memory. According to them, the plan is loaded into a motor or output buffer before the starting signal is given. The effects they obtained occur because, before producing each element, the subject must search the whole plan or program to find the part of it responsible for that element, and larger plans take longer to search through. The authors suggest that the fact that the increases occurred even when all elements were identical eliminates alternative accounts of their effects. You may ask why it does not eliminate theirs too. Why should a search be necessary if all items being searched are identical? They assume that a program for a sequence of identical items is placed in the output buffer in just the same way as one for a sequence of non-identical ones, and that there is no way of determining whether or not sub-programs in the buffer are for producing a sequence of the same or different items.

3 Information about action

We know where our limbs are. We know how fast they are moving and where they will be at some later point in time if we continue to move them in the same way. How do we know all this? Where does the information come from and what routes does it travel by? Figure 3.8 shows some of the routes which are possible. We know that the routes (1-4) exist but are not sure what they are used for. The very existence of the others (5-8) has been the subject of much controversy. In this section, we shall describe both the known and suggested routes. In the next section we shall discuss what the known ones might be used for.

3.1 *Extrinsic feedback (route 1)*

We may know what we are doing because of what another person or a machine tells us. Feedback which depends on some sort of mediation in this way has been called *extrinsic* feedback by Annett and Kay (1957) and Greenwald (1970). It is also occasionally referred to as *augmented* feedback because it augments other types of feedback which do not require such mediation. This mediated feedback may provide us not only with knowledge about what movement we have made but also with *knowledge of results* or consequences of that movement. The other types of feedback described below are *intrinsic* to performance because they depend on no more than the correct functioning of the sensory apparatus.

3.2   Exteroceptive feedback (route 2)

We may know what we are doing because we can see or hear ourselves doing it. Intrinsic feedback such as this is information which we have output into the environment before feeding it back into our nervous system via exteroceptors (receptors sensing things in the environment). It is therefore called exteroceptive feedback. Other types of intrinsic feedback are interoceptive because they depend on receptors which provide us with information about what is going on inside our own bodies.

3.3   Interoceptive feedback (route 3)

We may know what we are doing because we can feel ourselves doing it. Two types of interoceptive feedback are important here. Vestibular feedback gives us information about how our actions have altered our bodily orientation in the environment. Kinaesthetic feedback provides us with information about how they have changed the relative positions of our limb and body segments. The main proprioceptors were outlined above.

3.4   Spinal feedback mechanisms (route 4)

Even if our brain does not know what we are doing, our spinal cord might. The three cerebrally mediated types of feedback described above can help us to choose the appropriate movement for reaching a particular goal. Spinal feedback mechanisms help us to ensure that the chosen movement is the one that is actually carried out. We have already described the way they do this.

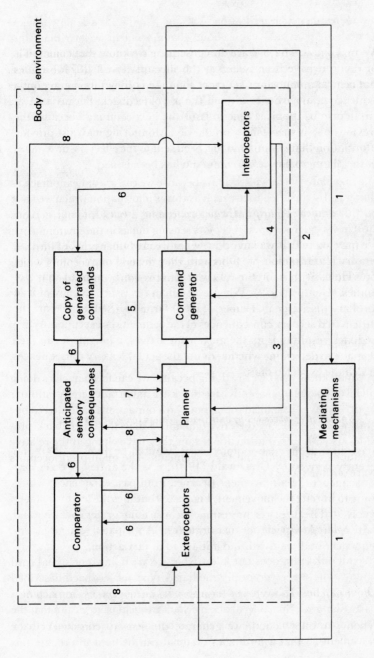

FIGURE 3.8 Transmission routes for information controlling action

3.5   *Efferent copy (route 5)*

We may know what we are doing because we know that commands for doing it have been issued to the effectors. Jones (1974a) argues that central monitoring of efferent commands allows us to carry out a sequence of movements without the use of feedback. For instance, it can inform us that it is time to issue the next command because the previous one is successfully on its way. Monitoring may just provide information that *a* command has been sent to the effectors, or it might let the planner know *which* command has been issued.

3.6   *Generation of anticipated sensory consequences (route 6)*

We may know that we have done what we intended to do because the sensory effects of doing it fit in with what we told our effectors to do. Von Holst's (1954) notion of efferent copy can be applied to motor control (Gentile, 1972). When a command is issued, a copy of it (a corollary discharge in Teuber's (1966) terms) is used to generate the anticipated sensory consequences of the command's execution. When feedback resulting from the movement arrives, a judgment can then be made to determine whether or not the actual sensory consequences match the expected ones.

3.7   *Initiation of movement by anticipated sensory consequences (route 7)*

According to the ideo-motor theory favoured by James (1890) and recently revived by Greenwald (1970), it is the anticipated sensory consequences of a movement (learned from past experience) which come to initiate the movement. Figure 3.9 outlines the learning stages involved. The theory is interesting because it integrates cognitive and motivational aspects of performance. Anticipated sensory consequences both motivate and initiate voluntary action.

3.8   *Feedforward to receptors from anticipated sensory consequences (route 8)*

When planning action, we generate the sensory consequences of movement so that a feedforward signal can be used to prepare the

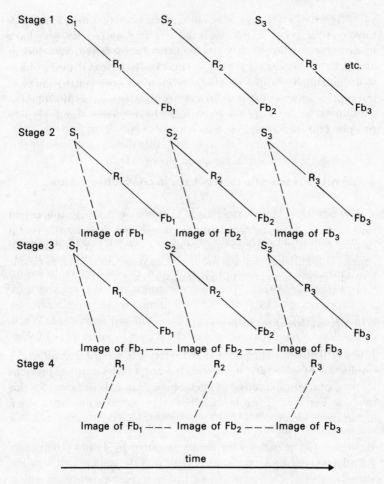

FIGURE 3.9 Acquisition of the ideo-motor mechanism (after Greenwald, 1970): Fb refers to feedback

receptors for input. This preparation may take the form of the introduction of a specific bias or it may just be a temporary increase in sensitivity (Kelso, 1977). Kelso and Wallace (1978) suggests that use of routes 7 and 8 can together account for why blindfolded subjects are better at reproducing their own movements when they had chosen the parameters of those movements in the first place than when the experimenter had chosen and constrained them. In the former case subjects have had to set up the anticipated sensory consequences of a movement in order to produce it the first time, and so they only have to preserve a store of those consequences in order to reproduce it again. In the latter case the subject may not have stored, or may have stored ineffectively, the passively received sensory consequences of the experimenter-constrained movement, and so anticipation of those consequences in order to reproduce the movement and prepare receptors for its consequences would be difficult.

4 The role of kinaesthetic feedback in controlling action

Everybody agrees that some aspects of motor control (e.g., movement initiation) must be independent of feedback, but that all aspects of it cannot be. (Otherwise proprioceptors would be redundant.) Of course, this still leaves much room for disagreement. Different people have different views about what feedback is for.

4.1   Appreciation of passive movement

Jones (1974b) has suggested that feedback is not used at all in the production of voluntary movement. Instead, as we saw in the previous section, central monitoring of efferent commands is sufficient for this purpose. For Jones, the role of feedback is restricted to the appreciation of passive movement.

4.2   Learning to move

If movement is planned in advance and executed without involvement of feedback, a *fixed* plan of action must be stored in memory. (Such a plan is sometimes misleadingly called a motor program (Keele, 1968) but, as Sternberg *et al.* (1978) point out, programming implies advance planning but not insensitivity to feedback.) Lashley (1917) was among the first to advocate this idea, but it has been recently modified by Keele (1968, 1973) and Keele and Summers (1976). The latter authors suggest that feedback is important for the acquisition of a fixed plan of action, but that it is largely unnecessary once that learning has taken place.

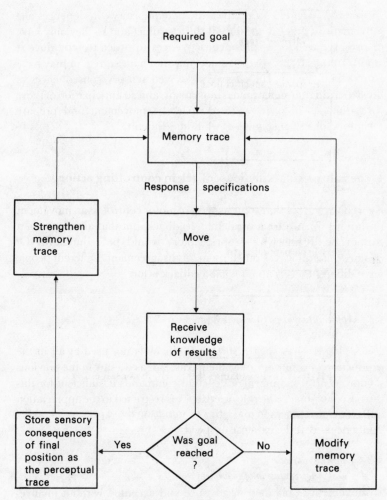

FIGURE 3.10 Adams's theory: (a) verbal-cognitive stage

4.3 *Slow but precise termination of movement*

Bindra (1976) and Keele and Summers (1976) have suggested that feedback may have a role in making the termination of a movement more precise. Firing of alpha (and, perhaps, gamma) motoneurons is under the control of a fixed program to initiate a movement and produce an approximate termination of it. Feedback from gamma

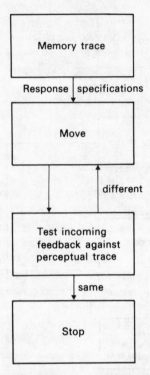

FIGURE 3.11   Adams's theory: (b) motor stage

afferents just serves to make this termination more precise – and then only does so at the expense of speed.

4.4   *Ongoing regulation of movement*

Sherrington stressed the importance of proprioceptive feedback for the ongoing regulation of walking as long ago as 1906. However, it is Adams (1971, 1976, 1977) who has developed this idea and integrated it into one of the more comprehensive theories of motor control. For Adams, there are two memory states involved in the production of a movement. The *memory trace* is a motor program which does no more than initiate the movement at some speed in some direction. The *perceptual trace* is a store of the sensory consequences of the limb being in the correct position. Both traces are acquired during a *verbal-cognitive stage* by strengthening them when knowledge of results signals that the goal of the movement has been obtained (Figure 3.10). After acquisition of these two traces, KR (knowledge of results) becomes redundant and the *motor stage* has been reached. Movement is then produced as shown in Figure 3.11. The memory trace initiates the movement, and then incoming feedback is compared with the perceptual trace to determine whether the limb is in the correct final position. If a match is obtained, movement stops. Otherwise further movement is made. In other words the memory trace is used to *recall* the correct TOTE unit and the perceptual trace is used in the test stage of that unit to recognize whether the goal has been reached.

It is to this question of whether or not kinaesthetic feedback is used in the ongoing regulation of movement that most empirical studies of the role of feedback in motor control have been addressed. However, experimenters trying to distinguish inflow or closed-loop theories (which hold that feedback is used for this purpose) from outflow or open-loop theories (which hold that it is not so used) are faced with a serious problem. It is possible to remove or distort exteroceptive feedback to examine its importance for behaviour, but analogous manipulations of kinaesthetic feedback in humans are rarely possible. Of course, removal of kinaesthetic feedback may occasionally take place by non-experimental means and its effects on motor control can then be observed. In fact, it was on the basis of one such case history that Lashley formulated his views. He observed that a soldier, who, after a gun shot wound, had lost all kinaesthetic input from one of his limbs, could, in the absence of visual feedback, accurately duplicate voluntary movements of that limb. In this respect, he did not need kinaesthetic input to control his movement. Furthermore, he was capable of making 'confidence' judgments of his performance.

This observation led to a host of neurophysiological experiments on animals in which kinaesthetic and/or exteroceptive feedback were surgically disrupted and the resulting motor behaviour observed. The majority of these 'deafferentation' studies appeared to support the initial observations of Lashley. However, the results of these experiments must be interpreted with caution because, although the animals can still move following, say, dorsal root section, there are differences in their movement and the occasions on which they use the affected limbs. Furthermore, the deafferentation paradigm is fraught with methodological difficulties. It is well nigh impossible to eliminate *all* feedback that may accompany a movement. For instance, Knapp *et al.* (1963) were able to condition an arm flexion movement in a deafferented limb. However, visual cues were available and it has been shown that recovery of movement in deafferented limbs is largely dependent on visual feedback (Bossom, 1974; Bossom and Ommaya, 1968). Taub (1973) attempted to remedy this by blinding the de-afferented monkeys. The animals gained accurate and co-ordinated movements and so it was concluded that their behaviour was not under feedback control. But, once again, there were still alternative feedback sources available to the animals. Levine and Ommaya (1974) have suggested that the monkeys may have matched the correct muscular output in the deafferented limb with tension in a non-deafferented muscle, such as one in the jaw. Finally, and perhaps more importantly, there is evidence that kinaesthetic feedback may travel to the brain via the still intact ventral roots (Dinsdale and Kemp, 1966; Ryall and Piercy, 1970).

The second series of studies relating to the role of kinaesthesis comes from psychological observations on kinaesthetic reaction time. Chernikoff and Taylor (1952) found that subjects took 150 milli-seconds to reverse the downward movement of an arm after it had been released from being passively held in a sling. If this were to be taken as an adequate measure of kinaesthetic reaction time, kinaesthetic control of movements made more rapidly than it would be precluded, and Lashley's (1951) argument that a pianist who moves his fingers at a rate of sixteen movements per second is not using such control would be supported. Furthermore, there would be reason to agree with Higgins and Angel (1970) that the error corrections made in their two-choice step-tracking task with a latency in the range 80-120 milliseconds were based on feedforward rather than feedback mechanisms. However, Chernikoff and Taylor's result may not provide a satisfactory measure of kinaesthetic reaction time. Neuro-physiological research has demonstrated the existence of a knaesthetic feedback loop with a loop time of 10 milliseconds – a far cry from 150 milliseconds. This loop was between the eye muscles and the brain (Fuchs and Kornhuber, 1969). More pertinent to limb movements, however, is the work of Evarts (1973) and Dewhurst (1967). Evarts (1973) investigated the sensory input of learned hand movements in monkeys who were trained to position a lever correctly after it had been displaced. Their cortically mediated electromyograph (EMG) responses had latencies of the order of 30-40 milliseconds. (Their movements were not, as some have suggested, spinally mediated reflexes, for they involved the animals *either* pushing the lever forward *or* pulling it back.) Dewhurst (1967) obtained a similar result in man. Each of his subjects had his elbows flexed at 90° while holding a weight in the palm of his hand. Dewhurst demonstrated that, on an unexpected increase or decrease in the weight, the subject's arm began to move back to its original position after about 50 milliseconds, and a change in EMG response in the experimental limb started after approximately 30 milliseconds. Both studies show that central processing of kinaesthetic information could have provided the basis for the detection and correction of error in Higgins and Angel's study, and even for the performance of Lashley's pianist. Spirduso (1978) has outlined the central pathways thought to subserve the misleadingly-termed 'long-loop or transcortical reflex' mechanism responsible for triggering movement in these and other similar experiments (see also Desmedt, 1978).

The methodological problems besetting the deafferentation studies and the recent discoveries of fast-acting kinaesthetic feedback loops do not falsify the outflow theories, but they do immobilize two of their major weapons against the inflow theories. Also, rather more direct support for the latter models has come from Schmidt and Christina's (1969) and Christina's (1970) findings that certain (notably temporal) characteristics of performance can be enhanced by the provision of extra kinaesthetic feedback. However, although the balance of power may have changed, neither type of model can yet be said to have won the war.

5 Flexibility of action

Cognitive psychologists must account for the flexibility of a learned skill. This flexibility is demonstrated in two ways.

5. *Within a muscle group*

Execution of some skill may always involve a particular group of muscles. In each performance, that muscle group is unlikely to reproduce the pattern of movements made on any previous occasion. This is because both initial conditions and desired outcomes are bound to vary slightly. Thus, when Bartlett (1932) played tennis, he observed that in making a stroke he did not produce something absolutely new and 'never merely repeated something old'. Adams's theory is unable to account for this, but a variation of it produced by Schmidt (1975, 1976) can do so.

It will be recalled that, for Adams, each memory trace associates a particular response specification to a particular goal, and each perceptual trace associates the sensory consequences of one particular correct limb position with the same outcome or goal. These discrete associations are built up during the verbal cognitive stage. Figure 3.12a is intended to portray the fact that twelve different memory states must be represented in LTM in order to produce three different outcomes under two different initial conditions.

(a) *Schematic specification of memory states in Adams's model after experience with three required outcomes and two initial conditions*

	Initial condition (I)	Outcome required (O)	Response specification (R)
Memory trace 1	1	1	1
Memory trace 2	1	2	4
Memory trace 3	1	3	9
Memory trace 4	2	1	2
Memory trace 5	2	2	8
Memory trace 6	2	3	18

	Initial condition (I)	Outcome required (O)	Sensory consequences (S)
Perceptual trace 1	1	1	1.00
Perceptual trace 2	1	2	2.00
Perceptual trace 3	1	3	3.00
Perceptual trace 4	2	1	0.5
Perceptual trace 5	2	2	1.0
Perceptual trace 6	2	3	1.5

(b) *Schematic specification of recall and recognition schema in Schmidt's model as derived from experience with the same three required outcomes and two initial conditions given above*

Recall schema $R = I (O^2)$
Recognition schema $S = O/I$

Here imagine I could include level of fatigue, O strength of response required, R effort needed and S intensity of feedback.

FIGURE 3.12   Adams's and Schmidt's models

In Schmidt's model, learning produces rules, not associations. All response specifications are related to all required outcomes and initial conditions by a single rule, the recall schema. This replaces the separate memory traces of Adams's model. Similarly, all sensory consequences are related to all required outcomes and initial conditions by another single rule, the recognition schema. This replaces all the separate perceptual traces in Adams's model. Thus the same experience which, according to Adams, would produce the twelve memory states in Figure 3.12a would, according to Schmidt, produce the two rules in Figure 3.12b. Once acquired, these rules allow the subject to use his past experience to produce response specifications and the expected feedback appropriate for initial conditions and desired outcomes which he has never encountered before. Furthermore, they take up less storage space in LTM.

Schmidt's recall and recognition schemata specify a motor programme which will produce the correct response together with expected feedback which will arise from it. He differs from Adams in assuming that the feedback mechanism is only used for the *ongoing* control of slow responses. Fast responses terminate before feedback can be matched with the output of the recognition schema, and the results of the comparison can therefore only be used to provide information about the correctness of already completed responses. Otherwise, his model is quite similar to that of Adams. It also bears a strong resemblance to another schema model which has been outlined by Pew (1974)

For both Adams (1971) and Schmidt (1976), movement depends on information contained in two separate independent memory stores. The various movement parameters, such as timing, amplitude, location, direction, speed, outcomes, etc. are thought to be exclusive to one or other of the memories. For instance, Adams considers that movement direction is stored in the memory trace, whereas movement extent is stored in the perceptual trace. Is this the case? Are there two independent stores that selectively share parameters? Christina and Merriman (1977) have provided experimental support for such proposals. They trained subjects to move a stylus in particular directions and amplitudes. They could thus look at subjects' performance when they manipulated independently the two variables of direction and amplitude. The data showed that, during learning, extent could be learned even though direction was varied, and vice versa. This was taken as support for two independent memories for these parameters.

Other experiments have attempted to distinguish Adams's and Schmidt's proposals. In Schmidt's model, a recall schema is developed as an abstract rule for each movement's initial condition, response specifications and actual outcome, and this development is a function of variability in practice. McCracken and Stelmach (1977) required subjects to perform arm movements under high and low variability practice conditions and then looked at the transfer of training to a new instance of the movement. The data supported Schmidt's theory: the high variability group performed better.

5.2   Between muscle groups

After having learned to reach a goal using particular muscle groups, we are able to reach the same goal using *quite different* muscle groups.

> Thus, the letter A may be written without moving any muscles or joints other than those of the fingers. Or, it may be written through large movements of the whole arm with the muscles of the fingers serving only to grasp the writing instrument. Or, more radically, one can write the character without involving the muscles or joints of either arms or fingers, by clenching the writing instrument between one's teeth or toes (Turvey, 1977, p. 213).

Hebb (1949) called this phenomenon 'motor equivalence'. It raises the question of how movement information is stored in long-term memory.

For behaviourists, the motor cortex was the 'keyboard upon which the sensory mind played to produce behaviour. The only question concerned whether the keys encoded a representation of individual muscles or represented more complex movements and combinations.' (Weimer, 1977, p. 273). Modified versions of this 'keyboard' view are still espoused (e.g., Bindra, 1976). The motor areas of the brain store motor commands for muscles. Choice of the correct command requires information about the absolute position of the limbs. As Boyd and Roberts (1953) had shown that different joint receptors fire for different limb positions, these receptors play a major role in such theories. For instance, Adams (1977) goes so far as to suggest that their firing characteristics are stored in the cortex for use in interpreting current firing rate in terms of the parameters used by physiologists to study them. In other words, joint receptor firing characteristics are the perceptual traces in his model, discussed above. Muscle commands presumably form the memory traces.

A number of empirical and theoretical problems arise if one adopts this type of model (Greer and Harvey, 1978). Recent work has shown that although different joint receptors do fire for different limb positions, they do so only at the extremes of limb movement (Burgess and Clark, 1969). Amputees possess knowledge about the position of their artificial limbs although no joints but only muscles are present to provide them with this information (Grigg *et al.*, 1973). Finally, and most important, it is difficult to see how 'keyboard' theories can account for motor equivalence.

That proprioceptors can code position, amplitude, velocity, acceleration and force of movement, does not indicate that those parameters of movement are stored in long-term memory. We have seen that movement information may be recoded from one form to another as it passes from one level of the nervous system to another. A number of workers (Lashley, 1951; Pribram, 1971; Turvey, 1977; Russell, 1976) have suggested that, for the purposes of long-term storage, motor patterns are centrally encoded within a 'space co-ordinate' system. For cognitive psychologists, this mode of storage has the advantage of being able to account for 'motor equivalence'. The *pattern* of movements is the same, however they are produced.

The 'space co-ordinate' hypothesis was developed in some detail by those interested in the control of articulation. This is not surprising. Production of a phoneme requires the tongue (and other articulators) to move to a particular position from any other previous position. If neural commands to muscles were stored centrally, a vast number would have to be retained to accomplish this (MacNeilage, 1970). MacNeilage and MacNeilage (1973) argue that it is the location of a target within a spatial co-ordinate system which is encoded in memory. A command to reach this target enables lower centres to generate afresh the appropriate movements each time they are required. Movement information *per se* is not stored — it is spontaneously generated by lower centres whenever it is needed. Sussman, in 'What the Tongue Tells the Brain' (1972), argues that the result of this generation process is the specification of a set of tuning parameters which can be used as feedforward by gamma-motoneurons to bias the reflex loop. The loop acts to cancel out the bias and the target is reached.

If the tongue can operate in such a way without joint receptors, perhaps a similar system can control limb movement. For articulation it can be argued that the moving part (the tongue) operates from the same base within a constant environment (the mouth). This is not true for limb movement. Thus we cannot immediately operate on the environment with our limbs by specifying a target position within our egocentric space co-ordinate system. Before we can do so, we must identify (or update) the relation between this system and our environment. Thus updating or rescaling must rely on exteroception, particularly vision. Indeed, it is presumably a function of that part of the visual system identified by Trevarthen (1968) as specialized for dealing with relationships in extensive space (ambient vision) rather than that part specialized for identification of things (focal vision). Turvey (1977) has discussed how it may be carried out.

To test these spatial co-ordinate theories of motor LTM, experimenters have studied whether the *location* of a target, the end position of a movement, is stored rather than the distance of the target from a starting point or the force required to get from that point to the target. Russell (1976) reports an experiment in which subjects in one group made movements from different starting locations to the same terminal location, and subjects in a second group made movements from a single starting location to that same terminal location. After this training, during which knowledge of results was given, subjects in both groups made a criterial movement to the terminal location from the same starting position that subjects in the second group had moved from during training. There was no difference in accuracy of the two groups, but both were better than a third group that had received no training. In other words, the performance of subjects in the first group, who had to depend on storage of location information because no specific movement information had been available to them during training, was as accurate as that of those in the second group, who did have access to specific movement information. Russell argues that this result and similar ones obtained by Martenuik and Roy (1972) and Laabs (1973) favour the spatial co-ordinate theories.

6 Timing of action

When throwing a grenade, it is just not sufficient to perform the correct movements in the correct order. Each movement (especially the last one) must be precisely timed. How is this done?

6.1 Feedback dependent timing

We have seen that feedback may specify *whether* a response is correct (Adams, 1971), or *which* response should be produced next (Gagné, 1965). In the latter case, it also specifies *when* that response will be produced; i.e., the grenade is thrown as soon as proprioceptive feedback from the removal of the pin has been received. In this case, input of proprioceptive information provides the basis for the timing of motor responses.

Adams and Creamer (1962) suggested that it is not the *input* of proprioceptive information which triggers a response. Instead it is the extent to which the memory trace of that information has *decayed*. For example, a response may be produced when feedback from the previous response has decayed to, say, 50 per cent of its original level. This hypothesis has the advantage of being able to account for delays between responses which are longer than the time required to input feedback and retrieve the response associated with it. Furthermore, different responses in a sequence may be triggered by different degrees of proprioceptive decay, and so the intervals between them may also be different. Adams (1977) identifies the firing functions of slowly adapting joint receptors not only as the perceptual trace in his 1971 model for positioning (see Section 4.4), but also as the proprioceptive information in his earlier model for timing. These firing functions show decay to a steady-state frequency over a period of about seven seconds from a movement and so the model can account for the timing of intervals up to that length. Longer intervals must be timed by producing redundant movements which will produce proprioceptive feedback for timing purposes but which are otherwise irrelevant to the task at hand (e.g., foot or finger tapping during the interval). (Adams also suggests that, as these receptors fire differentially for different velocities of movement, storage of their firing functions would allow regulation of that parameter too.)

The relative merits of the proprioceptive input and proprioceptive decay hypotheses have been reviewed by Schmidt (1971), Dickinson (1974) and Christina (1976).

6.2 Feedback independent timing

Timing need not involve the use of feedback information. It may arise as the automatic consequence of the execution of a series of motor commands as they are 'run off' in the order in which they are specified. However, without the introduction of redundant commands, such a system would not allow timing of intervals longer than the time to output a command. Hence it is more likely that timing parameters are separately specified in or with the plan for the sequence of movements and executed with the use of a timekeeper or pacemaker. Such a proposal raises two important issues.

Firstly, what is the nature of the pacemaker or clock which, in conjunction with the stored timing parameters, governs the speed of movements and the intervals between them? According to Jones (1974b), an effective clock would be provided by circulating efferent copy round a motor cortex-cerebellum loop. However, as Ornstein (1969) has pointed out, no satisfactory evidence for a central biological clock has been forthcoming. Even so, lower-level mechanisms capable of generating rhythmic pulses to act as a basis for locomotion have been identified. Relevant work is clearly reviewed by Pearson (1976).

Secondly, are timing parameters stored as an integral and inseparable part of the plan which specifies the sequence of movements, or are they stored independently and attached to each motor command as it is executed? Unlike Michon (1974), Summers (1977) favours the former possibility. He suggests that the relative timing of movements within a sequence is stored in the plan to produce that sequence, but that the overall speed of execution may be determined separately. (Gibbs (1970) suggested that one role of the cerebellum may be to act as this overall speed regulator by determining the relative use of the fast alpha- and the slower gamma-motoneurons.) To test his proposal, Summers trained two groups of subjects to learn a sequence of movements in response to visual events. In the 'no timing' group, the inter-event interval varied within the entire sequence. In the 'timing' group, this interval was constant throughout the sequence. Summers considered that in the 'timing' group, the constant inter-event interval made time an integral component of the skill. These groups were later tested in an experimental condition, during which their movement sequences were interrupted by an unexpected event that occurred at various points of the sequence. The data showed that the 'timing' group was more affected by this occurrence than the no-timing group – a finding that supports an 'integral' approach to the representation of time in the movement plan. Summers also observed that the speed of responding to the unexpected event was similar in both groups, but the overall execution speed of the movement sequence altered in the 'timing' group. (A finding that would support Schmidt's view that overall execution speed is a separate parameter put into effect on execution of the motor program.)

6.3 Compromise models

Wing (1977) has proposed a compromise model. A clock, together with stored timing parameters, generates the intervals to be produced, but feedback is occasionally used to alter the clock rate. The size of some movements may be governed by the time taken to produce them and these movements would be affected by alteration in clock rate. Handwriting may be produced by such movements and so the observation that it increases in size when nitrous oxide is inhaled may be explained either by assuming that the drug affects input of proprioceptive feedback (Legge, 1965), or by assuming that it affects the clock rate directly (Wing, 1978).

7 Acquisition of skilled action patterns

A number of authors (e.g., Fitts and Posner, 1967; Adams, 1971) have suggested that as a skill is learned, reliance shifts to faster and faster feedback loops. Initially, during the *verbal* stage, augmented feedback providing knowledge of results is essential to performance. Later, during the *association* stage, rules are learned to relate this feedback to that which is intrinsic to the task. When this has occurred, the *final or autonomous* stage has been reached and augmented feedback is no longer necessary. This transition from verbal to autonomous stages seems to correlate with a reduction in the individual's conscious involvement in the performance of his task. For Legge and Barber (1976), this reduction indicates a decreasing role for the central planner in the ongoing of the action and the increasing development and use of a special faster route to bypass it. They argue that such routes are specifically set up for the purposes of performing particular skills and that they connect together particular types of input (e.g., visual) with particular types of output (e.g., manual). This allows two well-learned skills to be performed as well simultaneously as separately when (and only when) they employ different inputs and outputs

(Allport *et al.*, 1972). Legge and Barber's view that a skill is developed by creating a special route or autonomous channel for processing information is not dissimilar to Fowler and Turvey's (1978) suggestion that, in acquiring a skill, the actor learns to turn himself into a special-purpose device. He does this by developing autonomous organizations of muscle groups (co-ordinative structures) that can be controlled as complete units, and by discovering the best combination of these co-ordinative structures for *bending* the force function provided by the environment (which would include gravitational and reactive forces) to produce the force function that is desired.

There has been some discussion concerning the type of intrinsic feedback which is used once the need for knowledge of results has dropped out. If both visual and proprioceptive feedback can provide sufficient information for performance, one would expect that with increasing competence subjects would come to rely more and more on the latter because of its faster transmission rate. Initially, knowledge of results may be mapped on to visual feedback, in which case we would expect vision to be especially important for learning the skill prior to removal of knowledge of results (Kelso and Stelmach, 1976). Afterwards, however, visual feedback itself may be mapped on to proprioceptive feedback so that the perceptual trace eventually stores information from the latter modality, as Adams (1971, 1977) suggests. Of course, as we noted in Section 4.2, some authors (Keele and Summers, 1976) suggest that, with really high levels of skill, the need for any sort of feedback is reduced to a minimum and performance becomes wholly reliant on the execution of a fixed motor program.

8   The study of action placed in a wider context

We have endeavoured to provide a broad but brief review of important issues in the study of action. Where we have not fully elaborated on some point, we hope we have provided the reader with the information he would require to access a more detailed discussion. To conclude, we would like to try to outline the relation between the study of action and the rest of cognitive psychology, to specify what seem to us to be potential growth points in the subject and to sketch a few of the many practical applications of it.

8.1 Interrelations

Many of the problems we have discussed closely parallel those faced by cognitive psychologists interested in other areas. Solutions too have been similar. So they should be. In general, cognitive psychology emphasizes the *active* nature of the individual, his dependence on hierarchic/heterarchic knowledge structures and his use of rules or schemata to transform and exploit that knowledge.

For us, the active nature of the individual is stressed by our rejection of the behaviourists' cued-movement theories in favour of advanced planning (Section 2). The hierarchic/heterarchic nature of knowledge is emphasized by the suggestion that such a structure represents the resulting plan in different levels of the nervous system (Section 1). The use of rules or schemata was found to be a satisfactory way of coping with the problems of accounting for the flexibility of action (Section 5.1).

Other chapters in this book refer to the active 'hypothesis testing' view perception (Chapter 2), the use of hierarchical/heterarchical knowledge structures by theorists interested in language and semantic memory (Chapter 6), and the empolyment of rules or schemata to account for the generation of novel but grammatical sentences (Chapter 7).

Finally, we have not only been viewing different areas in similar ways. In some cases, we may have been viewing related areas. We saw, for example, that movement may be generated by specifying target positions in a space co-ordinate system on to which the environment has been mapped by exteroceptors. Perhaps it would not be too far off the mark to describe such a model as a perceptual theory of motor control. In any case, it is particularly interesting to compare it with motor theories of speech and pattern perception (Liberman *et al.*, 1967; Weimer, 1977). According to these models the same rules are used to generate an event as to perceive it. Input is recognized after a successful match between it and an internally generated replica of it. Both types of model recognize the similarity, if not the identity, of processes involved in perceiving events and those involved in producing them. Allport in Chapter 2 has already pointed to this 'obvious parallel between the idea of *input*-pattern-specific recognition demons and *ouput*-pattern-specific *action demons*'. In fact, his discussion of the question of how 'action demons' are evoked by the appropriate combinations of 'goal demons' and 'cue demons' concerns processes which are directly antecedent to the ones we have been outlining. Specifically, we have been concerned with the effects of evoking an 'action demon', and with the processes that occur after it has been evoked.

8.2   New directions

Growth points in the area appear to be at its interfaces with other disciplines, particularly physiology, artificial intelligence, linguistics and phonetics.

The failure to find a neural correlate for the motor program is one of the major weaknesses of motor theories. We need detailed knowledge not only about what is in the program but also about how it is formulated. There is no explanation as yet, let alone evidence, for the way in which the program accesses the efferents. How does the target specified in the space co-ordinate system get recoded by successively lower levels of the nervous system to end up as an efferent signal to muscles? Psychologists and neurophysiologists need much more combined effort in order to investigate problems such as these. We now have a great deal of information about efferent and afferent pathways in the motor system, but we still do not know, for instance, how information about different movement parameters travels in these pathways. Reynolds, *et al.* (1972) observed that dogs subjected to bilateral sectioning of the dorsal columns had grossly impaired ability to produce symmetrical distribution of their weight when standing still, yet they could adjust to sudden displacements of the platform on which they stood. Any number of different pathways may have been used to do this. Many psychological experiments deal with highly constrained motor tasks, yet in everyday life many of our skilled movements are performed under a variety of conditions which may affect the control of the behaviour, and this information is not as yet under experimental control.

Progress has been made in some areas. For example, a major difficulty in research in kinaesthesis has been the inaccessibility of kinaesthetic input. It could not be measured and manipulated in the same way as visual and auditory stimulation. Recently some pioneering work in Scandinavia has succeeded in recording joint afferents firing to stimulation from nerves in conscious human subjects. This has enabled psychophysical measurements to be correlated with neural measurements taken at the same time in response to the same stimuli (Järvilehto, 1977).

Artificial intelligence (AI) studies have made important contributions to other areas of cognitive psychology. Until recently, they have been notable in the motor control literature only by their virtual absence. As Ernest Kent (1978) has pointed out,

> Our big fast machines can do elegant and complex mathematics, even proofs, far beyond our own powers, yet we have the greatest difficulty making them display even the slightest degree of common sense. The System 370 can do amazing things with numbers, but it wouldn't have the intelligence to duck if you swing a club at it. A dog could do better at dealing with its environment.

Now, however, work such as that of Greene (1972) and Turvey *et al.* (1978) indicates a growing awareness of the potential contribution of AI to the study of action. Allport (Chapter 2) has already mentioned possible applications of 'Production System' models in this and other areas.

We feel that language theorists and motor control theorists must get together, for many of the 'behaviours' in language are similar to those in motor control (e.g., we can generate novel utterances, just as we can generate novel movements). Dance, mime and signing systems also convey 'linguistic' information. Perhaps movement and language are based on the same underlying rules. Hughlings Jackson once postulated that the anatomical substrate of all higher intellectual processes is sensori-motor in origin, and language is one of the ways in which we might investigate the underlying basis of motor control. His ideas may be viewed ontogenetically (cf. Piaget, 1953; Bruner, 1964) or phylogenetically. In the latter case, an examination of them would involve looking at how the development of man's ability to use his limbs has paralleled his evolution in social and intellectual spheres. This would necessitate an interdisciplinary approach with contributions from psychologists, neurologists and anthropologists.

Eye movements (Brooks and Bajandas, 1977; Carpenter, 1977; Ditchburn, 1973; Senders *et al.*, 1978), locomotion (Herman, *et al.*, 1976; Stein *et al.*, 1973) and speech production (Kent, 1976; MacNeilage and Ladefoged, 1976) tend to be viewed as specialized topics in motor control. They all contain peculiar problems of their own. For example, consider speech production – an area within which the two

of us are working with a colleague, Pete Howell. Whereas we
know which muscles produce limb movements (e.g., the biceps flex
the arms) but do not know exactly how they do it, in many cases we do
not even know which muscles are responsible for changes in vocal
output. There has, for instance, been much discussion concerning the
identity of the muscles used to lower the pitch of the voice (Harvey
and Howell, in press). It is not surprising, therefore, that there is no
current model which will provide an adequate account of the main
phenomena of speech production. MacNeilage (1970) produced one
of the most flexible models, but he (MacNeilage, 1972) has acknowledged the validity of Nooteboom's (1970) criticisms of it. This model,
in which a sequence of phonemes specifies a sequence of targets
which, in turn, specifies a sequence of muscle lengths that are produced
under alpha-gamma loop control, provided a parsimonious account
of how articulators can reach the positions needed to produce a
particular phoneme from any previous positions. Nooteboom (1970)
pointed out, however, that it cannot account for our ability to speak
with clenched teeth (pipe speech) because in that situation many
muscles would have to assume different lengths to reach the same
targets. (In fact, there is no evidence that they actually reach the same
targets. Harshman, *et al.* (1977) have shown that, even in normal
speech, the same phonemes can be produced by a number of completely different target combinations.) Furthermore, prosodic aspects
of speech, such as rate and intonation, affect the acoustic specification
of each phoneme (i.e., the formants or vocal tract resonances which
characterize each vowel and the transitions between them which
characterize many consonants). Howell (1979), for instance, has
shown that the formants which are produced for a particular vowel
depend on the pitch of the voice. Hence the targets which are specified
for a particular phoneme must depend on higher-level prosodic features
(e.g., intonation, rate of speech) as well as on lower level ones concerning the articulatory environment. (The articulatory environment
is changed from normal when you have a pipe in your mouth, when
you've left your false teeth in the glass, when you have a cold, when
you're breathing a mixture of gases such as helium and oxygen rather
than air, when you have food in your mouth, etc.)

It should be possible to modify MacNeilage's (1970) model to cope
with both Nooteboom's (1970) criticisms and the above phenomena.
It will be recalled that Turvey (1977) suggested that the egocentric space
within which targets are specified to produce limb movements can be

rescaled on the basis of exteroceptive information. Similarly, it should be possible to rescale either the representation of the vocal tract within which targets are specified or else the actual target and/or muscle length specifications within that representation. This rescaling would be performed on the basis of factors specified by higher-level (prosodic) features, and by lower-level (articulatory environmental) ones. Scaling factor specification on the basis of higher level features and perhaps some lower-level ones would depend on corollary discharge from the efferent commands specifying these features in the first place, but specification on the basis of other lower-level ones (e.g., breathing a helium/oxygen mixture) would probably require interoceptive feedback.

It is important to emphasize three things. First, this rescaling model bears no resemblance to Wickelgren's (1969) context-sensitive allophone model, according to which each phoneme has a whole set of internal representations responsible for its production in all its various contexts (e.g., there would be one stored representation for producing a 'p' between an 'a' and a 't', and another for producing it between an 'a' and an 's'). In the rescaling model outlined here, there is no more need for each phoneme to possess a set of different stored targets for each state of the articulatory environment than there is for each movement to possess a set of differently stored targets for each state of the external environment in Turvey's (1977) model.

Secondly, a number of possible target combinations may produce the required phoneme, and which combination is actually specified (prior to rescaling) may depend on some least effort principle. In a completely new task situation (e.g. singing) the actor may discover that rescaling the old combination of targets on the basis of the features of the new situation produces movements which require more effort than those produced after selecting a completely new combination of targets from the set of possible combinations specified by the phoneme. This may be why a speaker appears to change the pitch of his voice by raising and lowering the larynx (Ohala, 1978); but a singer appears to do so by keeping the larynx stationary and altering the configuration of muscles inside it (Sundberg, 1973; Harvey and Howell, 1979). Discovering that use of a completely new combination of targets requires less effort than use of the rescaled old one corresponds to one of the processes involved in acquiring a skill, and parallels what Fowler and Turvey (1978) refer to as 'designing an effective bio-kinematic chain'.

Finally, it should be emphasized that the claim that a sequence of phonemes specifies a sequence of targets leaves open the question of the size of the phoneme sequence responsible for each specification. However, other data indicate that it may be quite large and that it probably corresponds to a tone group or syntagma (a stress pattern forming the basic unit of the speech rhythm). For instance, co-articulation (the dependence of the target specified for one phoneme on that specified for another) can extend across six consonants (Benguerel and Cowen, 1974); spoonerisms tend to occur within but not across tone groups (Boomer and Laver, 1968); and speech onset time increases with the number of primary stresses to be produced (Sternberg *et al.*, 1978). The tone group certainly appears to be the most economical segment for the rescaling model. Rescaling could occur when necessary but would not have to take place any more frequently than that. This is because changes in prosodic features, such as pitch or rate of speech, or in the articulatory environment, may often occur across tone groups but are unlikely to occur within them.

Experimental examination of models of speech production requires close co-operation between psychologists, physiologists, phoneticians and acousticians. In fact, throughout this section, we have tried to emphasize the need for integrated inter- and intradisciplinary approaches to the problems of motor control.

8.3   Practical applications

There are dozens of practical applications of work on action and motor control. What follows is just a miscellany of some of them.

The development of artificial limbs has progressed considerably in the last twenty years, and has used some aspects of motor control research in this development. Motor theorists in turn can benefit from studying the control of these limbs, especially when considering what type of feedback can be used to control behaviour, for various forms of feedback can be substituted in the limb and their efficacy observed. For example, Grigg, *et al.* (1973) studied patients who had been given artificial hip joints. Patients had little if any impairment in their ability to detect movement about the joint, indicating that joint receptor feedback was not necessary. Recently there has been a similar fruitful interaction between those concerned with developing artificial larynxes and theorists interested in speech production.

Recent pharmacological research has indicated that the motor system and brain structures underlying motivation may rely on the same neurotransmitter, dopamine. Parkinsonism, a disease of the motor system, may therefore also affect motivation when chronic. A link between this disease and schizophrenia would not be unexpected. In fact, the effects of anti-Parkinsonism drugs (e.g., L-dopa) and anti-schizophrenic drugs do not appear to be unrelated.

Many motor theories of perception and cognition (Weimer, 1977), as we have seen, suggest that if schemata can be created for generating movement they could also be used more generally in perception and thought. Forms of movement therapy to help the emotionally and physically disabled have been proposed (e.g., Morgan and Kalakian, 1974) and some have had a modicum of success (i.e., the motor schemata have 'transferred' to intellectual processes – another reflection of integration of other areas of cognitive psychology with the study of action).

This chapter has dealt solely with skeletal musculature present in the limbs and body. Autonomic or smooth muscle is also under feedback control but as yet little is known about the mechanisms of the autonomic control systems. However, there has been some success in training high-risk heart cases to control their heart rate using biofeedback.

8.4 Further reading

We have tried to convey, perhaps prematurely, the emerging coherence of the cognitive psychology of action. As we mentioned at the outset, these developments are even more recent than corresponding ones in other areas. Consequently, there is still a paucity of texts which describe them more fully than we have been able to do here. However, the following three collections of theoretical and review articles are particularly important.

G. Stelmach (ed.) (1976), *Motor Control: Issues and Trends,* Academic Press, New York, London.

G. Stelmach (ed.) (1978), *Information Processing in Motor Control and Learning,* Academic Press, New York, London.

G. Stelmach (ed.) (in press), *Tutorials in Motor Behaviour,* North Holland, Amsterdam.

References

Adams, J. A. (1971), 'A closed loop theory of motor learning', *Journal of Motor Behaviour, 3*, pp. 111–50.

Adams, J. A. (1976), 'Issues for a closed loop theory of motor learning', G. E. Stelmach (ed.), *Motor Control: Issues and Trends*, Academic Press: London.

Adams, J. A. (1977), 'Feedback theory of how joint receptors regulate the timing and positioning of a limb', *Psychological Review, 84*, 6, pp. 504–23.

Adams, J. A. and Creamer, L. R. (1962), 'Anticipatory timing of continuous and discrete responses', *Journal of Experimental Psychology, 63*, pp. 84–90.

Allport, D. A., Antonis, B. and Reynolds, P. (1972), 'On the division of attention: a disproof of the single channel hypothesis', *Quarterly Journal of Experimental Psychology, 24*, pp. 225–35.

Annett, J. and Kay, H. (1957), 'Knowledge of results and "skilled performance"', *Occupational Psychology, 31*, pp. 69–79.

Bartlett, F. C. (1932), *Remembering*, Cambridge University Press.

Benguerel, A. P. and Cowen, H. A. (1974), 'Coarticulation of upper lip protrusion in French', *Phonetica, 30*, pp. 41–55.

Bindra, D. (1976), *A Theory of Intelligent Behavior*, Wiley: New York.

Boomer, D. S. and Laver, J. D. M. (1968), 'Slips of the tongue', *British Journal of Disorders of Communication, 3*, pp. 2–12.

Bossom, J. (1974), 'Movement without proprioception', *Brain Research, 71*, pp. 285–96.

Bossom, J. and Ommaya, A. K. (1968), 'Visuo-motor adaptation (to prismatic transformation of the retinal image) in monkeys with bilateral dorsal phizotomy', *Brain, 91*, pp. 161–72.

Boyd, I. A. and Roberts, T. D. M. (1953), 'Proprioceptive discharge from stretch receptors in the knee joints of the cat', *Journal of Physiology, 122*, pp. 38–58.

Brooks, B. A. and Bajandas, F. J. (1977), *Eye Movements*, Plenum: London.

Bruner, J. S. (1964), 'The course of cognitive growth', *American Psychologist, 19*, pp. 1–15.

Burgess, P. R. and Clark, F. J. (1969), 'Characteristics of knee joint receptors in the cat', *Journal of Physiology, 203*, pp. 317–35.

Carpenter, R. S. H. (1977), *Movements of the Eyes*, Pion Press: London.

Chernikoff, R. and Taylor, F. V. (1952), 'Reaction time to kinaesthetic stimulation resulting from sudden arm displacement', *Journal of Experimental Psychology, 43*, pp. 1–8.

Christina, R. W. (1970), 'Proprioception as a basis for the temporal anticipation of motor responses', *Journal of Motor Behaviour, 2*, pp. 125–33.

Christina, R. W. (1976, 'Proprioception as a basis of anticipating timing behaviour', in G. E. Stelmach (ed.), *Motor Control: Issues and Trends*, Academic Press: New York, London.

Christina, R. W. and Merriman, W. J. (1977), 'Learning the direction and extent of a movement: a test of Adams's closed-loop theory', *Journal of Motor Behaviour, 9*, pp. 1–10.

Desmedt, J. E. (1978), *Cerebral Motor Control in Man: Long Loop Mechanisms*, S. Karger: Basle.

Deutsch, J. A. (1960), *The Structural Basis of Behavior*, University of Chicago Press.

Deutsch, J. A. and Deutsch, D. (1963), 'Attention: some theoretical considerations', *Psychological Review, 70*, pp. 80–90.

Dewhurst, D. J. (1967), 'Neuromuscular control system', *IEEE Trans. Bio-Med. Eng.*, BME-14, pp. 167-71.

Dickinson, J. (1974), *Proprioceptive Control of Human Movement*, Lepus Books: London.

Dinsdale, J. A. and Kemp, J. M. (1966), 'Afferent fibres in ventral nerve roots in the cat', *Proceedings of the Physiological Society, 187*, pp. 25–6.

Ditchburn, R. W. (1973), *Eye Movements and Visual Perception*, Clarendon Press: Oxford.

Dixon, N. F. (1971), *Subliminal Perception: the Nature of a Controversy*, McGraw-Hill: Toronto.

Evarts, E. V. (1973), 'Brain mechanisms in movement', *Scientific American, 229*, pp. 96–103.

Fitts, P. M. (1964), 'Perceptual motor skill learning', in A. W. Melton (ed.), *Categories of Human Learning*, Academic Press: New York.

Fitts, P. M. and Posner, M. I. (1967), *Human Performance*, Brooks Cole: Belmont.

Fowler, C. A. and Turvey, M. T. (1978), 'Skill acquisition: an event approach with special reference to searching for the optimum of a function of several variables', in G. E. Stelmach (ed.), *Information Processing in Motor Control and Learning*, Academic Press: London.

Fuchs, A. F. and Kornhuber, H. H. (1969), 'Extraocular muscle afferents to the cerebellum of the cat', *Journal of Physiology, 200*, pp. 713–22.

Gagné, R. M. (1965), *The Conditions of Learning*, Holt, Rinehart & Winston: New York.

Gentile, A. M. (1972), 'A working model of skill acquisition with applications to teaching', *Quest, 17*, pp. 3–23.

Gibbs, C. B. (1970), 'Servocontrol systems in organisms and the transfer of skill', in D. Legge (ed.), *Skills*, Penguine: Harmondsworth, pp. 211-26.

Greene, P. H. (1971), Introduction to I. M. Gelfand, V. S. Gurfinkel, S. V. Fomin and M. L. Tsetlin (eds), *Models of the Structural-Functional Organisation of Certain Biological Systems*, MIT Press: Cambridge, Mass., pp. xi–xxxi.

Greene, P. M. (1972), 'Problems in the organization of motor systems', in R. Rosen and F. M. Snell (eds), *Progress in Theoretical Biology*, vol. 2, Academic Press: New York.

Greenwald, A. G. (1970), 'Sensory feedback mechanisms in performance control: with special reference to the ideomotor mechanisms', *Psychological Review, 77*, pp. 73–9.

Greer, K. (1977), PhD thesis, University of London.

Greer, K. and Harvey, N. (1978), 'Timing and positioning of limb movements: comments on Adams' theory', *Psychological Review, 85*, pp. 482–4.

Grigg, P., Finerman, G. A. and Riley, L. H. (1973), 'Joint-position sense after total hip replacement', *Journal of Bone and Joint Surgery, 55*(A), pp. 1016–25.

Harshman, R., Ladefoged, P. and Goldstein, L. (1977), 'Factor analysis of tongue shapes', *Journal of the Acoustical Society of America, 62*, pp. 693–707.

Harvey, N. and Howell, P. (in press), 'Isotonic vocalis contraction as a means of producing rapid decreases in Fo', *Journal of Speech and Hearing Research.*

Hebb, D. O. (1949), *The Organization of Behavior,* Wiley: New York.

Henneman, E. (1974), 'Organization of the motor system: a preview', in V. B. Mountcastle (ed.), *Medical Physiology,* vol. 1, 13th edn., Mosby: St Louis.

Henry, F. M. and Rogers, E. E. (1960), 'Increased response latency for complicated movements and a "memory drum" theory of neuromotor reaction', *Research Quarterly for the American Association for Health, Physical Education and Recreation, 31*, pp. 448–58.

Herman, R. M., Grillner, S., Stein, P. S. G. and Stuart, D. G. (1976), *Neural Control of Locomotion,* Plenum: London.

Higgins, J. R. and Angel, R. W. (1970), 'Correction of tracking errors without sensory feedback', *Journal of Experimental Psychology, 84*, pp. 412–16.

Howell, P. (in press), 'Change in phoneme targets with different phonation type', in G. E. Stelmach (ed.), *Tutorials in Motor Behaviour,* North Holland: Amsterdam.

James, W. (1890), *The Principles of Psychology,* Holt, Rinehart & Winston: New York.

Järvilehto, T. (1977), 'Neural basis of cutaneous sensations analysed by microelectrode measurements from human peripheral nerves: a review', *Scandinavian Journal of Psychology, 18*, pp. 348–59.

Jones, B. (1974a), 'Is proprioception important for skilled performance?' *Journal of Motor Behaviour, 6*, pp. 33–45.

Jones, B. (1974b), 'The role of central monitoring of efference in motor short-term memory', *Journal of Experimental Psychology, 102*, pp. 37–43.

Keele, S. W. (1968), 'Movement control in skilled motor performance', *Psychological Bulletin, 70*, pp. 387–403.

Keele, S. W. (1973), *Attention and Human Performance,* Goodyear: Pacific Palisades, Cal.

Keele, S. W. and Summers, J. J. (1976), 'The structure of motor programs', in G. E. Stelmach (ed.) *Motor Control: Issues and Trends,* Academic Press: New York, London.

Kelso, J. A. S. (1977), 'Planning and efferent components in the coding of movement', *Journal of Motor Behavior, 9*, pp. 33–48.

Kelso, J. A. S. (1978), 'Joint receptors do not provide a satisfactory basis for motor timing and positioning', *Psychological Review, 85*, pp. 474–81.

Kelso, J. A. S. and Stelmach, G. E. (1976), 'Central and peripheral mechanisms in motor control', in G. E. Stelmach (ed.), *Motor Control: Issues and Trends,* Academic Press: London.

Kelso, J. A. S. and Wallace, S. A. (1978), 'Conscious mechanisms in movement', in G. E. Stelmach (ed.), *Information Processing in Motor Control and Learning,* Academic Press: London.

Kent, E. (1978), 'The brains of men-machines: biological models for robotics', *Byte, 3*, pp. 11–106.

Kent, R. D. (1976), 'Models of speech production', in N. J. Lass, *Contemporary Issues in Experimental Phonetics,* Academic Press: London.

Kerr, B. (1978), 'Task factors that influence selection and preparation for voluntary movements', in G. E. Stelmach (ed.), *Information Processing in Motor Control and Learning*, Academic Press: London.

Knapp, H. D., Taub, E. and Berman, A. J. (1963), 'Movement in monkeys with deafferented forelimbs', *Experimental Neurology, 7*, pp. 305–15.

Laabs, G. J. (1973), 'Retention characteristics of different reproduction cues in motor short-term memory', *Journal of Experimental Psychology, 100*, pp. 168–77.

Lashley, K. S. (1917), 'The accuracy of movement in the absence of excitation from the moving organ', *American Journal of Psychology, 43*, pp. 169–94.

Lashley, K. S. (1951), 'The problem of serial order in behavior', in L. A. Jefress (ed.), *Cerebral Mechanisms in Behavior: The Hixon Symposium,* Wiley: New York.

Legge, D. (1965), 'Analysis of visual and proprioceptive components of motor skill by means of a drug', *British Journal of Psychology, 56*, pp. 243–54.

Legge, D. and Barber, P. J. (1976), *Information and Skill*, Methuen: London.

Levine, D. and Ommaya, A. K. (1974), 'Precision of motor control after dorsal rhizotomy', *Archives of Neurology* (Chicago).

Liberman, A. M., Cooper, F. A., Shankweiler, D. and Studdert-Kennedy, M. (1967), 'Perception of the speech code', *Psychological Review, 74*, pp. 431–61.

McCracken, H. D. and Stelmach, G. E. (1977), 'A test of the Schema theory of discrete motor learning', *Journal of Motor Behaviour, 9*, pp. 193–202.

MacNeilage, P. F. (1970), 'The motor control of serial ordering of speech', *Psychological Review, 77*, pp. 182–96.

MacNeilage, P. F. (1972), 'Speech physiology', in J. H. Gilbert, *Speech and Cortical Functioning*, Academic Press: New York.

MacNeilage, P. F. and Ladefoged, P. (1976), 'The production of speech and language', in E. C. Carterette and M. P. Friedman (eds), *Handbook of Perception*, vol. 7, Academic Press: New York.

MacNeilage, P. F. and MacNeilage, L. A. (1973), 'Central processes controlling speech production during sleep and waking', in F. J. McGuigan and R. A. Scheonover (eds), *The Psychophysiology of Thinking*, Academic Press: New York, pp. 417–48.

Martenuik, R. G. and Roy, E. A. (1972), 'The codability of kinaesthetic location and distance information', *Acta Psychologica, 36*, pp. 471–9.

Mathews, P. B. C. (1977), 'Muscle afferents and kinaesthesia', *British Medical Bulletin, 33(2)*, pp. 137–42.

Merton, P. A. (1964), 'Human position sense and sense of effort', *Symposium of the Society of Experimental Biology, 18*, pp. 387–400.

Merton, P. A. (1972), 'How we control the contraction of our muscles', *Scientific American, 288*, pp. 30–7.

Michon, J. A. (1974), 'Programs and "programs" for sequential patterns in motor behaviour', *Brain Research, 71*, pp. 413–24.

Millar, J. (1975), 'Flexion-extension sensitivity of elbow joint efferents in cat', *Experimental Brain Research, 24*, pp. 209–14.

Miller, G. A., Galanter, E. and Pribram, K. H. (1960), *Plans and the Structure of Behavior*, Holt, Rinehart & Winston: New York.

Morgan, J. M. and Kalakian, L. H. (1974), *Movement Experiences for the Mentally Retarded or Emotionally Disturbed Child*, Burgess Press: Minneapolis, Mn.

Nooteboom, S. A. (1970), 'The target theory of speech production', *IPO Annual Progress Report, 5,* pp. 51–5.

Ohala, J. J. (1978), 'Production of tone', in V. A. Fromkin (ed.), *Tone: A Linguistic Survey,* Academic Press: London.

Ornstein, R. E. (1969), *On the Experience of Time,* Penguin: Harmondsworth.

Paillard, J. (1960), 'The patterning of skilled movements', in J. Field, H. W. Magour and V. E. Hall (eds), *Handbook of Physiology, 3,* American Physiological Society: Washington.

Pearson, K. (1976), 'The control of walking', *Scientific American, 235,* 6, pp. 72–86.

Pew, R. W. (1974), 'Human perceptual motor performance', in B. Kantowitz, (ed.), *Human Information Processing: Tutorials in Performance and Cognition,* Lawrence Erlbaum: Hillsdale, N.J.

Piaget, J. (1953), *The Origins of Intelligence in the Child,* Routledge & Kegan Paul, London.

Pribram, K. H. (1971), *Languages of the Brain: Experimental Paradoxes and Principles in Neuropsychology,* Prentice-Hall: Englewood Cliffs, N.J.

Reynolds, P. J., Talbott, R. E. and Brookbank, J. M. (1972), 'Control of postural reactions in the dog: the role of the dorsal column feedback pathway', *Brain Research, 40,* pp. 159–64.

Russell, D. G. (1976), 'Spatial location cues in movement production', in G. E. Stelmach (ed.), *Motor Control: Issues and Trends,* Academic Press: New York.

Ryall, R. W. and Piercy, N. H. (1970), 'Visceral afferents and efferent fibres in sacral ventral roots in cats', *Brain Research, 23,* pp. 57–65.

Schmidt, R. A. (1971), 'Proprioception and the timing of motor responses', *Psychological Bulletin, 76,* pp. 383–93.

Schmidt, R. A. (1975), 'A schema theory of discrete motor skill learning', *Psychological Review, 82,* pp. 225–80.

Schmidt, R. A. (1976), 'The schema as a solution to some persistent problems in motor learning theory', in G. E. Stelmach (ed.), *Motor Control: Issues and Trends,* Academic Press: New York.

Schmidt, R. A. and Christina, R. W. (1969), 'Proprioception as a mediator in the timing of motor responses', *Journal of Experimental Psychology, 81,* pp. 303–7.

Senders, J. W., Fisher, D. F. and Monty, R. A. (1978), *Eye Movements and the Higher Psychological Processes,* Lawrence Erlbaum: Hillsdale, N.J.

Sherrington, C. S. (1906), *The Integrative Action of the Nervous System,* Scribners: New York.

Skoglund, S. (1973), *Handbook of Sensory Physiology: Somatosensory system,* A. Iggo (ed.), vol. 2, Springer Verlag: Berlin, pp. 111–36.

Spirduso, W. W. (1978), 'Hemispheric lateralization and orientation in compensatory and voluntary movement', in G. E. Stelmach (ed.), *Information Processing in Motor Control and Learning,* Academic Press: London.

Stein, R. B., Pearson, K. G., Smith, R. S. and Redford, J. B. (1973), *Control of Posture and Locomotion,* Plenum: London.

Sternberg, S., Monsell, S., Knoll, R. C. and Wright, C. E. (1978), 'The latency and duration of rapid movement sequences: comparisons of speech and typewriting', in G. E. Stelmach (ed.), *Information Processing in Motor Control and Learning,* Academic Press: New York.

Summers, J. J. (1977), 'The relationship between the sequencing and timing components of a skill', *Journal of Motor Behaviour, 9,* pp. 49–60.

Sundberg, J. (1973), 'Data on the maximum speed of pitch changes', *Quarterly Progress and Status Report,* Speech Transmission Laboratory, Stockholm, 4/1973, pp. 39–47.

Sussman, H. M. (1972), 'What the tongue tells the brain', *Psychological Bulletin, 77,* pp. 262–70.

Taube, E. (1973), 'Behavioral development after forelimb deafferentation on the day of birth in monkeys with and without blinding', *Science, 181,* pp. 959–60.

Teuber, H.-L. (1966), 'Alteration to perception after brain injury', in J. C. Eccles (ed.), *Brain and Conscious Experience,* Springer Verlag: New York.

Trevarthen, C. B. (1968), 'Two mechanisms of vision in primates', *Psychologische Forschung, 31,* pp. 299–337.

Turvey, M. T. (1977), 'Preliminaries to a theory of action with reference to vision', in R. Shaw and J. Bransford (eds), *Perceiving, Acting and Knowing: Toward an Ecological Psychology,* Lawrence Erlbaum: New York.

Turvey, M. T., Shaw, R. and Mace, W. (1978), 'Issues in the theory of action: degrees of freedom, co-ordinative structures and coalitions', in J. Requin (ed.), *Attention and Performance, 7,* Lawrence Erlbaum: Hillsdale, N.J.

Von Holst, E. (1954), 'Relations between the central nervous system and the peripheral organs', *British Journal of Animal Behaviour, 2,* pp. 89–94.

Watson, J. B. (1929), *Psychology from the Standpoint of a Behaviorist,* 3rd edn., Lippincott: Philadelphia.

Weimer, W. B. (1977), 'A conceptual framework for cognitive psychology: motor theories of the mind', in R. Shaw and J. Bransford (eds), *Perceiving, Acting and Knowing: Toward an Ecological Psychology,* Lawrence Erlbaum: New York.

Wickelgren, W. A. (1969), 'Context-sensitive coding associative memory, and serial order in (speech) behavior', *Psychological Review, 76,* pp. 1–15.

Wing, A. M. (1977), 'Perturbations of auditory feedback delay and the timing of movement', *Journal of Experimental Psychology: Human Perception and Performance, 3,* pp. 175–86.

Wing, A. M. (1978), 'Response timing in handwriting', in G. E. Stelmach (ed.), *Information Processing in Motor Control and Learning,* Academic Press: London.

4 Attention and performance

D. Alan Allport

Introduction

This chapter is a critical review and reappraisal of current theories of 'attention'. In particular it offers a critique of the idea of general-purpose processing capacity as a metaphor for understanding human performance limitations in concurrent tasks. The chapter does not pretend to put forward, in its place, a complete theory of 'attention'. Indeed, one of its objectives is to show how various phenomena that have been attributed to the limitations of something called 'attention' demand quite diverse sorts of explanation.

The first section traces the recent history of the idea of processing 'capacity'. The second reviews a variety of behavioural phenomena that have been attributed to 'capacity' limitations, and suggests some alternative explanations. The third section recapitulates and summarizes an alternative approach towards experimental research on the limitations of dual-task performance.

Attention and capacity

Beginnings

The way scientific problems are initially posed has a powerful effect on the way we think about them thereafter. If consciousness is thought of as, in some sense, a compartment of the mind, a *container* having contents, then it is reasonable to ask how much it can contain. What is its 'capacity'? Equally, if the metaphor of a container – even a container of information – is fundamentally inappropriate, then so is the question.

Information-processing psychology has been obsessed with the idea that the mechanism repsonsible for 'the limitations of attention' is analogous to a limited reservoir (a container) whose capacity for holding, or 'processing', information of all sorts has narrow limits. My aim in this chapter is, first, to document this obsession, and then to try to weaken its hold.

First, a word of warning. The study of 'attention' began in phenomenology. 'Everyone knows what attention is', wrote William James in 1890. Ninety years later the word is still used, by otherwise hard-nosed information-processing psychologists, as a code name for consciousness. Questions regarding the limitations of concurrent human *performance* easily get confused with another, hidden agenda concerning the limitations of *consciousness*. Worse, 'attention' (or 'consciousness'?) is sometimes discussed as though it were yet another – but always unspecified! – information process. Theories that include 'attention' (or 'consciousness') as an essential component, but in which the process denoted by this label is simply left unspecified, can not seriously be distinguished from *homunculus* theories: theories of a little man inside the head.

The general-purpose limited-capacity central processor

The revivial of scientific interest in topics such as attention, in the 1950s and 1960s that had remained taboo throughout the behaviourist era, was directly indebted to the availability of a new language in which to represent mental processes: the language of computation. However, as I pointed out in Chapter 2, the first generation of information-processing theories in psychology, and especially those concerned with the overall organization of cognition, tended to reflect in a curiously literal way the functional architecture of the sequential, digital computer itself: a 'central processor' whose size, or 'capacity', was a basic limiting factor both in the type of processes possible and in the time taken to perform them; and a separate, content-independent, passive 'memory'.

This literal computer metaphor was nowhere more directly evident than in early theories of the nature of 'attention'.

Undoubtedly one of the most formative landmarks in the rise of information-processing psychology was the publication in 1958 of Donald Broadbent's book, *Perception and Communication*. Starting from the proposition that man (or woman), like any other physical system, must be limited in the rate at which he or she can 'process' information, Broadbent's central thesis was that this, quite theoretical, upper limit on information capacity, in bits-per-second, was the direct physical basis for the selective nature of conscious attention.

This metaphor for attention, in terms of the limited capacity to process information, was to dominate psychological thinking on the subject for the next twenty years.

Broadbent's theory was directed towards the analysis of human performance, thought of as essentially a matter of the transmission of information, through a succession of transformations, from senses to effectors. This line of thought naturally led to the question: Which of the successive stages of processing was rate-limiting? 'Where is the bottleneck?' 'Where is capacity limited?' became the principal subject of dispute among rival theories of attention.

Following from the 'bottleneck' approach, a secondary set of questions presented themselves: How did the vulnerable, rate-limiting mechanisms (whatever they might be) protect themselves from overload? This too became a question of almost hypnotic power in shaping research on attention.

Broadbent's answer, proposed in 1958, to the first of these questions (Where is the bottleneck?), was: in the 'perceptual system', or *P*-system. Transmission through the *P*-system was necessary for all access to memory (and hence, presumably, also for retrospective perceptual reports), as well as for the control of action. In other words – as in many restatements of this model – the *P*-system was the limited-capacity central processor of the human computer. This position was essentially unchanged in Broadbent's major restatement of the theory, thirteen years later, in his book *Decision and Stress*. The perceptual system could accept only so much information per unit time, in response to which it generated 'category states'.

In Broadbent's model the limited-capacity central processor received its inputs (as in the computer) from a variety of independent sensory peripherals and buffer stores, which were able to take in information in parallel, and in which that information could be held for brief periods while the *P*-system was otherwise occupied. The *P*-system was able to protect itself from 'overload' by setting these earlier, non-capacity-limited stages to pass on information only about stimuli possessing certain, relatively simple, 'password' sensory attributes ('coloured red', 'coming from top left', 'spoken in a female voice').

One obvious and important implication of this password hypothesis was that those attributes that could be used as passwords, to separate wanted from unwanted incoming information, must themselves be detected 'pre-attentively', before the stage at which selection became necessary. Thus, for the password hypothesis, the answers to both sets of questions were complementary. The type of cues that could be used to 'select' or 'reject' stimuli tell us about the level of analysis to which 'pre-attentive', non-capacity-limited processing can go.

Nearly ten years after Broadbent's *Perception and Communication,* Neiser published his eloquent and influential book *Cognitive Psychology* (Neisser, 1967). As far as attention was concerned, Neisser's view was extraordinarily similar to Broadbent's, though he differed from him in emphasizing the 'constructive' nature of perception. But, like Broadbent, he asserted that perception and attention were essentially identical: 'This constructive process (i.e., the process of perception) is itself the mechanism of attention' (p. 213). Furthermore, *'attention is serial*: only one object can be attended to at any moment' (p. 301). For example, 'if a whole row of letters is to be identified, they must be synthesized one at a time' (p. 103).

Other theorists maintained, on the basis of differing sorts of evidence, that the capacity bottleneck occurred at some other, usually later, hypothetical stage in the system. Welford (1952, 1968), for example, and subsequently Keele (1973), argued for a bottleneck only at the stage of selection of, or 'translation' to overt actions. The proposals of Deutsch and Deutsch (1963) have also sometimes been interpreted in this way. On the other hand, in what was also offered as a restatement of the Deutsches' position, Norman (1968, 1976) put forward a model of human information processing that, paradoxically, lacked any explicit reference to the control of action. In Norman's model, all familiar sensory stimuli gained access to their 'memory representations'. Following this, a diagram of the model showed a box labelled 'Selection and attention', the nature or function of which was not explained.

The most recent attempt to restate the Deutsches' hypothesis is by Duncan (in press). He proposes the existence of a limited-capacity system (unspecified: 'For present purposes it may be seen simply as a passage between levels') controlled by a 'selector', and through which all information must pass if it is to reach awareness or gain control of a response. As in Norman's model, prior to the limited-capacity bottleneck, all familiar stimuli are 'fully identified' without divided attention limitations. The source of all divided attention effects, in Duncan's model, is the limited capacity passage from 'level 1' to 'level 2' ('awareness'), which cannot deal effectively with more than one stimulus at a time.

The neuronal power supply

As more and more experiments were directed towards the problem of 'locating the bottleneck', the site of the (supposed) limited-capacity mechanisms came to look, to many people, increasingly Protean: now here, now there, now almost everywhere. (Some of this evidence is reviewed, though from a rather different viewpoint, later in this chapter.) Signs of interference between concurrent processing of different messages could show up at almost any logical level, from processing apparently the most elementary sensory attributes right through to the fine control of muscular movements.

Nevertheless, there was a strong presumption that such diverse performance limitations are derived from one common source: *attention*. (Though what that was, no one seemed to have any particularly clear ideas.) Once committed to the assumption that interference was the consequence of overloading capacity in some way, later proponents of such a view arrived at the conclusion that the capacity of the human information-processing system must be limited somehow *as a whole,* rather than in any specific stage. Moray (1967), and following him Kahneman, proposed as a basic assumption 'a *general* limit on man's capacity to do mental work' (Kahneman, 1973). That is, they proposed a completely general-purpose capacity, that must be competed for, and allocated around among all different ongoing cerebral processes. The natural analogy that presented itself for this sort of capacity was not that of a passive container, or a bottleneck, but a limited power supply. Once the supply is fully loaded, any more watts consumed by one part of the system mean less for all the rest, regardless of what they want it for. 'In the capacity model, interference is non-specific, and depends only on the (combined) demands of both the tasks' (Kahneman, 1973, p. 11).

Kahneman suggested that 'capacity' (or 'attention' or 'effort'; he used the terms interchangeably) might be related to 'physiological arousal'. The higher the arousal the more the 'capacity' available. The evidence that he invoked referred almost exclusively to autonomic arousal (heart-rate, pupil dilation, etc.). At the end of it I find myself still in the dark as to what Kahneman held the nature of the relationship between 'arousal' and 'capacity' to be. Presumably he did *not* mean to imply that 'arousal' was *itself* the limited power supply? (The more 'arousal' provided to some physiological sub-systems, the less available for any others?)

Kahneman went on to provide an extensive and valuable review of the experimental literature on attention up to 1972, ending with some studies of simultaneous performance of independent tasks. From these results Kahneman had to acknowledge that some at least, of the pattern of interference between concurrent processes must be 'structural'. That is, it must result from incompatible demands on the same *specific* components of cerebral mechanism. Nevertheless, his conclusion was still that 'interference must occur *whenever* two distinct tasks are performed together' (p. 200). Such interference must occur, he argued, 'even when the two activities do not share *any* mechanisms of either perception or response' (p. 178-9).

'There's a hole in my bucket'

These are strong claims. How are they to be tested? In particular, how can we measure the non-specific demand on general capacity, made by a particular task, and from which predictions of residual capacity, or performance, on some *other* simultaneous task or performance could be derived? Kahneman calls this 'a basic problem for experimental psychology'. Well, it is certainly a basic problem for his theory.

In general terms, Kahneman's answer to this basic problem is that task demands must be a direct function of task 'difficulty'. So how is 'difficulty' to be measured? 'The most sensitive test', according to Kahneman (p. 189), is the amount of interference in competition with another simultaneous task! In fact, that appears to be the only test that he can offer. The theory, at least in its application, appears to be entirely circular.

Some two years after the publication of Kahneman's book, Norman and Bobrow (1975) attempted to come to his rescue, elaborating on Kahneman's ideas in a way that, they hoped, could overcome Kahneman's 'basic problem' in the analysis of concurrent tasks. The issues involved are sufficiently central to the theme of this chapter that we shall need to go into them in some detail.

The principal idea in Norman and Bobrow's paper is a distinction between what they call 'Resource-limited' and 'Data-limited' processes. 'Resources,' they say, are 'such things as processing effort, the various forms of memory capacity, and communication channels. Resources are always limited' (p. 45). By 'processing effort' they appear to denote the same hypothetical construct as Kahneman's 'general processing capacity'. Accordingly, the central section of Norman and Bobrow's paper is headed 'Limited Capacity Central Processing'. The other resources they hint at ('various forms of memory', 'communication channels') are presumably what Kahneman referred to as 'structural' capacity limitations.

At the outset, at least, Norman and Bobrow clearly acknowledge that 'resources' are not all of the same kind. 'Because processes can simultaneously compete for a *number of different resources* (my italics), a full analysis of interprocess competition requires examination of each resource competition separately' (p. 45). So far, so good. However, 'in this paper we explore the interprocess interaction that results when there is competition for a *single* resource' (ibid.).

Now wait a minute! Obviously there is a problem of how we know when we are dealing with competition for a single resource. Indeed, for theories such as Kahneman's this is the central question at issue: When (if at all) are the observable conflicts between concurrent activities the result of competition for one common resource ('attention', 'processing effort', 'general-purpose capacity', or whatever) and when for many different, specific resources? But it is a problem that Norman and Bobrow simply ignore. In fact their whole argument rests on the failure to distinguish between competition for resources in general (and undifferentiated), and competition for any specific resource, call it Resource x or Resource y.

Once one accepts the idea of general-purpose processing capacity as a working hypothesis, it becomes temptingly easy to assume, without further ado, that almost any instance of dual-task interference is a result of competition for this same general resource, for 'attention'. The kind of tangle that Norman and Bobrow get themselves into in this paper illustrates how easy it is to fall into this trap. The result is a strategy of research that can do nothing but chase its own tail. (Notice, as you go, how their discussion slides between the idea of competition for resources (in general) and competition for one specific resource.)

'All that is needed to use these ideas', they write, 'is the ability to distinguish between resource-limited and data-limited operations, and to know at any time which one is taking place' (p. 62). This distinction is evidently to be defined over all processing resources available to the individual. Thus, 'whenever an increase in the amount of processing resources can result in improved performance, we say that the task (or performance on that task) is *resource-limited*' (p. 46). Otherwise, 'once *all* the processing that can be done has been completed, performance is dependent solely on the quality of the data' and is therefore called *data-limited* (ibid.).

So how are we to tell whether performance on Task A, over the range of performance we can investigate, is resource-limited or data-limited, in the sense they have defined? Well, they say, 'The only way to insure that performance is resource-limited is to demonstrate that it (performance on Task A) is affected by changes in *resource*' (p. 62). At this point we are back to Kahneman's 'basic problem': how are we to measure, or control, the demands made by Task A on any particular resource (or even on resources in general)? Hmm. 'This is not easy to do,' they say. 'Perhaps the best way to control resource,' Norman and Bobrow propose, 'is to require subjects to perform two tasks simultaneously.' (It sounds familiar.) 'One task is the interfering task. It should require a fixed amount of resource. The other is the primary task. It is *assumed* to use *all* the remaining available resource' (p. 52). What is more, 'To do this set of experiments, we need to have an interfering task whose resource requirements can be systematically and consistently varied over a wide range' (ibid.).

At this point Norman and Bobrow's proposals encounter two obstacles, one practical, the second logical and fatal.

1 First, to measure the demands made by Task A (on Resource x) we already need a second, interfering task, B, whose demands (on the same resource) we can somehow 'systematically and consistently vary over a wide range'. Well, *how?* 'Few tasks meet this requirement', Norman and Bobrow gravely add. Nothing daunted, however, let's pretend!

'Consider any task in which we *can* control the amount of resource required. The best way to exert control is to establish a narrow range for errors . . .' 'Thus,' they say, in a tracking or shadowing task, 'we might monitor the shadowing behavior and require subjects to maintain a fixed error rate. . . . Once we are able to control the error rate of the subject, we can vary the resource (specific? or general?) expended upon the task, and *therefore the amount available for other tasks*' (pp. 52–3).

Can we so? An implicit assumption seems to be that the more errors made by the subject in (say) shadowing, the less 'processing resource' (or 'resources'?) he must have been expending on it. If this is the assumption, it implies a curiously naive view of what is involved in shadowing. After all, following an error, the subject now has the additional problem of recovery from the error. If he is shadowing prose, the error will presumably violate in some way the linguistic or contextual constraints that permit him to anticipate what will follow. If anything, more (and possibly different) resources will be needed, rather than less. Moreover, if he is required to 'maintain a fixed error rate', then more – and different – resources again will be required by the subject to monitor and regulate his own performance in this respect.

2 Even suppose (let's pretend!) that by controlling error rate in Task B we could directly vary the amount of Resource x expended on that task. For their research strategy to contribute anything useful to Kahneman's 'basic problem', as Norman and Bobrow stoutly confess, 'we need to know how to transform the error rate on the competing task (Task B) to resource allotment for the task of interest (Task A). In general, we do not know the appropriate tranformation' (p. 53).

The problem this time is more fundamental. It is not just that we happen not to know the appropriate formulae, yet. The alchemy of transforming errors (in one task) into resources (in another) clearly requires that both tasks 'must share the *total* capacity of available processing resources'. Any such transformation, that is, can only be meaningfully computed if we can *assume* 'complete complementarity of processing resources for the two processes'. 'When process (i.e. Task) A uses some amount of resources, r, process B uses an amount L-r' (p. 51).

And that was more or less where we came in. What possible grounds could there be for this assumption, in any particular instance, except the prior assumption that *all* processing resources are indeed one and the same, namely, 'general-purpose capacity'?

What if Task B, the 'interfering task', is resource-limited in respect of Resource x, and Task A, the one we are interested in, is resource-limited in respect of Resource y? Once their theoretical distinction between 'data-limited' and 'resource-limited' processes is defined, not in respect of unspecified 'resources' in general, but of any specific resource, it ceases to be the neat dichotomy that it first purported to be. That is, when performance on Task A is independent of Resource x, there is no reason whatever to infer that performance on this task is therefore 'data-limited'. It may be limited by Resources y and z.

'Automatic' v. 'controlled processing', or How does your homunculus do it?

Norman and Bobrow will not be the last psychologists to hold, as a working assumption essential to their experimental methodology, that general 'processing resources', or 'capacity', or 'attention' is some limited quantity, L, which must be shared around among all simultaneously active psychological processes. By going into their proposals in some detail, I have tried to show how easy it is to slide into this assumption, almost without noticing. However, I am inclined to believe that this working assumption has been a singularly un-productive heuristic for the discovery of the architectural constraints on concurrent psychological processes. The reason is this.

Whenever two simultaneous task-demands conflict with one another, we have a comfortable, ready-made explanation: both must be competing for limited, general-purpose capacity (for 'attention'). When a pair of tasks is found that *can* be performed at the same time, independently (i.e., without evidence of mutual competition), that too is easily explained. One or both of the tasks evidently does not 'require attention'; it must be 'automatic' (or perhaps only 'data-limited'). As long as the same tasks are not studied in different combinations, the story will almost always appear to fit.

My principal complaint is that so anodyne an heuristic does not prompt further questions; it merely soothes away curiosity by the appearance of providing an explanation, even before the data have been obtained. It is therefore a fatally unproductive heuristic (or 'direction') for research. Indeed, by diverting us from what I believe to be the really interesting and fruitful questions – questions about the multiplicity of specific mechanisms that are competed for in different task combinations – it has been actively counter-productive.

I conclude this section with one further illustration of the way in which the hypothesis of a general-purpose limited-capacity central processor (GPLCCP) diverts its proponents away from serious attempts at specifying *mechanism*. In its place we are offered a cure-all nostrum, to the effect that all mental processes either 'require atten-tion' (whatever that may mean) or else they are 'automatic'.

Using an experimenter-paced serial visual search task, Shiffrin and

Schneider (1977) provide some spectacular demonstrations of a radical difference in performance between two conditions of target allocation. In one condition, individual stimulus-types (letters and numerals) are consistently allocated as 'targets' or 'non-targets'. Under this regime, with extended content-specific practice, the speed and accuracy of search becomes essentially independent both of the number of characters presented in each frame and of the number of currently valid targets. Shiffrin and Schneider call this 'automatic processing'. In another condition, the targets to be detected (and therefore the non-targets to be ignored) are allocated anew on each trial in a way that conflicts with their specification on preceding trials (so-called 'varied mapping', VM), so that *all* stimulus types, both currently valid targets and non-targets, come to be weakly associated with the detection response. In this case, performance is much poorer, and the accuracy of detection decreases monotonically both with the number of relevant character-positions to be searched and with the number of currently valid targets. Shiffrin and Schneider call this mode of performance 'controlled processing'. They make a number of ingenious and interesting experiments to explore these conditions, and I shall refer to them again later. What I am concerned with, in this section, is their theoretical discussion of these two modes of performance – 'automatic' and 'controlled processing' respectively – for which, they say, they have presented 'a specific, detailed model' (p. 184), providing 'a general framework for human information processing'.

Automatic processes, according to Shiffrin and Schneider, are essentially associative, and are *'activated without the necessity of active control or attention by the subject'* (p. 156). They are not affected by the capacity limitations of short-term store (STS). Do they affect the STS capacity for *other* processes? We are told little about the nature of these capacity limitations, except that the rate of loss of any informational element from STS increases with the number of 'similar' elements (undefined) active at the same time. No particular motivation is given for this assumption; and no reason at all is suggested why automatic processes – which must also entail activation of elements 'in STS' – are not subject to the same STS constraints as are controlled processes.

Controlled processes, on the other hand, are *'activated under control of, and through attention by, the subject'* (p. 156). What can these terms mean? Is 'the subject' equivalent to the whole system, long-term memory and all? (But *all* processes within a system are determined – in that sense, controlled – by the system-as-a-whole: that is part of the meaning of 'system', and would not exclude automatic processes.) Or does 'the subject' refer to some sub-part of the system, a ghost-in-the-machine? Shiffrin and Schneider do nothing to clarify this. And how does 'attention' affect the nature of the processes, associative or otherwise, that can occur? Again, Shiffrin and Schneider give us no clues. (Guy Claxton has also discussed this type of theorizing in Chapter 1.)

Under the heading of Controlled Processing, Shiffrin and Schneider principally discuss what they call 'control processes'. (Are these the same thing? Or are 'control processes' the processes that control the 'controlled processing'? Once more, this is not made clear.) Anyway, 'common examples of control processes,' we are told, 'include . . . rote rehearsal . . . serial search, long-term memory search, and decisions and strategies of all kinds' (p. 160). Moreover, these control processes are 'limited-capacity processes requiring attention . . . these limitations prevent multiple control processes from occurring simultaneously' (p. 160). In other words, the theory asserts that none of the procedures enumerated as examples of control processes, say 'rote rehearsal', can occur simultaneously with any other, say long-term memory search, or even 'decisions of all kind'. So stated, the theory is surely wrong. For example, in respect of 'rote rehearsal', a counter-demonstration is provided by Hitch and Baddeley (1976) Experiment II, already referred to in Chapter 2. Likewise, explicit rehearsal has been found to have no effect on the speed or accuracy of verifying auditorily presented syllogisms (Smith, 1976); neither, it appears, does it affect normal silent reading comprehension (Baddeley, 1979; Levy, 1978). In respect of 'memory search', Okada and Burrows (1978) found that rate of searching an LTM list (i.e., the rate of increase in RT with list size: 8-16 words) is unaffected by concurrently searching an STM (varied) list of 2-6 words. The catalogue can easily be extended. A number of demonstrations that provide further severe difficulties for Shiffrin and Schneider's hypothesis are described later in this chapter.

We must also ask, what is the *mechanism* of any of these 'control processes', which are thus supposedly constrained by 'attention limitations' to sequential, one-at-a-time operation? Can it be the general-purpose limited-capacity processing system? Shiffrin and Schneider provide, as an example, a brief account of 'controlled search' in the retrieval of information from long-term store. 'How does the subject exert control over LTS retrieval?' they ask (p. 159). The answer is as follows: 'On each cycle, (a) *the subject* generates probe information and places it in STS . . . (c) *the subject* searches the STS set; (d) *the subject* decides whether the appropriate information has been found . . .' (p. 159, my italics). That is to say, in Shiffrin and Schneider's model, the *mechanism* of 'control processes' and presumably therefore of 'attention' (which control processes supposedly require) is quite simply 'the subject'! I sometimes wonder whether all those psychological theories that propose, as their central mechanism, a GPLCCP are not similarly *homunculus* theories, though sometimes better disguised.

A look ahead

In Chapter 2 I have outlined a general approach to cognition, starting from the assumption that processing capacity, and memory, is *distributed* throughout the nervous system, in the form of autonomous, special-purpose or *content-specific*, modular sub-systems. Everything that we have been able to discover about neural organization, both at the cellular level and at the level of gross functional anatomy, points to the great specialization of function in the brain. Individual neurons and different anatomically defined populations of neurons, are responsive to highly specific forms or patterns of information, and appear to compute highly specific functions on the inputs that they accept.

In sharp contrast with this, there appears to be rather wide acceptance, among information-processing psychologists, of a radically different assumption. This is the hypothesis, whose recent history I have just briefly reviewed, that the central mechanism of cognition is a general-purpose processor (or at least a common reservoir of *non-specific* processing resource) of sharply limited capacity. The evidence that motivates this hypothesis is almost exclusively concerned with those behavioural phenomena typically described as 'attentional'. It is important, therefore, to ask: In what way does the behavioural evidence really demand this hypothesis?

We can also examine this issue the other way around. Given the fundamental assumptions about distributed, content-specific, parallel processing in the nervous system, outlined in Chapter 2, the question of course arises: *Why should there be any 'attentional' limitations at all?* The answers to these two questions, in various forms, will occupy the remainder of this chapter.

As a preliminary it will be important to keep in mind a distinction between limitations that concern, on the one hand, the ability for conscious, retrospective reports by a subject about his experience, and on the other hand that concern limitations on concurrent performance. These are by no means always equivalent. The majority of the discussion will refer to limitations on performance rather than on the capacity for conscious commentary. The argument will, of course, require some relatively detailed attention to laboratory experiments. Behavioural experiments cannot investigate the capacity limitations of 'attention', or any other internal process, directly. Whatever the internal states or processes we wish to explore, we must always find some means of coupling them with externally observable actions. As we shall see, the kinds of action we employ, and still more their compatibility with the conditions that are to elicit them, can radically affect the apparent limitations of these hidden processes.

One other note. There are quite evident limitations on how much of our immediate environment we can actively explore at one and the same time. These are limitations imposed by the directional nature of senses such as vision and touch – the relatively narrow region that can be explored by hand or eye at any instant – and by the geo-metrical optics of a world of opaque bodies. They are part of our finitude. Which parts of his environment a man or an animal chooses actually to explore can doubtless be a matter of critical importance for his survival. How these choices are made, how strategies of selective exploration are acquired and how they are adapted to different situations, are questions of central importance for our understanding of almost any skilled performance. But the fact that hand or eye or tongue cannot be everywhere at once is not, in the terms of this chapter, an 'attentional' limitation.

Performance and attention: a review of experiments

Simultaneous monitoring

Suppose that you have to detect the presence or absence of particular sensory patterns, coming potentially from several clearly separated sources (input channels). How is the efficiency of discrimination affected if all *n* channels must be monitored *simultaneously*, in contrast to the case in which the critical channel is known in advance and so can be given undivided attention? The results of many experiments which have been addressed to this question are singularly easy to summarize. There is no effect at all.

Of course, to make the comparison appropriately, we must ensure that the results are not affected by such things as shifting the direction of gaze favouring the 'attended' stimulus source, or by the simultaneous demands for the same kinds of overt responses. Shiffrin (1975) has reviewed an impressive series of experiments of this kind, with attention distributed respectively either between sensory modalities (visual, auditory and tactile) or over differing spatial channels within the same modality. The results were uniformly the same. When attentional 'capacity' had to be distributed over many different inputs, compared to when attention could be concentrated on just one, there was no added cost to the efficiency or accuracy of monitoring. As Shiffrin concluded, 'certainly our results indicate that no subject-controlled attenuation or filtering occurs during perceptual processing' (p. 189).

A possible artefact in this interpretation is that, in the successive-channels condition, the subject may need to store the results of all *n* successive observations in order to compare them and select his response. Thus possible 'memory' losses may be traded against increased capacity. However, an essentially identical pattern of results has been found, by many different experimenters, in situations where the subject is free to make his monitoring response immediately.

A favourite form of within-modality multi-channel monitoring experiment has messages directed separately to the two ears: 'dichotic listening'. When sufficiently carefully analysed, here too the efficiency of monitoring turns out to be equivalent, whether the subject is allowed to concentrate on just one ear, or whether he must listen concurrently for target events on both ears (e.g., Moray *et al.*, 1976; Ostry *et al.*, 1976; Sorkin *et al.*, 1973). That is, with practice, the efficiency or sensitivity (d') of detecting targets on one ear is unaffected by the simultaneous, correct decision that the event on the contralateral ear is a non-target. This holds true when the discriminations to be made involve such physically simple dimensions as the loudness or pitch of a tone, and when the targets are complex or abstract categories, such as spoken digits among letters, or animal names among other nouns.

Similar conclusions have been reached from numerous visual monitoring, or visual search experiments, where the number of spatially separate objects among which the target is concealed is the principal variable. Under appropriate conditions the accuracy (Shiffrin and Gardner, 1972) as well as the latency (Egeth *et al.*, 1972) of correct detection responses is essentially unaffected by the number of simultaneous non-target items. This too holds good when the target is specified categorically, for example as 'any digit' among a background of letters (Sperling *et al.*, 1971; Jonides and Gleitman, 1972), and even when successive arrays of characters are displayed, one after another, at up to 26 frames per second (Schneider and Shiffrin, 1977).

With extended practice the same result can be obtained for arbitrarily specified categories of target, even though target and non-target sets include mutually visually confusable items, such as letters in the first versus the second half of the alphabet (Shiffrin and Schneider, 1977). Also with practice, reaction time (and accuracy) in detecting a target becomes independent of the size of the target category as well as of the number of non-target items in a simultaneous display, so long as, throughout training, the target and non-target sets are kept scrupulously separate (ibid.).

The important point about practice is that it should be *content specific*. Only then is it possible for condition→action rules (see Chapter 2) to become established between particular classes of stimuli and their designated monitoring response. No amount of practice at the search task in general will suffice, if the specification of targets and non-targets is made contradictory from one trial to the next.

The above results remain valid, so long as two or more stimuli do not call simultaneously for the same kind of rapid classificatory response. When they do, even though the response to one is being made in error, as a false alarm, the probability of making a correct detection-response to a target simultaneously present on another input channel is substantially reduced (e.g., Moray *et al.*, 1976). That is, there is a significant negative correlation between correct responses to target events occurring simultaneously from different sensory sources. It does not matter whether the targets are simple physical stimulus-properties or complex forms. The competing call need not even result in an overt physical response, so long as the distracting stimulus is one that has come to be associated with the class of detection-response now demanded by another concurrent event, as illustrated in a neat experiment by Shiffrin and Schneider (1977: Experiment 4d). When searching/monitoring for a specified letter among other non-target letters, the appearance of an item from what had formerly been the target category for that subject, in a previously well-practised search condition, (e.g., a *digit*) caused a substantial reduction (from 84 per cent to 62 per cent) in the probability that their subjects would successfully report the presence of a simultaneously occurring valid letter target.

As we shall see, these sorts of result bear a striking similarity to ones reported in an earlier tradition, under the label of the 'psychological refractory period'. An experiment with obvious conceptual kinship to Shiffrin and Schneider's was reported by Roy Davis in 1959. This kind of competition appears to depend on concurrent, implicit demands for speeded *responses*. On the other hand, when perceptual judgments, in respect of simultaneously and briefly available stimuli, can be signalled without time constraints, two or more different types of discrimination can apparently be made independently: i.e. without capacity limitations (e.g., Gardner, 1973; Wing and Allport, 1972). We shall turn to questions of competition between response-evoking patterns in the next section of this chapter.

So long as no immediate, explicit response or commentary is evoked or required, simultaneous complex patterns on different sensory channels can be identified (and remembered) without mutual conflict. Kahneman (1973) cites an experiment by Levy (1971) that is to the point: the subject is asked simply to listen to a sequence of dichotic word-pairs in a 'passive, receptive attitude', and then probed subsequently for memory of the words by a recognition test. A subject's memory of any given word, heard in one ear, was *independent* of his or her memory for the word that coincided in time with it on the other ear. There was no sign of a negative correlation between the two.

In summary, there is evidence that sensory patterns coming simultaneously from separate spatial locations or separate modalities can be identified without conflict and without capacity limitations. Identification here evidently includes the semantic classification of such complex stimuli as spoken or written words (cf. Chapter 2, 'Unconscious' information-processing). The major qualification on the 'no conflict' generalization is that the concurrent stimuli should not each represent 'conditions', or calling-patterns for the same, currently activated class of overt rapid action. When this latter situation does arise, it appears that responding to, or even actively 'ignoring', one or other of the concurrent events can have an appreciable cost on the efficiency of response to the other.

Conflict between calling-patterns for explicit responses

Ignoring sensory events: We must now examine this matter of 'ignoring' a sensory event. To what extent can we succeed in doing so? And, to the extent that we can, does this mean that recognition of the unwanted event is curtailed, that the stimulus is somehow not fully identified; or is it rather a question of de-coupling the products of stimulus processing from the control of current action?

Neisser (1967) argued from his experiments in visual search that, with practice, the processing of unwanted, non-target patterns could be limited to the analysis of simple physical features – just sufficient to distinguish these patterns from the target category – and that the recognition process of non-target items then proceeded no further. A number of more recent experimental results exist to challenge this conclusion in a variety of situations (e.g., Eriksen and Eriksen, 1974; Keren *et al.*, 1977), among them the results of Shiffrin and Schneider's (1977) Experiment 4d, mentioned earlier. Numerous experimental results, some of which are described in the next two sections, provide ample evidence for the identification of 'ignored' or 'unattended' stimuli.

Nevertheless, when the *location* of irrelevant information is known in advance, subjects can learn quite rapidly to disconnect their processing of this information from any manifest, direct effects on behaviour. Shiffrin and Schneider's visual search task (with rates of presentation far too rapid to permit changes of fixation within a frame) again provides a good illustration. Certain locations of the display were specified as consistently 'irrelevant', and to be ignored. With a little practice (even with constant target mappings), the occurrence of an intruding target symbol in one of the 'irrelevant' locations simultaneously with a different (or even the same) target character in a 'relevant' location had *no* effect on the subjects' hit rate in detecting the 'relevant' targets (Experiment 4c: see footnote 4).

Similarly, in the ecologically more familiar task of reading alphabetic text in a left-to-right line on a page, there is evidence that the normal reader actively assimilates information up to twenty letter-spaces to the right of fixation, but that his overt behaviour is remarkably insensitive to even quite radical intrusions in the text that appear more than three or four letter-spaces to the left of fixation (McConkie and Rayner, 1976; McConkie, 1979).

Varieties of the Stroop phenomenon: A striking demonstration of the obligatory nature of pattern recognition, even of such abstract and arbitrary learned patterns as written words, can be seen in the so-called Stroop phenomenon. In its best known variant, the colour-word test (Dyer, 1973), the subject is confronted with a row of letters written, say, in red ink and is required to name the colour of the ink. When the letters form a word, the act of naming takes longer to initiate than if they form some unfamiliar sequence. The response is delayed still more if the letters spell one of the words used to name the ink colours (say, GREEN).

The Stroop task is a microcosm of 'selective responding'. Similar results are found in a great variety of analogous situations. To itemize just a few: they can be observed when the subject attempts to say how many characters are present, and the characters are themselves numerals (Morton, 1969); when he must indicate whether a word is spoken in a high- or low-pitched voice, by saying 'high' or 'low', and the words he hears are, respectively *low* and *high* (Cohen and Martin, 1975); or cross-modally, when the subject tries to name a written word or letter while a conflicting word is spoken to him (Greenwald, 1970); or vice versa (Lewis, 1972; Navon, 1977).

The interference is commonly, though not always, asymmetrical. The stimulus pattern that represents the more direct, or stronger or more compatible calling-cue for the naming response will interfere *more* with the production of the desired response to the *less* direct calling-cue, than vice versa. Similarly, a commonly occurring word, or one that has recently been 'primed' from another context, causes more interference than an uncommon word, or one not recently primed (e.g., Warren, 1972, 1974).

A fundamental feature of these Stroop-like situations appears to be the existence of a previously established condition→action link between the to-be-ignored base-stimulus and the domain of representation needed to access (or control) the overt response. A colour word that is not included among the set of responses actually used to name the ink colours produces less interference than a word taken from the currently primed response set, though still more than a neutral word (Klein, 1964; Stirling, 1979). When the mapping between the relevant stimulus aspect and its required response does not involve the domain of intermediate code evoked by the irrelevant aspect, the Stroop conflict can be eliminated altogether (Flowers and Blair, 1976; see also Morton and Chambers, 1973; Friedman and Derks, 1973; Seymour, 1975).

Dichotic shadowing and monitoring: Dichotic shadowing represents another laboratory microcosm of selective responding, analogous to the Stroop conflict situation. In the dichotic shadowing task, familiar to psychologists since the pioneering work of Colin Cherry in 1953, the subject is asked to repeat ('shadow') a sequence of words presented to one ear, while refraining from repeating those delivered to the other ear. As in other Stroop-like situations, the unwanted stimuli constitute, in principle, equally direct, or 'compatible' calling-cues for the vocal response.

To my knowledge no one has directly compared the minimum latencies of the shadowing response with and without an irrelevant dichotic message. However, when the words presented to the two ears are related to one another in meaning, then, as in other Stroop situations, additional delays in naming the 'attended' words can be observed – at least when the subject is shadowing with a relatively short lag (Lewis, 1970; Bryden, 1972; Treisman *et al.*, 1974). Such results, of course, could not occur unless the 'unattended' word had also activated some representation of its meaning. (See also Chapter 2.)

The strategy by which subjects typically succeed in isolating the outputs of word recognition units, activated by the to-be-rejected message, from control of the vocal 'shadowing' response apparently has the effect of also decoupling that information from the control of other voluntary responses,* as well as from retrospective 'commentary'.

A well-known experiment by Treisman and Geffen (1967) provides an illustration of this. At the same time as shadowing one of two dichotically presented prose texts, they asked their subjects to monitor both messages for various types of word target inserted in the text. Their subjects correctly responded to 89 per cent of (in context)

---

*This effect is greatly reduced after extended practice at shadowing (Underwood, 1974). Some very interesting dissociations of overt discriminative action, but in the absence of available retrospective commentary ('awareness'), have been described by Cumming (1972).

targets in the shadowed text, but to only 9 per cent in the non-shadowed text. By contrast, as we have already seen, without the selective shadowing constraint, monitoring for semantically, or categorically defined targets can operate for dichotic inputs in parallel, with no sign of conflict or capacity limitations.

In a subsequent experiment, this time using sequences of digit-names presented to the right and left ears in computer-synchronized pairs, Treisman and Riley (1969) obtained results broadly similar to Treisman and Geffen's. As well as repeating the sequence heard in one ear only, the subject's task was to monitor both ears for the occurrence of occasional letter names among the sequence of digits. On detecting a letter name he was to indicate this by immediately stopping shadowing; that is, he was to signal his detection specifically *within* the response-domain that crucially had to be decoupled from one of the two dichotic inputs.

These two experiments were originally intended to provide evidence relevant to the controversy, outlined in the first part of this chapter, about the 'locus of selective attention', or the 'bottleneck'. However, it is clear that, in these conditions (a) the selectivity of monitoring is contingent on the demands of selective shadowing, not the consequence of built-in 'capacity' limitations (except in the sense that a human cannot vocally produce two streams of speech concurrently); and (b) the speech presented to the non-shadowed ear is not just passively 'unattended'; it has to be specifically isolated (decoupled) from potential command of the shadowing response.

Yet both these points appear to have been persistently overlooked. In discussing these two experiments, Kahneman (1973) calls them 'the two critical experiments in this area' (p. 143); and he asserts that they provide 'strong evidence against the Deutsch and Deutsch theory', according to which (in Kahneman's words) 'attention merely determines which of the currently activated recognition units will be allowed to control awareness and response' (ibid.). On the contrary, when we contrast these results (a) with subjects' ability (when *not* also shadowing) to monitor dichotic inputs for semantically defined targets, without capacity limitations; (b) with the evidence, in shadowing tasks, for lexical or semantic interpretation of the words presented to the non-shadowed ear (Chapter 2), then the implications of these experiments and Kahneman's conclusion appear to be precisely reversed.

The 'double-bind' task of dichotic shadowing and monitoring would not deserve so much space here except for the fact that information-processing theorists have tried, in the past, to obtain so much mileage from dichotic shadowing experiments for theories of 'attention'. Before leaving this topic, one further question should be raised.

Granted that behavioural effects specific to the *meaning* of the non-shadowed words can be observed, can we characterize more precisely what kind of semantic interpretation of the message, thus decoupled from vocal response, is going on? In Treisman and Geffen's (1967) experiment, subjects did occasionally respond to digit-names in the non-shadowed text; but, in doing so, they were apparently unable to distinguish these from homophones of the target category: for example, they responded to the preposition 'for' as well as to the number 'four'. In the spoken message these quite distinct morphemes are physically more or less identical. They can be discriminated (their meanings disambiguated) only by the context. Their subjects' failure to make this discrimination therefore suggests that while recognition units can be activated by individual words in the non-shadowed text, the process whereby these semantic structures, evoked by individual words, are dis-ambiguated, and integrated into a complete phrase- or sentence-meaning is not completed for the non-shadowed dichotic text.

Further support for the same view comes from a dichotic shadowing experiment described by Underwood (1977). The latency of the vocal shadowing response was facilitated by prior verbal context presented *either* to the shadowed *or* to the non-shadowed ear. However, *increasing* the amount of prior context, from a single content-word to a whole sentence, had no further facilitating effect, if the context was in the unattended channel, although it produced substantial further facilitation if it was in the shadowed channel. The facilitation produced by a single content-word in the unattended ear was about 70 per cent of that due to the same amount of context in the shadowed ear. This figure seems to put a lower bound on the proportion of unattended content-words gaining semantic interpretation. (The remaining 30 per cent difference could easily be due to the larger shadowing lags when the semantic context is in the unattended ear, and the subject is therefore shadowing a sequence of unrelated words).

The 'psychological refractory period': Consider now the situation in which two environmental events (either simultaneously, or in close temporal succession) *both* call for separate, overt actions. That is, *both* actions are explicitly demanded by 'the task'. Early demonstrations showed that, in certain circumstances, subjects could indeed produce separate responses to both stimuli simultaneously. However, if the subject was instructed to respond to one of the two specified events with a fixed sequence of priority, and the second event (S_2) followed within some 200 milliseconds of the first event (S_1), then the response to S_2 (and often both responses) typically suffered some delay. As the onset-interval between the stimuli decreased towards simultaneity, so the delay in response to S_2 systematically increased. The range of onset-intervals over which this effect occurred became known, rather infelicitously, as the 'psychological refractory period' or PRP. Much as the family of Stroop tasks served as a miniaturized paradigm for 'selective attention', so did the refractory period for 'divided attention'. Indeed, the PRP was the original motivation for the 'single-channel hypothesis'. Readily accessible reviews of this literature can be found, for example, in Welford (1968) and Kantowitz (1974).

It is typical of many laboratory experiments in this tradition that, in *both* of the concurrent tasks, the 'choice-responses' to be made (for example, pushing buttons with one or other of the first two fingers, respectively, of the right and left hands) as well as the 'stimuli' that are to cue them (for example, lamps illuminated in one of two positions, respectively, in each of two adjacent panels) are *similar*. That is, the two responses (and sometimes the stimuli and the mappings between them) arguably fall within the *same domains* (see pp. 144–5).

A well-known experiment within this tradition was reported by Posner and Boies (1971). It has frequently been cited as showing evidence of competition for non-specific 'effort' or 'capacity' in the selection of responses. Their experiment involved two simple tasks. The primary task was to compare two letters presented in succession, one second apart, on a screen. As soon as possible after the second letter appeared, the subject was to press one of two keys with the first or second finger of his *right* hand, to indicate whether the two letters were, respectively, the 'same' or 'different'. The secondary task was to press another key with the forefinger of his *left* hand in response to a brief auditory singal, which could occur at any one of a number of temporal positions during the course of a letter-matching trial. The main result was that, when the auditory 'probe' signal coincided with, or just preceded, the arrival of the second letter (and therefore overlapped with the period in which the subject was deciding about, and making his 'same' or 'different' response) there was a very sharp increase in the reaction time to the probe. At all other times, including the period when the subject was presumably 'encoding' the first letter preparatory to comparing it with the second one, the response to the probe was as rapid as when the probe was presented outside the course of a letter match trial altogether. Both Kahneman (1973) and Norman and Bobrow (1975) quote this result as important evidence of two unrelated processes sharing 'effort' (whatever that is) from the same limited reservoir.

Some recent simple variations on the same design indicate that the conclusions from this particular experiment have been over-generalized. McLeod (1977a, 1978) repeated Posner and Boies's experiment. The primary letter-matching task was as before, but for half of his subjects he introduced one apparently small alteration in the secondary task. Instead of pressing a key in response to the auditory probe the subject was asked simply to respond by saying 'bip' as rapidly as possible. In this condition the sharp peak in probe response times, when the probe coincided with the second letter, now simply disappeared. That is, merely changing the modality of response to the auditory probe was apparently sufficient to eliminate the specific rivalry ('refractoriness') induced by eliciting two manual key-pressing responses at once. (Megaw and Armstrong, 1973, had similarly shown that independent movements of hand and eye to a visual target could also be initiated without mutual conflict.)

Possibly the greater 'compatibility' of a vocal response to the auditory stimulus contributed also to the separation of the two tasks in McLeod's experiment. Other results suggest that the cue-response relationships — their 'compatibility' — both *within* and even more importantly *between* any two temporally overlapping tasks can be crucial to the occurrence, respectively, of rivalry or independence between them.

For example, Greenwald and Shulman (1973) examined various combinations of eye-voice RT tasks within the PRP paradigm. When the tasks to be combined were each, individually, either spatially or I-M compatible (Chapter 2), there was no evidence of 'refractoriness'. In particular, when the stimuli for both tasks occurred simultaneously, responses to both cues were as rapid as when either task was performed alone. By contrast, when one or both the tasks involved relatively abstract or arbitary mappings of cues to responses (hear 'A'—say 'one', etc.), then refractory delays were found in one or both of the tasks. Modality separation alone, between eye or ear at input and between hand or voice at response, was not sufficient to eliminate them.

On the other hand, modality separation at output, anyway, may be a necessary condition for the elimination of response rivalry in simple S-R tasks. Brebner (1977) has shown that when one I-M compatible task (button-pressing in response to upward movement of the response-button against the fingertip) is paired with another, essentially identical I-M task (the equivalent button-pressing task with the other hand) then 'the usual PRP effect' is obtained. As yet there is far too little known about the degrees of freedom that can be exercised in much higher-level skills, such as playing a keyboard instrument, where competence manifestly depends on a very high degree of independence (as well as interdependence) in the control of individual finger-movements. Perhaps an essential feature in such skills involves the differentiation of new, independent domains of control.

Concurrent skilled transcription tasks

Let us now look at some comparatively highly skilled transcription tasks, such as copy-typing, reading aloud, or playing the piano from sight. These differ from the sorts of laboratory RT tasks previously discussed, in that (a) they are typically supported by many hundreds, or thousands, of hours of practice outside the laboratory, and (b) they lend themselves to the measurement not only of the lag (RT) between input and output but also of the working rate.

Given the evidence, thus far reviewed, of apparently specific rivalries within task-domains, and their release, consequent on domain separation, it seems appropriate to look, first, for combined performance, without general capacity limitations, in tasks from arguably distinct domains: language and music, for example.

Many pianists of even quite casual competence are aware that they can continue to play a well-known piece, or to improvise in a familiar idiom, while carrying on a conversation. More serious musicians may disapprove of such apparent lack of commitment, perhaps because at deeper levels of musical or emotional interpretation both speech and music begin to call upon the same human resources. But at the level of purely 'technical' performance there is remarkably little conflict.

Patricia Reynolds and I (Allport *et al.*, 1972) showed that competent keyboard performers could play examination pieces they had not seen before, on sight, while shadowing English prose presented to them over headphones, at 150 words per minute. Shadowing at that rate is subjectively highly demanding of 'concentration'. For our subjects, playing an unfamiliar piece of music from sight was equally subjectively taxing. Neither task is possible unless the performer has command of a rich working knowledge of the structure respectively of English prose and of classical harmony. At the onset, the rhythmic patterns of the music sometimes appeared in the subject's speech, as he shadowed; and from time to time performance of both tasks would abruptly break down. But with remarkably little practice, and certainly by the second thirty-minute session of combined piano-playing and shadowing, both activities were being performed concurrently without loss of speed or of accuracy of phrasing, and still with good comprehension of the passages transcribed.

By the second session, too, varying the technical difficulty of the music, or of the text to be shadowed, though it affected performance on the task concerned, had no influence on the level of performance of the other task being executed at the same time. This is a critical pointer to the *independence* of whatever mechanisms are limiting performance on each task individually. Peterson (1969) provides another example. He asked his subjects to read aloud a row of eight letters or numerals as rapidly as possible, at the same time as cumulatively adding a series of digits, presented by ear. The combined performance — with next to no practice at the combination — was less efficient than when the tasks were done individually. However, the interesting feature of the results was that varying the difficulty of either tasks alone had no effect on the concurrent performance level of the other. (See also, for example, Gardner 1973, Experiment I.)

In our piano-playing-plus-shadowing experiment it appeared that, for each of our performers, one or both tasks underwent some minor reorganization so that neither task made demands on the resources needed for the other. For example, speech rhythms can be controlled by musical rhythms, as in singing, and for this particular combination of tasks the speech rhythm had to be decoupled from potential command by the music. While this turned out to be easy for our performers, other pairings of particular skilled tasks may require much more radical reorganization before they can be combined. One interesting example will be discussed shortly. It was also very noticeable that the one subject for whom comprehension of, and memory for, the prose passage shadowed was as good in the combined task as when shadowing alone (in fact, as good as the memory of other subjects who merely listened to the texts) was also the most competent of our pianists. For all the rest, most of the piano pieces to be played presented some degree of technical challenge. Moments of emergency occurred; for example, when the particular fingering a performer had embarked on for part of a phrase left him badly placed for the next, and where recovery from such a momentary emergency called for relatively unpractised applications of his keyboard technique.

Precisely such emergencies call on resources that are difficult to anticipate in advance, and which therefore may not be pre-allocated to one task or another. Indeed, aspects of the problem-solving involved in *recovery from error* in otherwise very different tasks may well share the same, *specialized* processing resources, even though *error-free* performance of the same tasks entails no structural competition for specific resources. For the same reason, in using the dual-task technique to probe for functional overlap of processing resources, it may be inappropriate to push the performance of high-level skills into the region of incompetence, where gross qualitative errors are being made.

Another demonstration of independence of cerebral processing resources between tasks in intuitively distinct domains of processing has been made recently with Japanese abacus operators (Hatano *et al.*, 1977). Their young, skilled performers had had typically one or more hours of practice every day for several years. For the most expert of them, 'mental' calculation without an abacus was significantly faster than with one. These subjects were able to answer general knowledge questions, presented aurally during the course of a long mental calculation, without reducing its speed or accuracy, so long as the question had no numerical or arithmetical content. Vocal repetition of a three-digit number concurrently with calculation also had no deleterious effect. By contrast, presentation of a relatively simple arithmetical question, to be answered orally, often temporarily blocked performance on the 'mental abacus' operation altogether, even for the most expert operators.

These results suggest that, for these abacus experts, the cerebral mechanisms used in 'mental abacus' calculations are functionally entirely separate from the mechanisms of speech comprehension and production, and of information retrieval, involved in question answering. These distinct, high-level tasks do not draw on any common 'power supply'. And the same appears to be true as between speech shadowing and piano playing. In both combinations, the rules for mapping calling-patterns to actions (including, of course, entirely 'mental' actions) are strongly established. What is more, there is little risk of *data specific interference*, or 'cross-talk', between these pairs of tasks. That is, the cueing conditions proper to one task are unlikely to elicit the categories of action demanded by the other (see pp. 145–6).

Given the evidence of functional dissociations between musical and linguistic performance in neurological patients (cf. Chapter 2), laboratory demonstrations of their functional independence in intact, normal subjects should perhaps not occasion great surprise. Luria (1966) describes a distinguished Russian composer who, having suffered a haemorrhage of the left temporal lobe that deprived him of the ability to comprehend speech, nevertheless continued to perform, and indeed to compose outstanding symphonies.

The neuropsychological literature also contains evidence of highly specific dissociations of function, even within the sphere of language: for example, between reading and writing, between listening and speaking (again, see Chapter 2). How far are similar dissociations evident in dual-task performance by normal subjects?

Concurrent performance of linguistic tasks

In 1896 Solomons and Stein reported that they had been able to train themselves to write 'automatically' to dictation, while at the same time reading silently, at least to their own satisfaction. Much more recently Spelke *et al.* (1976) conducted an extended study of two college-student volunteers, who practised reading silently while at the same time writing to dictation, over a total of 85 hours spread over seventeen weeks. At first, writing a series of unrelated words to dictation interfered substantially with both the speed and the efficiency of their reading, in terms of comprehension and recall. But after some tens of hours of practice at the combined task their reading performance was no longer measurably impaired by the concurrent dictation, and there was no discernible trade-off between the two tasks. The same two subjects later practised writing, in response to each word they heard, the name of its superordinate category ('animal', 'furniture', etc.). Again, following practice at the combination, they were able to do this while reading at normal speed and comprehension.

So far, few if any task combinations have been explored under anything like the extent of practice that Spelke *et al.* gave their two subjects. The results of their marathon study provide a valuable warning: if a given pair of skilled tasks shows some mutual interference when first combined, that does not license us to infer that it will necessarily continue to do so, once the novel combination has itself been adequately practised. But it *may* do so. It would certainly be premature to assume that, for *any* pairing of tasks, some strategy can eventually be acquired which will enable them to be successfully performed together.

Different combinations of language-based skills reveal very sharp contrasts. Certain pairings of skilled tasks can be performed together, with little or no mutual interference, even after minimal practice at the combination, while others appear to be catastrophically difficult to combine. Studying a recently qualified audio- and copy-typist, Marjorie Tierney (1973) showed that she could maintain her normal speed of typing from a visual copy (about 50 words per minute) at the same time as repeating aloud (shadowing) an unrelated auditory text played to her over headphones. By contrast, when the mapping of inputs to outputs was swapped around, so that she was required to read aloud at the same time as audio-typing, performance on both tasks tumbled to around half the level of performance she could achieve, doing either task singly. That is, her audio-typing (at 50 words per minute) dropped from 95.4 per cent correct to 48.4 per cent; at the same time the number of words correctly read aloud in a one-minute period fell from an average of 145 to only 67. In both cases, over 90 per cent of the errors on these tasks were simply omissions. Essentially, the best she could do, even after three days of practice, was to alternate between short phases of either task. Shaffer (1975) has described a wide variety of similar observations, employing a very highly skilled (100 words per minute) typist. He showed that, in addition, audio-typing suffered radical interference if the subject attempted concurrently to recite well-known rhymes, or to spell words aloud, or even to vocalize the same word repeatedly. Typing from a visual copy, by contrast, was scarcely at all impaired by concurrent reciting.

One must enter the proviso that none of these task combinations were practised to anything like the extent that Spelke *et al.* (1976) gave their subjects. On the other hand, in Tierney's (1973) experiments performance at simultaneously typing and shadowing improved extremely rapidly towards independence, whereas, over three days of practice, there was negligible improvement at the combination of audio-typing and reading aloud.

How should we understand these results? First, they are extremely hard to reconcile with any notion of a truly general-purpose limitation on processing resources or non-specific capacity. Second, just keeping separate the modalities of the two tasks at both input and output clearly is not itself a sufficient condition of successful dual-task performance. What is more, in certain circumstances people can listen satisfactorily to one message while speaking another. Simultaneous interpreters, for example, can operate with a temporal overlap of at least 75 per cent between their speech output, in one language, and the sentences that they are listening to, in another (Gerver, 1974). So the suggestion that it is having to listen and speak at the same time that makes these task-combinations so difficult for the audio typist may not capture the crucial point.

The peculiar difficulty of speaking (i.e. reading aloud) one text while listening to another may derive from the fact that the auditory speech message provides such strongly compatible calling-cues for speech output that, so long as (a) speaking (in the same language?) is demanded in the combined task, and (b) the auditory speech input has to be 'attended' for some other purpose within the combined task (i.e., it cannot be decoupled from action demons altogether), then the speech output is constantly vulnerable to capture by the spoken input. The problem here, in other words, is not 'capacity limitation' but *data-specific limitation*. The data, or calling-patterns, nominally belonging to one task are also very strong calling-patterns for the domain of action that is needed (goal-activated) for the other task.

A similar problem may occur whenever the same domain of action (or even implicit action?) is required by two concurrent tasks. By contrast, when this problem of cross-capture, or data-specific limitation, is removed, many interesting combinations of language-based tasks appear possible. Recall the severe conflicts that were found in monitoring tasks, when independent inputs simultaneously evoke the same category of detection response. In contrast to this, when rapid visual monitoring for semantically-defined targets was combined, for example, with audio-shorthand transcription, given appropriate task weightings, Dennis (1978) found essentially no mutual competition.

Further systematic research along these lines, I believe, could be very rewarding.

Reappraisal

The phenomena just reviewed obviously do not exhaust the varieties of performance limitations that have been attributed, at one time or another, to the limitations of 'attention'. However, within the space available I have tried to include those experimental paradigms most often invoked in favour of a general-purpose limited-capacity central processor (GPLCCP) or – which may or may not be the same thing – in favour of a common pool of general-purpose processing resources.

Before embarking on this review of experiments I raised two questions. First, 'In what way does the behavioural evidence demand the hypothesis of a GPLCCP?' Second, given the contrasting theoretical orientation outlined in Chapter 2, 'Why should there by any "attentional" limitations at all?' Let us now return to each of these questions, in order.

Evaluating theories of general-purpose processing capacity

It is now clear that the results of several experimental paradigms, that have been deployed in the past to motivate the GPLCCP hypothesis, appear to have been over-generalized, Repeatedly, the conflicts or processing 'bottlenecks' revealed by these experiments can be seen to arise from *specific* or local competition, rather than arising from *general* limitations in the supply of non-specific processing capacity. In the preceding section there was space only to illustrate this motif from a limited number of examples. Nonetheless, I believe that a rather general reappraisal to this effect is inescapable, in respect of both discrete S-R tasks and continuous transcription, as well as in at least some forms of concurrent inputs to episodic memory. Moreover, in addition to the monitoring experiments reviewed here, there is substantial other evidence that independent stimuli activate multiple internal (conceptual) codes in parallel, without mutual conflict (e.g., Keele and Neill, 1976). (This is not to deny that, when stimuli are alike in various respects, and particularly when they are closely spaced, a diversity of interference or masking phenomena can be observed. However, masking effects have not generally been attributed, in themselves, to general-capacity limitations, and – although certainly of great interest – I shall not consider them further.)

There is one major obstacle to evaluating theories of general-purpose 'attention' ('processing capacity', 'effort', GPLCCP, universal resource, etc.). Most if not all theories of this kind with which I am familiar, permit themselves an all-important escape clause. If two tasks can in fact be performed concurrently, each independently of the manipulated difficulty of the other, then perforce one or both of the tasks must be 'automatic'. That task is therefore, by definition, irrelevant to the evaluation of the theory.

Kahneman, for example, introducing his 'capacity' model of attention, asserts that 'Not all activities of information processing require an input of attention.' In particular, he says (though this crucial disclaimer is tucked away in a figure-caption), 'Activities that can be triggered by an information-input alone are not considered in the model' (p. 16). The problem, of course, is that without some independent basis for deciding which activities are, or are not, of this kind, and therefore to which the model does or does not apply, the theory (and of course others like it) risks becoming unfalsifiable.

There is another, albeit unspoken implication, to the effect that 'automatic' processes are somehow no longer in need of explanation. (Certainly – by definition – they are not to be explained by these general 'attention' theories.) Even those processes that supposedly 'require attention' – once such a conclusion is arrived at – also risk thereby being absolved from further scrutiny. The theory has already accounted for them!

My fundamental complaint, therefore, is that this kind of approach provides an inadequate heuristic for driving research. It does not provoke further questions.

As knowledge increases, we may well identify certain processes, and certain limited-capacity mechanisms that embody them in the nervous system, that are indeed called upon – and therefore competed for – by a very diverse range of information-processing tasks. The real prize, then, will be to establish what (if any) these specific yet multi-purpose processes are. In the meantime, I suggest, it will be most fruitful, as a working assumption, to assume that *any* limitations in the performance of concurrent tasks are the result of quite *specific* sources of interference, function-specific or data-specific limitations. Systematic exploration of the same skilled tasks in many different task-combinations then appears to offer a powerful strategy for identifying these different, specific sources of interference, and hence (in conjunction with the evidence of neuropsychology) for revealing the functional anatomy of the tasks we have selected for study.

Why are there any 'attentional' limitations at all?

Many conflicts between concurrent tasks evidently result from quite specific forms of inter-process interference, as I have already argued. I conclude this chapter by listing some possible categories of specific interference.

Function-specific limitations: Separate domains of action: The constraints of the human body set upper bounds on the degrees of freedom of our physical action. A limb cannot be in two positions at once. We cannot shift our gaze simultaneously to right and left, nor vocalize two different syllables at the same time.

Shallice (1972, 1978) has argued that the necessity of preventing physically incompatible actions from being simultaneously commanded by separate action demons has forced the evolutionary development of a mechanism that enables one and only one high-level action demon (what he calls an 'action system') to be dominant at any one time. However, the observation that highly complex actions, such as speaking and piano-playing, or speaking and typing, can in fact be sustained concurrently without mutual interference, is obviously a major difficulty for any hypothesis of this sort.

Besides, the mechanism that Shallice has proposed for producing *unique* dominance among action systems depends on lateral reciprocal inhibition between 'internally self-exciting cell assemblies'. Clearly, to ensure moment-by-moment dominance by only one cell assembly would require that '*all* the assemblies mutually inhibit each other' (Shallice, 1978). Yet on physiological grounds, arguing for an otherwise very similar system, Walley and Weiden (1973) estimate the maximum inhibitory radius for a given cell assembly as only around 4 millimetres, in comparison with the 160,000 square millimetres of surface area of the human cortex.

Nonetheless, *within* such categories of action as speech utterance, or the direction of gaze, alternative actions are, clearly, mutually incompatible. Within systems such as these – conceivably even as between similar categories of action by the right and left hands – mechanisms of reciprocal inhibition could play an important role in establishing moment-by-moment dominance. Moreover, within a given category of actions the calculus of 'fixed capacity' may adequately model the response-delays that are observed (e.g., McLeod, 1977b), although the calculus in itself does not seem to offer any particular insights into possible mechanisms.

Certainly, many of the phenomena attributed hitherto to 'attentional' or 'general-capacity' limitations can be seen to depend on situations in which separate inputs compete for or share control of the same category of action. Separate the domains of action, and, in many instances, these 'attentional' limitations disappear.

In general, competition for the same, functionally specialized subsystem is a form of 'function-specific' limitation.

It seems plausible that function-specific limitations are not confined to the control of overt actions, but can arise from competition for many different kinds of specialized 'analysers' (Treisman, 1969). Possible examples of function-specific limitations in visual information processing are described by Allport (1970) and Wing and Allport (1972), and by Bjork and Murray (1977). Tasks that compete for a specialized auditory-verbal short-term memory (Chapter 5) similarly illustrate function-specific limitations.

Data-specific limitations: As already discussed in relation to various dual-task and Stroop-like situations, it can happen that the inputs (or the intermediate products of processing) proper to one task are also potential eliciting conditions for the domain of action required by the other, with consequent risk of crosstalk between the two tasks. The strategy most often adopted for coping with situations of this kind apparently has the effect of decoupling one set of inputs (or intermediate products) from potential command of *all* categories of action (although, with extended practice, other more effective strategies of data segregation appear possible: e.g., Spelke *el al.*, 1976; Underwood, 1974).

Again, there is no obvious reason why data-specific limitations should affect only the direct control of *action*. Certainly, in the classical Stroop task, there is evidence that interference, and facilitation, can occur at a stage prior to overt response selection (Seymour, 1977; Stirling, 1979).

The difficulty in making sense of two unrelated prose passages presented simultaneously to eye and ear (e.g., Mowbray, 1953) plausibly reflects both function-specific limitations (e.g., in respect of auditory-verbal STM?) and data-specific limitations. By way of illustration, in processing a noun phrase in English, the system must be prepared to accept an indefinitely long succession of modifiers, whose conceptual representations must ultimately be adapted and attached to the conceptual representation of the head noun, when it arrives (cf. Riesbeck, 1975; Gershman, 1977). Clearly, the availability of linguistic/conceptual information from another source presents a serious risk of attaching the wrong information, unless it can somehow be kept separate.

Analyses of concurrent text comprehension have for the most part used rather global methods, such as retrospective 'commentary' questions, and randomly paired texts. More sophisticated techniques, using indirect methods for probing text-processing, as well as detailed manipulation of the relationships between concurrent inputs, may provide a prime tool for the analysis of the information processes involved in language comprehension.

Limitations in keeping different goals active: A given object or event can potentially cue many different actions. Which action, if any, actually evoked must depend on the individual's currently active goals (cf. Chapter 2 and the 'cueing of actions'). To restate this, all condition→action rules that have, as their action term, a physically overt act are necessarily goal-dependent. These must include, in their conditions for execution, a particular, currently active goal.

Part of the difficulty in 'dividing attention', I suggest, is in maintaining goals appropriate to several different tasks independently active. This is especially so in discrete (e.g., RT) tasks, where there is not a continuous flow of contextual information and feedback to keep each of the task-goals primed.

M. Noble (personal communication) has shown that, even in combinations of very 'simple' tasks, the very fact of maintaining readiness for one of them (e.g., discriminating one of two, briefly presented, line orientations, even when this can be done without error) can exert a small but constant time-cost on a concurrent simple RT task. It appears that the stimulus for Task A (line discrimination) need not arrive at all, for this small, constant delay in Task B (simple RT) to show up.

This appears to be something rather different from the usual interpretation of 'processing effort' or 'processing capacity' shared between tasks. While it is seldom clearly spelled out, 'processing' implies something that is *done* to 'information'. Less information transmitted – allowing the error-rate to go up in a transduction task, such as tracking or shadowing, is Norman and Bobrow's suggested example – means less 'processing resources' allocated, fewer bits-per-second. In contrast to this, the cost of maintaining a given goal-demon activated will be independent of whether any (or how much) information is being transmitted by the organism.

So much of the difficulty of psychology has to do with getting clear what it is we are talking about.

A possibly related effect has been found when a list of letter-names must be held, for subsequent ordered recall, during performance of a choice RT task (Egeth *et al.*, 1977; Logan, 1978) Interestingly, some of this delay occurs even on those trials when no memory list is presented (and the subject therefore has only *that* simple fact to 'remember').

We know singularly little about this third variety of 'divided attention' effect, although, of the three, it is the one that seems closest to the conjectures about limited control processes, that have sometimes been invoked as the basis of 'attention' limitations.

Is the effect specific to discrete tasks? If not, is there a corresponding cost to be found, in continuous tasks, not only in lag (RT) but in working rate, or accuracy? Is the effect specifically to do with maintaining multiple goals (or intentions)? Indeed, is the intention to (re)produce a sequence of vocal or other acts (from STM) in the same sense a matter of maintaining multiple goals? What happens if the goals are related? And so on. We do not know.

Conclusion

None of the above three categories of limitation in the division (or selectivity) of 'attention' can be described in terms of competition for a universal channel of limited capacity, nor even for a limited pool of general purpose 'processing effort' or for a GPLCCP. The third category – the difficulty of keeping multiple goals active – is the one we know least about. Perhaps it will be claimed that this was, after all, what the old theories of general 'attention' were about, all along. If so, it seems surprising that their proponents have directed so little research effort to investigating this kind of limitation hitherto. Perhaps our limited ability for keeping independent goals concurrently active (How is it limited? We scarcely begin to know.) will turn out to be a special case of what I have called function-specific limitations. That is, there may turn out to be one special-purpose and limited-capacity mechanism, whose function is to keep track of current goals. It may be so.

In *Cognition and Reality,* Neisser (1976) argues forcefully against the idea of a general-purpose central capacity. However, he is also critical of postulating specialized sub-systems that can themselves only handle one message (or serve one goal?) at the same time. Such a postulate, he says 'would merely lead to a restatement of the problem' (p. 102), *viz.* Why cannot the postulated sub-system follow two messages (or maintain *n* goals) at once? Neisser is correct, I believe, in seeing such a step as a reformulation of the problem. It is a reformulation, however, that changes the problem from a diffuse and intractable one into one that is much sharper and more specific. In scientific advances, reformulation of the problem is very often the essential step.

In our present state of ignorance, the most conspicuous reason for investigating performance under 'divided attention' in the laboratory is not so much with a view to understanding 'attention', nor to diagnosing whether a given task is 'attention-demanding' or 'automatic', as for what it can tell us about the specialized sub-systems themselves that are called on and may be competed for by the particular tasks that we choose to investigate. It may be that, until we have a better description of what is being done by at least some of the sub-systems, questions about the overall architecture will just be premature.

References

Allport, D. A. (1970), 'Parallel encoding within and between elementary stimulus dimensions', *Perception and Psychophysics, 10,* pp. 104-8.
Allport, D. A., Antonis, B. and Reynolds, P. (1972), 'On the division of attention: a disproof of the single-channel hypothesis', *Quarterly Journal of Experimental Psychology, 24,* pp. 225-35.

Baddeley, A. D. (1979), 'Working memory and reading', in P. A. Kolers, M. Wrolstad and H. Bouma (eds), *Processing of Visible Language, 1,* Plenum: New York.

Bjork, E. L. and Murray, J. T. (1977), 'On the nature of input channels in visual processing', *Psychological Review, 84,* pp. 472-84.

Brebner, J. (1977), 'The search for exceptions to the psychological refractory period', in S. Dornic (ed.), *Attention and Performance, 6,* Lawrence Erlbaum: Hillsdale, N.J.

Broadbent, D. E. (1958), *Perception and Communication,* Pergamon: London.

Broadbent, D. E. (1971), *Decision and Stress,* Academic Press: London.

Bryden, M. P. (1972), 'Perceptual strategies, attention and memory in dichotic listening', University of Waterloo, Department of Psychology, Research Report no. 43.

Cherry, E. G. (1953), 'Some experiments on the recognition of speech, with one and with two ears', *Journal of the Acoustical Society of America, 25,* pp. 975-9.

Cohen, G., and Martin, M. (1975), 'Hemisphere differences in an auditory Stroop test', *Perception and Psychophysics, 17,* pp. 79-83.

Cumming, G. D. (1972), 'Visual perception and metacontrast at rapid input rates', unpublished DPhil thesis, Oxford University.

Davis R. (1959), 'The role of "attention" in the psychological refractory period', *Quarterly Journal of Experimental Psychology, 11,* pp. 211-20.

Dennis, I. (1978), 'Rate limitations in understanding words and sentences', unpublished PhD thesis, University of Reading.

Deutsch, J. A. and Deutsch, D. (1963), 'Attention: some theoretical considerations', *Psychological Review, 70,* pp. 80-90.

Duncan, J. (in press), 'The locus of interference in the perception of simultaneous stimuli', *Psychological Review.*

Dyer, F. N. (1973), 'The Stroop phenomenon and its use in the study of perceptual, cognitive and response processes', *Memory and Cognition, 1,* pp. 106-20.

Egeth, H. E., Jonides, J. and Wall, S. (1972), 'Parallel processing of multi-element displays', *Cognitive Psychology, 3,* pp. 674-98.

Egeth, H. E., Pomerantz, J. R. and Schwarz, S. P. (1977), 'Is encoding really effortless?' paper presented at the 18th Annual Meeting of the Psychonomic Society, Washington, D.C., November.

Eriksen, B. A. and Eriksen, C. W. (1974), 'Effects of noise letters upon identification of targets in a nonsearch task', *Perception and Psychophysics, 16,* pp. 143-9.

Flowers, J. H. and Blair, B. (1976), 'Verbal interference with visual classification: optimal processing and experimental design', *Bulletin of the Psychonomic Society, 7,* pp. 260-2.

Friedman, H. and Derks, P. L. (1973), 'Simultaneous motor and verbal processing of visual information in a modified Stroop test', *Perception and Psychophysics, 13,* pp. 113-15.

Gardner, G. T. (1973), 'Evidence for independent parallel channels in tachistoscopic perception', *Cognitive Psychology, 4,* pp,. 130-55.

Gershman, A. V. (1977), 'Analysing English noun groups for thier conceptual content', Yale University, Department of Computer Science, Research report no. 110.

Gerver, D. (1974), 'Simultaneous listening and speaking, and retention of prose', *Quarterly Journal of Experimental Psychology, 26,* pp. 337-41.

Greenwald, A. G. (1970), 'A double stimulation test of ideomotor theory with implications for selective attention', *Journal of Experimental Psychology, 84,* pp. 392-8.

Greenwald, A. G. and Shulman, H. G. (1973), 'On doing two things at once: II. Elimination of the psychological refractory period', *Journal of Experimental Psychology, 101,* pp. 70-6.

Hatano, G., Miyake, Y. and Binks, M. G. (1977), 'Performance of expert abacus operators', *Cognition, 5,* pp. 57-71.

Hitch, G. J. and Baddeley, A. D. (1976), 'Verbal reasoning and working memory', *Quarterly Journal of Experimental Psychology, 28,* pp. 603-21.

James, W. (1890), *Principles of Psychology,* vol. 1, Henry Holt, New York. Reprinted by Dover Publications: New York, 1950.

Jonides, J. and Gleitman, H. (1972), 'A conceptual category effect in visual search: O as letter or as digit', *Perception and Psychophysics, 12,* pp. 457-60.

Kahneman, D. (1973), *Attention and Effort,* Prentice-Hall: Englewood Cliffs, N.J.

Kantowitz, B. H. (1974), 'Double stimulation', in B. H. Kantowitz (ed.), *Human Information-Processing: Tutorials in Performance and Cognition,* Lawrence Erlbaum: Hillsdale, N.J.

Keele, S. W. (1973), *Attention and Human Performance,* Goodyear: Pacific Palisades, Cal.

Keele, S. W. and Neill, W. T. (1976), 'Mechanisms of attention', in E. C. Carterette and M. P. Friedman (eds), *Handbook of Perception,* vol. 9, Academic Press: New York.

Keren, G., O'Hara, W. P. and Skelton, J. M. (1977), 'Levels of noise processing and attentional control', *Journal of Experimental Psychology: Human Perception and Performance, 3,* pp. 653-64.

Klein, G. S. (1964), 'Semantic power measured through the interference of words with colour-naming', *American Journal of Psychology, 77,* pp. 576-88.

Levy, B. A. (1978), 'Speech processing during reading', in A. M. Lesgold, J. W. Pellagrino, S. D. Fokkema and G. Glaser (eds), *Cognitive Psychology and Instruction,* Plenum: New York.

Levy, R. (1971), 'Recognition of dichotic word lists in focused and divided attention', unpublished MA thesis, Hebrew University, Jerusalem (Hebrew).

Lewis, J. L. (1970), 'Semantic processing of unattended messages using dichotic listening', *Journal of Experimental Psychology, 85,* pp. 225-8.

Lewis, J. L. (1972), 'Semantic processing with bisensory stimulation', *Journal of Experimental Psychology, 96,* pp. 455-7.

Logan, G. D. (1978), 'Attention in character-classification tasks: evidence for the automaticity of component stages', *Journal of Experimental Psychology: General, 107,* pp. 32-63.

Luria, A. R. (1966), *Higher Cortical Functions in Man,* Basic Books: New York.

McConkie, G. W. (1979), 'On the role and control of eye movements in reading', in P. A. Kolers, M. Wrolstad, and H. Bouma (eds), *Processing of Visible Language, 1,* Plenum: New York.

McConkie, G. W. and Rayner, K. (1976), 'Asymmetry of the perceptual span in reading', *Bulletin of the Psychonomic Society, 8,* pp. 365-8.

McLeod, P. D. (1977a), 'A dual-task response modality effect: support for multiprocessor models of attention', *Quarterly Journal of Experimental Psychology, 29,* pp. 651-67.

McLeod, P. D. (1977b), 'Parallel processing and the psychological refractory period', *Acta Psychologica, 41,* pp. 381-96.

McLeod, P. D. (1978), 'Does probe RT measure central processing demand?' *Quarterly Journal of Experimental Psychology, 30,* pp. 83-9.

Megaw, E. D. and Armstrong, W. (1973), 'Individual and simultaneous tracking of a step input by the horizontal saccadic eye movement and manual control systems', *Journal of Experimental Psychology, 100,* pp.18-28.

Moray, N. (1967), 'Where is capacity limited? A survey and a model', *Acta Psychologica, 27,* pp. 84-92.

Moray, N., Fitter, M., Ostry, D., Favreau, D. and Nagy, V. (1976), 'Attention to pure tones', *Quarterly Journal of Experimental Psychology, 28,* pp. 271-83.

Morton, J. (1969), 'Categories of interference: verbal mediation and conflict in card sorting', *British Journal of Psychology, 60,* pp. 329-46.

Morton, J. and Chambers, S. M. (1973), 'Selective attention to words and colours', *Quarterly Journal of Experimental Psychology, 25,* pp. 387-97.

Mowbray, G. H. (1953), 'Simultaneous vision and audition: the comprehension of prose passages with varying levels of difficulty', *Journal of Experimental Psychology, 46,* pp. 365-72.

Navon, D. (1977), 'Forest before trees: the precedence of global features in visual perception', *Cognitive Psychology, 9,* pp. 353-83.

Neisser, U. (1967), *Cognitive Psychology,* Appleton-Century-Crofts: New York.

Neisser, U. (1976), *Cognition and Reality,* Freeman: San Francisco.

Newstead, S. E. and Dennis, I. (in press), 'Lexical and grammatical processing of unshadowed messages: a re-examination of the Mackay effect', *Quarterly Journal of Experimental Psychology.*

Norman, D. A. (1968), 'Toward a theory of memory and attention', *Psychological Review, 75,* pp. 522-36.

Norman, D. A. (1976), *Memory and Attention,* 2nd edn., Wiley: New York.

Norman, D. A. and Bobrow, D. G. (1975), 'On data-limited and resource-limited processes', *Cognitive Psychology, 7,* pp. 44-64.

Okada, R. and Burrows, D. (1978), 'The effects of subsidiary tasks on memory retrieval from long and short lists', *Quarterly Journal of Experimental Psychology, 30,* pp. 221-33.

Ostry, D., Moray, N. and Marks, G. (1976), 'Attention, practice and semantic targets', *Journal of Experimental Psychology: Human Perception and Performance, 2,* pp. 326-36.

Peterson, L. R. (1969), 'Concurrent verbal activity', *Psychological Review, 76,* pp. 376-86.

Posner, M. I. and Boies, S. J. (1971), 'Components of attention', *Psychological Review, 78,* pp.391-408.

Riesbeck, C. K. (1975), 'Conceptual analysis', in R. C. Schank (ed.), *Conceptual Information Processing*, North Holland: Amsterdam.

Schneider, W. and Shiffrin, R. M. (1977), 'Controlled and automatic human information processing: I. Detection, search and attention', *Psychological Review, 84*, pp. 1-66.

Seymour, P. H. K. (1975), 'Semantic equivalence of verbal and pictorial displays', in A. M. Kennedy and A. Wilkes (eds), *Studies in Long-Term Memory*, Wiley: London.

Seymour, P. H. K. (1977), 'Conceptual encoding and locus of the Stroop effect', *Quarterly Journal of Experimental Psychology, 29*, pp. 245-65.

Shaffer, L. H. (1975), 'Multiple attention in continuous verbal tasks', in P. M. A. Rabbitt and S. Dornic (eds), *Attention and Performance, 5*, Academic Press: New York.

Shallice, T. (1972), 'Dual functions of consciousness', *Psychological Review, 79*, pp. 303-93.

Shallice, T. (1978), 'The dominant action-system: an information-processing approach to consciousness', in K. S. Pope and J. L. Singer (eds), *The Stream of Consciousness: Psychological Investigations into the Flow of Private Experience*, Plenum: New York.

Shiffrin, R. M. (1975), 'The locus and role of attention in memory systems', in P. M. A. Rabbitt and S. Dornic (eds), *Attention and Performance, 5*, Academic Press: New York.

Shiffrin, R. M. and Gardner, G. T. (1972), 'Visual processing capacity and attentional control', *Journal of Experimental Psychology, 93*, pp. 72-82.

Shiffrin, R. M. and Schneider, W. (1977), 'Controlled and automatic human information processing: II. Perceptual learning, automatic attending, and a general theory', *Psychological Review, 84*, pp. 127-190.

Smith, M. C. (1976), 'Evidence for speech recoding when reading for comprehension', paper presented to the Psychonomic Society, St Louis, November.

Solomons, L. and Stein, G. (1896), 'Normal motor automatism', *Psychological Review, 3*, pp. 492-512.

Sorkin, R. E., Pohlmann, L. and Gilliom, J. (1973), 'Simultaneous two-channel signal detection: III. 630 and 1400 Hz signals', *Journal of the Acoustical Society of America, 53*, pp. 1045-51.

Spelke, E., Hirst, W. and Neisser, U. (1976), 'Skills of divided attention', *Cognition, 4*, pp. 215-30.

Sperling, G., Budiansky, J., Spivak, J. G. and Johnson, M. C. (1971), 'Extremely rapid visual search: the maximum rate of scanning letters for the presence of numerals', *Science, 174*, pp. 307-11.

Stirling, N. (1979), Stroop interference: an input and an output phenomenon', *Quarterly Journal of Experimental Psychology, 31*, pp. 121-32.

Tierney, M. (1973), 'Dual task performance: the effects of manipulating stimulus-response requirements', unpublished BA thesis, University of Reading.

Treisman, A. M. (1969), 'Strategies and models of selective attention', *Psychological Review, 76*, pp. 282-99.

Treisman, A. M. and Geffen, G. (1967), 'Selective attention: perception or response?', *Quarterly Journal of Experimental Psychology, 19,* pp. 1-17.

Treisman, A. M. and Riley, J. G. A. (1969), 'Is selective attention selective perception or selective response? A further test', *Journal of Experimental Psychology, 79,* pp. 27-34.

Treisman, A. M., Squire, R. and Green, J. (1974), 'Semantic processing in dichotic listening? A replication', *Memory and Cognition, 2,* pp. 641-6.

Underwood, G. (1974), 'Moray vs. the rest: the effect of extended shadowing practice', *Quarterly Journal of Experimental Psychology, 26,* pp. 368-72.

Underwood, G. (1977), 'Contextual facilitation from attended and nonattended messages', *Journal of Verbal Learning and Verbal Behavior, 16,* pp. 90-100.

Walley, R. E. and Weiden, T. T. (1973), 'Lateral inhibition and cognitive masking: a neuropsychological theory of attention', *Psychological Review, 80,* pp. 284-302.

Warren, R. E. (1972), 'Stimulus encoding and memory', *Journal of Experimental Psychology, 94,* pp. 90-100.

Warren, R. E. (1974), 'Association, directionality, and stimulus encoding', *Journal of Experimental Psychology, 102,* pp. 151-8.

Welford, A. T. (1952), 'The "psychological refractory period" and the timing of high-speed performance: a review and a theory', *British Journal of Psychology, 43,* pp. 2-19.

Welford, A. T. (1968), *Fundamentals of Skill,* Methuen: London.

Wing, A. M. and Allport, D. A. (1972), 'Multidimensional encoding of visual form', *Perception and Psychophysics, 12,* pp. 474-6.

5 Developing the concept of working memory

Graham J. Hitch

1 Introduction

In the current memory literature the human subject is often characterized as making an 'effort after meaning', relying on short-term memory or 'shallow' levels of processing only when his options are restricted, as, for example, when he is presented with relatively meaningless material to remember. Outside the laboratory, the usual illustration of short-term memory in operation is the by now rather dreary and time-worn example of remembering telephone numbers. This chapter sets out to show that the short-term memory system is of far greater interest and importance than these observations seem to suggest. The method adopted consists of first identifying some of the mechanisms of short-term memory, and then ascertaining the functions of these mechanisms in several examples of everyday cognitive processing. The whole effort can be regarded as an attempt to develop and extend the concept of short-term memory as a general-purpose 'working memory system' occupying a central role in human information processing (Baddeley and Hitch, 1974). Such an approach has the potential advantages of establishing theoretical links between topics within cognitive psychology that are sometimes all too widely separated, and providing a relatively broad context within which to formulate questions about the nature of basic mechanisms. Hopefully it, will exemplify one aspect of the New Directions we are trying to identify in this book.

The plan of the chapter is as follows. The next section examines the discontent which Guy Claxton expresses about the current state of cognitive psychology and suggests some lessons we can learn from our failures in the past. Section 3 introduces the topic of short-term memory by reviewing the background to current research and identifying some of the major issues. Section 4 goes on to consider evidence from the literature on memory and develops the view that short-term memory consists of a set of interacting sub-systems. Section 5 then examines some everyday activities and suggests hypotheses about the functions served by the various sub-systems in these tasks. Finally, Section 6 goes on to discuss the relations between these ideas and some of the other topics dealt with in this book.

2   Reasons for discontent and some lessons to be learned

It is easy to sympathize with many of Guy Claxton's dissatisfactions with cognitive psychology, in particular his charges that it is excessively phenomenon-driven, that it uses artificial situations, ignores many important aspects of behaviour, consists of many unrelated topics, and fails to offer an integrated conceptual framework for theorizing about cognitive processes. However, Claxton omits to discuss *why* the subject is so extraordinarily difficult. This is clearly worth considering.

Two fundamental difficulties are evident to all students attempting to use empirical techniques in order to understand cognitive processes. First is an appreciation that the processes we are trying to understand are exceedingly complex (a fact that surely requires no substantiation). Second is an acknowledgment that our experimental methods for testing models of cognitive processes are extremely limited. There is unfortunately no 'direct window' on mental processes, and for the most part we must make inferences about them from observations of overt behaviour.

Many researchers attempt to reduce the complexity problem by choosing to investigate limited task environments which are thought to reflect the operation of a small (and thus hopefully manageable) set of 'basic processes', such as 'attention' or 'iconic memory'. The usual experiment consists of varying a relatively small number of parameters in the laboratory task and examining their effect on behaviour. The hope is that by isolating sub-problems, changes in behaviour as a function of task variables will be an intelligible consequence of the operation of the basic processes and the way they interact. In the long run, there is the further hope that a complete picture of the cognitive system will be built up in this way.

Although many researchers will disagree with this particular thumbnail sketch, I think it fair to say that it is not an inaccurate description of a large percentage of research in cognitive psychology. It is relatively easy to see the limitations of this methodology. For example:

1 It is exceedingly difficult to decide what *are* the basic processes to be investigated and how to design laboratory tasks which do indeed focus on one or a small sub-set of them. To do this pre-supposes the existence of a generally accepted theoretical frame-work within which such processes and their possible interactions can be represented. Unfortunately, we do not yet have such a general theory of 'intelligent systems'.

2 It is impossible to test hypotheses relating observed behaviour to particular underlying mechanisms without making assump-tions about the role of other mechanisms in influencing behaviour. Often the experimenter has to make working assumptions that are in fact more weighty than the hypotheses he is directly setting out to test.

3 The search for simple, tractable sub-problems leads inevitably to the fragmentation of research topics.

4 The need for adequate control of the factors determining behaviour and the search for intelligible laws push the investigator more and more towards the study of highly artificial laboratory tasks which often bear little resemblance to normal everyday behaviour.

5 Given only fairly simple measures of overt behaviour (such as the frequency and latency of different types of response) and the usual manipulation of only a small number of task variables, only fairly simple hypotheses can be subjected to empirical test. This accounts for the often very considerable gap between theories of cognitive processes and the evidence which can be cited in direct support of their various assumptions.

6 Given the difficulty of making genuine advances in cognitive psychology, it is hardly surprising that much research is phenomenon-driven.

What then are the lessons we can learn from this rather bleak picture? One could argue that our fundamental need is for a sufficiently powerful conceptual framework within which to theorize about cogni-tive processes. Although the study of artificial intelligence may eventually supply us with such a system, there are unfortunately no immediate signs that such a framework is about to appear (despite Alan Allport's optimism). However, there are, I believe, two important methodological lessons that can be learned from our past experience. The first of these concerns the desirability of studying 'ecologically valid' tasks that are representative of normal everyday cognition, in addition to more conventional laboratory tasks (Baddeley, 1976; Neisser, 1976). An awareness of ecological validity has several advantages. It discourages the over-investigation of isolated phenomena and favours the consideration of how different aspects of the cognitive system interact to give rise to everyday behaviour. It therefore acts directly against the fragmentation and isolation of topics within cognitive psychology. In addition, it encourages an appreciation of man as an agent in his environment, and raises the important issues of evolutionary and cultural inferences on cognitive processes. The second methodological lesson we can learn from our past failures is that we need to consider evidence from as wide a variety of sources as possible in order to provide 'converging operations' for testing models and hypotheses. For example, if a cluster of related variables affects performance in a particular task in a similar way we may be justified in assuming that they affect a common sub-system or domain of processing. This justification would be increased if the effects were found to be common to a relatively wide range of tasks which could be grouped together in conceptual terms. If, in addition, it were possible to identify a group of brain-damaged patients whose behaviour could be described in terms of damage to the hypothetial sub-system, we would then have further corroboration. The technique of searching for converging evidence should lead to conclusions that have considerable power and generality, and should, once again, act against the fragmentation of topic areas within cognitive psychology.

To summarize, I have made the rather obvious point that New Directions in cognitive psychology should learn from some of the errors and limitations of our past efforts at research. While I find it hard to identify particularly fruitful lines of theoretical development, it has proved possible to suggest two methodological criteria for productive research. The first of these is the need to move beyond the bounds of typical laboratory experimentation by considering the issue of ecological validity. The second is to search for converging operations which hold over a range of experimental and observational contexts. These may be hard disciplines to adopt since both of them seem to reduce the importance of the contribution that can be made by any single experiment. However, this itself may not be a bad thing.

We shall now lay these considerations temporarily on one side to see what conclusions can be drawn about the particular topic of short-term memory on the basis of traditional research paradigms. This necessitates shifting from the present fairly general level of discussion to a more particular and detailed analysis. Subsequently, we shall illustrate the proposed methodology by trying to identify the presence and function of common short-term memory systems across a range of everyday tasks.

3 Background and issues in short-term memory

Throughout the chapter the phrase short-term memory (STM) will be used to refer in a general way to the processes responsible for retaining information over short intervals, typically of the order of seconds rather than minutes. Thus the processes involved in retention over longer intervals are excluded. A reference point for the issues that will be discussed is the 'modal' model of memory (Murdock, 1967) which was widely accepted in the late 1960s. In the generally quoted Atkinson and Shiffrin (1971) version of this class of models, memory was seen as consisting of a bank of modality-specific registers, a common limited-capacity short-term store (STS) and a more permanent long-term store (LTS). A stimulus entering the system creates a short-lived trace in one of the sensory registers, followed by entry of its name-code into the STS. Once in STS there is both rapid forgetting and a more gradual process of autonomous transfer to LTS. The model also proposed that the flow of information through this structure can be modified by control processes such as rehearsal or recoding, assumed to originate in the STS system.

The modal model achieved particular success in explaining free recall, a task where a long list of words is presented and followed by either immediate or delayed recall of the items (paying no attention to getting their order correct). The delay is usually filled by a distractor task such as counting backwards by threes for of the order of 15 to 30 seconds. Figure 5.1 presents idealized results from free recall and shows retention as a function of an item's position in the list. As can be seen, the effect of delay is restricted to the last items in the list. The 'recency effect', the relatively high level of recall of final items in immediate recall, is drastically lowered by the filled delay. According to the modal model, recency corresponds to output of the last items

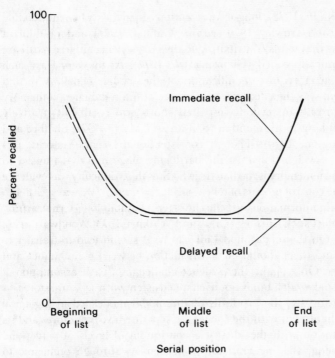

FIGURE 5.1   Effect of a short filled delay on free recall (idealized curves)

from STS and the delay task removes recency by displacing them from STS. Demonstrations that the recall of early (i.e. LTS) items in a free recall list can be affected by a number of task variables without any concomitant changes in the size of the recency effect support the two-component view (e.g., Glanzer, 1972). Further support came from results suggesting that short-term retention is typically mediated by a phonemic (or speech-related) code, whereas long-term retention is mediated by semantic coding (see, e.g., Baddeley, 1966a, 1966b). It was generally supposed that these results reflected differential coding in STS and LTS.

Though the language of the modal model continues to be used as a convenient shorthand, its shortcomings are now widely acknowledged. A major problem was the identification of coding differences in STS and LTS. Short-term retention can involve semantic coding (Shulman,

1970; Raser, 1972), long-term retention can involve phonemic coding (Bruce and Crowley, 1970; see also Shulman, 1971), and it is difficult to show that items contributing to the recency effect in free recall are phonemically coded (Glanzer *et al.*, 1972). At the very least such phenomena require modification of the modal model. A second problem was the effect of certain types of brain damage on memory which result in severely impaired short-term recall but relatively normal long-term retention (Saffran and Marin, 1975; Shallice and Warrington, 1970). Though consistent with separate stores, this evidence weighed against the particular suggestion that transfer to long-term memory is mediated via STS. A third difficulty was evidence that the control process of rehearsal can be used in two ways, either to maintain information over the short-term without long-term learning or to effect such learning (Craik and Watkins, 1973; Woodward *et al.*, 1973). On the modal model all rehearsal should lead to transfer to LTS, and there should be no distinction between maintenance and transfer. Once again, the evidence challenges a basic assumption of the modal model, but is not itself inconsistent with separate stores.

Historically, the problems of the modal model led to a general disenchantment with the concept of separate box-type stores and its substitution with the idea of a continuum of levels of perceptual processing, shading gradually from sensory through phonemic to semantic levels of analysis (Craik and Lockhart, 1972). Memory was regarded as a by-product of perceptual analyses, and retention was seen as a function of 'depth of processing', semantic analyses being the deepest and thus giving the most durable traces. To account for control processes Craik and Lockhart proposed a separate 'primary memory system', a limited-capacity processor capable of operating at any depth and able either to maintain information at a given level or to transfer it to deeper levels.

The major influence of levels of processing has been to encourage tests of the hypothesis that retention is a function of depth of processing (e.g., Craik and Tulving, 1975), and this has meant a shift of emphasis towards long-term retention. Although the general framework is attracting growing criticism (Baddeley, 1978; Nelson, 1977), its view of short-term memory remains interestingly different from the modal model. Basic to the levels of processing view is the separation of a limited-capacity processor from the 'domain' in which short-lived phonemic traces are represented, and the assumption that control processes can operate at any level of coding. The model sees the storage and processing aspects of short-term memory as properties of a common system. However, both approaches regard phonemic coding as being subsequent to sensory analyses and prior to semantic analyses within the general flow of information-processing operations on environmental inputs.

It would be unnecessarily tedious to go through all the many further attempts to explain the nature of short-term memory, and instead only the major issues will be mentioned. First is the question whether short-term memory is a unitary or a multiple system. It is still possible to find examples of the unitary viewpoint (Glanzer, 1977), but most authors accept the need to postulate more than one mechanism. One of the more popular candidates is that of a limited-capacity central processor (Baddeley and Hitch, 1974; Bjork, 1975; Craik and Lockhart, 1972; see also Broadbent, 1971; Shallice, 1975), although this assumption is not always made (Morton, 1970; Waugh and Norman, 1965). Another issue is that of coding. The concept of a phonemic store is often used, either as a store for verbal *inputs* (Shallice, 1975) or as a store for verbal *output* (Baddeley and Hitch, 1974; Morton, 1970). Alternatively, phonemic storage is assigned to a particular level of perceptual processing rather than a separate store (Bjork, 1975; Craik and Lockhart, 1972; Shiffrin, 1975). There are also differences in the way STM is linked to LTM. Sometimes information passes through STM in order to reach LTM (Atkinson and Shiffrin, 1971; Glanzer, 1977), sometimes there is a parallel access to STM and LTM (Shallice and Warrington, 1970), and sometimes STM is regarded as an activated sub-set of LTM (Shiffrin, 1975). The mysterious property of consciousness also proves elusive. Sometimes it is to be found in the central processor (Craik and Lockhart, 1972), at others it lives in the short-term store (Waugh and Norman, 1965; Erdelyi, 1974), and more often than not it is homeless.

Clearly, most theorists are agreed on the need to postulate a reasonably complex short-term memory system, but beyond this there is disagreement on virtually every issue. In our present search for New Directions, we shall begin by examining the short-term memory literature to see what kinds of sub-system must be postulated to account for the experimental evidence. This is a somewhat laborious task, but it is essential and unavoidable if we are to establish a starting point for assessing the ecological validity of short-term memory mechanisms.

4   Short-term memory mechanisms

In this section we shall suggest that short-term memory phenomena reflect the operation of a 'working memory system' (cf. Baddeley and Hitch, 1974) consisting of separable sub-systems, rather than a single system. An important modification to the view expressed by Baddeley and Hitch (1974) concerns the need to distinguish between a sub-system for the temporary storage of verbal *inputs* and a sub-system for storing verbal *outputs*. The output system is involved in holding information about potential verbal responses, is used in articulatory rehearsal, and will be referred to as the 'response buffer' (Morton, 1970) or the 'articulatory loop' (Baddeley and Hitch, 1974). The 'input register' holds information about recent verbal inputs and has similarities with Waugh and Norman's (1965) concept of primary memory. Two additional components of the working memory system that will be discussed are a limited-capacity system for the selection and firing of control processes, corresponding to the 'central executive' of Baddeley and Hitch (1974), and a separate non-verbal store for visuo-spatial information. These four suggestions are an attempt to identify the domains of processing that are likely to be the subject of future research in short-term memory rather than to suggest a formal model. The use of the term 'working memory' for the system as a whole is intended to emphasize its role in many aspects of cognition besides conventional short-term recall, as will be argued in Section 5.

4.1   The input register

Although we have mentioned the problems faced by the modal model, it is worth asking whether some aspects of it are worth saving. It fared reasonably well as an explanation of the two-component task of free recall by assuming that STS acts as an input register for the last few items presented, and it was principally as a more general account of short-term memory phenomena that the model failed. We can therefore ask whether there are any alternatives to the proposition that the recency effect in free recall is indeed due to the operation of an 'input register' type of store.

Perhaps the most serious alternative is the suggestion that recency effects result from the use of a particular type of retrieval strategy in which ordinal position cues are used to access items, these cues being particularly distinctive for items at the end of a list (Baddeley and Hitch, 1977; Bjork and Whitten, 1974; Craik and Jacoby, 1975; Tulving, 1968). On this view there is no need to postulate a separate store for the final items. Evidence in its favour comes from demonstrations of long-term recency effects under conditions where it is hard to imagine short-term storage systems being involved. For example, a rugby player attempting to recall the games he has played in a season does much better on the last few games than earlier ones (Baddeley and Hitch, 1977). A better-known example comes from a modification of the free recall task known as the 'continuous distractor' paradigm. In this paradigm, each item in the memory list is both preceded and followed by a period of distractor activity, of the type known to abolish recency when used as a delay task in standard free recall. Surprisingly, these conditions produce a pronounced 'long-term' recency effect extending across several items in the list (Aldridge and Farrell, 1977; Bjork and Whitten, 1974; Poltrock and MacLeod, 1977; Tzeng, 1973).

Recency then, is clearly not a *special* consequence of short-term memory mechanisms. However, while the retrieval strategy hypothesis provides a viable general account of recency effects, it in no way rules out the possibility that the standard short-term recency effect results from the application of this strategy to a short-term store (Baddeley and Hitch, 1977). To argue for this possibility, it is necessary to show that there are differences between short-term and long-term recency effects. One self-evident difference is, of course, that the standard recency effect is wiped out by a short filled delay prior to recall, while the long-term effect is largely unaffected by this manipulation (Bjork and Whitten, 1974). A similar result is that the standard recency effect is obtained only when the last items in the list are recalled first (Dalezman, 1976), whereas long-term recency is present regardless of whether recall starts with the beginning, middle or final items of the list (Whitten, 1978). Further evidence that short- and long-term recency effects reflect different storage systems comes from comparing the effects of varying list-length in standard free recall and the continuous distractor task. Figure 5.2 shows results collected from a range of broadly comparable studies. It can be seen that the short-term recency effect retains a constant profile across different list lengths, whereas long-term recency becomes weaker as list length increases. This is consistent with the operation of a buffer store in the case of short-term recency and not long-term recency. Assuming

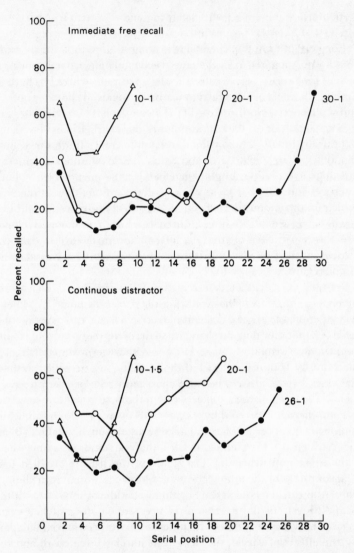

FIGURE 5.2 Effect of list-length on the recency effect in immediate free recall and the continuous distractor paradigm. Immediate free recall data from Postman and Phillips (1965); continuous distractor data from Bjork and Whitten (1974) and Tzeng (1973). Parameters refer to list-length and presentation rate: i.e., 10–1.5 indicates a list of 10 words, each word being presented for 1.5 seconds. Data from adjacent serial positions have been pooled

therefore that there is a buffer operating in short-term recency, what can be said about its properties? To anticipate, the evidence points to a relatively passive 'input register' storing information about recent events and separate from systems responsible for control processes such as rehearsal.

First, the effect of a concurrent task performed during the presentation of a free recall list impairs the LTS component of recall but leaves recency unaffected. This is true across a range of tasks including mental arithmetic (Silverstein and Glanzer, 1971), card-sorting (Baddeley *et al.*, 1969; Bartz and Salehi, 1970; Murdock, 1965) and choice reaction time (Anderson and Craik, 1974). Given such a heterogeneous range of tasks, perhaps the one thing they can be said to have in common is the execution of 'control processes'. Assuming, as will be argued later, a limited capacity for such processes, it follows that the registration of stimulus information in the buffer does not involve control processes and is therefore automatic. For this reason it can be regarded as a relatively 'passive' input register.

Second, it is evident that registration in the input store is not dependent on the *particular* control process of articulatory rehearsal. When people are asked to rehearse aloud in a free recall experiment it turns out that they only rarely rehearse the items that contribute to the recency effect (Rundus, 1971). Further evidence comes from effects of 'articulatory suppression', a technique of interfering with rehearsal processes by requiring the repetition of an irrelevant speech sound such as the word 'the' during list presentation. In free recall, articulatory suppression leaves the recency effect intact while lowering the long-term component of recall (Richardson and Baddeley, 1975), suggesting again that storage in the input register is not a function of rehearsal.

Assuming that the input register is a passive store, we can enquire about the further issues of its coding and capacity. Studies of free recall for lists of unrelated words suggest that the recency effect consists of between two and three items. However, when slightly less atypical material is used, such as a list of unrelated sentences, recency is found to extend over as much as a sentence or so (Glanzer and Razel, 1974). This important result suggests that the input register contains the last few 'meaningful units' or 'chunks' (cf. Miller, 1956) of a verbal input, rather than a fixed number of words. This property will be taken as a strong clue to the function of the input store when it is discussed in Section 5.

The question of coding in the input register is best considered in the context of the arguments for differentiating it from a second component of short-term storage, the response buffer or articulatory loop.

4.2   The articulatory sub-system

It is of some significance that most of the evidence that phonemic coding is characteristic of short-term retention comes not from free recall but from the 'memory span' paradigm, where the task is the immediate reproduction of a relatively short sequence of unrelated items in their order of presentation. Sequences made up of similar sounding items are more difficult to recall than control sequences (Baddeley, 1966b; Conrad and Hull, 1964; Murray, 1968), and errors tend to be items that have a similar sound to the correct items (Conrad, 1964). Both effects are strong and reliable characteristics of the memory span task.

A crucial problem for the modal model was the evident lack of convergence between the phonemic store implied by the memory span and the store underlying recency in free recall (Broadbent, 1971). Several attempts have been made to test the proposition that items contributing to the recency effect are phonemically coded, but with only mixed success. For instance, phonemic similarity of the items presented for free recall, either to one another or to post-list distracting activity, appears to have no influence on the recency effect (Glanzer *et al.*, 1969, 1972). On the other hand misrecalls do tend to be phonemically related to correct items for the final but not the earlier items of free recall lists (Craik, 1968b; Shallice, 1975). And studies where, instead of free recall of the whole list, a single 'probe' item is used to prompt recall of the item which followed it during list presentation, phonemic similarity impairs the recall of final items but not earlier ones (Kintsch and Buschke, 1969; Levy and Murdock, 1968; Woodward, 1970).

One response to this mixture of evidence is to claim that the mechanisms underlying memory span and recency in free recall are the same (cf. Shallice, 1975). Since phonemic similarity exerts its effect primarily on order errors in the span task (Wickelgren, 1965), its somewhat elusive effect in free recall might reflect the irrelevance of order information to the task; its clearer effect in probed recall might be because order is relevant in that case. However, further considerations militate against this conclusion.

The most telling results come from an experimental paradigm in which a memory span task is performed simultaneously with the presentation of a free recall list, one task being presented visually the other auditorily (Baddeley and Hitch, 1974, 1977). Increasing the difficulty of the memory span task by changing the list length from one to three to six items impaired the long-term component of free recall, but left recency intact. Since six items is close to the limit on memory span, the results demonstrate that the 'memory span mechanisms' can be fairly fully occupied and yet have no influence on the recency effect. If the two systems were one and the same some influence on recency would have been expected.

A second line of evidence concerns the differential capacities of the two systems. For lists of random words, the size of the recency effect is uninfluenced by the phonemic variable of word length (Craik, 1968a; Watkins, 1972). Indeed, memory for more complex material suggests that recency extends over the last few meaningful 'chunks' of input, even when these contain several words (see Section 4.1). In contrast, memory span for unrelated words is systematically dependent upon word-length, recall being limited to as many words as can be read aloud in about two seconds plus a small constant amount that is independent of word-length (Baddeley *et al.*, 1975).

Further findings help to identify the nature of the system underlying the span. The word-length effect disappears under 'articulatory suppression', the technique where rehearsal is prevented by forcing articulation of irrelevant speech sounds during list presentation (Baddeley *et al.*, 1975), and the effect of phonemic similarity on memory span also disappears under articulatory suppression (Murray, 1968; Levy, 1971). Thus a simple interpretation of the span is that it is mediated by a rehearsal buffer or 'articulatory loop' (Baddeley and Hitch, 1974), whose effective capacity is determined by the interaction of rate of rehearsal and the rate at which information decays. Since some items can still be recalled even under articulatory suppression, and there is a corresponding component of recall which is independent of word length it is necessary to postulate an additional factor in the memory span besides the articulatory loop. This second component will be discussed in a later section.

To sum up, the memory span appears to reflect active use of an articulatory sub-system which is subject to temporal decay and sensitive to effects of word-length, phonemic similarity and articulatory suppression. On the other hand, the recency effect in free recall is item-based rather than time-based (cf. Waugh and Norman, 1965), insensitive to articulatory suppression (Section 4.1.) and word-length, but shows a mixture of evidence in relation to phonemic coding. These differences seem sufficient to distinguish a relatively passive 'input register' underlying recency from a more actively controlled system for retaining sub-vocal output, the 'articulatory loop'. In Section 5 we shall take the distinction one stage further by assigning quite different functions to these two systems.

An important question is how two apparently quite similar short-term memory paradigms could possibly reflect fundamentally different systems. The reason would appear to be straightforward. In free recall experiments subjects are unconstrained as to the order of recall and tend to retrieve the final list items first. This would correspond to retrieving the contents of the input register before searching other domains within memory. In the memory span, on the other hand, subjects must begin their recall with the first items presented. The effect of this is to produce loss of information from the input register, which cannot therefore make an effective contribution to recall. Interestingly, this argument suggests that the second factor involved in the memory span cannot correspond to retrieval from the input register.

As a final comment, it would be unfair not to admit that there are some difficulties with the present argument. One is that the power of articulatory suppression to abolish word-length and phonemic similarity effects on memory span is contingent upon visual presentation of the material and is absent with auditory presentation (Baddeley *et al.*, 1975; Murray, 1968). This is not expected on the basis of a common output buffer accepting inputs from either modality, and requires extra assumptions about the processes of input to the articulatory loop.

4.3 *The concept of a central executive*

Another component of short-term memory performance that is quite widely postulated is the idea of a limited-capacity central processor (Baddeley and Hitch, 1974; Bjork, 1975; Craik and Lockhart, 1972). The concept has its roots in countless studies of divided attention and dual-task performance, which generally show that there is a limit on our ability to do more than one thing at the same time (Broadbent, 1971; Kahneman, 1973; Norman, 1968; Welford, 1968). It has also been argued that these results do not necessarily imply a general-purpose limited-capacity system (see Alan Allport's Chapter 4, and Neisser, 1976). Needless to say, the issue is a complex one. What I shall do here is, first outline some of the reasons for supposing that there is a limited-capacity processor operating in short-term memory experiments. Second, I shall defend the notion that the processor is a general-purpose one.

My own interest in the concept of a 'central executive processor' came from a series of experiments studying the role of the short-term memory system across a range of information processing activities (Baddeley and Hitch, 1974). It was concluded that the two components of memory span performance consisted of retrieval from the articulatory loop, as already described, and items retained by a limited capacity processor interacting with other (as yet unspecified) domains of the memory system. A pattern of observations led to the adoption of this position. First were the results of a number of dual-task experiments where a memory span task was required to be performed concurrently with another task such as verbal reasoning, prose comprehension or free recall. Across all combinations, interference was observed when the span task involved sequences of six items but was minimal for sequences consisting of three or four items. It was reasoned that a small number of items could be held in the articulatory loop without burdening the limited-capacity common processor, but that large memory loads would place demands on the processor and hence give rise to substantial dual-task interference. Further experiments showed that combining articulatory suppression with verbal reasoning or free recall produced only minimal interference, confirming that the interference associated with high memory loads was at a level other than that of the articulatory loop. However, a crucial question is whether a limited capacity *general-purpose* processor is necessarily implied by these results. It would appear not, since the source of interference might reflect overload of a specific system common only to the particular combinations of tasks investigated.

Assuming that the cognitive system can be conceptualized in terms of several separable but interacting domains of processing, tasks that compete for any specific domain are clearly likely to interfere. This corresponds to what Kahneman (1973) describes as 'structural' inter-ference. Opponents of the idea of a general-purpose processing limitation (e.g., Allport *et al.*, 1972) take the view that *all* dual-task interference is structural and highly specific to particular task combinations, there being no 'general domain' common to all tasks. To make matters more complicated, structural interference is not denied by supporters of the concept of a general-purpose capacity, but is seen as an extra source of dual-task interference over and above competition for the central capacity (cf. Kahneman, 1973). Resolution of this issue is probably impossible without a clear understanding of the domains of proces-sing that are involved in tasks that are combined in experiments on divided attention. What evidence we do have is highly suggestive of limited processing capacity of a fairly general nature.

In one study McLeod (1977) combined a continuous visuo-motor tracking task with two-choice tone identification which required either manual or vocal responses in two separate conditions. Analysis of the temporal relations between response execution within the two streams of activity showed cross-talk in the case of the auditory-manual task, but independence in the case of the auditory-vocal task. However, even though the tasks were temporally independent in the latter case, there was an overall decrement in tracking performance as compared to a control condition involving tracking alone. A plausible interpretation is to assign the overall decrement in performance to competition for a resource common to both tasks, but not involved in the detailed processing operations of either. The apparent paradox this presents can be resolved by assuming that the common resource is a 'high-level' system such as an executive, involved only in initiat-ing largely autonomous processing routines and monitoring their progress in order to be able to recover from any errors that might occur. With highly practised input-output tasks such as those used by McLeod, one might expect an executive to perform just this function and little more. In novel, more complex tasks the same executive might be more heavily involved in co-ordinating the various com-ponents of performance.

This possibility is indicated by the results of experiments by Egeth and colleagues (1977) and Logan (1978) (described in Chapter 4). Both experiments combined a short-term memory task with reaction-time tasks whose performance could be analysed in terms of a sequence of separate stages of processing (cf. Sternberg, 1969). In both cases short-term memory load produced a general slowing of reaction times, but in neither case was the interference associated with any particular stages of processing. The best way of understanding this interference seems to be once again in terms of a single high-level resource that co-ordinates stages of processing (see Logan, 1978). The alternative notion of a set of separate resources, one for each stage, all suffering equal interference from the concurrent task seems highly implausible. A similar type of result was found when two levels of difficulty of a tapping task were combined with short-term retention (Roediger *et al.*, 1977). Recall was independent of tapping difficulty, but was poorer than when the memory task was performed alone. Once again, the two tasks appear to be limited by independent resources but there is nevertheless an overall dual-task decrement.

It should be more than clear that in arguing for a common capacity limitation it has been necessary to abandon the strong assumption that *all* mental operations draw on the common resource. The general conclusion is instead that 'lower-level' processes can proceed without drawing on general capacity and that only 'high-level' processes, those of control and co-ordination, require access to the common resource.

A useful analogy may be that of the manager of a large office. In order to control and supervise the activities of the organization he must be untrammelled by the need to be aware of all the details of what is going on at any instant. However, he must also be able to switch from his general supervisory role to deal with specific problems when circumstances dictate, such as the occurrence of an unusual pattern of demand on the office resources or inefficiency in a particular department. Nevertheless, even in cases such as these, he is still prevented by the rules of the organization from undertaking low-level tasks for himself (such as typing letters or operating the switchboard). In other words, the manager still behaves as an executive even when general supervision is abandoned in favour of local intervention. Of course, helpful though the analogy is, we need a much clearer mapping onto cognitive processes in order to make it more than a useful illustration. Further comments on the question of distinguishing different levels of control appear in Section 5.4.

Since we have by now moved some distance from the specific context of short-term memory, let us try and sum up the argument of this section. First, it was argued that memory span and a range of verbal tasks compete for a common limited-capacity processing resource.

Second, several dual-task experiments, including situations in which one of the tasks requires short-term retention, show that even when the detailed processing associated with each of the tasks appears to be performed independently, there is still a decrement when single- and dual-task performance are compared. The concept of a 'central executive', a common, limited capacity for high-level processes of control and co-ordination, was used to interpret these results. Such an executive, whilst being a crucial component of short-term retention, is of course conceptually distinct from temporary stores such as the input register and articulatory buffer. Its only 'short-term' characteristic is its limited capacity for doing several types of operation at the same time, whereas the short-term characteristic of the stores refers to the durability of the information they contain.

As a postscript, it is worth remembering that dual-task experiments in which one of the tasks is free recall (see Section 4.1.) show interference with the long-term component of free recall but not the recency effect. It seems therefore that while the executive is involved in control processes such as rehearsal and recoding, it is not essential for the entry of information into the input register. Indeed, given also that a concurrent memory span task does not interfere with the recency component of free recall, access to the input register must be not only relatively automatic, but parallel for different input streams. Following Shiffrin (1975), the suggestion is that the input register has a larger instantaneous capacity than measures of recall would imply.

4.4 Short-term visual memory

Sensory storage for visual information, or iconic memory, is well documented (see reviews by Baddeley, 1976; Crowder, 1976). It has a large instantaneous capacity, a brief duration (of the order of a few hundred milliseconds), and is sensitive to masking by subsequent visual input (Turvey, 1973). There is, however, growing evidence of short-term visual representations which outlive the icon, are not subject to masking and are sharply limited in capacity (Phillips, 1974; Phillips and Christie, 1977a, 1977b; Posner, 1969). In the interests of keeping this chapter at least relatively readable, we shall not discuss this work in detail and shall merely point out this possible further component of the short-term memory system.

5 Functions for short-term memory mechanisms

The arguments so far have been concerned with the task of separating the various sub-systems that must be identified in order to begin an account of the phenomena of short-term memory. The time has now come to assess the usefulness and appropriateness of these ideas in relation to a wider range of activities, and to consider what function the various systems serve in everyday cognition. Success would give the concepts some ecological validity and would help to draw relationships between different areas of research. It would also, incidentally, re-inforce the spirit of the suggestion that short-term memory mechanisms can be profitably viewed collectively as a general 'working memory system' (Baddeley and Hitch, 1974). Failure would mean that we are still a long way from bringing the study of short-term memory to life. Since everyday activity defines a virtually limitless set of situations, I shall confine myself to the particular skills of speech perception, language production, reading, and performing arithmetic. In each case the view will be selective and will concentrate on those aspects of the skills which seem to enable a function to be mapped onto a specific sub-system of short-term memory. In no case will it be feasible to go into the tasks themselves in the detail that they each merit in their own right.

5.1 Speech perception

There are generally recognized *prima facie* grounds for supposing that some form of short-term memory is necessary for comprehending both spoken and written language. In each case the input is sequential and its meaning is dependent upon integration over time. Interestingly, this argument can be applied at each of the possible levels at which the linguistic input can be described. In order to comprehend speech we might imagine a cascade of temporary stores integrating distinctive features into phonetic segments, phonetic segments into syllables, syllables into words, words into sentence constituents, and so forth and so on. Clearly, the short-term memory sub-systems that we have identified here are described far too globally to have implications for the detailed nature of these processes. On the other hand, it would be rather odd if the systems served no function at all in speech comprehension. One plausible possibility is that the input register corresponds to an identifiable junction in the process of perceiving speech, acting as a buffer between relatively automatic analyses on the input and subsequent processing that is more flexible and situation-dependent, involving some measure of co-ordination by the central executive.

What support is there for such a view? First, it has the merit of corresponding to at least some psycholinguists' attempts to conceptualize the comprehension process. Thus Clark and Clark (1977) propose that sentence constituents are stored in a buffer memory. Comprehension then proceeds by constructing propositional representations from the constituents and then relating these representations to a propositional structure for the preceding discourse as a whole. Could sentence constituents therefore form the units stored in the input register? While experiments on memory for lists of random words suggest not, since recency is confined to just two or three words, experiments on memory for unrelated sentences (Glanzer and Razel, 1974) suggest a greater capacity, corresponding to perhaps two or three sentence constituents. The suggestion is therefore feasible. It receives support from experiments in which continuous speech is interrupted and listeners are asked for immediate verbal recall of the most recent input (Jarvella, 1970; Jarvella and Herman, 1972). When plotted as a function of word position, recall exhibits a general recency effect extending over several words, with marked discontinuities in the curve at clause and sentence boundaries. The shape and extent of the curves imply a register storing the last one or two clauses of the discourse at any given instant. Thus there is at least suggestive evidence that the input register serves the important function of holding the results of preliminary parsing processes during speech comprehension, even though it is not yet clear what the precise definition of the syntactic units should be.

A second implication of the present proposal is that it should be difficult, if not impossible, to use control processes to modify or even monitor automatic stages of stimulus analysis prior to the input register. Confirmation of this prediction comes from experiments in which subjects are required to monitor spoken sentences for the occurrence of a particular phoneme or word designated as a target (Warren, 1971). If stimulus analysing mechanisms could be tapped directly by task-specific control processes, we would expect phonemes to be detected faster than words, since phonemic analysis presumably occurs more peripherally than word analysis. In fact the reverse is found, suggesting that phonemic information has to be 'recovered' from a higher-level description which is closer to the word. Support for this interpretation comes from the observation that phoneme monitoring is facilitated when the transitional probability of the word containing the target in the context of the preceding utterance is relatively high (Morton and Long, 1976). Such probabilities can only operate at the level of word recognition and beyond, and are uninterpretable in terms of a phonemic level of description. In terms of the present short-term memory structure, the 'recovery' of phonemic information would be assigned to control processes interrogating the stimulus representation in the input register.

An obligatory parsing process would also imply that in shadowing a spoken message there should be an obligatory lag between input and output of a sentence constituent, or at least a word, and this is typically found to be so (Treisman, 1965). However, it is now known that certain selected individuals can in fact shadow a spoken message at very short lags corresponding to little more than the duration of a syllable (Marslen-Wilson, 1973). If control processes are 'blind' to stimulus analyses taking place prior to the input register, such performance ought not to be possible. The fact remains that most people cannot shadow at such short lags, suggesting that close shadowers are utilizing a somewhat atypical mode of speech processing.

In summary, the input register can be identified as a buffer holding a parsed representation of the most recent words of a speech input, upon whose contents control processes involved in comprehension, presumably requiring the central executive, subsequently operate. There are also grounds for supposing that control processes do not normally have the power to modify earlier levels of stimulus analysis, though the the extent to which this is true may be a function of individual differences.

5.2 Speech production

Given that sub-vocal rehearsal involves recirculating information through an articulatory loop, it is natural to suggest that this sub-system also serves as an output buffer in the production of overt speech (cf. Morton, 1970). Evidence supporting this view comes from the study of speech errors, which can be regarded as due to occasional misfunctions of the normal production mechanisms. The analysis of speech errors suggests that several words are simultaneously activated prior to their production, supporting the general concept of an output buffer. More detailed analyses show correspondences between the properties of speech errors and errors of recall in the memory span paradigm, suggesting that the speech buffer can be identified with the articulatory loop. We shall consider these points in turn.

Perhaps the most well-known class of speech errors are Spoonerisms, which typically involve an unintended interchange between the initial consonants of a pair of words, as in:

Wasted the whole term—Tasted the whole worm.

For such errors to occur there must be a level of representation in which words that have yet to be produced can interact with words currently being produced (Lashley, 1951), presumably corresponding to a store which maintains the contents of an utterance in between its planning and its execution (e.g., Fromkin, 1966; Mackay, 1970). Some idea of the capacity of the store can be obtained from considering the intervals over which paired exchanges take place, which, according to Fromkin (1971), are seldom more than six or seven words. Does this correspond to the properties of the articulatory loop? Recall first that the capacity of the loop was defined in terms of the number of words that could be read aloud in about two seconds. The two measures can be approximately related by taking Foulke and Sticht's (1969) estimate that typical reading rates are about three words a second. Thus it appears that the capacity of the loop is indeed the right order of magnitude to be compatible with the known distribution of speech errors. However, this analysis belies the hierarchic structure of speech errors (see below) and can only be regarded as suggestive.

More convincing evidence comes from the demonstration of fine-grain correspondences between the properties of speech errors and intrusion errors in the memory span paradigm (Ellis, 1979). Spoonerisms are more likely to involve consonant reversals than vowel reversals, and more likely to involve vowel reversals than syllable reversals. Precisely the same pattern is observed in the immediate recall of syllable sequences. Second, Spoonerisms are more likely to involve the exchange of adjacent elements than elements that are widely separated. The same is true of order errors in short-term recall. Third, consonant Spoonerisms are affected by vowel context and feature similarity in just the same way as consonant transpositions in short-term recall. Ellis cites many more correspondences, but it is unnecessary to list them all here.

In summary, there are strong grounds for supposing that speech errors reflect the operation of the articulatory sub-system identified from experiments on short-term memory, suggesting that the function of the sub-system is to serve as an output buffer enabling speech plans to be translated into utterances. However, as with the input register in the case of speech perception, it is obvious that the concept of the articulatory buffer requires considerable elaboration. Slips of the tongue typically occur at several levels of linguistic representation, involving exchanges between distinctive features, consonants, vowels, syllables and even whole words (Clark and Clark, 1977). While the same is also true of short-term memory intrusions, it is clear that the concept of the articulatory buffer needs considerable development in order to account for the actual forms that errors take. Presumably what will be required is a fairly detailed model of articulatory programmes (cf. Fromkin, 1971).

The identification of the articulatory buffer with speech production has interesting implications for understanding the type of memory disorder described by Shallice and Warrington (1970) and Warrington *et al.* (1971). The patients in question exhibit impaired short-term memory in the form of a reduced recency effect in free recall and a very low memory span, while measures of long-term memory such as their recall of early items in free recall lists are typically normal. According to Baddeley and Hitch (1974) the disorder was interpreted in terms of impairment to the articulatory buffer while the central executive remained intact. However, this view was put forward in a theoretical context which did not recognize the input register as an additional component of verbal short-term memory, and before the appearance of evidence that the disorder can occur in the absence of any measurable disfluency in speech production (Shallice and Butterworth, 1977). This evidence must be taken to suggest that the articulatory buffer is unaffected by the disorder, in contradiction to the Baddeley and Hitch hypothesis. In our present context, a more plausible alternative is to propose that the impairment is associated with the input register rather than the articulatory buffer. This would directly account for the patients' poor recency effect in free recall. Their poor memory span would be an indirect consequence, as follows. Storage in the articulatory output buffer or via the central executive (the two components of span), would depend on both these systems being 'fed' by an intact input register. Thus, even though memory span performance does not involve retrieval from the input register at the time of recall, an intact register is nevertheless a crucial precondition for normal retention in this paradigm. Finally, a deficit to the input register would imply some impairment of speech comprehension. This is typically found to be the case for messages that are beyond all but the very lowest levels of linguistic complexity. Indeed, the patients' much greater difficulty with comprehension as opposed to production of speech can be taken as a direct suggestion of impairment at an input rather than an output storage location.

We have seen that considerations of language behaviour suggest that rather different functions can be assigned to the input register and the articulatory buffer, and furthermore, that these functions can in turn to be used to interpret the neurological impairment of short-term memory. In addition, the complexity of language itself suggests that the notion of simple box-type stores will eventually need to be substituted by concepts that are more closely related to linguistic function.

5.3   Reading

Ever since Huey's (1908) famous pronouncements, considerable attention has been devoted to considering the role of 'inner speech' during reading. What function, if any, does it serve? Over the years, two quite separate issues have emerged. The first concerns the problem of how the meanings of individual words become available during reading. The evidence here suggests at least two distinct ways, one in which a graphemic description of the printed word maps directly onto meaning, and one in which the graphemic code is first translated into a phonological code which in turn maps onto meaning (see, e.g., Levy, 1978). We shall be concerned here with a second, quite different issue, the role of sub-vocalization in reading continuous text, where the processing of meaning goes beyond the level of individual words.

Electrophysiological recordings confirm that activity in the speech musculature increases during the reading of continuous text. Interestingly, the level of activity increases with the rated difficulty of the material (McGuigan, 1970); and training people to inhibit sub-vocalization by monitoring feedback from their speech-muscle activity impairs comprehension of difficult texts but not easy ones (Hardyck and Petrinovich, 1970). We seem therefore to be dealing with a process that is only called upon under certain circumstances. However, the precise component of 'difficulty' that triggers sub-vocalization cannot be identified from these experiments. Clearer evidence is available from studies by Kleiman (1975), who studied the effects of interfering with sub-vocalization on a range of tasks designed to tap different aspects of the reading process. One of these required a judgment about the meaning of an individual word in terms of a decision whether or not it belonged to a particular conceptual category. Another required judgment about whole sentences in terms of a decision whether or not each sentence was semantically acceptable. An acceptable sentence might be 'Noisy parties disturb sleeping neighbours', while 'Pizzas have been eating Jerry' would be unacceptable. Interfering with articulation caused much greater interference with the second type of decision. Kleiman interpreted his experiments in terms of a comprehension process which is normally fed by an input store but is supplemented by a separate articulatory store when the input store is overloaded, as is the case when a whole sentence has to be held in order to make a decision. Clearly one might interpret the increase in sub-vocal activity during reading difficult texts in a similar way by assuming that the crucial component of difficulty is that it increases the simultaneous storage load necessary for comprehension. In terms of the memory structure we have proposed here, Kleiman's interpretation of reading maps onto our earlier claim that the input register plays a crucial role in the comprehension of spoken language, adding the extra assumption that the articulatory loop is also used during reading. This mapping requires us to be explicit in stating that the input register is not specific to the auditory modality but can also be accessed by visual inputs, a proposition that we have not had space to support by detailed argument.

Interestingly, Kleiman's technique may underestimate the point at which the input register becomes overloaded since his interfering task involved auditory shadowing, a more complex task than 'pure' articulatory suppression, and his sentence judgment task seems somewhat atypical of normal reading. Experiments by Alan Baddeley, Vivien Lewis and myself (Baddeley, in press) tend to confirm this conclusion, since we found no measurable effect of the more usual manipulation of articulatory suppression on judgments of the truth of sentences such as 'Robins move around searching for food'. It is as yet unclear under what conditions the articulatory loop becomes necessary for supplementary storage during reading.

It is also of some interest to consider *why* supplementary articulatory storage seems necessary in reading, when , so far as is known, it is not involved in listening. One possibility is that the longer-lasting sensory memory for auditory inputs (which we have not included in the present discussion) fulfils the supplementary storage function for speech inputs. A second possibility arises from the suggestion that reading is parasitic upon listening, since we learn to read long after we learn to understand spoken language. The need for supplementary storage in reading may therefore reflect a system which is biologically unsuited for dealing with the highly grammatical, intonation-free input provided by written as opposed to spoken language, and is therefore more frequently overloaded.

To sum up this section, it is plausible to suppose that the articulatory loop provides supplementary short-term storage in the case of reading, though the conditions under which this occurs have yet to be fully explored. Since the loop seems also to be involved in speech production, it would appear to be an important general aspect of verbal cognition.

5.4   Arithmetical calculation

In arithmetical calculation the case for supposing that some form of short-term storage is involved is almost self-evident. Of more crucial importance is whether the storage involves the same underlying systems as more conventional short-term memory tasks.

In a series of experiments (Hitch, 1978) I explored the nature of the short-term memory component in mental additions where people were required to write down the sum of two auditorily presented numbers (such as 321 and 493). Problems of this type involve a sequence of operations on individual pairs of digits (Dansereau and Gregg, 1966), and thus in general there are delays between the initial presentation of any digit and its subsequent processing. Further analysis reveals that there are also delays between generating partial results and either producing them as overt responses or incorporating them into subsequent operations, for example as a consequence of carrying. The results of the experiments showed that under a variety of conditions the pattern of errors could be predicted by assuming that stored information decays or suffers interference during the delay intervals imposed by the particular sequence of operations required by the task. Furthermore, the rate of forgetting was broadly comparable with that observed in laboratory studies of short-term forgetting, suggesting that arithmetic does indeed use the same underlying system. The experiments were not designed to answer the question of what sub-systems of short-term memory are involved in mental arithmetic, and this interesting question remains open. In subsequent as yet unpublished experiments I have begun to explore this issue in the context of written arithmetic, where the problem information is continuously available for visual inspection. The fallibility of memory is therefore probably only crucial for the storage of intermediate results. One experiment compared the effect of articulatory suppression on two types of problem matched in arithmetical complexity but differing with respect to the duration for which intermediate results had to be held in store. Examples of the two types are: $(3 + 2) \times (2 + 6 + 1)$ and $(2 + 6 + 1) \times (3+2)$. Articulatory suppression produced a greater impairment in solving the first type of problem, where the result of the first bracket must be stored over a longer interval, suggesting that in arithmetic, as in reading, the articulatory loop serves an identifiable storage role.

A further aspect of arithmetical skill is that it highlights the general problem of the organization of control processes. In considering the role of STM in arithmetic, the elementary operations were regarded as the individual digit-pair transformations (such as $2 + 3$ or $1 + 4$). However, when children do arithmetic, studies of the speed of these elementary operations suggest that they have an information-processing structure of their own (Parkman and Groen, 1971; Parkman, 1972; Svenson *et al.*, 1976). One common strategy appears to be a process involving counting on from the larger digit by a number of steps equal to the smaller (Parkman and Groen, 1971). Such a process implies deciding which of the digits is the larger and keeping track of the count, and is clearly non-trivial. When a child adds two numbers such as $421 + 369$ the control processes would appear to range from the general command 'start the adding routine' through intermediate instructions such as 'add this pair of digits' to the specific operation 'check the count'. How are these various types of operation organized?

One solution is provided by a general theory of human problem-solving, that of Production Systems (Newell and Simon, 1972). A Production System consists of three elements: a short-term memory storing 'conditions', a serial processing device for executing 'actions', and a long-term memory containing 'productions' consisting of 'condition-action' pairs. When the contents of STM match the conditions for a particular production the processor executes the action associated with it. This action in turn modifies the contents of STM, causing another production to fire, and so forth and so on. In simulating the performance of an arithmetic calculation, the processor would step sequentially through all the operations one by one until the calculation was complete. In this system all control processes are treated in the same way regardless of their hierarchical level in relation to the task. An alternative system, more in line with the present concept of a 'high-level' executive, is one in which the more detailed processing operations are highly automatized and do not require any control other than initiation and monitoring for feedback about their completion. A consequence of this would be that the executive is ignorant of the detailed levels of processing and free to initiate other, parallel processes. There is some evidence to suggest that highly practised arithmetical calculation becomes more like this than the scheme proposed by production systems. Thus the speed with which adults add pairs of digits suggests that they either perform child-like counting operations exceedingly rapidly or retrieve many of the answers as known facts from semantic memory (Parkman and Groen, 1971). This strongly suggests automatization of the lower-level operations.

The question of parallel processing during highly practised arithmetic has not been investigated, but suggestive evidence is available in the introspective accounts of Professor Aitken, the celebrated calculating prodigy (see Hunter, 1962). According to these accounts he was apparently able to carry out running checks on accuracy during the solution of complex calculations without experiencing any distraction from the extra processing involved. Whether this constituted parallel processing or rapid alternation between checking and calculating is of course impossible to tell on the basis of introspection alone. While it seems meaningful to differentiate between different levels of control in the particular skill of arithmetic, the question has not yet been fully explored by experiment. Finally, it must be observed that the general problem of control is one of considerable complexity (see, e.g., Broadbent, 1977), and the present discussion has touched on only one aspect of this important topic.

6   The place of STM in a total cognitive psychology

In the previous section we have argued that one of the functions of short-term memory mechanisms is to support the perception and production of spoken language. Over and above this the total system appears to function as a 'working memory' in activities like reading and performing arithmetic. We can extrapolate from these particular conclusions and make the further suggestion that the system acts as a working memory in *all* activities which require the temporary storage of symbolic information and the execution of control processes, such as learning, problem-solving, and routine skills like typing and writing (cf. Baddeley and Hitch, 1974). In order to capture the way in which the system is involved in activities such as these the concepts of input register, output buffer and central executive will require considerable elaboration. For example, we have observed that linguistic tasks involve the representation of information at many levels, from the distinctive feature to the proposition and beyond. How do these levels map onto short-term stores? Should the concept of a 'store' be abandoned? A second example is that of control processes. Is the same executive involved in all types of control (e.g., motor as well as verbal skills) and how can different levels of control be conceptualized? Is there a relationship between the central executive and selective attention? These are challenging questions, especially when contrasted with the questions that used to be asked about STM some years ago. Their solution ought to make for a more integrated approach to the problem of explaining human cognition. In the following sections we will comment on some of the links which relate the concept of a working memory to the other topics that are dealt with in this book.

6.1   *Working memory and perception*

In the case of perception the working memory system might be thought irrelevant. Clearly, nothing that we have said has implications for the way pattern-recognition operates at the earliest levels, such as analysing the spatial frequencies present in a visual stimulus or the phonemes in a speech signal. Nevertheless we have found it necessary to assume that analyses such as these can proceed largely in parallel and are largely unmodifiable by control processes. Hopefully the study of perception can contribute to a better understanding of the usefulness of these generalizations.

Short-term memory mechanisms may also have implications for the way perception is studied. In the case of language comprehension, for example, our analysis suggested that perception cannot be regarded as terminating at any clear point of reference within the cognitive system. Thus, while it may be useful to consider word recognition as the result of activation in lexical 'recognition units' or 'logogens' (cf. Morton, 1970), the comprehension of a prose passage cannot be conceptualized in such a general way. A complete model of perception will therefore include the contribution made by short-term memory mechanisms and will need to specify what these mechanisms are. There may also be an interesting methodological consequence of this proposition. In many perceptual tasks the observer is asked to make a judgment about a sensory attribute of a stimulus. It is often assumed that such judgments are directly based on the level of sensory representation appropriate to the task, so that analysis on the latencies for various types of judgment will enable the different stages of perceptual processing to be mapped out. In the case of phoneme monitoring experiments, however, we have seen that this is probably a false assumption. It is probably incorrect to assume that control processes can have direct access to early levels of sensory representation, and in many cases it may be necessary to conceptualize a process of recovery of information from subsequent levels of analysis. This general point is discussed by Marcel (in press).

6.2 *Working memory and attention*

Short-term memory has been given importance in the study of attention, from the very earliest days of work on selective listening (see, e.g., Broadbent, 1957). Indeed there are quite clear points of correspondence between this chapter and Alan Allport's (Chapter 4). We both find it necessary to assume parallel and automatic processes of pattern recognition to a fairly high level of analysis. Alan Allport suggests that such patterns can be at least as complex as individual words and their meanings; here I have suggested that the level extends to small groups of words in the case of a connected linguistic input. Although I have not referred specifically to the analysis of meaning, the arguments that Allport cites strongly suggest that the meanings of individual words exert their influence 'automatically', and the entailments of this conclusion certainly need to be incorporated in any development of the current approach. A point of apparent contrast between the chapters concerns the suggestion of a limited-capacity central executive (seen here as crucial to an account of dual-task performance), versus Allport's rejection of this view in favour of what he terms distributed processing. In a distributed processing system the only source of interaction between two concurrent activities arises when they compete for specific domains of processing rather than general-purpose resources.

However, the conflict turns out to be more apparent than real. In Allport's system the selection of an action is seen as depending on the activation of its characteristic 'calling-pattern', consisting of a set of external stimulus conditions (its 'CUE') and the specification of an internal parameter corresponding to the current 'GOAL'. In order to explain some aspects of dual-task performance it is postulated that there is a limitation on the number of GOALS that can be simultaneously activated. Since the goal-setting mechanism is clearly a general-purpose device, this assumption is actually isomorphic with the concept of a central executive. It is important to be clear that our use of the term 'general-purpose' here and throughout this chapter implies involvement in a wide range, if not all *tasks*, rather than involvement in all information processing *operations*. Thus despite differences of terminology and emphasis, the present approach to short-term memory shares some common features with Alan Allport's analysis of attention. Perhaps the most important distinction is that of emphasis. The aim here has been to identify some of the mechanisms that are common to a range of activities, rather than to emphasize the ways in which the activities call upon separate and independent mechanisms. Presumably, however, the clear relationship between the topics is a sign that they will both continue to develop in close connection with one another.

6.3   Working memory and long-term memory

As most theorists have appreciated, the relationship between short-term and long-term memory is of crucial importance in conceptualizing the nature of the memory system as a whole. Hopefully, however, it has been justifiable to concentrate here on the sub-problem of short-term memory without worrying too much about the detailed nature of long-term memory. In attempts to model the interaction between these different aspects of memory, two issues have traditionally arisen. First is the question of the connections between STM and LTM in the general flow of information processing. Second is the question of whether the short-term memory system should be thought of as a separate 'box-type' store (or stores), or as a set of currently activated nodes or locations in LTM.

A common assumption is that information must pass through a unitary short-term store in order to reach long-term storage (Atkinson and Shiffrin, 1971) or that the phonemic level of processing precedes the semantic level (Craik and Lockhart, 1972). A major problem for this view is that it fails to account for the disorder of memory described by Shallice and Warrington (1970) in which impairment in short-term retention is not associated with impairment to long-term retention. In terms of the approach here, the question of 'placing' the two systems in an information-flow diagram is meaningless, since STM is regarded as a working memory consisting of several separate systems and arguably the same is also true of LTM. Thus the pattern-recognition procedures prior to the input register correspond to one form of long-term memory, which, following Alan Allport's arguments about the processing of word-meanings, may be thought of as part of 'semantic memory'. The central executive must also have access to LTM since it can activate sets of learned procedures. In this case we might want to talk about a store of 'procedural knowledge' or a set of 'productions' (Newell and Simon, 1972), though Claxton, in Chapter 6, argues against the implicit distinction. In addition, the articulatory output buffer must also be closely connected to a further aspect of LTM, knowledge of articulatory programmes, which Harvey and Greer have discussed. Finally, we may also wish to postulate a further, episodic component of LTM whose 'place' in the present system must remain obscure.

The further issue of whether STM should be thought of as 'activated LTM' (Shiffrin, 1975) is probably best regarded as a notational one, given our present state of knowledge. However, the odds would seem to favour some form of LTM-activation, since the assumption of a working memory system containing a number of short-term storage mechanisms raises the important problem of conceptualizing how the system keeps track of where all the information is and how it is related, especially if traces of the same item are assumed to be in different sub-systems at the same time.

In sum, short-term and long-term memory are clearly closely related, but the suggestion that both systems consist of separable components considerably complicates the issues involved in spelling out their relationship; any simple answers will clearly not be sufficient.

6.4 Working memory and language processes

We have already discussed in some detail the suggestion that the proposed working memory system is part of the normal processes of comprehending and producing language. Indeed, given that language has been around much longer than the memory span and free recall, the *primary* function of temporary storage mechanisms may be their role in language processes. Barnard (in preparation), argues this case in some detail and presents a formal model which aims to account for short-term memory phenomena in terms of the operation of a system designed for understanding language.

6.5 Working memory and cross-cultural cognition

Since it has been argued that short-term memory mechanisms are an important component of many cognitive activities, it would be surprising if the basic mechanisms were not common to all cultures, especially since all groups make use of language. It would be equally surprising if there were not many aspects of the use of memory which *were* culture-specific. An interesting hypothesis which captures both suppositions is that control processes may be culturally determined, while memory structure is universal (Wagner, 1978). Wagner studied free recall in Moroccan children as a function of age, schooling and urbanization, and found that the recency effect was unaffected by cultural variables whereas recall of early list items was, lending support to his hypothesis. This type of work may exemplify a fruitful means of linking cross-cultural studies with traditional cognitive psychology.

6.6 Working memory and problem-solving

The limits on human problem-solving ability appear to have much to do with limitations on control processes and short-term storage over and above the particular nature of the procedural and factual knowledge required for any given problem. Interestingly, it is from an analysis of problem-solving behaviour that one of the most powerful general approaches to human information processing has developed, that of 'production systems' (Newell and Simon, 1972). As described in Section 5.4, a production system consists of a single short-term store interacting with a long-term store via a central processor. Using this approach it has proved possible to simulate behaviour in situations as varied as playing chess, solving cryptarithmetic problems and verifying sentences (Hunt and Poltrock, 1974; Newell and Simon, 1972).

The architecture of production systems bears a broad but not detailed resemblance to the structure we have proposed for working memory. One major difference is production systems' assumption of a single short-term store as opposed to working memory's separate components of input and output stores for verbal information and a further visuo-spatial system. A second difference is that most production system simulations require a much greater short-term storage capacity than can be reasonably inferred from experimental studies of short-term memory. A third is that production systems postulate a single serial processor involved in firing all productions whereas the central executive of working memory is not committed to seriality and is believed to be involved in only 'high-level' control processes. Nevertheless, the ability of production systems to simulate complex behaviour in a range of contexts provides at the very least a successful formal implementation of the general hypothesis that short-term memory mechanisms may serve as a general-purpose working memory. Perhaps a general 'theory of production systems' which compared different sets of storage and processing assumptions would provide a useful conceptual framework for many areas of cognitive psychology. It would certainly help in going from the present sketch of working memory towards a more rigorous model of the system.

6.7   *Working memory and action*

In the present treatment, the control of 'action', whether overt or covert, has been viewed as the function of the central executive. Such basic issues as how one set of processes gain dominance over others, and how control is exercised, remain to be tackled seriously in the current approach. It is not proposed to go into these complex issues here except to mention once again the importance of defining different 'levels' of control in relation to the concept of a central executive. Some discussion of the control of action is to be found in Chapters 3 and 4, and in Shallice (1972).

7 Conclusions

We began this chapter by suggesting that New Directions in cognitive psychology will consider ecological validity more seriously than in the past, and will search more actively for converging operations to identify common mechanisms across a range of situations. It was argued that this strategy should ensure a less fragmented, more integrative approach to the problem of modelling cognitive processes. We then temporarily put this dictum aside and considered the traditional memory literature to try and separate out the sub-systems involved in short-term recall. These sub-systems were regarded as the major components of a general-purpose working memory system. It was concluded that verbal information is stored in at least two locations, an input register and an articulatory output buffer. It was also suggested that there is a separate limited-capacity central processor and a further component corresponding to visual short-term memory. We then illustrated the type of approach which New Directions might follow by considering the use of these components of working memory in understanding and producing spoken language, reading and performing arithmetic. In each case it was possible to identify a sub-system serving a particular function. Thus the articulatory system was seen as serving the primary function of an output buffer for speech responses and the additional function of providing temporary storage in reading and arithmetic. The input buffer on the other hand was seen as being involved in the process of understanding language. One benefit of the process of assigning functions to sub-systems was to suggest further questions about the systems themselves, questions that would not immediately have arisen within the more restricted context of traditional research into short-term memory. Issues about the nature of control processes arose from considering arithmetical skill, while the analysis of language processing suggested how the nature of the verbal stores needs to be elaborated. Finally, some of the links between the working memory system and other cognitive processes were touched upon in a general way, and in some cases, such as the study of attentional processes, the links were found to be particularly strong.

The deficiencies of the approach are many, and, as the introduction pointed out, have much to do with the limited experimental techniques that are currently at our disposal, and the lack of a principled conceptual framework within which to conduct research. Nevertheless, I am persuaded that the attempt to isolate domains of processing and identify their function in both laboratory studies and everyday cognition is a worthwhile enterprise and encourages us to ask useful questions. I hope that the outcome of this effort will be moves toward a greater synthesis, in which the current fragmentation of topics in experimental psychology such as perception, memory, attention and psycholinguistics, will seem curiously old-fashioned.

Acknowledgment

I would like to thank Guy Claxton and Tim Shallice for their comments on earlier drafts of this chapter.

References

Aldridge, J. W. and Farrell, M. T. (1977), 'Long-term recency effects in free recall', *American Journal of Psychology, 90,* pp. 475-9.

Allport, D. A., Antonis, B. and Reynolds, P. (1972), 'On the division of attention: a disproof of the single-channel hypothesis', *Quarterly Journal of Experimental Psychology, 24,* pp. 225-35.

Anderson, C. M. B. and Craik, F. I. M. (1974), 'The effect of a concurrent task on recall from primary memory', *Journal of Verbal Learning and Verbal Behavior, 13,* pp. 107-13.

Atkinson, R. C. and Shiffrin, R. M. (1971), 'The control of short-term memory', *Scientific American, 225,* pp. 82-90.

Baddeley, A. D. (1966a), 'The influence of acoustic and semantic similarity on long-term memory for word sequences', *Quarterly Journal of Experimental Psychology, 18,* pp. 302-9.

Baddeley, A. D. (1966b), 'Short-term memory for word sequences as a function of acoustic, semantic and formal similarity', *Quarterly Journal of Experimental Psychology, 18,* pp. 362-5.

Baddeley, A. D. (1976), *The Psychology of Memory,* Harper and Row: New York.

Baddeley, A. D. (1978), 'The trouble with levels: a re-examination of Craik and Lockhart's framework for memory research', *Psychological Review, 85,* pp. 139-52.

Baddeley, A. D. (in press), 'Working memory and reading', in P. A. Kolers,

M. E. Wrolstad and H. Bouma (eds), *Proceedings of the Conference on the Processing of Visible Language,* Plenum: New York.

Baddeley, A. D. and Hitch, G. J. (1974), 'Working memory', in G. Bower, *The Psychology of Learning and Motivation,* vol. 8, Academic Press: New York.

Baddeley, A. D. and Hitch, G. J. (1977), 'Recency re-examined', in S. Dornic (ed.), *Attention and Performance, 6,* Academic Press: London.

Baddeley, A. D., Scott, D., Drynan, R. and Smith, J. C. (1969), 'Short-term memory and the limited capacity hypothesis', *British Journal of Psychology, 60,* pp. 51-5.

Baddeley, A. D., Thomson, N. and Buchanan, M. (1975), 'Word-length and the structure of short-term memory', *Journal of Verbal Learning and Verbal Behavior, 14,* pp. 575-89.

Barnard, P. J., 'Interacting cognitive subsystems: a psycholinguistic approach to short-term memory' (in preparation).

Bartz, W. H. and Salehi, M. (1970), 'Interference in short- and long-term memory', *Journal of Experimental Psychology, 84,* pp. 380-2.

Bjork, R. A. (1975), 'Short-term storage: the ordered output of a central processor', in F. Restle *et al.* (eds), *Cognitive Theory,* Lawrence Erlbaum: Hillsdale, N.J.

Bjork, R. A. and Whitten, W. B. (1974), 'Recency-sensitive retrieval processes in long-term free recall', *Cognitive Psychology, 2,* pp. 99-116.

Broadbent, D. E. (1957), 'A mechanical model for human attention and immediate memory', *Psychological Review, 64,* pp. 205-15.

Broadbent, D. E. (1971), *Decision and Stress,* Academic Press: London.

Broadbent, D. E. (1977), 'Levels, hierarchies and the locus of control', *Quarterly Journal of Experimental Psychology, 29,* pp. 181-201.

Bruce, D. and Crowley, J. J. (1970), 'Acoustic similarity effects in retrieval from secondary memory', *Journal of Verbal Learning and Verbal Behavior, 9,* pp. 190-6.

Clark, H. H. and Clark, E. V. (1977), *Psychology and Language: An Introduction to Psycholinguistics,* Harcourt, Brace, Jovanovich: New York.

Conrad, R. (1964), 'Acoustic confusions in immediate memory', *British Journal of Psychology, 55,* pp. 75-84.

Conrad, R. and Hull, A. J. (1964), 'Information, acoustic confusion and memory span', *British Journal of Psychology, 55,* pp. 429-32.

Craik, F. I. M. (1968a), 'Two components in free recall', *Journal of Verbal Learning and Verbal Behavior, 7,* pp. 996-1004.

Craik, F. I. M. (1968b), 'Types of error in free recall', *Psychonomic Science, 10,* pp. 353-4.

Craik, F. I. M. and Jacoby, L. L. (1975), 'A process view of short-term retention', in F. Restle *et al.* (eds), *Cognitive Theory,* vol. 1, Lawrence Erlbaum: Hillsdale, New Jersey.

Craik, F. I. M. and Lockhart, R. S. (1972), 'Levels of processing: a framework for memory research', *Journal of Verbal Learning and Verbal Behavior, 11,* pp. 671-84.

Craik, F. I. M. and Tulving, E. (1975), 'Depth of processing and the retention of words in episodic memory', *Journal of Experimental Psychology: General, 104,* pp. 268-94.

Craik, F. I. M. and Watkins, M. J. (1973), 'The role of rehearsal in short-term memory', *Journal of Verbal Learning and Verbal Behavior, 12,* pp. 599-607.

Crowder, R. G. (1976), *Principles of Learning and Memory,* Wiley: New York.

Dalezman, J. J. (1976), 'Effects of output order on immediate, delayed, and final recall performance', *Journal of Experimental Psychology: Human Learning and Memory, 2,* pp. 597-608.

Dansereau, D. F. and Gregg, L. W. (1966), 'An information processing analysis of mental multiplication', *Psychonomic Science, 6,* pp. 71-2.

Egeth, H. E., Pomerantz, J. R. and Schwarz, S. P. (1977), 'Is encoding really effortless?' Paper presented at the 18th Annual Meeting of the Psychonomic Society, Washington, D.C., November.

Ellis, A. W. (1979), 'Speech production and short-term memory', in J. Morton and J. C. Marshall (eds), *Psycholinguistics Series, vol. 2: Structures and Processes,* Elek Science Press: London.

Erdelyi, M. H. (1974), 'A new look at the new look: perceptual defense and vigilance', *Psychological Review, 81,* pp. 1-25.

Foulke, E. and Sticht, T. (1969), 'Review of research on the intelligibility and comprehension of accelerated speech', *Psychological Bulletin, 72,* pp. 50-62.

Fromkin, V. A. (1966), 'Some requirements for a model of performance', University of California at Los Angeles, *Working Papers in Phonetics, 4,* pp. 19-39.

Fromkin, V. (1971), 'The non-anomalous nature of anomalous utterances', *Language, 47,* pp. 27-52.

Glanzer, M. (1972), 'Storage mechanisms in recall', in G. H. Bower (ed.), *The Psychology of Learning and Motivation,* vol. 5, Academic Press: New York.

Glanzer, M. (1977), 'Commentary on "Storage mechanisms in recall",' in G. H. Bower (ed.), *Human Memory: Basic Processes,* Academic Press: New York.

Glanzer, M., Gianutsos, R. and Dubin, S. (1969), 'The removal of items from short-term storage', *Journal of Verbal Learning and Verbal Behaviour, 8,* pp. 435-47.

Glanzer, M., Kopenaal, L. and Nelson, R. (1972), 'Effects of relations between words on short-term storage and long-term storage', *Journal of Verbal Learning and Verbal Behavior, 11,* pp. 403-16.

Glanzer, M. and Razel, M. (1974), 'The size of the unit in short-term storage', *Journal of Verbal Learning and Verbal Behavior, 13,* pp. 114-31.

Hardyck, C. D. and Petrinovich, L. R. (1970), 'Subvocal speech and comprehension level as a function of difficulty level of reading material', *Journal of Verbal Learning and Verbal Behavior, 9,* pp. 647-52.

Hitch, G. J. (1978), 'The role of short-term working memory in mental arithmetic', *Cognitive Psychology, 10,* pp. 302-23.

Huey, E. D. (1968), *The Psychology and Pedagogy of Reading,* MIT Press, Cambridge, Mass. (originally 1908).

Hunt, E. B. and Poltrock, S. E. (1974), 'The mechanics of thought', in B. H. Kantowitz (ed.), *Human Information Processing: Tutorials in Performance and Cognition,* Wiley: New York.

Hunter, I. M. L. (1962), 'An exceptional talent for calculative thinking', *British Journal of Psychology, 53,* pp. 243-58.

Jarvella, R. J. (1970), 'Effects of syntax on running memory span for connected discourse', *Psychonomic Science, 19*, pp. 235-6.

Jarvella, R. J. and Herman, S. J. (1972), 'Clause structure of sentences and speech processing', *Perception and Psychophysics, 11*, pp. 381-4.

Kahneman, D. (1973), *Attention and Effort*, Prentice-Hall: Englewood Cliffs, N.J.

Kintsch, W. and Buschke, H. (1969), 'Homophones and synonyms in short-term memory', *Journal of Experimental Psychology, 80*, pp. 403-7.

Kleiman, G. M. (1975), 'Speech recoding in reading', *Journal of Verbal Learning and Verbal Behavior, 14*, pp. 323-39.

Lashley, K. S. (1951), 'The problem of serial order in bahavior', in L. A. Jeffress (ed.), *Cerebral Mechanisms in Behavior*, Wiley: New York.

Levy, B. A., (1971), 'The role of articulation in auditory and visual short-term memory', *Journal of Verbal Learning and Verbal Behavior, 10*, pp. 123-32.

Levy, B. A. (1978), 'Speech processing during reading', in A. M. Lesgold, J. W. Pellegrino, S. D. Fokkema and R. Glaser (eds), *Cognitive Psychology and Instruction*, Plenum: New York.

Levy, B. A. and Murdock, B. B., Jr. (1968), 'The effects of delayed auditory feedback and intralist similarity in short-term memory', *Journal of Verbal Learning and Verbal Behavior, 7*, pp. 887-894.

Logan, G. D. (1978), 'Attention in character-classification tasks: evidence for the automaticity of component stages', *Journal of Experimental Psychology: General, 107*, pp. 32-63.

McGuigan, F. J. (1970), 'Covert oral behavior during the silent performance of language tasks', *Psychological Bulletin, 74*, pp. 309-26.

Mackay, D. G. (1970), 'Spoonerisms and the structure of errors in the serial order of speech', *Neuropsychologia, 8*, pp. 323-50.

McLeod, P. (1977), 'A dual-task response modality effect: support for multiprocessor models of attention', *Quarterly Journal of Experimental Psychology, 29*, 651-67.

Marcel, A. J. (in press), 'Unconscious perception: the effects of visual masking on word processing', *Cognitive Psychology*.

Marslen-Wilson, W. D. (1973), 'Linguistic structure and speech shadowing at very short latencies', *Nature, 244*, pp. 522-3.

Miller, G. A. (1956), 'The magical number seven plus or minus two', *Psychological Review, 63*, pp. 81-97.

Morton, J. (1970), 'A functional model for memory', in D. A. Norman (ed.), *Models of Human Memory*, Academic Press: New York.

Morton, J. and Long, J. (1976), 'Effect of word transitional probability on phoneme identification', *Journal of Verbal Learning and Verbal Behavior, 15*, pp. 43-51.

Murdock, B. B., Jr. (1965), 'Effects of a subsidiary task on short-term memory', *British Journal of Psychology, 56*, pp. 413-19.

Murdock, B. B., Jr. (1967), 'Recent developments in short-term memory', *British Journal of Psychology, 58*, pp. 421-33.

Murray, D. J. (1968), 'Articulation and acoustic confusability in short-term memory', *Journal of Experimental Psychology, 78*, pp. 679-84.

Neisser, U. (1976), *Cognition and Reality: Principles and Implications of Cognitive Psychology*, Freeman: San Francisco.

Nelson, T. O. (1977), 'Repetition and depth of processing', *Journal of Verbal Learning and Verbal Behavior, 16*, pp. 151-72.

Newell, A. and Simon, H. A. (1972), *Human Problem Solving*, Prentice-Hall: Englewood Cliffs, N.J.

Norman, D. A. (1968), 'Toward a theory of memory and attention', *Psychological Review, 75*, 522-36.

Parkman, J. M. (1972), 'Temporal aspects of simple multiplication and comparison', *Journal of Experimental Psychology, 95*, pp. 437-44.

Parkman, J. M. and Groen, G. J. (1971), 'Temporal aspects of simple addition and comparison', *Journal of Experimental Psychology, 89*, pp. 335-42.

Phillips, W. A. (1974), 'On the distinction between sensory storage and short-term visual memory', *Perception and Psychophysics, 16*, pp. 283-90.

Phillips, W. A. Christie, D. F. M. (1977a), 'Components of visual memory', *Quarterly Journal of Experimental Psychology, 29*, pp. 117-33.

Phillips, W. A. and Christie, D. F. M. (1977b), 'Interference with visualization', *Quarterly Journal of Experimental Psychology, 29*, pp. 637-50.

Poltrock, S. E. and MacLeod, C. M. (1977), 'Primacy and recency in the continuous distractor paradigm', *Journal of Experimental Psychology: Human Learning and Memory, 3*, pp. 560-71.

Posner, M. I. (1969), 'Representational systems for storing information in memory', in G. A. Talland and N. C. Waugh (eds), *The Pathology of Memory*, Academic Press: New York.

Postman, L. and Phillips, L. W. (1965), 'Short-term temporal changes in free recall', *Quarterly Journal of Experimental Psychology, 17*, pp. 132-8.

Raser, G. A. (1972), 'Recoding of semantic and acoustic information in short-term memory', *Journal of Verbal Learning and Verbal Behavior, 11*, pp. 692-7.

Richardson, J. T. E. and Baddeley, A. D. (1975), 'The effect of articulatory suppression in free recall', *Journal of Verbal Learning and Verbal Behavior, 14*, pp. 623-9.

Roediger, H., Knight, J. and Kantowitz, B. (1977), 'Inferring decay in short-term memory: the issue of capacity', *Memory and Cognition, 5*, pp. 167-76.

Rundus, D. (1971), 'Analysis of rehearsal processes in free recall', *Journal of Experimental Psychology, 89*, pp. 63-77.

Saffran, E. M. and Marin, O. S. M. (1975), 'Immediate memory for word lists and sentences in a patient with deficient auditory short-term memory', *Brain and Language, 2*, pp. 420-33.

Shallice, T. (1972), 'Dual functions of consciousness', *Psychological Review, 79*, pp. 383-93.

Shallice, T. (1975), 'On the contents of primary memory', in P. M. A. Rabbitt and S. Dornic (eds), *Attention and Performance, 5*, Academic Press: London.

Shallice, T. and Butterworth, B. (1977), 'Short-term memory impairment and spontaneous speech', *Neuropsychologia, 13,* pp. 729-36.

Shallice, T. and Warrington, E. K. (1970), 'Independent functioning of verbal memory stores: a neuropsychological study', *Quarterly Journal of Experimental Psychology, 22,* pp. 261-73.

Shiffrin, R. M. (1975), 'Short-term store: the basis for a memory system', in F. Restle, R. M. Shiffrin, N. J. Castellan, H. R. Lindman and D. B. Pisoni (eds), *Cognitive Theory,* Lawrence Erlbaum: Hillsdale, N.J.

Shulman, H. G. (1970), 'Encoding and retention of semantic and phonemic information in short-term memory', *Journal of Verbal Learning and Verbal Behavior, 2,* 499-508.

Shulman, H. G. (1971), 'Similarity effects in short-term memory', *Psychological Bulletin, 75,* pp. 399-415.

Silverstein, C. and Glanzer, M. (1971), 'Concurrent task in free recall: differential effects of LTS and STS', *Psychonomic Science, 22,* pp. 367-8.

Sternberg, S. (1969), 'The discovery of processing stages: extensions of Donders' method', in W. G. Koster (ed.), *Attention and Performance, 2,* North Holland: Amsterdam.

Svenson, O., Hedenborg, M-L. and Lingman, L. (1976), 'On children's heuristics for solving simple additions', *Scandinavian Journal of Educational Research, 20,* pp. 161-73.

Treisman, A. M. (1965), 'The effects of redundancy and familiarity on translating and repeating back a foreign and a native language', *British Journal of Psychology, 56,* pp. 369-79.

Tulving, E. (1968), 'Theoretical issues in free recall', in T. R. Dixon and D. L. Horton (eds), *Verbal Behavior and General Behavior Theory,* Prentice-Hall: Englewood Cliffs, N.J.

Turvey, M. T. (1973), 'On peripheral and central processes in vision: inferences from an information-processing analysis of masking with patterned stimuli', *Psychological Review, 80,* pp. 1-52.

Tzeng, O. J. L. (1973), 'Positive recency effect in delayed free recall', *Journal of Verbal Learning and Verbal Behavior, 12,* pp. 436-9.

Wagner, D. A. (1978), 'Memories of Morocco: the influence of age, schooling and environment on memory', *Cognitive Psychology, 10,* pp. 1-28.

Warren, R. M. (1971), 'Identification times for phonemic components of graded complexity and for spelling of speech', *Perception and Psychophysics, 9,* pp. 358-61.

Warrington, E. K., Logue, V. and Pratt, R. T. C. (1971), 'The anatomical localization of auditory verbal short-term memory', *Neuropsychologia, 9,* pp. 377-87.

Watkins, M. J. (1972), 'Locus of the modality effect in free recall', *Journal of Verbal Learning and Verbal Behavior, 11,* pp. 644-8.

Waugh, N. C. and Norman, D. A. (1965), 'Primary memory', *Psychological Review, 72,* pp. 89-104.

Welford, A. T. (1968), *Fundamentals of Skill,* Methuen: London.

Whitten, W. B., II (1978), 'Output interference and long-term serial position effects', *Journal of Experimental Psychology: Human Learning and Memory, 4,* pp. 685-92.

Wickelgren, W. A. (1965), 'Short-term memory for phonemically similar lists', *American Journal of Psychology, 78,* 567-74.

Woodward, A. E. (1970), 'Continuity between serial memory and serial learning', *Journal of Experimental Psychology, 85,* pp. 90-4.

Woodward, A. E., Bjork, R. A. and Jongewaard, R. H., Jr. (1973), 'Recall and recognition as a function of primary rehearsal', *Journal of Verbal Learning and Verbal Behavior, 12,* pp. 608-17.

6 Remembering and understanding

Guy Claxton

1 Introduction

> RECOLLECT, *v.* To recall with additions something not
> previously known.
>
> Ambrose Bierce, *The Devil's Dictionary*

The study of memory is the most fundamental of the concerns of
cognitive psychology, for it attempts to elucidate the structures and
mechanisms on which all cognitive processes depend. Perception
looks at the way stored experience enables us to classify new sensations as examples of familiar concepts. Attention studies how aspects
of stimulus situations and contexts influence which parts of memory
will be selectively activated. Short-term memory investigates the
temporary maintenance of activation of long-term memory, and
temporal and capacity limitations of this activation. Problem-solving
looks at the lining-up of pre-existing knowledge in order to generate
answers to questions that are not immediately obvious. Cognitive
theories of action study the structure and operation of motor memories.
And so on.

Inasmuch as these areas are concerned at root with the way our
knowledge can be represented, extended and used, the whole of
cognition may be said to be the study of memory. What then is
'memory' as a separate topic about? Roughly, it is the study of
memory — as defined above — as manifest in, and therefore in-
ferrable from, two particular uses to which it can be put: remembering and understanding language. It is on these two functions that the
present chapter focusses – though we should note in passing that their

197

study gives no more privileged access to 'memory itself' than many other areas.

My intention is to identify an underlying drift in memory research and to extrapolate some possible new emphases therefrom, rather than to review the novel areas of experimentation in depth. 'Metamemory' (knowledge about one's own memory processes), memory for real-life events, the development of memory, and comprehension of text (which David Green looks at in the next chapter), to name just a few, are all currently hot potatoes. Yet it seems to me, while these diversifications are most welcome, that the conceptual drift in the way *all* these operations are understood is ultimately more important. For the current foci of hyperactivity, the reader is referred to Gruneberg, Morris and Sykes's interesting volume *Practical Aspects of Memory* (1978).

At the risk of spoiling a good story, I will give away the conclusions at the beginning. The framework that emerges is a 'two-power' one. Let me explain by analogy. To understand living tissue it helps to have a microscope on which you can vary the level of magnification. Low power is useful to help dissection, for it reveals boundaries and structures that seem solid and well-defined. It shows the 'overall picture'. Too much detail at this stage is a nuisance. But when one wishes to investigate the functional properties of the tissue, how it works, the fine detail becomes crucial. Boundaries that had seemed like walls become, under higher magnification, more vague. They are not impermeable barriers, fixed in time and space, but distributed concentrations of actions, sites of intense and continuous *inter*action and *trans*action between the two sides.

The same two complementary magnifications are necessary to dissect and understand memory performance. The low-power model (what I shall call the 'associative metaphor') is useful for describing relatively gross features of the memory system. The high-power model (the 'integrative metaphor') is necessary to reveal the micro-processes of memory function. The stagnant smell that still hangs over much memory research is due to the persistence with which theorists have tried to get the low-power model to do a high-power job, a job for which it is too crude and too limited by half. Even when the existence of high-power models is acknowledged, the usual reaction (as we shall see) is to try to test, empirically, which power is 'right': which is as misguided as to ask 'which is right, a mallet or a watch-maker's screwdriver?' Physics and biology have been at ease with complementarity for some time, but it remains a lesson to be learned by psychologists.

I shall proceed by outlining the associative and integrative metaphors, and then show how, and more importantly when and where, they apply. I start by contrasting them, and end by reconciling them.

2 The associative and the integrative metaphors

In this section I want to try to clarify some of the theoretical issues in memory research by describing a number of contrasts that can be made between different models. Although many of these contrasts are logically independent of each other, in practice sets of assumptions have tended to hang together, these groupings following more or less naturally from more fundamental, pre-theoretical attitudes. We may isolate two of these underlying prejudices. The first, already familiar from the earlier discussions by Alan Allport and myself, is that memory can be divided into general-purpose chunks, or stores, and that processes are stored to a great extent independently of the contents or materials to which they can be applied. The second is that the process of storing events in memory is one of creating associations between locations within these stores that do not produce any modifications of what is stored at these locations. When these two assumptions are taken together, they create what may be called the 'associative metaphor' for memory. Conversely, we may assume on the one hand that memory is *integrated* (i.e., there are no major structural or functional distinctions), and on the other that its function is very often *integrative*, that is that learning requires the integration and modification of what is stored, not just its interconnection. These latter assumptions seem to be emerging as guiding principles of the 'new direction' in memory research: taken together we might call them the 'integrative metaphor'.

The purpose in creating these two metaphors is not to show that one is new and right and the other old-fashioned and wrong. They are fictitious and sterotypical in the same way that 'traditional' and 'progressive' teachers are, for example. Most real teachers, and most real memory models, fall somewhere between the two poles. But if we do not make the mistake of trying to force a complex world to jump through a simple conceptual hoop, such stark contrasts *are* useful. It may help to sort out a tangle of string by gripping it firmly in two places and pulling it open — but the creation of this antagonism does not commit the unraveller to the belief that the tangle actually consists of two bits. I am using my metaphors with the same pragmatic attitude.

What then are the threads exposed by this tug? The associative metaphor rests on the postulation of some basic distinctions in storage, of which two are pre-eminent. The first is between what are now called 'declarative' and 'procedural knowledge': roughly, knowing that and knowing how, or in computer language, data-base and program-store. The former is the prototypical memory store which simply contains facts and associations in the way that a warehouse contains packages, or an aviary birds. Often represented as a large network, like a piled-up fishing net, this knowledge is passive: it cannot organize or activate itself in an intelligent or appropriate manner. This is the province of the active, programme-store, part of memory, which, like the storekeeper or the bird-fancier, operates on the declarative part in a purposeful way. The latter is *extrinsically manipulated* by the former.

If we deny the split between the programme-store and data-base, however, stored knowledge must be *intrinsically active:* it must be self-organizing, self-activating and self-directing. Its own structural and functional properties must be sufficient to determine how it works. As we shall see, a 'conceptual nervous system' provides just the right basis for such an integrated memory.

The second distinction that the associative metaphor has thrown up is that between *episodic* and *semantic* memory (Tulving, 1972). These tend to be seen as a further sub-division of declarative knowledge. Some of our knowledge is generalized, or conceptual, and therefore proactive. 'The formula for salt is NaCl' 'Thursday is early closing day in Fulham', 'Budapest is divided into Buda and Pest by the Danube' are facts about the world that may be useful to me in some future context. Likewise 'Anita takes two sugars' or 'Term ends on 14 December' are facts about *my* world that, although being of more personal, circumscribed relevance, still look to the future rather than the past. In contrast, 'Last night I went to see The Mighty Sparrow at the Rainbow with Max, and there was a bomb scare' refers to a record of past experience that does not as it stands signify anything about the future. I may deduce from this episodic memory the semantic fact (accurate or not) that 'The Rainbow is a dangerous place', but that involves an additional operation. While Tulving explicitly denied that he was proposing two separate stores, the seductive power of the associative metaphor led inevitably to experiments to see whether the distinction was 'real' or not (e.g., Shoben, *et al.*, 1978). We shall see that such attempts are misconceived, because to understand how sentences are recognized, verified or comprehended we have to go beyond the very distinction that these tasks are being used to demonstrate. In the integrative metaphor, some memories of the things we have learned remain attached to memories of when and where they were learned; others, either because they are inferences from a range of experience, or through the passage of time, do not have such a place in our autobiography. Things we know may be connected conceptually, or contextually, or both. But we do not have to make a cut down the middle and say 'these are episodic' and 'these are semantic'. Other authors have made suggestions similar to Tulving's, but in a way that is closer to the integrative spirit. Bruner (1969), for example, talks about memories 'with record' and 'without record'.

The two views lead to different methodological outlooks. Because in the associative metaphor 'content' and 'process' are separable, its concern has been with hypothetical general properties of structure and operation that are *content-free*. So the specific properties of stimuli can be largely ignored — they simply constitute 'items' or 'examples' — and the interest focusses on 'the' characteristics of processes like 'rehearsal', or stores like 'semantic memory'. The reality of a structural distinction between 'short-term memory' and 'long-term memory', for example, discussed by Graham Hitch, is itself only at issue within the associative metaphor. In the integrative metaphor, a general distinction between process and content is not made. We can say that every process is indissociable from a learned specification of the range of stimuli, contexts and tasks to which it is appropriate: what Allport called in Chapter 2 its 'condition'. The operation of the system is always *content-linked*. It follows that within the integrative view so-called 'strategies' are the primary object of investigation, while for the associative view they are secondary, and are often treated as something of a nuisance.

Let us now look at how the two metaphors see the micro-structure of the memory system: how do they represent individual word-meanings, or concepts? The associative metaphor views them as 'net-lets', small parts of the overall network. So to define 'zebra', for example, we might imagine a node labelled ZEBRA, with radiating from it, relational links to its defining properties, such as 'is an animal', 'like a horse', 'has stripes', 'can run fast', and so on (Collins and Quillian, 1969). Various other authors such as Rumelhart *et al.* (1972) and Anderson and Bower (1973) have proposed more sophisticated variants of this basic approach. The integrative approach appears on the surface to differ more in quantity than quality from this. Its image of a concept is that of a 'fuzzy set' of features: a useful term of Zadeh's (1965) that has been taken up by Labov (1974) and Rosch (1977), amongst others. It sees concepts as inherently fuzzy clusters of features and associations and not, as many of the associative models tend to imply, if they do not actually state it, well-defined. The essential indeterminacy of word meanings, while it may seem to be only a matter of emphasis, leads integrative theorists to a very different way of approaching language comprehension from that of their associative counterparts.

The difference comes into focus when we look at the way in which different concepts are connected to each other. Perhaps one of the most basic assumptions of the associative metaphor is that a compound event (a sentence) or idea (a proposition within semantic memory) can be construed as a collection of more elementary concepts that are not themselves altered by being members of this collection. The very representation of a sentence, for example, as a network of *associations* between ideas presupposes that the ideas themselves (be they objects, actions, locations or whatever) are immutable, atomic and bounded: every distinct sense of a word has a meaning that does not vary with its linguistic (or non-linguistic) environment. The process of understanding a sentence, therefore, is one of linking the concepts of a sentence together in ways that are permitted by the syntax – and possibly of elaborating by adding some extra associations as well.

The integrative view is quite different. The vast majority of our experiences, it says, are not collections but *gestalten:* a sentence cannot be reduced to 'A *and* B *and* C *and* D *and* . . .', because the meaning that we have to give to A, B, C and D is modified by the presence of the others. The basic connection is not an association (an 'and') but a relationship, which does not exist as something separate from the things related, but as modifications of their meanings. Concepts, though fuzzy in themselves, are sharpened and completed in different ways by the different scenarios in which they appear. So one central problem in explaining how we understand a sentence is to do with these processes of *integrating* and *modifying*. Not only does the integrative metaphor have to concern itself with specific contents: it is also *centrally* concerned with context, where the associative view tends to treat context-effects as *peripheral* and again, as something of a nuisance which obscure the (postulated) essential cleanliness and invariance of the mechanisms under study.

Another question concerns how knowledge is accessed, and events recalled. If one's view of memory is a divided one, it is natural to see the active part as somehow deciding what is required, and then searching and selecting within the passive part. This raises, as we shall see in detail in Section 4, further questions about how exactly the search is conducted and how the active search decides whether a candidate is or isn't the thing it is after. In the intrinsically active and self-directing memory of the integrative metaphor, however, the 'state' of the system at any moment (i.e., what parts are active, and what connections are available) determines how the activity will flow and change in the next moment. Active parts are constantly 'calling' or recruiting other parts to become active. Thus, if part of an event is reactivated by the presentation of retrieval cues and reminders, the rest of the event may be recruited, and we have the experience of remembering something.

A final corollary of these contrasts concerns the question of wherein lies the basic creativity of language. The associative focus is on its combinatorial nature: *syntax* allows us to generate and comprehend novel juxtapositions of ideas. The integrative metaphor leads to an interest in truly *semantic* forms of creativity such as metaphor itself—another issue that David Green takes up in the next chapter.

Models of the associative and integrative kinds

It will help to make subsequent discussions easier if we clothe the bones of these two sets of assumptions with a little flesh, so that we may breathe some life into them, and see how they respond when confronted with real data. The associative model is easier to outline, because it is more familiar. It contains a memory for facts and propositions (which may be divided into 'general' and 'autobiographical' components) and a set of strategies and processes for putting things in, taking things out, and re-jigging the contents of the store. The main job of the model is to register and recall language: text, sentences or lists of words. It does this by setting up associative

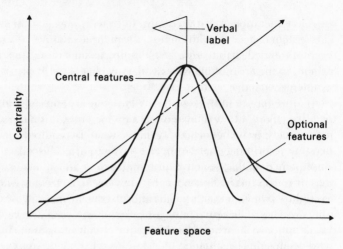

FIGURE 6.1   A conceptual mountain

structures that are 'tagged' for the recency and/or context of their occurrence. We shall meet several variants of this prototype in what follows.

An integrative model derives its inspiration more from biology than electronics, and therefore has an organic rather than technological air to it. In Hebb's (1949) theory of cell assemblies, for example, which is reappearing as the Godfather of such approaches, concepts and ideas are represented as more-or-less tightly bound aggregates of simpler features, what we called before 'fuzzy sets'. We can visualize the fuzziness better if we look at it in three dimensions (Figure 6.1) as a mountain with a flag at the summit. The flag bears the 'name' of the word, which is just a shorthand way of representing appropriate connections to the linguistic (e.g., articulatory) parts of the memory system. The mountain consists of all the features and ideas, many of them experiential rather than verbal, that are associated with the concept, or *diagnostic* of it. The ones at the summit are central to the meaning, those on the foothills are more loosely connected, or optional. Part of the mountain comprises dictionary features of the concept, that serve to describe and identify it, and to discriminate it from other, neighbouring mountains. And part is more encyclopaedic, connecting the concept to others with which it has been associated in experience.

These sets, or circuits, are connected one with another, through sub-sets of features that they share, to form a large central system. This system receives activation from the internal and external sensory receptors and distributes it, in an indirect and much transformed fashion, to the areas of motor control. Any part of the system may be completely inactive, it may be 'primed' (active at a sub-threshold level), or it may be fully active. Activity in one area tends to flow into the adjacent area that is most easily excited, or most highly primed. So the precise sequence of activity that a stimulus initiates depends on the state of priming of the system on which it falls. One particular consequence of this selective priming idea is worth noting in the present context. When a word occurs in context, some of its optional, less tightly bound, features will have been primed by the context, and others will not. The actual pattern of features that fires, therefore, will reflect not only the word, but the unique circumstances in which the word occurred. The situation modifies the meaning which is given to the word itself. The importance of this will appear in a minute.

The fundamental principle of learning is the establishment of a measure of facilitation between all the features that are concurrently active. Recall occurs when reactivation of a part of such a set leads to the recruitment of the whole, or at least of substantial other parts. This total feature set may then have to be broken down again – in verbal recall of a sentence, for example – into sub-sets that correspond to the words originally heard.

This will, I hope, be sufficient to give an idea of the ways in which the two clusters of assumptions lead to perspectives on memory that in some ways diverge quite radically. The rest of the chapter presents some areas of experimental and theoretical concern where they have both been applied, and tries to evaluate their relative suitability, and also some areas of study that each has generated in its own right. We shall see that many current issues and controversies stem from demonstrations of the importance of different kinds of context on memory; demonstrations that are problematic for the associative metaphor, but which are not only explained but required by the integrative approach.

3 Understanding sentences

Our words spoken to a listener are like the cryptic directions a playwright provides for a play director, from which a

competent director is expected to construct an entire setting,
an expressive mood, or an action sequence . . . What the
sentence does is merely mention a couple of signposts . . .
along the way; the listener interpolates or fills in all the
interstitial events between the mentioned signposts.
                                        Anderson and Bower, *Human Associative Memory*

Sentences: collections or Gestalts?

In the early days of psycholinguistics it was assumed that understanding a sentence was rather like constructing a model of a molecule
with one of those kits that we used to use in school chemistry. The
content words were the balls, of different sizes and colours, and the
syntax prescribed the way they should be fitted together. There were
also some semantic contraints on which balls could go together (e.g.,
Katz and Fodor, 1963). These rules and constraints might be difficult
to describe, but the process of comprehension was essentially
mechanical and regular (i.e. rule-governed). This bare associative
picture has been shown to be more and more inadequate by the
demonstration that, interacting with these basic processes, and often
overlapping them, or making them redundant, are other processes of
modification, integration and *elaboration*. Sentences in general are not
reduceable to collections, they are Gestalts.

A Gestalt, whether it be a picture, a sentence or whatever, is not
something mysterious. There is no magic property which emerges
when certain sets of components are put together. All that happens is
that the appearance or behaviour of some 'parts' is altered by the
presence of other 'parts'. This is the basic fact of *relationship* (Asch,
1969): when two things bear a relationship to each other, each is itself
modified by the relationship. The relationship is not something that
exists independently of two immutable parts, it exists precisely in the
mutation of each part by its partner. If 'Ian is the boyfriend of Alison'
the relationship between them alters one's understanding of each of
them. There are innumerable relationships that things may bear to
each other, all but one of which significantly alters the natures of the
'terms' of the relationship. This one special pseudo-relationship is
'and'. It is as near as we can get to a specification of pure co-existence
without mutual influence or modification. It is the overwhelmingly
preponderant relationship present in verbal learning experiments,

and it is largely because of this that this literature seems so specialized.

Some attempts have been made to test directly whether sentences are stored as Gestalts or as associative structures, with generally inconclusive results. Anderson and Bower (1971), for example, claimed to have demonstrated that sentences were associative structures, and went on to invest much effort (Anderson and Bower, 1973; Anderson, 1976) in describing these structures, despite the fact that they themselves (1972a) had produced evidence in favour of a Gestalt interpretation. In fact it seems to turn out that those tasks and materials that permit integrative processes (using plausible sentences like 'The doctor prescribed the medicine', and allowing recall of the gist) make sentences look as if they are Gestalts, while those that do not ('The doctor kissed the computer', and verbatim recall) favour the associative metaphor.

Modification

Consider the meaning of 'to eat', used as an example by R. C. Anderson and Ortony (1975), in the following sentence-contexts:

> Lord Raleigh ate the steak
> Lord Raleigh ate the apple
> Lord Raleigh ate the soup
> The tramp ate the soup
> The baby ate the steak
> The dog ate the steak

In every one of these, the action referred to is different: the contexts create different suppositions about the location, circumstances, manner, speed, instrumentality and antecedents and consequences of the action. The core of meaning is there — of putting food into one's mouth and swallowing — but the form that that action takes varies widely. Anderson and Ortony provide an empirical demonstration of this phenomenon. Subjects were shown sentences like 'The accountant pounded the stake' and 'The accountant pounded the desk', and their recall prompted with either the word 'hammer' or 'fist'. Although neither appeared in the original sentences, 'hammer' was an effective cue for the first sentence, and 'fist' for the second. They argue that an associative model like J. R. Anderson and Bower's HAM (1973) cannot account for this unsurprising result, nor can it be easily modified to do so.

We must accept, then, that the process of creating a memory representation for a sentence involves the creation of a novel structure that derives from, but is not reduceable to, the core meanings of the individual words that the stimulus contains. Comprehension is an activity more akin to problem-solving than to the simple establishment of links between well-defined words and meanings. Bransford and Franks (1976) for example, in an extremely thought-provoking paper, say:

> There does not seem to be any limit on the number of different contexts within which a given item (e.g., a word) can occur. Each of these different contexts can lead to differences in what is comprehended. Novelty is inherently involved in comprehending . . . Our use of novelty involves changes in the significance or meaning of individual elements, terms, relationships, etc., rather than the novel recombination of old information.

Integration

The fact that people tend to compile a composite representation of a sentence, from which some of the 'surface' information is lost, is now very well-established. Within a sentence Green (1975), for example, has shown that phrases like 'a large, heavy stone' tend to be integrated into a composite set of features that corresponds closely to the stored conceptual set for 'boulder': thus when asked to recall the sentence containing the original phrase, people tend to produce the word 'boulder' rather than the original, or to be slow at deciding that it was not shown. Likewise Bransford and Franks (1971) showed that a set of simple sentences, like 'The rock rolled down the hill', 'The rock was green', 'The house was at the bottom of the hill', 'The rock smashed the house' and so on, are integrated together, so that other sentences ('The green rock smashed the house') that can be drived from the integrated representation but which were not actually shown, tend to be falsely recognized. Where normal language processing habits can be applied, and especially where integration can occur within the experiential base of memory (see Section 5), these phenomena occur.

These qualifications are important. Some researchers have tried to 'cast doubt on' the notion of integration by showing that it doesn't happen with different stimuli, such as letters or numbers (e.g., Reitman and Bower, 1973). But here we have the makings of another sterile controversy, based on an ignorance of the fact that the performance you get always depends on what operations ('strategy') your particular stimuli have called. Results using any other stimuli than sentences can have nothing binding to say about how we understand sentences.

Another point may need clarifying. To claim that sentence comprehension involves integration is not to claim that other, more 'veridical', processes are not operating, nor to assert that people have no memory for the particular events that have occurred to them. To show, in a Bransford and Franks task, that people do have *some* memory for the actual sentences they saw does not refute the fact that integration occurs.

Elaboration

People also tend to flesh out their understanding of a sentence, quite unconsciously, with inferences, that are not required, not even strictly logical, but plausible. And the more 'natural' the stimuli you choose to show them, the greater the wealth of potential elaborations, and the more likely the phenomenon is to be observed. For example, from the sentence 'Three turtles sat on a log and a fish swam beneath them' it is plausible to infer the similar sentence 'Three turtles sat on a log and a fish swam beneath *it*'. It has been shown (Bransford *et al.*, 1972) that people do tend (falsely) to recognize the second sentence if they earlier saw the first. They elaborate the original representation, gratuitously and automatically, with the information that makes the second sentence true.

J. R. Anderson (1976) has tried to show how an associative model can account for elaboration by adding to the representation that the form and content of the sentence requires, additional and associated propositions that are already present in memory. But he gives the lie to this model of selection of elaborations rather the construction of them himself when discussing memory for paragraphs and stories.

'These units', he says, 'are novel and it is not going to be the case that a subject has these already represented in memory with a stock of potential elaborations stored with them. One needs some general procedures for elaboration which can apply to novel material.' And, once brought into existence, there is no reason why these general procedures should not apply to individual sentences, as well as to text.

Remembering stories

Lists of sentences fall somewhat ambiguously between lists of words on the one hand and text on the other, as psychological stimuli. Each individual sentence forms a Gestalt, and thus calls processes of integration. But the *list* of sentences usually is more of a collection, with each having little influence on the form of encoding of the others. Anderson (1976) reports some experiments investigating what he calls 'fan', which is the number of sentences that share a common elements, such as the verb. Not surprisingly, the choice of this rather superficial variable for linking sentences together leads to results that can be handled by an associative framework.

In stories, however, each sentence has to be understood within the context of what has gone before. Pronouns have to be 'cashed' correctly ('And then she said to him "He doesn't want it: you'd better take it over to her place in the High . . .".'). References to individuals have to be interpreted so that their characters develop in a consistent way. Ambiguous words are disambiguated ('So off they went to the bank . . .'). Overall expectancies, so-called 'frames', which suggest the general form of content and development of the story, are activated and guide the interpretation of new sentences. And so on. The existence of frames – to take just one of these – is illustrated by an experiment of R. C. Anderson and Pichert (1978). Subjects read a story from the perspective of either a house-buyer or a burglar, recalled what they could, and were then told to try to recall more from the other perspective. Giving a new frame provided alternative ways of accessing the story, and of decomposing composite representations into individual propositions: it therefore aided recall. In other circumstances, where the new perspective given at retrieval cannot activate a frame capable of recruiting the representation (as, for example, in Bransford and Johnson, 1973) then recall is not helped.

It is unfortunate that much of the current work on memory and comprehension of text, as well as sentences, takes an associative line, and misses these essential aspects of creativity, integration and problem-solving (Frederiksen, 1972; Mandler and Johnson, 1977; Thorndyke, 1977). The next chapter looks into the processing of text in greater detail.

Depth of processing

One context in which the idea of elaboration has often been used is that of the 'depth of processing' hypothesis (Craik and Lockhart, 1972), which suggests that the more deeply you process something the better you will retain it. The depth of processing research is exemplified by an experiment by Hyde and Jenkins (1973). Subjects studied lists of words and were asked to perform one of the following five tasks: rate the pleasantness of the word, rate its frequency of usage, check for occurrences of certain letters, indicate its part of speech, or decide if the word fits into either of the sentence frames 'It is ...' or 'It is the ...'. They found much higher recall, and much better organization of recall, in the first two tasks than in the other three. They argued, quite plausibly, that the first two tasks required a 'deeper' level of processing, and that this was responsible for the superiority in retention.

Unfortunately it is the very plausibility of the notion of depth, its intuitive appeal, that has got it into trouble, for it is one thing to appeal to the intuitions of a sympathetic audience, and another to provide any firm and explicit rationale for the idea in either theoretical or experimental terms. Without such a rationale, the only evidence for variations in depth of processing is variations in the success of memory, and it lacks any explanatory value.

Theoretical attempts to interpret depth rely on the idea of elaborateness, or richness, of encoding (e.g., Anderson, 1976; Craik and Tulving, 1975). Anderson, for example, suggests that 'rich elaboration is critical because it produces multiple redundant paths for recall. This redundancy makes it more difficult to lose the memory traces.' Within a model like Anderson's ACT it is possible to specify the degree of elaboration of a memory trace quite precisely, and so anchor one's memory predictions in a set of theoretical statements that are independent of any particular experimental result. However, Anderson himself notes the fact that his model as it stands predicts memory solely on the basis of the quantity, not the quality of the elaborations: 'It seems that the advantage of deeper processing does not just lie in the fact that it provides a more elaborate graph structure. There is something in the *semantic cohesion* of the elaboration that contributes to good memory' (my emphasis). Elaboration *per se* is not the ultimate predictor of memory, it is elaboration in the service of integration of parts of the memory trace with each other, with the memory system itself, and with the traces of likely retrieval routes. But as Baddeley (1978) has pointed out, to cash one vague notion ('depth') in terms of another ('cohesion') does not in itself provide a solution. We are back again to the problem that words and concepts are signposts, not bricks – the problem that poses the biggest challenge to the construction of constructive models of memory and comprehension.

In our integrative model, modification and elaboration are not just explicable, they are expected: the rule rather than the exception. The representation that a sentence is given is the total pattern of features that were simultaneously active when it was read or heard, and this pattern will be *based on, but not reduceable to* the content words of the sentence. If, for example, an association between A and B is very strong, or if the context primes B strongly, then the presentation of a 'sentence' A may recruit the 'elaboration' B automatically, and B will become incorporated in the representation of the event. Likewise if the occurrence of one concept A selectively primes some of the optional features of a second concept B, then the exact pattern that becomes active when B is presented will include those features primed by A, but not others. We shall see a clear example of this latter effect when we discuss the 'encoding specificity' principle.

Verifying statements

So far we have considered the operations that attend the reception of a 'new' sentence. But suppose one's task is not just to register the sentence, but to see whether it corresponds to a known fact about the world, a proposition within 'semantic memory'. Which of our metaphors applies best here?

The very influential paper by Collins and Quillian (1969), which I reviewed in detail in Chapter 1, did two things. It introduced into cognitive psychology the associative network as a general model of semantic memory, and it also introduced the *semantic judgment task* as an experimental method for investigating the structural and functional properties of this associative net. The task involved giving people questions about their general knowledge, like 'Is a robin a bird?', 'Can pigs fly?', or 'Does a walnut have a shell?', and measuring how long they took to answer. Immediately this type of task was picked up by other workers who began to find fault with the details of both Collins and Quillian's methodology (e.g., Conrad, 1972; Wilkins, 1971) and their interpretation (Landauer and Meyer, 1972). A more fundamental difference of opinion emerged about whether the associative net, in which word meanings were represented by single nodes, was the best conception of semantic memory, or whether one should rather see words as sets of features. In the latter case the evaluation of a question like 'Is a robin a bird?' would be performed not by finding a path within the network linking the two nodes 'robin' and 'bird' to each other, as Collins and Quillian had suggested, but by a matching of two simultaneously active patterns of features to see whether one ('robin') included all the features of the other ('bird') (Schaeffer and Wallace, 1969).

It is interesting to look at the history of this issue, for it parallels that of most big 'either/or' questions in cognitive psychology, such as serial versus parallel processing (Feigenbaum, 1963; Selfridge and Neisser, 1960), or active versus passive models of word recognition (Morton and Broadbent, 1967). The issue is not solved, or even resolved, but dissolved, or perhaps transcended. In 1970 the 'net' protagonists were Collins and Quillian and their 'set' adversaries were Schaeffer and Wallace. The ensuing ten years saw the network conception developed by Collins and Quillian themselves (1972), Rumelhart *et al.* (1972), Collins and Loftus (1975), and most spectacularly by J. R. Anderson (1976). In the opposite corner have collected R. C. Anderson and Ortony (1975), Bransford and Franks (1971), and Smith *et al.* (1974).

From the vantage point of 1980, however, we can see that these positions can be reconciled. To start with, both Hollan (1975) and Anderson (1976) have reminded us that the set/net question is not an empirically decidable one. Hollan's logic showed that any theory of one sort can be recast into the other form. Anderson argued that while particular 'strong' versions of the two approaches *can* be distinguished empirically, there are many versions of both associative-net and Gestalt-set models that lead to identical predictions.

Second, it is clear that while the original authors thought that their experiments were testing different models of memory *structure,* the results can equally well be seen as reflecting different *processes,* different methods of activating and using the same structure. The question that is being asked is not 'Is memory net or set?' but 'Is it better to treat memory *as if* it were nettish or settish?' And the answer that emerges is, of course, 'It depends'. Here is a clear case where different metaphors like net and set can be seen as complementary, and mutually reinforcing, rather than as contradictory. The data on semantic memory judgments are interesting because many of them are explicable in either net or set terms: they form a class of phenonema that fall within the range of convenience of both metaphors. This is in contrast to the data we have just considered on understanding new sentences, which seems to require the integrative view, and to the results of experiments using lists of isolated words, many of which, as we shall see in a moment, fit most snugly within the associative picture.

4   Remembering words

> *Socrates:* 'Let us now, as it were, frame in each man's soul a dovecote of all manner of birds, some in flocks apart from the others, and some in small detachments, and some flying about anywhere and everywhere by themselves . . .
>
> 'Now shall we not compare (learning and retrieval) with the possession and recapture of the doves, and say that there was a double chase; one before the acquisition, in order to acquire it, and the other after possession, for the purpose of having in his hand what was already long acquired? . . .
>
> '(But) it is possible for him to have in his hand not the knowledge of the thing he wants; but some other knowledge instead, if, when he is hunting up some particular knowledge from his stock, others fly in the way and he takes one by mistake for the other . . . having caught, as it were, a ringdove for a pigeon.'
>
> Plato, *Theaetetus*

The storage metaphor and its implications

Still the most prevalent metaphor for memory, one firmly within the associative tradition, is that of storage: we could call it the 'warehouse' or, to continue Platonically, the 'dovecote metaphor'. A measure of the tenacity of its hold on the field is that it is often not seen as a metaphor at all, but as obvious or common-sense, fact rather than speculation. It is what Bransford and Franks (1976) call a dead metaphor. The essence of this view is that memory is a store (like an aviary), or a set of stores, into which things (birds) are put. The metaphor suggests questions like: how are stimuli (the incoming birds) placed in the store; what characteristics of the birds are relevant to their storage; what are the principles of organization of the aviary itself; how are the birds retrieved subsequently; how are specifications of the kind of bird to be recaptured used? The mass of studies on the recall and recognition of lists of familiar words that was carried out in the 1960s and early 1970s relied extensively on this metaphor to generate both experimental questions and hypothetical answers. One preoccupation, for example, was with the general principles of organization that characterized 'the store'. How is the mental depository arranged so that groups of related items can be encoded and retrieved with maximum ease? Thus we had Underwood's influential 1969 paper 'Attributes of Memory', in which he identified what seemed to be the major organizational dimensions that had been uncovered by research on verbal memory: time, space, frequency, modality, orthography, and verbal and non-verbal associations.

The process of encoding novel stimuli in this view simply involved examining them for the presence of attributes that matched storage dimensions, so that they could be shunted to, and deposited in, the appropriate places. Recognition involved being shown the same stimulus, extracting the same 'storage specification', and looking to see whether there was indeed something stored at that address. Recall was like recognition except that you were given not an exact address but some clues as to the whereabouts of the required items. You had to define, using some of these clues, the search space, and then search methodically through all the things stored within that space for those that satisfied the criteria for what was wanted. The operation was rather like an Air-Sea Rescue, with a target area being mapped out, and planes dispatched equipped with a description of the missing boat to search for it. Those aspects of the boat – like its last reported position – that could be used to delimit the search, were used to do so. Those that could not – like the number of funnels – were given to the pilots to aid their decision about any particular boat they came across. Or, to return to Plato, you may know that the bird you want is in a certain compartment, but then you have to catch the birds one by one and examine each more closely to see if it is exactly the one you require.

One presupposition of this model, that took some time to bring to light, and question, is that the typical verbal memory task requires a subject to store and retrieve novel, distinct stimuli that have never been seen before. This is not an accurate assumption, however. What is usually required of subjects in such a task is not the storage of new stimuli, but registration of the fact that a certain type of stimulus has been presented in a certain context. If I ask you to remember the words 'cat', 'picture', 'tea', 'blue', 'tinder', 'fun', what you are required to do is not remember the words – you know them perfectly well already – but to remember that those words have occurred in this situation. When I later ask you to recall 'those' words, it is only your memory of the context that enables you to tell which words 'those' are. Thus we need in the memory store both semantic information about what the contents are, and episodic, or what has been called 'occurrence information'; that is, some record of when and where particular words, for example, have been experienced. You are not buying new birds, but ringing some of the existing ones.

Strength

Two general methods for recording occurrences of examples of known concepts or words have been proposed. Usually they have been discussed as alternatives, though some recent models, as we shall see, accept the idea that they may be complementary. In the first type of model, we might imagine that words are inscribed in the head on little brass plates, which shine with a brightness that diminishes as the length of time since they were last polished increases. Every time a word is perceived – every time that plate is retrieved – it is given a quick polish. Thus the brightness of the plate is a cumulative index of the frequency and recency with which that word has been presented. This index, whose official name is the 'strength' or the 'familiarity' of the memory trace of that word, can be used to decide whether the word has been perceived sufficiently recently to count as one of those 'on the list'. The subject sets a criterion, saying, 'If I am presented

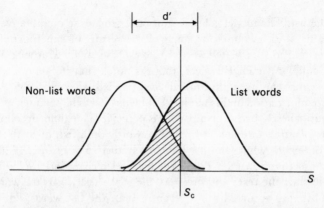

FIGURE 6.2   The signal detection model of recognition

with a word whose strength is greater than so much, then I shall say I have seen it recently. If it is less, I shall say I have not seen it recently: it was not one of the words on the list.' This decision process has been developed within the context of signal detection theory (Green and Swets, 1966) by authors such as Murdock (e.g., 1976) to a high level of mathematical sophistication. Conceptually the theory is simple. It assumes that the words on the list have had their strengths incremented, so that they are on average higher than for words not presented. However, there is some variability in the strength of both list and non-list words, so that we can conceive of two, possibly overlapping, distributions of strength, as in Figure 6.2. The subject's task is to set some criterion value, say S_c, of the strength that maximizes his chances of making a correct decision about any test item. The two important variables are S_c and the distance apart of the two distributions, a quality that has come to be called, for reasons now obscured by time, d' ('d primed'). By suitable mathematical juggling we can predict, given values of S_c and d', not only the probability of correctly deciding that a test word was or was not on the previously studied list, but also the relative likelihoods of the two kinds of error depicted by the hatched and solid areas in Figure 6.2 The hatched area represents those words that were on the list but whose strength values fall below the criterion: i.e., those list words that the subject fails to recognize. The solid area represents the proportion of non-list words that happen to have strength values higher than S_c, so that they are falsely recognized as having been on the list. The model is an elegant one, generating quantitative predictions, and accounts for some of the results of experiments on the recognition of isolated words quite well (see again Murdock, 1976, for a fuller review). However, there is much that it cannot cope with, because the strength/familiarity notion is such a crude one. There is no information in this model about what else is happening, or has just happened, when a certain word is perceived. It cannot account for the association of one word to other words on a list, or to the general context in which the list is being studied. For example, suppose a subject is shown a list of words for later recognition, then told 'Now we start the test', and given as one of the test words the word 'test'. This has occurred more recently than the list words, so its plate should be brighter, and it should be falsely recognized as one of the list words. It isn't (Anderson and Bower, 1972b). Clearly subjects can use another kind of occurrence information, a kind that identifies list words *as* list words, and thus discriminates them from other words, both less recent and more recent.

Contextual associations

Models that propose this second kind of information come in a variety of forms, but they all assume that when a word occurs its representation in memory becomes associated with other parts of memory which represent aspects of the spatial and temporal context in which the occurrence takes place. The two most important aspects of this context are the other words on the list, and the general features of the situation like the room in which the experiment is conducted, and 'internal' aspects of the subject, like how he is sitting, whether he feels hungry, and so on. The simplest versions of this approach assume that when a word occurs it has a label tied on to it that says 'This word was on List 1', or something like that. Recognition is then accomplished not by comparing its familiarity or strength with that of other words, but by checking its associations to see whether one of them corresponds to the appropriate label. Recall can be performed in one of two ways. Either a candidate word is located on the basis of some non-contextual clues (as in the Air-Sea Rescue model) and the list-tag is sought in the same way as for recognition. Or alternatively the word can be accessed from the list-tag, in which case it is, by definition, one of the words to be recalled. This is most likely to occur in so-called 'free' or

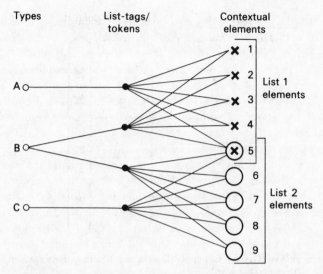

FIGURE 6.3 The relation between types, tokens and contextual elements for a situation in which A and B are members of one list, and B and C are members of a second (after Anderson and Bower, 1972b)

unprompted recall, where the clues for recall are the ambient, extra-list features of the situation that persist until, or are reactivated at, the moment of recall.

Perhaps the best model of this sort is that of Anderson and Bower (1972b), which they put forward in the same article in which they attack and try to eliminate all models of the strength sort. Their scheme is shown in Figure 6.3. Word A is a member of a list whose presentation is accompanied by the contextual features 1-5 which are present during the whole list. Thus A becomes associated, via a list-tag or 'token', with elements 1, 2, 3, 4 and 5. Likewise B, a member of the same list, becomes linked with the same elements. Now imagine B presented again in a later list, List 2. Here a new tag links B with a different (but partially overlapping) set of contextual elements 5, 6, 7, 8 and 9. And C, a member only of the second list, also becomes attached to 5, 6, 7, 8 and 9. Note that on this view the two occurrences of B can be kept separate – the subject can potentially recall or recognize B, with confidence, as having been a member of both lists – whereas in the strength models the two occurrences add together, serving only to increment a single index, so that more subtle

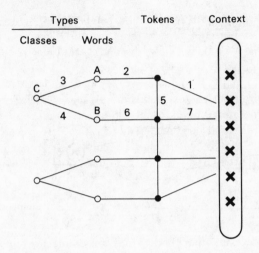

FIGURE 6.4   Conceptual, serial and contextual associations
between list words

information about places and times of occurrence is lost. Both
experimental data, such as that of Anderson and Bower themselves,
and common sense (we can, after all answer questions like 'What
were you doing the Christmas *before last?*') attest to the need for this
kind of contextually-based occurrence information.

Serial and conceptual associations

We can elaborate the model in Figure 6.3 to incorporate two other
kinds of associative information, serial and conceptual, which are
particularly important in recall tasks. The elaboration is shown in
Figure 6.4. The problem in recall, as we have said, is to find a path in
the memory network that links a specified context with a set of words.
This can either be performed directly, or indirectly. In Figure 6.4,
imagine that A has been retrieved by the activation of the direct
contextual pathway comprising associations 1 and 2. There are now
three ways of finding B. First, A and B may share a common conceptual link, C, such as a class of which they are both members. If A
and B are 'cat' and 'tiger', then C might be 'feline'. These associations
antedate the presentation of the list, being part of 'conceptual' or
'semantic' memory. B can be retrieved as a candidate for list member-

ship, therefore, via the path 3, 4. It must then be tested, by the same methods discussed in the context of recognition (see especially Atkinson and Juola's model, below). Second, the list may have been learned wholly or partly in serial sequences, so that A leads to B via the path 2, 5, 6. Finally, B could be retrieved independently of A via the direct path from the context elements 7, 6. This simple scheme is sufficient to generate accounts of most free and serial recall tasks where the words used are not 'redintegrative' (Horowitz and Prytulak, 1969); that is, where they cannot be integrated into a Gestalt; where they can be associated, but do not modify each other.

Composite models

It may be, however, that both kinds of occurrence information – both strength and associations – are necessary for a full account of how occurrence decisions are made. Some results are difficult to explain if we assume that 'items are recognized by retrieving certain kinds of contextual information originally stored along with the item in question' (Anderson and Bower, 1972b), and *only* in that way. For instance, Morton (1968) has demonstrated that judgments of recency can be confused by repeating items. If you present subjects with a string of digits like 3-7-5-4-*2*-9-*2*-*8*-6, and then enquire whether 8 or 2 was presented most recently there is a tendency to answer '2' mistakenly. A likely explanation is that two presentations of an earlier item can produce a cumulative strength that is greater than that produced by a single presentation of a later item. In this task all the digits occur in virtually identical extra-list contexts, so contextual associations will not help. Neither can the subject create any meaningful and integrated associative structure for the string of digits themselves. They are randomly arranged, and arriving too fast. So the cumulative strength value is the only available source of information, and that leads the subject into error. This explanation suggests that if the 'items' in the string could be built easily into an integrated representational structure, then this could be used as a basis for the recency judgment, and the confusion would disappear. I am unlikely to judge falsely 'the' more recent than 'girl' after hearing the equivalent sequence '*The*-boy-hit-*the-girl*-hard'.

One current model explicitly combines both strength and contextual-associative information in a two-stage model of recognition.

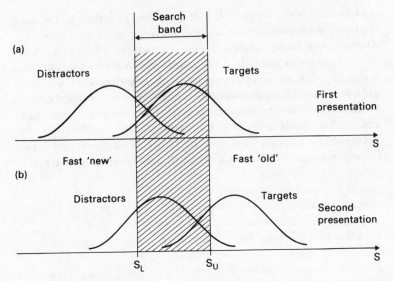

FIGURE 6.5   Atkinson and Juloa's (1973) model for long-term recognition memory

Its application is again to the recognition of lists of unconnected words in long-term memory. Atkinson and Juola (1973) start by postulating a strength index, and distributions of the strength for both words that were and were not studied on the list, with the mean of the former distribution being higher than the mean of the latter. So far, just like Murdock. But instead of a single criterion, Atkinson and Juola propose two: an upper one, S_U, above which the likelihood of falsely recognizing a new, 'distractor' word as having been on the list is negligible; and a lower one, S_L, below which the likelihood of erroneously failing to recognize a word that was on the list is likewise negligible (see Figure 6.5). If the strength value of a test word falls above S_U, the subject can rapidly and confidently respond, 'Yes, it was on the list', and if it falls below S_L, he can quickly respond, 'No, it wasn't on the list'. If the test item's strength is between S_L and S_U, there is a significant chance that, if he responds solely on the basis of strength, he will be wrong. In this case, it is suggested that subjects perform a lengthier, but ultimately less equivocal, search for an appropriate contextual association.

Atkinson and Juola present a number of predictions that follow from this picture, and experiments to test them. To give just one as an illustration: because decisions based purely on strength are faster than those in which associative information is used, it follows that mean reaction time will be a function of the proportion of items that fall within the 'search band'; that is, with strength values between S_L and S_U. Consider what will happen if both list words and distractor words are repeated within the test session. On their first presentation their strength distributions will be as in Figure 6.5a. On the second presentation, both distributions will have been shifted up the strength axis somewhat, because the previous test presentation will have increased the strength, as in Figure 6.5b. The effect of this, as you can see, is to lower the proportions of list to distractor words within the search band, and so to decrease the mean reaction time to list words, and increase it to distractors. The predicted phenomenon was observed by Atkinson and Juola.

The integrative view

If the integrative metaphor is a more highly magnified version of the associative metaphor, containing detail that the latter cannot represent, it must also be capable of reducing to an associative picture if we 'pan back' – just as Einstein's theory of relativity includes Newtonian mechanics, and reduces to it when certain simplifying assumptions are made. We can see quite readily that the forming of associations can be represented as the creation of facilitation between originally separate sets of features, so that activation of one set recruits, or tends to recruit, the other. Hebb (1949) has shown how 'cell assemblies' become associated into 'phase sequences', and his neuro-logic remains persuasive. But is there a way of making sense of strength as well?

There is such a way. Many models of perceptual identification (e.g., Morton and Broadbent, 1967) assume that the 'perception' of an object is subserved by the activation, or firing, of some unit or feature set in memory that corresponds to the long-term representation of the concept of which the object is being perceived as an example. These sets have a firing threshold and a resting level of activity, and the stimulus information increases the activity within the set until the threshold is exceeded and it fires off. The amount of information needed to fire a set is determined by the disparity between the *a priori* level of activity, and the threshold, which we might call its 'excitability'. The more excitable the set, the less sensory information is required to exceed the threshold, and the quicker it fires. Most theories of this sort assume that the excitability of a set depends on the frequency and recency with which it has been activated. Thus both excitability and strength are cumulative indices of occurrence, the former determining the speed of perception, the latter the speed and success of recognition memory. Could they not be the same? I do not see why they should not be combined into a single dimension that does both jobs. The implications of this are interesting and easily tested. For example, we can now see that recognition memory, when it uses this index and by-passes associative information, might be an inference from speed of perception. Words are recognized as having been on the list because they are identified faster. This assumption would seem to fit well with a two-stage model such as Atkinson and Juola's, in which excitability can sometimes be used as a rapid source of information which can by-pass the lengthier process of retrieving contextual associations. 'Strength' is no longer a dubious idea conjured up to do a rather narrow job: it is a by-product of a basic characteristic of perceptual recognition. It is conceived of not as a type of information appended to, or stored with, a concept, but as a process-characteristic of it. The use of this characteristic as a memory aid will be part of a person's 'meta-memory': that is, his knowledge about the way his own cognitive systems function.

This proposal, incidentally, provides an explanation for the perennially puzzling *déjà vu* phenomenon. The feeling of having witnessed an event before is a 'recognition memory' judgment, and could therefore be produced by the fact that the event has been perceived (for reasons that it would be interesting to explore) faster than one normally processes events of that kind. Comfort (1977) has suggested a somewhat similar explanation.

Integrative effects in word memory

Although the usual stimuli in verbal learning experiments do their best to disallow integrative processes, in fact even the most random list of words will spark off some relationships, associations and amplifications. It is as impossible to exclude relationships between items in a series as it is to make them meaningless. Trying to simplify experiments by banishing meanings (by using so-called 'nonsense syllables' like *gon* or *pov*) or relationships is like trying to legislate against prostitution: you may not approve of it, but all a ban does is to push it underground, and make its incidence and effects more difficult to assess. It does not make it go away.

This 'effort after meaning', as Sir Frederic Bartlett called it, operates quite involuntarily, although its effectiveness can be increased, in some circumstances, by instruction. The involuntary search for ways of making sense out of apparent nonsense was clearly shown by Prytulak (1971), who found that the ease with which people could remember a nonsense syllable was accurately predicted by the number of transformations that had to be applied to it to turn it into a 'natural language mediator', a familiar word, phrase, set of initials, etc. Thus *gon* is easily transformed into 'gone', while *pov* requires more complex and idiosyncratic transformation: it is therefore remembered much less well.

Meaning inheres not only in words but in collections of words, in their relationships, in the way they interact with and modify each other. In normal processes of language comprehension the integra-tion of the individual word-meanings proceeds smoothly and auto-matically. With less familiar stimuli, such as pairs or lists of nouns, either memory fails or special tricks such as the use of mnemonics or imagery have to be employed, analogous to the use of natural language mediators for single items. Instruction in both imagery and mnemonics is well-known to be highly effective in improving memory for not-readily-integrable material (Bower, 1972), but they work in slightly different ways. Imagine that the three words 'window', 'carrot', 'nurse' have to be remembered. An *imagery* solution constructs a superordinate context which coheres, and thereby associates, the three words. Starting with the three 'core' meanings, they are elaborated until a scenario emerges, in which, for example, Bugs Bunny is seen diving out of an upper-storey window into a garden, impaling himself (in one way or another) on a giant carrot, and being ministered to by a beautiful rabbit nurse. Provided the whole incident can be retrieved later, it can fairly readily be decomposed into the original components. A *mnemonic* solution provides integration to a number of isolated items not through an emergent scenario, but via the attachment of the items to an already learned sequence. In one famous mnemonic system called the 'orator's walk' (Yates, 1966) one learns a string of ideas by taking a mental stroll through a well-known building and placing the ideas, or symbols for them, at strategic points. Thus one might first construct a front door that had a fancy window in it, then find an umbrella stand with a long thin carrot in it in the hall, go on to see an accident and lots of nurses in the living room, and so on. In other systems the framework is provided by a well-learned list of rhymes such as 'one is a bun, two is a shoe, three is a tree . . .' and individual images or associations produced to link window and bun, carrot and shoe, and nurse and tree. It is now generally accepted that these *aides memoires* work by reducing the retrieval difficulty. A little extra work during learning, and the increased complexity of the memory trace, are small prices to pay for a record that, once found, can be readily broken down or followed, to reveal all the necessary information.

Two further experiments illustrate the necessity for considering processes of integration – and conversely of decomposition – even with non-sentential materials. The first, by Tulving and Thompson (1973) demonstrates the problem of retrieving a composite feature set; the second, by myself (Claxton, 1972) shows that even when retrieved such a composite may be difficult to decompose into its original constituents. In Tulving and Thompson's study subjects first saw a list of pairs of words, such as 'train-black', one of which ('black') was the word that would later have to be recalled, and the other ('train') a cue word that would be provided to assist recall of the first. Before the recall test, however, the subjects were given words like 'white' and asked to write down some free associations. These words were chosen so that the to-be-remembered word was very likely to be produced. They were then asked to look through their free association responses to see if they could recognize any of the to-be-remembered words. Finally the cue words were provided, and the anticipated recall of the to-be-remembered words required. The result, which is so robust that it even survives the strong test of replication in a student laboratory class, is that, while final recall in the context of the cue words is quite good (about 60 per cent), subjects' ability to recognize the to-be-remembered words in the different context of the word association task is strikingly bad, in some demonstrations as low as 10 to 15 per cent. What it appears they are doing is constructing a composite representation that can be recruited by the presentation of the expected cue word in the expected context, but which cannot be recruited by the target word when presented in the context of a different task.

In the second example – my own study – subjects were shown adjective-noun phrases, to which they were asked to give free association responses and were later required to recall the adjective given the noun. The phrases differed in the degree of conceptual relatedness of the adjective and noun. In *hi* pairs, such as 'sweet sugar' or striped tiger', the adjective itself formed part of the concept to which the noun referred. In *mid* pairs, like 'spilt sugar' or 'hungry tiger', the relationship was sensible, but not part of the definition of the noun. In two other conditions, *lo* and *nons*, the relationship was unlikely ('blue sugar', 'painted tiger') or nonsensical ('biased sugar', 'countersunk tiger'). On the simple associative model these pairs are remembered by creating, or tagging, a link between them. When given the noun prompt its associations are searched and recognized on the basis of occurrence information of some sort. Pairs like 'striped tiger' should be well remembered, because strong links already exist. On the integrative view, however, encoding requires activation of the feature sets corresponding to the two words, and their integration into one composite set that is in turn linked with features of the spatio-temporal context. At retrieval, this composite set must be recruited by the noun cue and then decomposed again into those features that correspond to the noun, and those that will identify the adjective. Memory failure may result from a failure either to create this feature set, or to locate it during the test, or to decompose it into the appropriate constituents. This latter source of difficulty is not present in the associative models, and it leads to a prediction of relative difficulty for the *hi* stimuli. The composite representation for 'striped tiger' is the same as the basic feature set for 'tiger': thus when the 'tiger' set is taken away, nothing is left to indicate what the adjective should be. This is what the data showed: *hi* pairs are less well recalled than *mid* pairs, which are the best remembered of all.

5   The upshot

Let me summarize the main conclusions of this survey, and then try to draw out some implications for the 'new directions' in memory research.

1   What I have called the associative and integrative metaphors represent low- and high-power specifications of the contents of memory. The former seems to suggest several distinctions that dissolve

under the closer scrutiny of the latter. For some purposes the associative view is adequate and economical. For others it is inadequate and clumsy. It may be able to contort itself to produce an explanation for some integrative phenomena, but the effort produces more problems than it solves (Claxton, 1978).

2   The situations where the associative metaphor is sufficient are rather different from those of everyday perception, comprehension and retrieval: they contain collections of words or objects that do not readily integrate with each other, and task demands, like lack of time or practice, that effectively prevent the emergence of integration. Normally events form Gestalts within which the presence of each object alters the perceived nature and significance of other objects. To such events the integrative metaphor is the more applicable.

3   Many of the developments of memory research in the last decade serve to emphasize the importance and ubiquity of integration. The depth of processing line shows that some tasks require more integrative processing than others. Research on mnemonics and imagery shows that instructions – particularly instructions to activate the experiential referents of words – promote integration. The 'encoding specificity' work of Tulving and his collaborators show that even impoverished materials like word-pairs can be rigged so that integration is required.

Where, then, is the study of memory going? We do not, I think, need to spend any more time simply demonstrating the existence of experiential, integrational and contextual effects. These demonstrations were necessary to loosen the grip of the associative tradition, but they would not come as much surprise to Herb Simon's character T. C. Mits (The Common Man in the Street). What does need to be done is to sharpen the focus on our higher-powered perspective. Because the integrative metaphor requires notions of fuzziness and probability, it does not mean that the theoretical approach itself is necessarily vague. The ability to produce precise formulations of intrinsic vagueness seems to be a symptom of this trend in the physical and biological sciences – Heisenberg's principle of uncertainty being perhaps the best known. It may be so in the human sciences as well, and in the next decade of memory research we should find out.

Beginnings have been made, although I have barely been able to hint at them in this chapter. Barbara Hayes-Roth (1977) has produced a model that has many integrative features, and fragments of a similar approach have appeared elsewhere. Smith *et al.* (1974) have suggested a distinction between 'characteristic' and 'defining' features of concepts that is a way of recognizing their fuzziness. The research of Meyer (e.g., Meyer and Schvaneveldt, 1976), which shows that recognition of a word is facilitated by the prior recognition of an associated word – the 'associative priming' effect – has been interpreted in terms of an active network system that routes activity from one location to another, without the help of any external control processes. Tulving (1976) has revived the idea that retrieval from memory need not reflect a recursive and implicit search-and-decision process – he points out that there is no *direct* evidence for this decision stage – but rests on the recruitment of a record by current reactivation of a part of it. Whether memory succeeds depends on whether the retrieval context is sufficient to reactivate the appropriate trace. This conforms better with our own experience of memory: only rarely are we aware of reviewing a list of candidates for the thing we want. Usually it either just 'pops into our heads', or it doesn't.

The declarative/procedural distinction has also come under fire, even from within its home ground of Artificial Intelligence. Thus we have Allen Newell (quoted in Anderson, 1976) saying:

> The wrong way to conceive of (memory) is with the Production System as the active net-interpreter and with the semantic net as an associative data structure. The right way is that the production system is the associative structure itself.

And Newell and Simon (1972) go on to suggest: 'If this were the case, the act of taking a new item into long-term memory would be equivalent to creating a new production (or productions).' Elsewhere (Claxton, 1978) I have examined the arguments for and against the procedural/declarative distinction and concluded that it is indeed unnecessary and hinders progress in understanding memory by creating a number of spurious and unhelpful questions, such as how do we decide to assign any particular piece of knowledge to one form or the other? 'Canaries are yellow' is certainly part of my declarative knowledge, but equally it refers to one of the procedures whereby I am able to recognize canaries.

The problem is that declarative and procedural knowledge are not basically different types of knowledge; they are different aspects of the same knowledge. They refer not to different stores but to different questions we can ask about what we know, that are, again, complementary ones. We can ask about *structure*, which, as we have seen, leads at the micro level to the fuzzy sets of features idea. Or we can ask about *function*, which tends to lead to answers couched in programme, or procedure, or 'production system' metaphors. But to say that these different views imply different types of knowledge is like saying that the fact that we can describe a knife either in terms of its structure or its function implies that there are two types of knife: one that is long and thin with a handle and a blade, and another for cutting things.

The same general point applies to Tulving's distinction between *semantic* and *episodic* memory (1972). Aside from the fact that there are many specific objections to Tulving's formulation of the distinction (see, e.g., Baddeley, 1976), he makes the same error as J. R. Anderson, in assuming that because people can make judgments about knowledge, these judgments directly reflect basic principles of storage. Once such a distinction is proposed, research energy becomes focussed on deciding whether the distinction is or isn't 'real', and on creating difficult test cases to embarrass its proponents. The fate of other chimerical distinctions like 'short-term' *v.* 'long-term' memory should make us wary of indulging in this misguided brand of psychologizing – one that we might call, in honour of Sir Frederic Bartlett, whose conduct in this regard was exemplary, 'The War of the Ghosts'. As Baddeley has remarked (1978): 'The most fruitful way to extend our understanding of human memory is not to search for broader generalizations and "principles", but is rather to develop ways of separating out and analysing more deeply the complex underlying processes.'

To conclude with a long-term hope, perhaps the greatest general advantage of the integrative metaphor is that it opens the way for a mature theory of *human* learning, that is neither derived second-hand from the study of animals, nor obsessed with the conscious, verbal, deliberate aspects of human cognition. Even if we restrict our attention to learning that happens through language, there is much more to be considered than simply understanding. Some things we hear or read have great 'significance' or 'impact' or 'meaning' for us; others do not. And these notions must refer to the intimacy of contact that such statements achieve with non-verbal, or better sub-verbal, aspects of ourselves that are not represented within the linguistic plane of knowing. There is much more to knowing than knowing about, much more to learning than learning about. The integrative, high-powered approach to memory may be a step towards a rapprochement of cognition with its lost complements of emotion, motivation, and ultimately, action.

Much of our knowledge is derived intuitively from our dealings with the world: it is inferred from our own immediate experience, and becomes automatically built in to the processes that subserve our perception, thought, feeling and action. This experiential knowledge is largely *non-verbal* and non-verbalizable, and also *tacit* in the sense that it is not directly available to conscious awareness. We can see its products – thoughts, acts or whatever – but not the processes whereby those products are produced. Jonathan Evans demonstrates in Chapter 8 the importance of this point in the context of reasoning and problem-solving. Most adults are fluent speakers of a language, but (unless they are linguists or psycholinguists) almost totally unaware of the processes that control their speech. It is to experiential knowledge that the integrative metaphor applies most naturally. It is the metaphor, as we saw before, of cell assemblies and 'mountains', rather than of flags.

The associative metaphor, however, arose from, and is primarily applied to, research on verbal material. We have seen that lists of words, the most widely used form of material in memory research, suggest an associative approach precisely because the normal operations of integration and modification cannot be applied. In addition, many of the words that can be used in such a task refer to objects or actions that have not been encountered by the learner, so that he has no readily available experiential currency that he can use to cash them. Many of the verbal concepts that we are taught remain defined only by other words. Eventually a chain of verbal 'associations' can lead to an image of the concept, but it may be hard to retrieve and then only an inadequate instantiation of its meaning. Try to form a visual image of 'independence' or 'morality', for example.

Let me make it clear what I am saying, and what I am not. I am not proposing two boxes, two stores, labelled 'Verbal Memory' and 'Experiential Memory', nor the allied process distinction between verbal coding and experiential coding which has been repeatedly propounded by Paivio (1971) and others. This would be heresy within the terms I have laid down for myself. My image of the relationship is more like that of Figure 6.6, where a verbal surface and an experiential surface possess many connnections within and

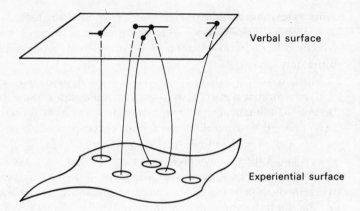

FIGURE 6.6 An interactive representation of two aspects of memory

between each other, but between which the mapping is incomplete, so that each level may contain concepts, processes and principles of organization that are not represented at all, or are distorted, in the other level. The degree of interrelationship depends crucially on the particular concepts or words one is using: in some places the levels may reflect each other very closely, while in others they may indeed *appear* to be separate stores. My suspicion, in brief, is that the associative metaphor and integrative metaphor apply best to the verbal and experiential surfaces respectively; and that when a verbal task activates only verbal connections and operations, memory will appear to be associative; when it penetrates to and activates experiential referents it will appear integrative; and where it does both, the metaphor will appear mixed.

References

Anderson, J. R. (1976), *Language, Memory and Thought,* Lawrence Erlbaum: Hillsdale, N.J.

Anderson, J. R. and Bower, G. H. (1971), 'On an associative trace for sentence memory', *Journal of Verbal Learning and Verbal Behavior, 10,* pp. 673-80.

Anderson, J. R. and Bower, G. H. (1972a), 'Configural properties in sentence memory', *Journal of Verbal Learning and Verbal Behavior, 11,* pp. 594-605.

Anderson, J. R. and Bower, G. H. (1972b), 'Recognition and retrieval processes in free recall', *Psychological Review, 79,* pp. 97-123.

Anderson, J. R. and Bower, G. H. (1973), *Human Associative Memory*, Winston: Washington, D.C.

Anderson, R. C. and Ortony, A. (1975), 'On putting apples into bottles: a problem in polysemy', *Cognitive Psychology, 7*, pp. 167-180.

Anderson, R. C. and Pichert, J. W. (1978), 'Recall of previously unrecallable information following a shift in perspective', *Journal of Verbal Learning and Verbal Behavior, 17*, pp. 1-12.

Asch, S. (1969), 'A reformulation of the problem of associations', *American Psychologist, 24*, pp. 92-102.

Atkinson, R. C. and Juola, J. (1973), 'Factors influencing speed and accuracy of word recognition', in S. Kornblum (ed.), *Attention and Performance, 4*, Academic Press: New York.

Baddeley, A. D. (1976), *The Psychology of Human Memory*. Harper & Row: London.

Baddeley, A. D. (1978), 'The trouble with levels: a re-examination of Craik and Lockhart's framework for memory research', *Psychological Review, 85*, pp. 139-52.

Bower, G. H. (1972), 'Mental imagery and associative learning', in L. W. Gregg (ed.), *Cognition in Learning and Memory*, Wiley: New York.

Bransford, J. D., Barclay, J. R. and Franks, J. J. (1972), 'Sentence memory: a constructive versus interpretive approach', *Cognitive Psychology, 3*, pp. 193-209.

Bransford, J. D. and Franks, J. J. (1971), 'The abstraction of linguistic ideas', *Cognitive Psychology, 2*, pp. 331-50.

Bransford, J. D. and Franks, J. J. (1976), 'Towards a framework for understanding learning', in G. H. Bower (ed.) *The Psychology of Learning and Motivation*, vol. 10, Academic Press: New York.

Bransford, J. D. and Johnson, M. K. (1973), 'Consideration of some problems of comprehension', in W. G. Chase (ed.), *Visual Information Processing*, Academic Press: New York.

Bruner, J. S. (1969), 'Modalities of memory', in G. A. Talland and N. C. Waugh (eds), *Pathology of Memory*, Academic Press: New York.

Claxton, G. L. (1972), 'Lexical and topical memory', paper delivered to the Experimental Psychology Society, Newcastle-upon-Tyne.

Claxton, G. L. (1978), 'Special review feature: Memory research', *British Journal of Psychology, 69*, pp. 513-20.

Collins, A. M. and Loftus, E. F. (1975), 'A spreading-activation theory of semantic memory', *Psychological Review, 82*, pp. 407-28.

Collins, A. M. and Quillian, M. R. (1969), 'Retrieval time from semantic memory', *Journal of Verbal Learning and Verbal Behavior, 8*, pp. 240-7.

Collins, A. M. and Quillian, M. R. (1972), 'How to make a language user', in E. Tulving and W. Donaldson (eds), *Organization of Memory*, Academic Press: New York.

Comfort, A. (1977), 'Homuncular identity-sense as a déjà-vu phenomenon', *British Journal of Medical Psychology, 50*, pp. 313-16.

Conrad, C. (1972), 'Cognitive economy in semantic memory', *Journal of Experimental Psychology, 92*, pp. 149-54.

Craik, F. I. M. and Lockhart, R. S. (1972), 'Levels of processing: a framework for memory research', *Journal of Verbal Learning and Verbal Behavior, 11*, pp. 671-84.

Craik, F. I. M. and Tulving, E. (1975), 'Depth of processing and the retention of words in episodic memory', *Journal of Experimental Psychology, 104*, pp. 268-94.

Feigenbaum, E. A. (1963), 'The simulation of verbal learning behavior', in E. A. Feigenbaum and J. Feldman (eds), *Computers and Thought*, McGraw-Hill: New York.

Frederiksen, C. H. (1972), 'Effects of task-induced cognitive operations on comprehension and memory processes', in J. B. Carroll and R. O. Freedle (eds), *Language Comprehension and the Acquisition of Knowledge*, Winston: Washington, D.C.

Green, D. M. and Swets, J. A. (1966), *Signal Detection Theory and Psychophysics*, Wiley: New York.

Green, D. W. (1975), 'The effects of task on the representation of sentences', *Journal of Verbal Learning and Verbal Behavior, 14*, pp. 275-83.

Gruneberg, M., Morris, P. and Sykes, R. (1978), *Practical Aspects of Memory*, Academic Press: London.

Hayes-Roth, B. (1977), 'Evolution of cognitive structures and processes', *Psychological Review, 84*, pp. 260-78.

Hebb, D. O. (1949), *The Organization of Behavior*, Wiley: New York.

Hollan, J. D. (1975), 'Features and semantic memory: set-theoretic or network model', *Psychological Review, 82*, pp. 154-5.

Horowitz, L. M. and Prytulak, L. S. (1969), 'Redintergrative memory', *Psychological Review, 76*, pp. 519-31.

Hyde, T. S. and Jenkins, J. J. (1973), 'Recall for words as a function of semantic, graphic and syntactic orienting tasks', *Journal of Verbal Learning and Verbal Behavior, 12, 3*, pp. 471-80.

Katz, J. J. and Fodor, J. A. (1963), 'The structure of a semantic theory', *Language, 39*, pp. 170-210.

Kelly, G. A. (1955), *The Psychology of Personal Constructs*, vol. 1, Norton: New York.

Kintsch, W. (1974), *The Representation of Meaning in Memory*, Lawrence Erlbaum: Potomac, Md.

Labov, W. (1974), 'The boundaries of words and their meanings', in C. J. Bailey and R. Shuy (eds), *New Ways of Analysing Variation in English*, Georgetown University Press: Washington, D.C.

Landauer, T. K. and Meyer, D. E. (1972), 'Category size and semantic memory retrieval', *Journal of Verbal Learning and Verbal Behavior, 11*, pp. 539-47.

Mandler, J. M. and Johnson, N. S. (1977), 'Remembrance of things parsed: story structure and recall', *Cognitive Psychology, 9*, pp. 111-51.

Marr, D. (1970), 'A theory of cerebral new-cortex', *Proceedings of the Royal Society, B, 176*, pp. 161-234.

Marr, D. (1971), 'Simple memory: a theory of archicortex', *Philosophical Transactions of the Royal Society, B, 262*, pp. 23-81.

Meyer, D. E. and Schvaneveldt, R. E. (1976), 'Meaning, memory structure, and mental processes', in C. N. Cofer (ed.), *The Structure of Human Memory*, Freeman: San Francisco.

Morton, J. (1968), 'Repeated items and decay in memory', *Psychonomic Science, 10*, pp. 219-20.

Morton, J. and Broadbent, D. E. (1967), 'Passive versus active recognition models, or is your homunculus really necessary?' in W. Wathen-Dunn (ed.), *Models for the Perception of Speech and Visual Form*, MIT Press: Cambridge, Mass.

Murdock, B. B. Jr. (1976), 'Methodology in the study of human memory', in W. K. Estes (ed.), *Handbook of Learning and Cognitive Processes, vol. 4: Attention and Memory*, Lawrence Erlbaum: Hillsdale, N.J.

Newell, A. and Simon, H. A. (1972), *Human Problem Solving*, Prentice-Hall Englewood Cliffs, N.J.

Paivio, A. (1971), *Imagery and Verbal Processes*, Holt, Rinehart & Winston: New York.

Prytulak, L. S. (1971), 'Natural language mediation', *Cognitive Psychology, 2*, pp. 1-56.

Reitman, J. S. and Bower, G. H. (1973), 'Storage and later recognition of exemplars of concepts', *Cognitive Psychology, 4*, pp. 194-206.

Rosch, E. (1977), 'Human categorization', in N. Warren (ed.), *Studies in Cross-Cultural Psychology*, Academic Press: New York.

Rumelhart, D. E., Lindsay, P. H. and Norman, D. A. (1972), 'A process model for long-term memory', in E. Tulving and W. Donaldson (eds), *Organization of Memory*, Academic Press: New York.

Schaeffer, B. and Wallace, R. (1969), 'Semantic similarity and the comparison of word meanings', *Journal of Experimental Psychology, 82*, pp. 343-6.

Selfridge, O. G. and Neisser, U. (1960), 'Pattern recognition by machine', *Scientific American, 203*, pp. 60-8.

Shoben, E. J., Wescourt, K. T. and Smith E. E. (1978), 'Sentence verification, sentence recognition and the semantic-episodic distinction', *Journal of Experimental Psychology: Human Learning and Memory, 4*, pp. 304-17.

Smith, E. E., Shoben, E. J., and Rips, L. J. (1974), 'Structure and process in semantic memory: a feature model for semantic decisions', *Psychological Review, 81*, pp.214-41.

Thorndyke, P. W. (1977), 'Cognitive structures in comprehension and memory of narrative discourse', *Cognitive Psychology, 9*, 77-110.

Tulving, E. (1972), 'Episodic and semantic memory', in E. Tulving and W. Donaldson (eds), *Organization of Memory*, Academic Press: New York.

Tulving, E. (1976), 'Ecphoric processes in recall and recognition', in J. Brown (ed.), *Recall and Recognition*, Wiley: London.

Tulving, E. and Thompson, D. M. (1973), 'Encoding specificity and retrieval processes in episodic memory', *Psychological Review, 80*, pp. 352-73.

Underwood, B. J. (1969), 'Attributes of memory', *Psychological Review, 76*, pp. 539-73.

Wilkins, A. J. (1971), 'Conjoint frequency, category size and categorization time', *Journal of Verbal Learning and Verbal Behavior, 10*, pp. 382-5.

Yates, F. (1966), *The Art of Memory*, RKP; University of Chicago Press.

Zadeh, L. A. (1965), 'Fuzzy sets', *Information and Control, 8*, pp. 338-53.

7 Psycholinguistics: cognitive aspects of human communication

David W. Green

Introduction

How do we understand and make ourselves understood? In everyday life we are faced constantly with a variety of communicational tasks ranging from reading notices and advertisements to giving directions to strangers. Some we solve fluently, others cause us to pause and consider. In using language as our medium of communication, whether as the source of messages for others, or as the receiver of messages from others, we are engaged in a form of personal action – communicative action.

Such actions can take many forms. We can speak or write, listen or read. More generally, we can produce messages (either as speakers, or writers) or we can receive them (either as listeners, or readers). Common to both activities is the process of relating sense to expression, which is the fundamental concern in this essay. However, in order to begin we need to talk concretely. As a start let us look at some aspects of reading.

Reading as communication

Take reading a page in a book. To a non-reader it might appear as a spatial array consisting of a series of black marks on a white ground. As readers, we perceive a series of printed words, graphemic signs, arranged in lines. As we move our eyes across the page meaningfulness increases: mysteriously the page begins to 'talk' to us, to communicate. It is not the page itself that talks, of course, but ourselves as the receivers of the message that treat the page as a message source out there. For us, the page is meaning arrayed spatially. What is involved in this amazing process through which we inform, persuade, and project ourselves?

It is evident that as readers we have to recognize the meanings of the graphemic signs before us, taking account of the sequence of letters comprising them ('not' as a sign does not equal 'ton'). We have then to organize these meanings according to the syntax of the sentences (the meaning of 'A boy kissed a girl' is not the same as the meaning of 'A boy is kissed by a girl'). We have to relate the meanings of successive sentences to derive their meaning in context. ('There it is' has a different sense preceded by 'Where's the book?' from 'Where's the planet?'). And there is more that we do. In order to grasp the sense of a page, we have to have some conception of what kind of text it is a part of. We read a page of a detective story differently from the way we read a page in a recipe book. In the first case we are involved in puzzling out 'who dun it'. The message or text is constructed to be potentially misleading, and as readers we are aware of this type of construction. In fact, our enjoyment derives from willingly entering into this construction. In the case of a cooking recipe, however, we anticipate that the procedures described to prepare a particular dish will in fact, if we carry them out, lead to *risotto* rather than to *boeuf bourgignon*. Our reading is guided by our conception of the text. And is that the end of it? No, it is not. For we read for many reasons, and our reasons also affect our activity. If we read simply to find a certain item of information or to derive a general impression, we read a page to detect certain kinds of meaning and do not dwell on others. If, on the other hand, we are interested in reading the page as part of a story or a novel, we are more concerned with the sense as a whole. Psychologically speaking, the nature of the receptive process depends on the aims of the receiver as well as on the nature of the material.

Accordingly it seems best to view the process not as a single inevitable sequence that is run off automatically, but as an activity comprising a number of interrelated processes that are organized to meet certain demands. Undoubtedly there are automatic aspects to it, but these aspects derive their meaning from the whole. Experiments on reading, and on communicative activity in general, are best seen as studies of adaptive organization. We shall treat this notion as one of the themes in the present examination of the field. The principal focus in what follows will be the immediate processing of sentences and texts.

The interpretation of sentences

Our understanding of sentence interpretation (the meanings of sign sequences) has developed on the basis of applying two interrelated analogies: one based on linguistic theory, transformational grammar; and the second, on the practice of computer programming. The first analogy was deployed because there were no alternatives within psychology itself, since the available mediation and conditioning theories had been shown to be defunct as possible candidates (Fodor, 1965). The second has been deployed to remedy certain deficiencies in the linguistic analogy as a psychological account.

Linguistic theory as an analogy of process

Essentially, transformational grammar is a theory of language as a product, rather than an account of language as a process. In our lives language presents itself to us in both aspects. It is a product for us in the sense that as children we have to acquire it and it is a process for us in the sense that we act in terms of it. Yet there are no logical grounds for assuming that a theory of product is directly relevant to a theory of process. We can describe the rules of chess without such a description informing us about the cognitive processes of playing chess. In the case of language the difference is more extreme, for we can speak and understand without knowing anything at all in an explicit sense about the rules governing the combination of words or sentences. We may act in conformity with rules, but there is no necessity that such rules play a part in explaining our activity (cf. Jonckheere, 1966, p. 85). But when did logic alone prevent human activity? We don't have wings but this doesn't stop us from flying. The theory offered an embracing conception of language. Although it idealized and tore language from its social context, the creative aspects of language seemed to have some place in it. It offered, not an associationist conception of man which at the time had acquired negative connotations, but man as grammatical machine that could generate a potentially infinite number of expressions with finite means. It proved formative not only in this area but also in language acquisition and other fields entirely, such as machine translation. Within psycholinguistics it offered a structure for thought. What was the theory this analogy was based on?

Outline of transformational grammar

The first point to make about transformational grammar is that it was developed through the method of systematic observation. Linguistics is an empirical science too. Although we cannot reconstruct the thought processes involved we can note some of the steps on the way. It is clear that the sound of a sentence depends on the order of its words and their arrangements into phrases and clauses – its surface structure. (In the sentence 'Before leaving, switch off all lights', 'all lights' is a phrase or constituent of the clause 'switch off all lights'.) At first sight it might seem that the ordering of words is sufficient for us to derive the meaning of a sentence. But as Chomsky (1965) noted, surface structure by itself is insufficient, for there are some sentences with distinct surface structures that are nonetheless related in meaning, such as the active and passive versions of a sentence (e.g., 'The man kissed the woman'; 'The woman was kissed by the man'), and other sentences with unique surface structures that can yield distinct interpretations such as 'I had a book stolen'. This led Chomsky to propose that sentences have both a surface structure and a deep structure. The triple ambiguity of 'I had a book stolen' (cf. Chomsky, 1965) arises because its surface structure is compatible with three alternative deep structures: that someone stole a book from me; that I incited someone to steal a book for me; and that I attempted to steal a book myself.

The deep structure captures the logical or functional relations amongst the words in a sentence in terms of such notions as subject and object. It is related to the surface structure by a series of transformations that permute and delete its elements. By postulating this structure the theory reveals unity in diversity. The active and passive versions of a sentence are similar in meaning because they derive from a common deep structure, bar the presence in the deep structure of the passive sentence of a symbol (or marker) specifying that a passive transformation is applicable. It has a further merit. It proposes that sentences with complex structures are derived (or generated) from a number of separate deep structure clauses. A sentence such as 'Invisible god made the visible world', for instance (see Chomsky, 1966), is derived transformationally from three such structures, corresponding to: god made the world; god is invisible; the world is visible. Transformational grammar offers a way, therefore, of describing the patterning of multiple ideas into unitary expressions. Is there any wonder that it exerted such a fascination for colleagues in the neighbouring discipline of psycholinguistics? The deep structure was held to specify all the syntactic information necessary to allow a sentence to be correctly interpreted. This information is utilized by a final semantic component that amalgamates the meanings of individual words (strictly, morphemes). A theory of word meaning was also developed (Katz and Fodor, 1963) in which the meanings of words were composed of various semantic features. For instance, the meanings of words such as 'woman', 'cat', 'man' and 'tiger' may be differentiated in terms of various combinations of the features animate, human, female and domestic. The theory has undergone change and modification as it faced new problems, but we must leave these changes on one side and proceed to its application within psychology (see Bresnan, 1978; Smith, 1979).

Applications of the analogy

Given this concept, what are the psychological implications of it? The relationship between expression and meaning is revealed to be complex rather than direct. Taken literally, the implication is that interpreting a sentence involves extracting its surface structure (identifying its constituents) and deriving its deep structure by unravelling the transformations that lead to it. Reception appears as the mirror-image of production and sense as derivative upon syntax.

The first problem facing researchers was to find suitable tasks and material to investigate the 'reality' of this description. Out of the enormous amount of productive activity expended in the search to test the description we illustrate one cycle of experimental formulation and reformulation.

Suppose we do organize the words of sentences into phrases and clauses according to surface structure, then extraneous information might be apprehended with respect to these units, rather than with respect to the words themselves.

Fodor and Bever (1965) seemed to observe exactly this phenomenon. When listeners were asked to locate the presence of a brief noise burst or 'click' relative to a speech stream, they tended to shift the click away (→) from its objective position (*) to a point between the boundaries of major constituents (/) as below:

$$*_{\rightarrow}$$

That he was happy/was evident from the way he smiled.

Such effects occur even when there are no clues to structure in terms of the intonation of the sentence. They presumed that structure is actively imposed and that the units derived 'resist' interruption. It seems more likely, though, that listeners detect the signal as it occurs but judge its location relative to constituents. However, there is a problem. Listeners had to write down the sentence before marking the position of the click, so relocation could occur through production rather than reception. Although this may contribute to the effect it does not account for it entirely (cf. Green, 1973).

Let's accept the effect here. Does it arise because listeners identify constituents? Relocations also occur when noise bursts replace the words of sentences (Reber and Anderson, 1970), suggesting that displacement cannot be taken as unequivocal support for the notion that constituents act as the units of perception. A more comprehensive view is that receptive processes in general act to collate and organize incoming information, and the reception of linguistic messages is one illustration of this more general phenomenon. Individuals seek to recode information into larger 'chunks'. In the case of language these chunks may correspond to constituents. According to the model there are two ways in which relocations could occur: they could occur either through the extraction of surface constituents or through the identification of deep structure constituents, since major surface boundaries are also boundaries in deep structure.

The next phase of experimentation (see Bever *et al.*, 1969) suggested that such relocations are largely attributable to divisions in the deep structure, for they do not occur in the absence of such breaks. Two types of sentence were found. In sentences of the first type such as 'They desired the general to fight' there is a boundary of an underlying clause between the verb and the noun as can be seen by reformulating the sentence into 'What they desired was for the general to fight'. In sentences of the second type, however, such as 'They defied the general to fight', which possesses similar wording, there is no such break since the object of the first verb is also the subject of the second. Such sentences cannot be reformulated on the lines above and remain intelligible. In the event, clicks located in verbs of the first type tend to be consistently relocated into the deep structure boundary:

$$*\rightarrow$$

They desired/the general to fight

There was no systematic trend for clicks in the other sentence type. Individuals appear actually to organize messages in terms of the underlying clauses.

But again, the model overdetermines the effect. It could equally well arise as a consequence not of syntactic processing but of semantic processing with the clause boundary being the focus of such activity (Johnson-Laird, 1970; Fodor *et al.*, 1974). But this suggestion seems to imply that receivers may not be deriving the meaning of a sentence continuously. In fact, on a direct interpretation of the theory, this is precisely what is implied (e.g., Bever and Hurtig, 1975).

Receivers must first determine the structure of a clause before they can interpret it. There are a number of experiments which seem to provide some support for this idea (Forster and Olbrei, 1973; Forster and Ryder, 1971). Yet this notion seems counter-intuitive. Any evidence in support of it, we must suppose, must have arisen either because the experimental test was inappropriate or because the demands of the task employed were such that syntactic and semantic processes that normally operate concurrently were dissociated in some manner.

If semantic processing does occur during the course of processing a clause, does this refute the serial relationship between syntax and semantics postulated by the linguistic model? Contrary to what is sometimes assumed, the answer is that it does not. Suppose that at the beginning of a clause an individual, on the basis of the first few words, conjectures that the structure of the clause will be of a certain type, we could then say that the deep structure is hypothetically complete or known. Individuals could then commence semantic interpretation right from the start, on the supposition that the deep structure is as they presume it to be, and still be acting in conformity with the linguistic model.

In fact, a notion compatible with this idea had to be developed for another reason. This reason was that aside from some work on an earlier version of the theory, there was no good evidence for the reality of transformations. In other words, the presumed connection between the surface and deep structure of a sentence could not be demonstrated empirically (cf. Greene, 1972 for details). In order to handle this problem it was proposed (see, for example, Bever, 1970) that individuals derived the deep structure of sentences directly from the surface structure by using various types of clue. Reception was a matter of deploying heuristics and strategies. Flexibility replaced rigidity. It was suggested, for instance, that (a) individuals might treat the first noun-verb-noun sequence of a sentence as a main clause unless it was marked as a subordinate one; and (b) they might consider the first noun of a sentence as the agent. The interpretation of sentences appears as a process of tentative construction that is subject to revision and reformulation, exactly as are theoretical concepts in science. Although such a notion does not entail that semantic processing should occur before the end of a clause, it is not incompatible with it.

But if it is the case that semantic processing is occurring continuously throughout the reception of a clause, as recent empirical work discloses (e.g., Marslen-Wilson, 1975; Marslen-Wilson *et al.*, 1978), what is it that accounts for the apparent organization of inputs in to clauses?

One possibility is that individuals seek to code the information into a different type of representation (Jarvella, 1971), or seek to relate it to other aspects of their knowledge (Haviland and Clark, 1974). They certainly appear to pause longer at the ends of clause boundaries relative to other points within sentences during reading (see Mitchell and Green, 1978). If, in fact, individuals do perform such operations, is it plausible that such operations are triggered solely on the basis of the completeness of the syntactic clause? Marslen-Wilson *et al.* (1978) have argued that it is more plausible to assume that the primary goals of the receiver are to identify *informationally* complete sequences. Normally, clauses may correspond to informationally complete units, but it is possible to manipulate informational completeness independently of syntactic completeness; and when this was done they found that effects related to clause boundaries on ongoing processing were obtained only for informationally complete sequences.

Given such results, it is necessary to consider whether or not there is any value in postulating an independent level of processing corresponding to deep structure. One suggestion that does not discard the insights and activity of our linguistic colleagues has been proposed by Miller and Johnson-Laird (1976). Their suggestion is to treat the generalizations of linguistics as consequences of the implicit workings of psychological processes. We need only add that such processes should be viewed in a collective sense. Once again, individuals can reasonably act in conformity with the rules, without these rules playing any direct part in explaining their activity.

We have considered the development of a psychological model based on linguistic theory. It is time now to turn to another more recent appraoch. In doing so, we shall go beyond the notion of isolated sentences and consider their processing in context. We shall also move to more theoretical considerations.

The programming approach

The aim of the linguistic analogy was to account for the interpretation of sentences. But the question of what the meaning of a sentence actually is was left in abeyance. If we look at the accounts of how individuals perform various tasks it is clear that these are largely formulated in terms of mental operations.

For example, consider the way we might change our understanding of some event on the basis of new information conveyed by a sentence. Suppose we read 'It was Lucy who brought the dessert'. This sentence conveys as *given* the information that someone brought the dessert and conveys as *new* information that the person concerned was called Lucy. According to a proposal by Clark (see Haviland and Clark, 1974; Clark and Clark, 1977), individuals move through a three-step process in recording this information. In step 1 they *divide* the sentence into given and new information. In step 2 they *search* for the given information in memory, and in step 3, assuming they locate it, they *add* the new information to memory. Where there is no direct representation of the given information, receivers are supposed to infer a suitable connection to what they already know. In other words, overt expression is converted into some type of mental representation that is suitable for performing the requisite operations, and then these operations are carried out.

This notion was made explicit by Miller and Johnson-Laird (1976) in their treatise on perception and language via an analogy to programming a computer. We shall consider the overall nature of their proposal first of all, and then examine one of their basic concepts in more detail.

One of their contentions is that understanding a sentence can be likened to the process of running a program on a computer. There are usually two phases involved in using a computer to perform a particular task. In the first phase the computer must compile a program written in some high-level language, such as Fortran or Planner, into some language that the particular machine can understand, the machine code. In the second phase it must execute this compiled program with respect to the data it is to operate upon. By analogy, they propose two phases in the psychological processing of a sentence. In the *translation phase* an individual translates the natural language input into a series of mental instructions concerning goals, objects and properties, that allow a question to be answered or a command to be carried out. In the *execution phase* an individual decides whether to answer the question or to carry out the command. If he or she does so decide then the instructions are executed. Such execution might involve searching memorial data or constructing a plan based on environmental input to perform some action.

It is perhaps worth emphasizing that the translation phase in this case is held to convert natural language into something equivalent to a high-level programming language, rather than into a machine code. Clearly, if such a program is to be run by the brain, which can be viewed as a neural computer, there must be a further process of translation which results in the compilation of the 'neural' machine code.

Without going into details, let us try to get a feel for these notions. The effect of translation is to unpack questions, commands or assertions in one language into a multiplicity of instructions or procedures in another.

We are offered a procedural semantics. By way of illustration, let us consider the process of translating a question such as 'Did Lucy bring the dessert?' Its procedural translation might be glossed as: *find* some event in memory such that the relationship between a person, called Lucy, and an object, dessert, is one of bringing. The notion of bringing itself, can be unpacked as a series of *tests* in which a person has to arrive somewhere and be holding something at the same time. Similarly the notion of person and dessert can be given a procedural specification. Having translated our sentence into this procedural package we can decide whether or not to carry out the requisite searches and tests. If we decide to, and the tests are confirmed, we can answer affirmatively. It may be, of course, that on hearing a question about Lucy we begin thinking about where we last saw her; i.e., we may execute a *find* instruction, even as we are beginning to translate the rest of the sentence. The two activities of translation and execution are dissociable and potentially concurrent.

Miller and Johnson-Laird organize the information used in executing instructions as a series of interlocked decision tables. A decision table factors knowledge into *conditions* for actions and *actions* to be taken. (This is the production system notion that Allport and Hitch have already discussed.) If an object, percept or memory satisfies a particular condition or series of conditions, then a certain action can be taken.

An example will clarify the matter (see also Miller and Johnson-Laird, 1976, pp. 283-90).

Suppose a simple world consisting of three items of furniture: a bed, a table and a chair. If a condition such as 'does the object have a seat?' is met, then a person could call the object a 'chair'. If it doesn't have a seat but has a worktop, the person could call it a 'table'. If it has neither a seat nor a worktop, then it can be called a 'bed'. Whole sets of words relating to various categories such as furniture can be represented in terms of such notions, and their interconnectedness revealed. The meaning of 'chair' arises through its differentiation from other kinds of furniture, in particular with respect to objects that are various types of seat such as 'sofas', 'benches', 'ottomans'. Such differentiation is captured by the different conditions that such objects have to meet. For instance, although sofas and benches are both seats they are distinguished in part because one of the conditions of calling an object a 'sofa' is that it be upholstered, but this requirement is not a condition for an object called a 'bench'. These conditions include information regarding what an object looks like (perceptual information) and information about what it is used for (functional information). We shall use this notion of two types of information later in our discussion of metaphor.

As a way of handling the enormous complexity of our unconscious knowledge, they propose in addition that one of the actions in a decision table can be to call another decision table that specifies further conditions and actions, that progressively differentiate the percept, memory or concept, and allow it to be signified by a single sign. Such orderings offer a way of representing the various semantic domains (e.g., vehicles, furniture, animals) and capture the hierarchic relationship that can obtain. 'Tulips' are examples of 'flowers', that are instances of 'plants', that are a sub-set of animate processes.

Before proceeding further we can note, first, that decision tables are really an alternative way of expressing a program of instructions; and second, that such programs can be used not only to trigger the production of a word but also to comprehend it. On encountering a condition such as the word 'table' the program will take the action of releasing the pertinent perceptual and functional information. The form in which such information is released may depend upon the goals of the receiver. Normally it might be released as a unit, to be used as such in the representation of the input. The internal structure of the unit would remain 'tacit' (see Claxton's Chapter 6) but vital to the course of understanding. On other occasions, however, we may need to use this information more explicitly, in which case we might well attend to the separate aspects of this information (see Miller, 1978). In either case the notion of interlinked decision tables captures rather elegantly the intuition that reception, like production, is a process that moves from the global to the particular (Werner and Kaplan, 1963), and it permits therefore a *dynamic* view of receptive processing.

In order to effect their idea of translation, Miller and Johnson-Laird (1976) wed their procedural analysis to a programming scheme called an Augmented Transition Network (ATN), that was developed initially in the field of machine translation to retrieve the surface and deep structure of sentences without recourse to transformations. Psychologists are great borrowers, and in this case use the scheme to derive meaning directly. Steedman and Johnson-Laird (1978) term this modification a Semantic Transition Network or an STN.

Basically, the device tests for the presence of certain syntactic features of incoming words and assigns roles such as subject and object to these words if the tests are passed. In the simplest case it comprises a main sentence network that specifies that sentences will contain noun-phrases and verb-phrases, and a subordinate network that handles the testing and procedural translation of noun-phrases. Control passes to and from the main network to the subordinate one. In understanding a noun-phrase at the beginning of a sentence the network would test at some point for the presence of a noun feature, and if the test was passed, retrieve its meaning. It would then label it a noun-phrase and return control to the main network, that would assign it the role of subject of the sentence and move on to consider the next word. This next word would be tested for being a verb and so forth.

One advantage of this approach is that it allows us to specify tests in a certain order and hence to capture the notions of a processing heuristic or strategy. Revision of interpretation is also possible. For instance, if a 'by-phrase' signalling the presence of a passive sentence is detected, the network can relabel its initial designation of the first noun-phrase as subject and call it an object. Within the orientation being developed here an STN can be viewed as a schema or a program for processing sentences that both permits adaptive response to different sentence continuations (it encodes sentence possibilities) and reflects an individual's learning of these multiple but cohesive possibilities (see also Wanner and Maratsos, 1978).

The use of sentences

In order to effect an appropriate translation of a sentence we need to know what kind of message is being conveyed. Questions specify searches; commands specify instructions to achieve something. Assertions may be treated in various ways: we might store the information they express, or generate some image on the basis of it. Miller and Johnson-Laird propose a dummy instruction, 'instruct', for which more specific instructions can be substituted. Our acts of asserting, questioning and commanding often correlate with particular sentence forms. Assertions are typically expressed as declaratives ('This is a book'), questions as interrogatives ('Are you reading?'), and commands as imperatives ('Give him the salt'). The structure or form of sentences follows from their communicative function. This correlation means that we can sometimes work out what we should do on the basis of structural cues, and these could be embodied with the transition network.

We can also question by using declarative sentences, command using interrogatives, and assert using imperatives. How then do we work out what to do? How is translation into a procedural description effected? The basic idea is that we use our knowledge of the social conventions underlying discourse. What are these conventions? We endeavour to make our messages *efficient* (clear, informative and relevant) and *true*. We try to act *co-operatively* (Grice, 1967), and assume that other sources are acting in this way too. Where this is the case we can infer what action needs to be undertaken. Take a direct request such as 'Open the door'. The source is believed to *desire* the outcome, to have *reason* for it, and to believe that the receiver has both the *ability* to effect the outcome, and the *will* or intention to effect it, if requested to do so. If normal use permits indirect use, then the ways we have of formulating indirect requests should match the assumptions underlying direct usage. And, in fact, this appears to be the case, as Searle (1968) has shown. Indirect requests can be achieved by asserting: *desire* ('I would like the door open'), *reason* ('You should open the door'), *ability* ('You can open the door') and *will* or intention ('You will open the door').

It is because we know how to use language appropriately that we can solve the problem of its indirect use. This suggests that the receiver first works out the direct meaning of a sentence, and checks to see if it is applicable. If it is not, then some other interpretation must be constructed. For instance, if a person says 'The door is open' and it is, we assume, if the percept is available to both parties, that some other 'speech act' other than an assertion is being performed. It is possible that the person is making a request for the door to be closed.

The relationship betweeen sense and expression has moved from an exclusive concern with what is given to a concern with how it is being used. It is the *functional* meaning that is psychologically relevant. This has been demonstrated experimentally by Clark and Lucy (1975) in a task in which subjects were asked to judge whether a picture (such as an open door) satisfied a particular request. In such a context a superficially positive sentence such as 'Why open the door' was treated like a negative sentence, 'Don't open the door'; whereas a superficially negative sentence, such as 'Why not open the door' was treated as a positive sentence, 'Open the door'. Moreover, the experiment suggested that receivers may determine the direct meaning of a sentence before its indirect meaning. Whether this sequence is invariably the case is open to question. It is possible that, given suitable context, individuals may grasp the indirect sense immediately. The importance of contextual factors in reception had been pointed out previously by Wason (1972) in connection with the processing of negatives. Out of context a sentence such as 'The train isn't late today' requires an individual to suppose that the train is normally late and that this is not the case today. In context, however, the knowledge that the train is normally late is shared by the source and receiver. Accordingly, the receptive processes must be different. In particular, in context the negative would be fulfilling its natural function of signalling the denial of some already presupposed or given information (see Wason, 1972), and when used appropriately it is known that negative sentences take no longer to comprehend than affirmative ones (see Greene, 1972). It seems plausible that context may exert a similar effect on the time needed to process indirect speech acts.

In summary, the central point of this section is that our translation and execution of linguistic messages is guided by our conception of the conventions underlying language use. Ultimately these conventions are rooted in the willingness and ability of sender and receiver to take into account one another's personal worlds. Such effort leads each to reorganize in an adaptive way. Communicative success rests on mutuality.

Some implications of the translation-execution strategy

One of the essential features of this strategy is that it seems to provide a way of distinguishing between understanding an utterance and any physical action entailed by it. We can understand a command but refuse to carry it out (Davies and Isard, 1972). How do we decide whether or not to carry out a particular command? One method would be to work out the implications of what it would mean to do so. If we do use such a method then we must obviously execute the instructions symbolically and evaluate the consequences for ourselves and others. It seems necessary therefore to distinguish the process of determining whether we could or would wish to achieve the goal of a command by internally simulating or imagining such an achievement from the process of actually achieving this goal by altering some state of affairs in the world. Alternately expressed, we need to distinguish between executing a program in the *intra*-personal world, from executing one in the *inter*-personal world.

This distinction was implicit in the previous discussion of the comprehension of indirect speech acts. The present contention is that the evaluation of possibilities and outcomes is a routine part of language comprehension and that theories of language comprehension must assume that the participants in any communicative exchange utilize models of the setting in which they find themselves.

Consider first of all the process of answering a question such as 'Is it possible for John to leave?' (see Johnson-Laird, 1978). The receiver must identify (or already know) the situations to which the question refers, and then must attempt mentally either to construct a sequel to it that leads to the event of John leaving (or to his definitely not leaving), or, if this procedure fails, the receiver must establish that the event cannot be ruled out in some sequel.

Similarly, in answering a question such as, 'Can you touch me?' (Johnson-Laird, 1977), the listener would have to determine amongst other things whether if he stretched out his arm, his fingers could just touch the speaker. In order to answer the question without any actual arm-stretching the listener must simulate the action, using an internal model that represents himself, the speaker and the space between them. Such examples suffice to show that in order to answer a question or to evaluate the significance of a remark the receiver may need to consider possibilities of one form or another. In grasping sense we seek not some literal or abstracted understanding but a functional, personal understanding. Such understanding involves cycles of symbolic activity in which various hypotheses and conjectures are tested out. Moreover, such activity may be carried out without conscious awareness.

In fact, there is a great deal of evidence showing that messages which we do not consciously apprehend can nonetheless affect our behaviour, if they are relevant to our current goals and our conceptions of ourselves (see Dixon, 1971 for a lucid review and theoretical exposition). However, it is possible, as Miller and Johnson-Laird appear to suggest, that some of these effects arise solely through translation. They discuss an experiment by Lackner and Garrett (1972). In this experiment individuals were required to paraphrase a sentence presented to one ear. In one condition, shortly after its onset, a second less audible sentence was presented to the other ear. Some of the sentences to be paraphrased were ambiguous, such as 'The spy put out the torch as our signal to attack' (did he extinguish it or relocate it?), and were accompanied in the other ear by an unambiguous counterpart ('The spy extinguished the torch in the window'). Although subjects revealed no conscious experience of this second sentence their paraphrases revealed that it had biassed the interpretation of the sentence for them. How could this come about? One possibility is that the verb 'extinguish' simply weighted one sense of 'put out' rather than the other. Such a weighting might then occur during translation. But since the two sentences could *logically* refer to distinct events, the use of such a weighting must be *motivated* psychologically and must be *mediated* by some mental operation.

The mental operation involves an act of textual inference, and such an inference is motivated because individuals given the paraphrasing task have to choose a particular meaning for this expression. They have to search for relevant disambiguating information and in doing so treat the two sentences as a text describing an event; e.g., 'The spy put out the torch as our signal to attack. He extinguished it in the window.' This search and inference is an executive action through which listeners construct a representation of a scene which allows them to solve the paraphrase problem. If we grant the possibility of such unconscious executive action, we have a way of accounting for unconscious fantasy, which we shall consider below.

Before proceeding it is perhaps worth taking stock of where we have got to. We have seen how the concerns of research have moved from a preoccupation with individual sentences to a consideration of the use of sentences in context. We have also seen how the field of psycho-linguistics has gradually recognized the necessity of including a wider variety of personal knowledge and knowledge of the meanings which individuals can intend when they use language. In addition, we have shown how it is possible to develop an alternative and possibly complementary account of comprehension which is tied more directly to information processing descriptions. In the following sections we shall utilize this account in our discussion of metaphorical language.

Metaphor as communicative action

A broad division may be made between literal and figurative language. We take this division psychologically to be based on the way language is used as a function of context and knowledge. Consider the role of context. In looking for somewhere to place our food during a picnic we might say, pointing to a tree stump, 'There's a table for us' (Miller, 1977). There is nothing metaphoric about this statement itself; its metaphoric value arises because of its context of use. Tree stumps are not tables as such, but may be used, or treated as if they were, for certain purposes. Metaphors meet pragmatic demands.

Consider, next, the role of knowledge. A sentence such as 'A chicken is a bird' is processed differently from a sentence with the same structure such as 'A person is a machine'. Whereas an instance-category relationship may be recognized for 'chicken' and 'birds', 'persons' and 'machines' are treated conventionally as categorically distinct. Accordingly, we construe the assertion 'A person is a machine' as meaning that persons are to be treated 'as if' they were machines (Turbayne, 1970). Without recognizing the 'as if' quality we are not grasping the sentence metaphorically at all. At the same time, unless we recognize that it asserts the direct relationship of two categorically distinct entities we also fail to appreciate its metaphoric value. It becomes a simile, and similes such as 'A person is like a machine', respecting categorical distinctions, commit no trespass.

In construing the sentence 'A person is a machine' as a metaphor we presupposed a conventional distinction. But distinctions change and evolve. Suppose that, as a result of the impact of modern tech-nology and psychological theorizing, the word 'person' refers to certain instances of 'adaptatively self-organizing information pro-cessing systems' and the word 'machine' to any 'information-processing system', then a sentence such as 'A person is a machine' ceases to elicit metaphorical construal and becomes interpretable on the lines of 'A chicken is a bird'. Receptive processing is a function of our personal knowledge. Given different presumed knowledge the use of the sentence changes. To assert 'A person is a machine', given this future context, would serve to remind the receiver of the commonalities obtaining among 'persons' and other 'machines' such as 'computers' and 'robots', rather than to cause the individual to construe such commonalities.

How might the process of metaphoric comprehension work? One possibility is that receivers first determine the literal meaning of the metaphorical sentence, check this meaning against prior context and, on finding an inconsistency, reconstrue this meaning in the light of the conventions underlying discourse. This proposal is consistent with the three stages proposed by Clark and Lucy (1975) to account for the interpretation of indirect speech acts. In both cases the receiver is seeking to work out what the source means from what is actually stated. However, Searle (in press; cited in Ortony *et al.*, 1978b) argues that there is a difference between metaphors and indirect speech acts. In the case of indirect speech acts an individual intends both the literal and the conveyed meaning of the utterance; whereas in the case of metaphor the speaker intends only to convey the metaphorical meaning of utterance.

There seem to be two issues here. First, is it really the case that individuals go through an additional process of reinterpretation, a further cycle of translation and execution, in order to grasp the sense of metaphor? If this is the case, then individuals should always take longer to derive a metaphorical compared to a literal reading of a sentence. Second, how is the metaphorical reading itself achieved and how is it to be characterized? We shall pursue these two questions in the present section, by considering briefly certain traditional theories and then by examining three recent psychological proposals in more detail.

Traditional theories of metaphor

From a psychological point of view each of the traditional theories of metaphor seem to presume the three-step procedure, noted above, for deriving the metaphorical meaning of an expression. Individuals are presumed to determine the literal meaning of an expression, detect its inconsistency with context and attempt to resolve this inconsistency. It is at the third step that the theories differ. Two broad theories of the nature of this resolution process will be discussed; monistic and dualistic theories (see Mooij, 1976). Monistic theories argue that the resolution eliminates any reference to the literal extension of the metaphorical term. Dualistic theories, on the other hand, suppose that it is only through the maintenance of the literal reference that the metaphorical meaning of the expression arises. Neither type of theory offers an effective procedure for deriving the interpretation of a metaphor. We present two versions of each theory below.

Our focus in what follows is to develop an understanding of the comprehension of simple metaphors of the form 'A person is a machine' variety. We shall presume a loose definition of metaphor as a word or sentence that is applied to an object or action to which it is not literally applicable. In addition we shall refer to the subject of the metaphor as the 'topic' and the metaphorical term itself as the 'vehicle'. Sometimes we shall call the relationship between the two of them, the 'ground' of the metaphor (see Verbrugge and McCarrell, 1977).

Monistic theories

One of the traditional views of metaphor, the *substitution* view, would suppose that in interpreting a metaphor we replace any metaphorical term(s) in an expression by a literal term(s) that can fit the same context. A basic objection to this view is that it is not clear how a literal substitute can be chosen without considering the sense of the metaphor, which is precisely what we are seeking to explain.

A second type of monistic theory, the *connotation* theory (e.g., Beardsley, 1962), supposes that in a metaphorical sentence there is a conflict between the central aspects of the meaning and reference of words, that is resolved by determining some more marginal aspects of the word's meaning or connotation. For example, the word 'sea' denotes a large body of salt water but connotes changeability and endless motion. Such connotations might be employed in understanding a metaphor such as 'The crowd was a sea of faces'. This theory is monistic since the literal referent of the metaphorical is considered only for the purpose of determining other marginal meanings. Psychologically, it supposes that the receiver first detects inconsistency between the topic and vehicle, according to their core senses, and then selects a suitable connotation of the vehicle in order to resolve this inconsistency. The question of how such selection occurs is left unanswered.

In summary, the substitution and connotation theories both presume that individuals detect inconsistency and seek to resolve it, either by finding some literal substitute for the metaphorical term (substitution theory) or by finding a suitable connotation of that term that renders the sentence literal (connotation theory). In both cases, the literal extension of the metaphorical word plays no part in the representation of the metaphor itself. it is considered only to be discarded. Finally, neither theory specifies a general procedure for determining a suitable literal translation.

Dualistic theories

In contrast to monistic theories, dualistic theories assume that it is only through literal reference that the metaphorical meaning of an expression arises. The first of these, *comparison* theory, when considered generally, asserts that metaphors are condensed or implied similes. For example, Henle (1958) describes metaphor as an analogy between things and situations in which one situation serves as an image for another. In the metaphor, 'The car beetles along the road', the movement of the car along the road is likened to the movement of a beetle. Psychologically, this theory suggests that we determine the general nature of the situation being described in a literal sense (e.g., the movement of a car along the road) and link this analogically to a more specific situation that we have inferred (e.g., the movement of a beetle). The outcome of processing is therefore to represent two subject matters, one pertaining to the topic and the other to the vehicle. According to this version, the outcome of processing is two potentially independent representations linked via some internal symbol of resemblance.

An alternative formulation would be to suppose that the metaphor is the compressed, surface representation of a more complex deep structure, which explicitly states the analogy (see Kintsch, 1976). In this case there would be a single representation that is related to the surface form by 'compression rules'. But again, this underlying structure would contain a general description plus a more specific description. Comparison theory presumes that we can infer the analogous situation on the basis of our practical knowledge of situations. Exactly which aspects of this knowledge are utilized remains unclear.

This notion of comparison is similar to the second class of dualistic theories, *interaction* theories, in that a metaphor is viewed as an integration of parts that are disparate initially in a categorial sense. In contrast to comparison theories, interaction theories stress the idea that there is an interaction between the topic and vehicle domains that results in a change in the conception of the topic (Richards, 1965). Black (1962) has argued that in metaphor the topic is 'seen through' the vehicle. A metaphor such as 'Man is a wolf' is processed, according to Black, by finding those aspects of wolves in our practical knowledge or schema of them, that may be applied without undue strain to man. Such aspects might be their presumed fierceness and hunger (see Beardsley, 1962). Any human traits that can be talked about in this way will become prominent, and others that cannot will be pushed into the background. The vehicle serves to *organize* our conception of the topic (man becomes more wolflike). Conversely, our conception of the vehicle may also be somewhat reorganized by virtue of the attempt to see the topic in the terms of the vehicle (wolves become slightly more human).

Both comparison and interaction theories seek to treat metaphor in its own terms rather than seeking to formulate an account in which it appears as a disguised literal statement. Both presume that the metaphorical reading of a sentence involves additional processing. Both speak in terms of the topic of the metaphor being seen in terms of the vehicle. The difference between them lies in the form of this relationship. For one the two items remain distinct, linked by analogy; for the other the two are fused in some way. Psychologically the theories make different predictions about the nature of the internal representation of metaphor. In contrast to comparison theory, an interaction theory such as Black's would suggest that those aspects of the topic that have been selected by the vehicle should be more salient in the representation of the metaphor than those which have not been so selected.

Having outlined some of the traditional theories, we shall now consider some psychological approaches. Our questions remain the same. First, does metaphorical interpretation invariably involve additional processing? Second, by what process do receivers derive a pertinent metaphorical interpretation?

Psychological approaches

Schema theory, version 1: Verbrugge and McCarrell (1977) have criticized previous psychological approaches based on the notion that the resolution of inconsistency involves identifying common properties or attributes of the topic and vehicle. Despite the fact that the number of shared properties affects the rated goodness of a metaphor (Johnson and Malgady, 1975), they propose that the notion of receivers searching through lists of attributes is inadequate to explain the comprehension of metaphors. They argue that a large number of metaphors draw attention to a system of relationship, a schema, rather than a fixed invariant list of attributes (Black, 1962). In order to grasp a metaphor such as 'Tree trunks are straws for thirsty leaves', the comprehender must perceive the role of 'straws' and 'tree trunks' as means for transporting fluid. The significance of this opposition between attribute and schema theories depends on what one means by these terms. For present purposes, it seems best to pursue their central idea rather than dwelling on this opposition, since some authors (e.g., Tversky, 1977) would allow a feature or an attribute to stand for any of a number of things, including the schemata of practical knowledge.

According to Verbrugge and McCarrell, in comprehending a metaphor such as 'Tree trunks are straws for thirsty leaves' individuals activate a schema associated with each of the words. The schema for 'straws', for example, would indicate that an object such as a straw is specified *perceptually* (or structurally, as they call it) as hollow and cylindrical in shape, with a small diameter relative to its length, composed of relatively rigid, non-porous material; and is specified *functionally* (or transformationally, as they call it) as a cylindrical space that channels fluid for the purpose of relieving thirst. A straw itself can be viewed as an instance, possibly an exemplary one, of such a relational system. In any concrete situation it presents itself as possessing particular attributes that mediate these abstract relations (for example, it might be six inches long and made of paper and be involved in transporting Coca-Cola from a glass to a pair of lips).

Interpreting a metaphor, in their view, involves applying the vehicle schema to the topic domain in order to create a similar relational system out of the entities in that domain. The notion that metaphorical comprehension involves additional interpretative activity seems implicit in this view. In addition, their view seems to be a dualistic theory of an interactionist type. It is dualistic, in that the application of the vehicle schema is held to involve both its structural and functional aspects. It is interactionist, in the tradition of Richards and Black, in that not only do they presume that the topic domain is restructured but presume that some restructuring can also take place in the vehicle domain.

In an interesting series of prompted recall experiments they established the importance of the vehicle in determining the ground of a metaphor. Prompting with a cue such as 'are tubes which conduct water to where it's needed' was effective in eliciting recall of the metaphor 'Tree trunks are straws for thirsty leaves and branches' but was ineffective in eliciting recall of the metaphor: 'Tree trunks are pillars for a roof of leaves and branches'. Conversely, a prompt capturing the ground of the latter metaphor elicited its recall, but was ineffective in eliciting the recall of the tree-trunks-leaves metaphor.

Although such findings are compatible with an interaction view they do not rule out other types of theory. Let us suppose that their schema interpretation is correct. How do individuals go about choosing an appropriate interpretation of the metaphor?

Given the suggestion that vehicles may be exemplary instances of a particular system of relations, it seems plausible that individuals would simply apply the most *salient* schema in the vehicle domain to the topic. This suggestion, of course, pushes the problem of how individuals select the appropriate aspects of the vehicle back to the nature of the specification of the vehicle itself. Perhaps this is where the problem is to be solved. This 'solution' still leaves unexplained, as they point out, why some types of schema can be applied successfully and others fail (e.g. tree trunks are baby pacifiers). They suggest that there must be some sort of compatibility rules, but leave open what they are.

Schema theory, version 2: A similar view of metaphoric comprehension has been proposed by Ortony *et al.* (1978a). They also appeal to the idea that readers activate schemata during the processing of a sentence, and propose a number of interesting extensions.

These authors define a metaphor as a contextual-anomaly that can be resolved. (This definition needs further refinement, since as it stands it would allow any resolvable textual inconsistency to be a metaphor.) Using what they call whole-sentence metaphors that occur when a sentence which is perfectly normal is placed in a context which requires it to be given a metaphorical reading, they suggest that the ease or difficulty in processing such a sentence does not depend upon how literal or metaphorical it is, but on whether it can be accounted for by prior context. They propose that, given sufficient context, a target sentence will be comprehended as rapidly in a metaphorical as in a literal sense.

This is an interesting prediction since it is counter to traditional views and the three-stage procedure that imply that metaphors should always take longer to process than literal statements. In fact, in an experiment on this issue, Ortony *et al.* (1978b) found that in minimal contexts subjects did take longer to derive the metaphorical compared to the literal sense of a target sentence, but that this difference disappeared in longer contexts. Such a finding suggests that the three-step procedure may have limited generality.

In order to explain their findings they argue that in reading material individuals activate schemata and generate expectations about the nature of what is to follow. Given sufficient context a metaphorical target can be readily understood, or accounted for, in terms of these expectations. As an illustration they suggest that in reading a passage about the criticisms of Spain's erstwhile dictator, Franco, readers activate schemata associated with Franco, dictator, Spain, resistance and persistence. On encountering the target sentence, 'The waves beat relentlessly against the shore', readers account for it in terms of the notions of resistance and persistence. They propose that similar schemata could be employed in understanding the target in a literal context that deals with the coastal region of Iceland. In short contexts, on the other hand, there is likely to be a processing advantage for a literal over a metaphorical interpretation. In such a case they suggest that readers may use the target sentence itself to determine an interpretation of the prior context. Where the prior context induces a metaphorical reading of the target sentence, this proposal means that the schemata from the vehicle domain (the target sentence) are applied to the topic domain (the prior context) in line with the suggestions of Verbrugge and McCarrell. In long contexts, their proposals seem to imply the reverse arrangement (but see below).

A number of comments seem in order. First, although Ortony *et al.*

(1978b) speak as if the length of the prior context was crucial, it seems more consistent with their proposal to say that the crucial factor is the extent to which that context activates *suitable* schemata. Second, it is not clear in what sense the target sentence in the long contexts actually restructures the topic domain, given that the necessary schemata are already present. One possibility is that, although prior context generates expectations about future input, the interpretation of the target sentence serves to make some of these more important than others; this would be compatible with the idea that the vehicle does in fact always restructure prior context. It remains an open question as to whether the literal referents of the target sentence are included in the developing representation. Their view seems to be that as long as there is a *reasonable* fit, other aspects of the input can be ignored. This seems to suggest that their theory is a *connotation* theory rather than a dualistic theory such as that of Verbrugge and McCarrell. Third, there seems to be a possible inconsistency between their view (Ortony *et al.*, 1978b) that metaphor is a contextual anomaly in which the 'tension' created is potentially eliminable, and their finding that in suitable contexts understanding a target sentence metaphorically takes no longer than understanding it literally. Ortony *et al.*'s (1978b) whole-sentence metaphors must involve tension-elimination, if they are to be counted as metaphors according to their own definition (Ortony *et al.*, 1978a). But this implies that in long contexts tension-elimination takes place in zero time. This conclusion is unacceptable, given the supposition that all cognitive operations take time to execute.

One way round this problem which preserves their definition of metaphor and that still predicts the obtained results is to assume that the process of detecting the anomaly is *concurrent* with the process of fitting the target sentence into prior context that mediates the elimination of tension. If we assume that it is the total processing activity of the individual that corresponds to the perceived significance of the material, then the fact that two processes occur concurrently is immaterial. In fact, these two processes are really aspects of one and the same process that relates the target sentence to prior context. Part of this processing activity is 'blocked', yielding the contextual anomaly, and part is carried through mediating tension-elimination. This proposal indicates that the findings cited earlier in connection with indirect speech acts, suggesting a stages model of comprehension, may have arisen because of the absence of contextual support. In fact

Ortony *et al.* (1978b) cite an experiment by Rumelhart (in press) showing that indirect speech acts do not take longer to process, given suitable context. Such findings are also compatible with the data that the time to process negative sentences depends on whether they are being used appropriately in context. It is the provision of a suitable framework for comprehending successive sentences that determines the time needed to comprehend the material, rather than the structure or metaphorical value of such material *per se*.

Although the papers by Ortony and colleagues are extremely provocative, they inevitably leave open certain problems. Their argument about the role of context seems to require that the current input is scanned in terms of all currently activate expectations simultaneously. However, this assumption does not mean that all aspects of the schemata activated during the reading of the target sentences are themselves equally available. There is considerable evidence that certain properties of objects are more frequently produced as descriptions than others (e.g., Ashcraft, 1976; Hampton, 1979). If these aspects become available before others, then the time needed to comprehend a metaphor even with adequate context may vary as a function of the salience of the information that is required to resolve the sense of the metaphor.

A procedural approach: It has been argued through this section that what is required is some procedure for constructing the resemblance between terms or expressions linked metaphorically. None of the traditional approaches offers an effective procedure and the current versions of schema theory leave this problem aside. In this section we shall consider one procedural possibility and integrate it with the idea that the information about an object is differentially accessible.

Miller (1977) hints at a procedural approach to the comprehension of metaphor in his paper on practical and lexical knowledge. It will be recalled from the section on Miller and Johnson-Laird's (1976) work that the perceptual tests used to determine whether a particular object is a table, say, are guided by our understanding of the functions that such an object fulfils in our culture. Accordingly, Miller (1977) proposes that if a particular object looks like a table and could possible function as one then we can call it a 'table' in a literal sense. Where the object meets only one of these criteria, then it may be called a metaphorical or figurative 'table'. So, for example, we can call a picture of a table a 'table', since it meets the perceptual criteria for table even though it does not meet the relevant functional criteria. Conversely, we can call a tree stump in a picnic scenario a 'table', even though the perceptual criteria are not met, because it could function as a table or afford table possibilities (Bransford and McCarrell, 1977).

Miller supposes that we use some procedure that determines whether or not the particular object can meet the relevant perceptual or functional criteria. We shall refer to such a procedure as a process of construal. In the case of functional criteria the construal process seeks to determine whether or not a particular function is possible for a given object. For example, we could not say, pointing to a flag draped over a bucket, 'There's a table for us', since we know that flags are incapable of giving the relevant support.

The merit of Miller's proposal is that it allows a slot for practical knowledge in the linguistic entry for words in the mental lexicon, and hence does not conflate the two types of information as seems to occur in schema theories. Like schema theory, it allows our knowledge of objects to be brought to bear in the task of comprehending metaphors. Moreover it is clear that such knowledge is necessary in order to understand literal statements. A classic illustration of the use of such knowledge is our ability to disambiguate sentences such as 'The Smiths saw the Rocky Mountains while they were flying to California', where we immediately assume that the pronoun 'they' refers to the Smiths rather than to the Rocky Mountains.

What type of theory does such an approach suggest? If we take the proposal as it stands, the internal representation of the sentence 'There's a table for us' in the context of a tree stump would consist of a characterization of the tree stump in terms of the functional properties of tables. (e.g., it would include information to the effect that the entity concerned can be used to support objects for purposes of eating.) No literal reference to 'tables' would be included. However, it could be argued that in applying the perceptual and functional tests individuals represent the topic in terms of such tests. So, for example, although certain perceptual criteria would not be met, such as the object possessing legs, others such as the object possessing a flat surface would be. (Under the guidance of functional information, perhaps, even the trunk itself could be viewed as a leg.) In short, such a procedural theory is potentially dualistic. Moreover since the application of various tests is complementary to reorganizing the input, such a theory is potentially interactionist as well.

What kind of predictions would such a theory make? It seems clear that the time needed to comprehend a metaphor in context should be some function of the time required to determine whether either the perceptual or functional criteria of the vehicle can be met by the topic. One factor which is likely to be important here is the salience of the information in the vehicle schema that permits the receiver to decide whether either the perceptual criteria are true or the functional criteria are possible. The time required to comprehend a metaphor should reveal a 'salience effect'. Correspondingly, the information utilized or proving 'diagnostic' (Tversky, 1977) in resolving the sense of a metaphor should be more accessible in its internal representation. The process of recalling or questioning the sense of a metaphor should therefore reveal a 'diagnosticity' effect. Other factors are likely to be important, such as the degree of dissimilarity between the topic and vehicle, but these two serve to show how it is possible to formulate conjectures concerning the interpretation of metaphors that would be revealed in the time required to process them and in the nature of the representation created.

Many problems remain unresolved. One of these is the question of how an individual determines whether or not he or she has understood the metaphor. In resolving the sense of indirect speech acts, an individual can run through a list of possible speech acts and find one that is consistent with the co-operative principle. Are there any such determinate rules which could be applied in the case of metaphors? Verbrugge and McCarrell (1977) seem to imply that receivers seek to maximize the quality of the match (see also Tversky, 1977); whereas Ortony *et al.* (1978b) suggest that receivers seek a minimal resolution. It would be unreasonable to propose one or the other as *the* rule. Rather the nature of the resolution would seem to depend on the individual's goals in comprehending the material. In the case of explanatory metaphors (e.g., 'The heart is a pump') the criteria of understanding is presumably that a formerly diverse set of factors become interpretable as a consequence of a single factor.

There is a second related problem. Is it the case that there is a single type of representation underlying the resolution of metaphors? This suggestion seems implausible. It seems more reasonable to suppose that the comprehension procedure produces different outcomes as a function of the input material and the goals of the receiver. From this point of view the various traditional theories appear as descriptions of such outcomes. In cases, for example, where the co-ordination of the topic and vehicle terms leads to a considerable reorganization of the topic domain, the outcome is appropriately described in interactionist terms (see also Mooij, 1976). Such reorganization may be more likely, the more unrelated the concepts involved.

Understanding the nature of metaphors is important for practical reasons as well as theoretical ones. One of the applied uses of metaphors is in the field of advertising. Consider for example the process of understanding the command 'Put a tiger in your tank', issued by a petroleum company. This command requires us to identify 'tigers' with 'petrol' by construing them in common terms. In a strictly physical-technical sense we cannot run a car using a tiger. Tigers do not afford petrol possibilities in this sense. They neither look like, nor can function as, petrol. Viewing in a wider psychological sense, however, we can discern a way of construing tigers and petrol as compatible. What is the psychological meaning of 'tiger'? Summarily, 'tiger' identifies an animal, living in certain habitats, that functions as a predator, and connotes for us vitality, power and possibly ferocity. It connotes powerful expressiveness. Next, consider 'petrol'. It is a liquid propellant used in energizing cars. Its psychological sense is a derivative of this function. Since cars are instruments through which we express ourselves to others (think of the connotations of a Rolls-Royce), petrol affords expressive possibilities. A common, if speculative, ground has emerged between the concept of petrol and tiger: both entities afford expressiveness. Viewed psychologically, tigers can afford petrol-possibilities. And not just any old petrol-possibilities, but tigerish ones – vital, assertive petrol-possibilities.

In resolving sense we motivate the purchase of the product, endowing it with greater power. For 'tiger' to refer to 'petrol', the petrol must be powerfully expressive. In making this identification, we restructure our concept of petrol, emphasizing its latent expressive possibilities and making less salient such properties as its chemical and liquid nature. At the same time we reorganize our concept of 'tiger', emphasizing its expressive value over its physical description, though of course we can use this description as a sign of the petrol's expessive value. We 'reciprocally rotate' our concepts, in the words of Werner and Kaplan (1963): we reorganize them adaptively.

In comprehending this metaphor, we translate it into some internal language and seek to work out the connection with petrol by executing a procedure that could establish such a connection. In this case the connection exists in terms of the psycho-functional meanings of the entities concerned. Our apprehension of this connection may not be conscious. In fact, since the action required to execute the command in the physical world requires us to think in terms of practical objects and activities it is perhaps no wonder that we may fail to recollect our mental journey. The petrol is good, it seems to us. It may allow us to overtake others. Perhaps unconsciously we may feel ourselves to be tigers (cf. Packard, cited in Reboul, 1974). But how and why may remain opaque to us. Like dreamers, we may forget our dreaming on waking to the world of practical action. Our apprehension of the sense we have made may be restricted in extent because of the demands of appropriate action (Green, 1977).

Our sally into speculative psychology suggests that the process of construing a sentence metaphorically is like telling ourselves a story. Of course, as individuals we may tell ourselves different stories. But communicative success does not require identity of reaction, which can never be achieved, but correspondence of reaction. As long as the sense of a story within differing personal contexts achieves a measure of correspondence, communication between source and diverse receivers is possible. For further aspects of the psychology of metaphor see Pollio *et al.* (1977).

This analogy between metaphorical interpretations and stories provides a link with our next topic: the comprehension of stories. Our aim is to capture the direction of current work and to provide a framework for its appraisal.

Stories as communications

Any particular sequence of connected sentences or utterances (a text) is formulated to serve a particular function. The kind of text produced as descriptions of a motor-cycle journey differs from that offered as a description of philosophical positions (see Pirsig's *Zen and the Art of Motorcycle Maintenance*), both in terms of its structural character and its content. Texts are selective accounts. They are selective first of all in the sense that they are orientated to convey particular *types of meaning*, rather than others. They are selective, second, in that they convey only a *sub-set* of the meaning that could *potentially* be conveyed. A text acts as a map, as it were (Hayakawa, 1974), of a situation, and in comprehending it we go beyond the information given (see Bransford, Barclay and Franks, 1972). Our account of the interpretation of a metaphor is an illustration of such enrichment. In understanding any such description, therefore, we have to deploy our wider knowledge of the kinds of situation (perceptual or conceptual) being described (see Schank and Abelson, 1977; Minsky, 1975), and use our practical knowledge that is coded as various types of schema. One problem is to work out how we organize our thinking about the successive sentences of a text.

We can think of a text as a series of instructions for constructing a particular symbolic reality or psychological representation. In order to construct such a reality we have to know (a) how successive sentences *connect* together and (b) how we are to *construe* their connectedness. As we noted at the beginning, reading a detective story is not the same as reading a recipe. Knowledge of the nature of the type of text, therefore, will be useful in organizing how we build our internal representation of it.

We shall presume that readers work out connections between successive sentences by searching for the information held to be *given* and integrating *new* information into what Kintsch (1976) has termed the 'text base'. This process of integration, together with the necessary inferential work, seems to occur during the course of reading a sentence (see Carpenter and Just, 1978). According to recent suggestions, readers work out the significance of such connections with respect to some conception or schema of how the text will evolve. This schema serves to organize the text base to create what may be termed the 'text core' or text macrostructure, which mediates our phenomenal experience of the text. It serves to structure the possibilities inherent in the connections among sentences. How these two aspects are related is not clear at the present time; but we shall assume that the text base is created through a process of forward scanning (one cycle of translation and execution) and the text core via a recoding or backward scanning of the text base (a further cycle of translation and execution).

What is the nature of this schematizing activity? Most of the work in this field has been concerned with the interpretation of simple stories. Such stories appear to possess, at least within the west European tradition, a characteristic structure (Rumelhart, 1975; Bower, 1976; Mandler and Johnson, 1977). Although there are various formulations, we can say that they comprise: a *scene* or stage-setting sequence, which identifies the main character; an exposition sequence comprising of a *theme*, stating what it is going to be about; a set of *episodes*, recounting the actions undertaken; and a *resolution* sequence.

Roughly speaking, they have a beginning, a middle and an end. The episodes themselves consist of *goals* to be obtained by the protagonist, the *actions* undertaken and the *outcome* or effect of these actions. Since a protagonist may have to achieve one goal in order to achieve another, episodes can be embedded within one another, creating an hierarchical structure. This structural characterization is held to be a description of the nature of the psychological schema deployed.

The tenor of the experimental work bears a remarkable similarity to the search for the psychological reality of syntactic structure alluded to earlier. Having formulated a conception, researchers sought experimental expression. They chose materials ranging from fables to the tales of Boccaccio and tasks such as recall and *précis*. Students and children have been the subject of study.

Taken as psychological models, the structural descriptions specify that certain sequences in the story are more critical to its overall development than others. In consequence, they might be expected to be psychologically more salient. In fact, the evidence so far appears to corroborate this supposition.

Subjects recall ideas critical to the story, its theme, principal actions and resolution with greater accuracy than subordinate details (Bower, 1976; Mandler and Johnson, 1977); and produce such ideas more frequently in summaries of stories (Kintsch, 1976). Such selectivity disappears, however, in the absence of a thematic sequence (Thorndyke, 1977). If readers are required to recall stories that do not conform to the west European stereotype (e.g., North American Indian tales) the number of ideas recalled tends to be similar but whole episodes are omitted (Kintsch, 1976).

All these findings could arise as a consequence of a schema guiding the retrieval of information rather than its immediate processing. It is intuitively plausible that such schemata might be involved in both activities. During encoding it accounts for our sense of anticipation and involvement in the story. How else can we account for our excitement unless we appreciate the possibility of dénouement or resolution? It might serve a number of functions during immediate processing, as pointed out by Mandler and Johnson (1977). It would alert attention to certain aspects of the story. It would allow individuals to keep track of prior events, serving to reduce memory load by allowing readers to summarize the input into higher-order units (see Kintsch, 1976; Van Dijk, 1977). It would inform readers when some component sequence is complete. Direct evidence for such functions is scant. Our evidence relates principally to the role of the textual schema during recall or reconstruction. During recall it might serve to select information from the text base, translating it into core statements for output. Many of the ideas on the role of the text schema derive from Bartlett's (1932) pioneering work on reconstructive memory. The current work is more specific in its prediction but largely promissory in terms of immediate processing (but see Shebileske, 1977). We shall consider below other evidence favourable to the general notions that receivers organize incoming messages according to certain conceptions. But, first, how shall we view the text schema?

Given our prior discussion, we can view the text schema as a 'text transition network', in which incoming messages from the 'text base' are tested for membership of particular text categories, such as scene-setting, theme resolution; and, if they match, are summarized as the 'text core'. All we are saying here is that our conception of the text guides the significance that we attach to successive messages. The pattern of activity described by the text transition network would subsume the activity of the semantic transition network.

Our conception of a text is certainly important to our reading of it. But our *goals* or *purposes* in reading are also vital, as we argued in the Introduction. The role of the pragmatic schema has been shown by Pichert and Anderson (1977). Presented with a description of a house and its furnishings, subjects adopting the viewpoint of a burglar rated facts such as the presence of a colour TV set more important than the presence of a damp cellar. Conversely, subjects adopting the position of a house-buyer rated the presence of a damp cellar as more important. Other subjects requested to recall the story, having read it from a particular perspective, showed superior recall for those elements salient to their perspective. The pragmatic schema appears to configure or structure information in the text base. The fact that such a base does exist, independent of a given structuring, is supported by a later experiment by these workers (Anderson and Pichert, 1978) in which they found that subjects, having recalled all they could of the description from one perspective, were nonetheless capable of retrieving more information when they adopted a second perspective. In turn this newly recalled information was related to that perspective. Within the present discussion this experiment indicates that pragmatic factors, together with textual factors, may govern our apprehension or phenomenal awareness of the meaning of a text, but they do not exhaust our psychological representation of it. Perceived significance is an aspect of conveyed significance.

Just as we treated the text schema as a transition network we can imagine the pragmatic schema as such a network. It would select messages relevant to the task in hand. The operation of such a process is a common feature of our everyday experience. Take a situation such as walking down the street in a city. Our experience of it changes as a function of our goals. If we are hungry smells of food and restaurant signs stand out as the attentional focus. If we are looking for clothes, dress and tailor shops are salient. Our needs and current tasks serve to configure our awareness of a scene or text.

Such selectivity does not exhaust our organizing activity. Our inner experience is affected by our feelings about what we are doing. Any task may be carried out in all sorts of different ways. In reading for instance, if we feel under some obligation our experience of the text changes. The simple is perceived as the trite, the difficult as the obscure. If we read out of interest, however, the author's words may strike us as charged with insight. We can distinguish between our styles of acting communicatively and the type of action we are engaged in. Both contribute to the perceived significance of a text. Exactly how we should capture the notion of styles of action is unclear. One stylistic aspect involves the extent to which we seek to confirm our prior sense of ourselves and our world, as opposed to enquiring into the intrinsic meanings of persons and objects. That is, the extent to which we act ego-centrically as opposed to allo-centrically. Through a concern with the individual structuring of experience psycholinguistics shares a common ground with psychoanalytic theory. A rapprochement of these areas of interest seems possible, given the attempt of certain theoreticians (e.g., Schafer, 1976) to translate Freudian concepts such as the ego, superego, and id into the language of action. A common tongue increases the chances of a unified view of man as sense-maker emerging.

According to the conception we have been pursuing, a receiver progressively organizes incoming information in order to construct an internal representation of the input. We can view the process as one in which an input suggests certain possibilities and these are then evaluated in terms of the organizing processes (Navon, 1975; discussed in Broadbent, 1977). We have seen how in order to describe this process of construction we have had to consider the use of practical knowledge and the ways in which individuals imagine and simulate possible actions in the world. We have concentrated here on looking at a relatively simple communicational setting in which the source is generally a page or a paragraph of text. Yet although such a setting has provided the focus of this essay, the data that have been described arose in experimental situations which are likely to be more complex in a communicational sense than any private reading situation. For example, in experimental situations subjects are aware of themselves not only as actors but also as objects of another's awareness (see Farr, 1978).

It seems fundamental that if we are to develop effective accounts of comprehension then psycholinguistics must develop models of the experimental situation in which particular tasks are located. It is only by specifying both the nature of the material we are using (for which we need an appropriate linguistics) and the perceived nature of the task in its full inter-personal sense (for which we need a socio-psychological description) that we can reach an understanding of the nature of adaptive processing in linguistic communication.

Acknowledgments

Among the people who kindly volunteered their thoughts on the first draft of this chapter I am especially indebted to the editor, Guy Claxton, and to Peter Wason. I should also like to thank Susan Churchill for her invaluable secretarial assistance.

References

Anderson, R. C. and Pichert, J. W. (1978), 'Recall of previously unrecallable information following a shift in perspective', *Journal of Verbal Learning and Verbal Behavior, 17*, pp. 1-12.

Ashcraft, M. H. (1976), 'Priming and property dominance effects in semantic memory', *Memory and Cognition, 4*, pp. 490-500.

Bartlett, F. C. (1932), *Remembering,* Cambridge University Press.

Beardsley, M. C. (1962), 'The metaphorical twist', *Philosophy and Phenomenological Research, 22*, pp. 293-307.

Bever, T. G. (1970), 'The cognitive basis for linguistic structures', in J. R. Hayes (ed.), *Cognition and the Development of Language,* Wiley: New York.

Bever, T. G. and Hurtig, R. R. (1975), 'Detection of a non-linguistic stimulus is poorest at the end of a clause', *Journal of Psycholinguistic Research, 4*, pp. 1-7.

Bever, T. T., Lackner, J. R. and Kirk, R. (1969), 'The underlying structures of sentences are the primary units of immediate speech processing', *Perception and Psychophysics, 5,* pp. 225-34.

Black, M. (1962), 'Metaphor', in M. Black, *Models and Metaphors: Studies in Language and Philosophy,* Ithaca: New York.

Bower, G. H. (1976), 'Experiment on story understanding and recall', *Quarterly Journal of Experimental Psychology, 28,* pp. 511-34.

Bransford, J. D., Barclay, J. R., and Franks, J. J. (1972), 'Sentence memory: a constructive versus interpretive approach', *Cognitive Psychology, 3,* pp. 193-209.

Bransford, J. D. and McCarrell, N. S. (1977), 'A sketch of a cognitive approach to comprehension: some thoughts about understanding what it means to comprehend', reprinted in P. C. Wason and P. N. Johnson-Laird, *Readings in Cognitive Science,* Cambridge University Press.

Bresnan, J. (1978), 'A realistic transformational grammar', in M. Halle, J. Bresnan and G. A. Miller (eds), *Linguistic Theory and Psychological Reality,* MIT Press: Cambridge, Mass.

Broadbent, D. E. (1977), 'The hidden preattentive processes', *American Psychologist, 32,* pp. 109-18.

Carpenter, P. A. and Just, M. (1978), 'Reading as the eyes see it', in M. Just and P. A. Carpenter (eds), *Cognitive Processes in Comprehension,* Lawrence Erlbaum, Hillsdale, N.J.

Chomsky, N. (1965), *Aspects of the Theory of Syntax,* MIT Press: Cambridge, Mass.

Chomsky, N. (1966), 'Cartesian linguistics', a chapter in the *History of Rationalist Thought,* Harper & Row: London.

Clark, H. H. and Clark, E. V. (1977), *Psychology and Language: An Introduction to Psycholinguistics,* Harcourt Brace Jovanovich: New York.

Clark, H. H. and Lucy, P. (1975), 'Understanding what is meant from what is said: a study in conversationally conveyed requests', *Journal of Verbal Learning and Verbal Behavior, 14,* pp. 56-72.

Davies, D. J. M. and Isard, S. D. (1972), 'Utterances as programmes', in D. Michie (ed.), *Machine Intelligence, 7,* Edinburgh University Press.

Dixon, N. F. (1971), *Subliminal Perception: The Nature of a Controversy,* McGraw-Hill: London.

Farr, R. M. (1978), 'On the social significance of artifacts in experimenting', *British Journal of Social and Clinical Psychology, 17,* pp. 299-306.

Fodor, J. A. (1965), 'Could meaning be an rm?', *Journal of Verbal Learning and Verbal Behavior, 4,* pp. 73-81.

Fodor, J. A. and Bever, T. G. (1965), 'The psychological reality of linguistic segments', *Journal of Verbal Learning and Verbal Behavior, 4,* pp. 414-20.

Fodor, J. A., Bever, T. G. and Garrett, M. F. (1974), *The Psychology of Language,* McGraw-Hill: New York.

Forster, K. I. and Olbrei, I. (1973), 'Semantic heuristics and syntactic analysis', *Cognition, 2,* pp. 319-47.

Forster, K. I. and Ryder, L. A. (1971), 'Perceiving the structure and meaning of sentences', *Journal of Verbal Learning and Verbal Behavior, 10,* pp. 255-96.

Green, D. W. (1973), 'A psychological investigation into the memory and comprehension of sentences', PhD thesis, London University.

Green, D. W. (1977), 'The immediate processing of sentences', *Quarterly Journal of Experimental Psychology, 29*, pp. 135-46.

Greene, J. (1972), *Psycholinguistics: Chomsky and Psychology*, Penguin: Harmondsworth.

Grice, H. D. (1967), *William James Lectures*, Harvard University. Published in part as 'Logic and conversation' in P. Cole and J. L. Morgan (eds), *Syntax and Semantics Vol. 3: Speech Acts*, Seminar Press: New York, 1975.

Hampton, J. (1979), 'Polymorphous concepts in semantic memory', *Journal of Verbal Learning and Verbal Behavior, 18*, pp. 441-61.

Haviland, S. E. and Clark, H. H. (1974), 'Acquiring new information as a process in comprehension', *Journal of Verbal Learning and Verbal Behavior, 11*, pp. 148-56.

Hayakawa, S. I. (1974), *Language in Thought and Action*, Allen & Unwin: London.

Henle, P. (1958), 'Metaphor', in P. Henle (ed.), *Language, Thought and Culture*, University of Michigan Press: Ann Arbor, Mi.

Jarvella, R. J. (1971), 'Syntactic processing of connected speech', *Journal of Verbal Learning and Verbal Behavior, 10*, pp. 409-16.

Johnson, M. G. and Malgady, R. G. (1975), 'Some cognitive aspects of figurative language: association and metaphor', unpublished manuscript.

Johnson-Laird, P. N. (1970), 'The perception and memory of sentences', in J. Lyons (ed.), *New Horizons in Linguistics*, Penguin: Harmondsworth.

Johnson-Laird, P. N. (1977), 'Procedural semantics', *Cognition, 5*, pp. 189-214.

Johnson-Laird, P. N. (1978), 'The meaning of modality', *Cognition Science, 2*, pp. 17-26.

Jonckheere, A. R. (1966), discussion in J. Lyons and R. J. Wales (eds), *Psycholinguistic Papers: Proceedings of the Edinburgh Conference*, Edinburgh University Press.

Katz, J. J. and Fodor, J. A. (1963), 'The structure of a semantic theory', *Language, 39*, pp. 170-210.

Kintsch, W. (1976), 'On comprehending stories', paper presented at the Carnegie Symposium.

Lackner, J. R. and Garrett, M. F. (1972), 'Resolving ambiguity: effects of biasing context in the unattended ear', *Cognition, 1*, pp. 359-72.

Mandler, J. M. and Johnson, N. S. (1977), 'Remembrance of things parsed: story structure and recall', *Cognitive Psychology, 9*, pp. 111-51.

Marslen-Wilson, W. D. (1975), 'Sentence perception as an interactive parallel process', *Science, 189*, pp. 226-8.

Marslen-Wilson, W. D., Tyler, L. K. and Seidenberg, M. (1978), 'Sentence processing and the clause boundary', in W. J. M. Levelt and G. B. Flores d'Arcais (eds), *Studies in the Perception of Language*, Wiley: New York.

Miller, G. A. (1977), 'Practical and lexical knowledge', in P. N. Johnson-Laird and P. C. Wason (eds), *Thinking: Readings in Cognitive Science*, Cambridge University Press.

Miller, G. A. (1978), 'Semantic relations among words', in M. Halle, J. Bresnan and G. A. Miller (eds), *Linguistic Theory and Psychological Reality*, MIT Press: Cambridge, Mass.

Miller, G. A. and Johnson-Laird, P. N. (1976), *Language and Perception,* Cambridge University Press.

Minsky, M. (1975), 'Frame-system theory', in R. C. Schank and B. L. Nash-Webber (eds), *Theoretical Issues in Natural Language Processing,* MIT Conference report, reprinted 1977 in P. N. Johnson-Laird and P. C. Wason (eds), *Thinking: Readings in Cognitive Science,* Cambridge University Press.

Mitchell, D. C. and Green, D. W. (1978), 'The effects of context and content on immediate processing in reading', *Quarterly Journal of Experimental Psychology, 30,* pp. 609-36.

Mooij, J. J. A. (1976), *A Study of Metaphor,* North Holland: Amsterdam.

Navon, D. (1975), 'Global precedence in visual recognition', unpublished doctoral dissertation, University of California, San Diego.

Ortony, A., Reynolds, R. E. and Arter, J. A. (1978a), 'Metaphor: theoretical and empirical research', *Psychological Bulletin, 85,* pp. 919-43.

Ortony, A., Schallert, D. L., Reynolds, R. E. and Antos, S. J. (1978b), 'Interpreting metaphors and idioms: some effects of context on comprehension', *Journal of Verbal Learning and Verbal Behavior, 17,* pp. 465-77.

Pichert, J. W. and Anderson, R. C. (1977), 'Taking different perspectives on a story', *Journal of Educational Psychology, 69,* pp. 309-15.

Pollio, H. R., Barlow, J. M., Fine, H. J. and Pollio, M. R. (1977), *Psychology and the Poetics of Growth: Figurative language in Psychology, Psychotherapy and Education,* Lawrence Erlbaum: Hillsdale, New Jersey.

Reber, A. S. and Anderson, J. R. (1970), 'The perception of clicks in linguistic and non-linguistic messages', *Perception and Psychophysics, 8,* pp. 81-9.

Reboul, O. (1974), 'Slogans and education', *Diogenes, 86,* pp. 55-72.

Richards, I. A. (1965), *The Philosophy of Rhetoric,* Oxford University Press: New York.

Rumelhart, D. E. (1975), 'Notes on a schema for stories', in D. G. Bobrow and A. Collins (eds), *Representation and Understanding,* Academic Press: New York.

Schafer, R. (1976), *A New Language for Psychoanalysis,* Yale University Press.

Schank, R. C. and Abelson, R. P. (1977), *Scripts, Plans, Goals and Understanding: An inquiry into human knowledge structures,* Lawrence Erlbaum: Hillsdale, N.J.

Searle, J. (1968), *Speech Acts,* Cambridge University Press.

Searle, J. (in press), 'Metaphor', in A. Ortony (ed.), *Metaphor and Thought,* Cambridge University Press.

Shebileske, W. L. (1977), 'Reading eye movements, macro-structure and goal processing', paper read at conference on Processing of Visible Language. Eindhoven.

Smith, N. V. (1979), 'Syntax for psychologists', in J. Morton and J. C. Marshall (eds), *Psycholinguistics Series 2. Structure and Processes,* Elek: London.

Steedman, M. J. and Johnson-Laird, P. N. (1978), 'A programmatic theory of linguistic performance', in R. W. Campbell and P. T. Smith (eds), *Recent Advances in Psycholinguistics,* vol. 11, Plenum: New York.

Thorndyke, P. W. (1977), 'Cognitive structures in comprehension and memory of narrative discourse', *Cognitive Psychology, 9,* pp. 77-110.

Turbayne, C. M. (1970), *The Myth of Metaphor,* U. of South Carolina Press.

Tversky, A. (1977), 'Features of similarity', *Psychological Review, 84*, pp. 327-52.

Van Dijk, T. A. (1977), *Text and Context: Explorations in the Semantics and Pragmatics of Discourse*, Longman: London.

Verbrugge, R. R. and McCarrell, N. S. (1977), 'Metaphoric comprehension: studies in reminding and resembing', *Cognitive Psychology, 9*, pp. 494-533.

Wanner, E. and Maratsos, M. (1978), 'An ATN approach to comprehension, in M. Halle, J. Bresnan and G. A. Miller (eds), *Linguistic Theory and Psychological Reality*, MIT Press: Cambridge, Mass.

Wason, P. C. (1972), 'In real life, negatives are false', *Logique et Analyse, 57-8*, pp. 19-38.

Werner, H. and Kaplan, B. (1963), *Symbol Formation: An organismic-development approach to language and the expression of thought*, Wiley: New York.

8 Thinking: experiential and information processing approaches

Jonathan St B. T. Evans

Introduction

The nature of thinking has been the object of serious study in philosophy and psychology since the time of Aristotle, but we still have very limited understanding of this phenomenon. Whilst recognizing the theoretical importance of understanding thought, comparatively few cognitive psychologists are studying it experimentally, preferring to concentrate on the 'simpler' problems associated with perception, memory and language. In my view it is conceptual, rather than methodological, problems which deter research into this important field. Consequently, this chapter will aim to clarify conceptual issues, and attempt to indicate the directions in which research can productively develop.

The important point is that psychologists use the term 'thinking' and related terms (e.g., strategy, image) in several quite distinct senses, which can too easily become confused. In historical order of development the main conceptions of thought are as (a) *mental experience*, (b) *behaviour*, and (c) *information processing*. A brief historical review of these conceptions is in order.

In the view of Aristotle and other early Greek philosophers, the mind or rational soul, being pure, could only be studied by itself; to study others by observation through the bodily, and hence impure, medium of the senses was simply not on. Thus the only method available to study thinking was introspection by the philosopher himself. If the method of study is limited to introspection, then the phenomena which may be studied can only be those which are introspectible, the 'contents of consciousness', or mental experience. By use of this method Aristotle concluded that the content of the mind

275

consisted principally of images which are reproductions of past sensations. The operations of the mind could be deduced from the temporal order in which such images presented themselves to the mind. Aristotle proposed several principles of organization, of which the most important was association by contiguity: those things which have been presented together in one's previous experience tend to be recalled together. This basic associationist theory of thinking, with a focus upon images as the content of the mind, was developed and embellished by the British Empiricist School (e.g., Hobbes, James, Mill, Locke) and was generally dominant until the late nineteenth century. For a review of associationist and empiricist philosophy from a psychological viewpoint the reader is recommended to Mandler and Mandler (1964).

The associationist theory, with its implicit emphasis on mental experience as an adequate definition of thinking, was not seriously challenged until psychologists started to study thinking by controlled experiment, albeit with an introspective methodology. Thus, for example, Galton (1883) by making serious introspective study of his own thought processes reached the following conclusions: 'Its (consciousness's) position appears to be that of a helpless spectator of but a minute fraction of automatic brain work'. It is a tribute to the genius of Galton that he discovered the undoubted limitations of the introspective method through using that method itself, without the benefit of the subsequently developed experimental techniques.

Similar conclusions were reached by psychologists of the Wurzburg school working in Germany at around the turn of the century (for a detailed review see Humphrey, 1951). Their methodology involved giving a subject a task to perform such as producing a word association, or making a psychophysical judgment, and then immediately asking him to introspect upon his mental experiences. According to the associationist theory they expected all such acts to be mediated by images; in fact some reports indicated no accompanying mental experience, and others experiences of an indescribable nature, the so-called 'imageless thoughts'. Despite vehement methodological criticism by Wundt, the Wurzburg work produced an impressive and important set of results, the more so since their methods have not been repeated in modern studies of thinking.

In the twentieth century the notions of thinking as an introspectible mental experience was further challenged by the concept of *unconscious* thinking: an idea made famous by Freud, but developed by others before him (see Reeves, 1965). In experimental psychology, however, the most important development was that of behaviourism, spearheaded by Watson (1914). The notion of mental experience and any other kind of unobservable entity was banished by the behaviourists with their stimulus-response approach. Although primarily concerned with learning, the behaviourists attempted to describe 'thinking' in similar terms, thus introducing a second conception of thought – a term used to describe certain complex forms of *behaviour*, such as those involved in problem-solving. While Watson was determined to explain away thinking as sub-vocal speech, behaviourists such as Skinner (1972) are happy to acknowledge mental experience, whilst denying that it has any role in explaining behaviour.

It is important to realize that the radically behaviourist approach implicit in our second definition of thought is not only anti-mentalistic but also opposed to any postulation of unobservable mechanisms or processes. There is, in fact, an intermediate position, the most recently developed, in which thinking is conceived of as a form of *information processing* which mediates between stimulus and response. This is the so-called *cognitive* approach with which the authors of this book are primarily concerned. The point is that the process postulated need not manifest itself as mental experience, and the methods used to infer the nature of these processes do not, in the main, rest upon introspection.

One of the first psychologists to exploit the now familiar computer analogy, and propose an information processing theory of thinking was Neisser (1963). He proposed that thinking had a main sequence analogous to an 'executive' program which was by its nature sequential; in addition, parallel or multiple thought processes were constantly in progress and liable to influence the main sequence. A computer simulation model was devised on very similar principles by Reitman *et al.* (1964). Neisser, however, proposed also that the main sequence relates to what we call 'conscious' thinking and the multiple process to 'preconscious' thinking (Kubie, 1958). In doing so he went beyond the cognitive conception, as defined here, and proposed a relationship between the cognitive and experiential definitions. It is the nature of this relationship, and the confusions associated with it, which will be the main concern of this chapter.

The best-known work on thinking using an information processing approach is probably that of Newell and Simon (1972). For the past fifteen to twenty years intensive efforts have been made to develop 'artificial intelligence' programs which will enable computers to solve mathematical problems, play chess, and generally, according to some definitions at least, to 'think'. The psychological value of this work is debatable, but some psychologists, at least, are optimistic. Thus, for example, in selecting readings on the subject of problem-solving, Johnson-Laird and Wason (1977) state, 'we have emphasized theories of problem-solving, and especially ideas from Artificial Intelligence because in the past brute empiricism has led to periods of stagnation in the area'. The viewpoint is, of course, controversial; there are many who believe that more systematic experimental study of thinking is needed.

At one level the Artificial Intelligence work has clearly made an important psychological contribution. In order to write a computer program to do something, one is forced to make a clear conceptual analysis of the thing which is to be done. Consequently, the nature of 'problem-solving' has been more clearly defined. In particular, it has been shown that the complex problem-solving behaviour which is characteristic of human intelligence cannot be achieved by exhaustive search procedures (algorithms) but requires *selective* search procedure (heuristics). Some of the heuristic programming techniques that have been developed, such as means-end analysis (see Newell and Simon, 1972), are of direct psychological relevance. It is interesting to note that one of the most general heuristic techniques, that of working backwards from the desired conclusion and setting up of sub-problems, was anticipated in the Gestalt study of problem-solving. For example, Duncker (1945) claims that erroneous attempts at solving problems are not valueless, but lead to the discovery of 'solution principles'. He concludes, 'The final form of a solution is typically attained by way of mediating processes, of which each one, in retrospect, possesses the character of a solution, and, in prospect, that of a problem.'

How, though, can we assess the value of a computer program as a psychological theory? From the viewpoint of a cognitive psychologist it is not sufficient to develop a program which does the same thing as people; it must also do it in a similar way. In some fields, such as chess playing, even the first requirement has not been met (programs are still below master standard). For programs which have simulated human behaviour reasonably well in certain situations (e.g., the General Problem Solver, Newell and Simon, 1963) attempts to meet the second requirement have relied heavily on protocol analysis (discussed in detail by Newell and Simon, 1972). Such protocols are obtained by asking subjects to 'think aloud' while solving a problem. Whilst detailed analysis of this work is beyond the scope of the present chapter, a couple of cautionary notes can be sounded. Like the introspective method, to which it is closely related, the 'thinking aloud' method severely restricts the type of thought that can be studied – specifically to that which can be verbalized. Worse, as Neisser (1963) points out, such a method may actually alter the nature of the thought process being studied: in terms of Neisser's theory, for example, by restricting thinking to the main sequence. For an interesting discussion on this form of protocol analysis, see Byrne (1977).

Having distinguished the three conceptions of thinking, we should consider their relevance in understanding contemporary studies of thought. All three conceptions are still with us, although rarely explicitly defined, and commonly confused. A problem which is of central concern to cognitive psychology is that of the relationship between experiential and information processing concepts. Upon our ability to resolve this problem rests, for example, any assessment of the value of subjective reports or introspective data of any kind. From a more theoretical point of view the question is raised as to whether or not the undeniable phenomenon of mental experience comes within the scope of experimental psychology. At a more personal level we may ask the question, 'Does my subjective experience tell me anything about the way in which I actually make decisions, solve problems, and so on?' Each of these questions will be considered.

First of all, however, I must define a potentially confusing term: 'mentalism'. As I shall use the term, mentalism does *not* refer to approaches which affirm the existence of mental experience, nor those which regard experience as a legitimate phenomenon for psychologists to study. Rather I shall use the term to refer to the assumption that mental events *cause* behaviour, or the supposition that subjective reports necessarily reveal 'underlying processes' which are functional in behaviour. A strong form of mentalism, which would clearly require that all cognitive acts were introspectible, hardly exists in modern psychology; it is too easy to refute. A weak form of mentalism in which *some* processes are considered introspectible, abounds, however. As Pylyshyn (1973) succinctly puts it,

> While most psychologists are willing to concede that not all
> important psychological processes and structures are available to

conscious inspection, it is not generally recognized that the converse may also hold: That what is available to conscious inspection may not be what plays an important causal role in psychological processes.

However, the weak mentalistic position rests critically on the assumption that all introspectible processes are functional in behaviour, as can be demonstrated by a simple logical argument. If only some experiences are functional, than we can only determine *which* by some independent measurement of the process; for example, by the use of 'converging operations'. However, if such an independent measure is available then we don't need the subjective report to explain the behaviour.

It can be seen from the above that an explicitly held mentalistic position is very hard to maintain. Our main concern will be more with inplicitly held mentalistic views that tend to creep unnoticed into various arguments in cognitive psychology. The position that will be argued here is not that introspective reports are useless, but that they have been misinterpreted. As Byrne (1977) points out, verbal reports are a form of data to be explained in their own right, not a means of explaining some other aspect of behaviour. The problems arise when we stop regarding the reports as one of the dependent variables, along with errors and response times, and start regarding them as descriptions of underlying processes.

In order to illustrate the nature of these problems it is necessary now to examine in detail some fields of current interest in the psychology of thinking. In view of space limitations we will focus selectively on investigations concerned with the phenomena of *imagery* and *reasoning*.

Contemporary studies

Imagery

Psychological research into mental imagery provides some of the clearest examples of approaches which are primarily concerned with mental experience, those which regard imagery as a constituent in information processing, and those which sadly confuse the two. The earliest systematic study of imagery as a mental experience was conducted by Galton (1883). His study, which was restricted to visual imagery, involved asking people to visualize their breakfast table and to describe the clarity of their image. Galton discovered large individual differences not only in the vividness of imagery reported but also in its controllability (i.e., the degree to which a subject could summon and direct it 'at will'). Subsequent research has confirmed that these are indeed the main dimensions of imagery as measured by self-report; for a review of work of this sort the reader is referred to Richardson (1977).

To some psychologists, imagery is by definition a mental experience; namely, one which is similar to a perceptual experience, in the absence of the appropriate sensory stimulation. There are, however, those who are entirely interested in imagery as a form of information-processing and make no use of introspective report at all. A good example of this can be found in a paper by Brooks (1968), who set out to test the 'notion that verbal and spatial information are handled in distinct, modality-specific manners'. Brooks showed that if asked to recall information of a spatial nature, subjects' performance deteriorated when a response task involving the visual modality (pointing) was used, compared with a response task of an auditory nature (speaking). Converse results were found if the information to be recalled was verbal and auditory in nature. One advantage of Brooks's results is that one can run the argument in reverse: if one wishes to find out the nature of the modality used in certain forms of information processing, one may use interference with a competing task in a certain modality as a 'converging operation' to measure this, an argument similar to that used by Allport in Chapter 4. For example, if a problem-solving process is supposed to involve imagery, then there ought to be more interference with a concurrent visual than auditory task. A recent experiment along these lines is that of Shaver *et al.* (1975).

It is clear that Brooks's concept of a modality-specific information-processing system is not dependent upon a phenomenological conception of imagery. Other research is less clear. Consider, for example, the work of Segal (1971) on the Perky phenomenon. The phenomenon discovered by Perky (1910) is that under certain circumstances subjects can be tricked into believing that their perception of a weak stimulus presented by the experimenter is actually a construction of their own visual imagination. Segal terms this a 'reality decision', analyses the data by signal detection theory, and manipulates dozens of independent variables which may be shown to affect the phenomenon. The impressive aura of scientism thus created might easily divert one from the realization that the whole problem is phenomenological in nature.

Some psychologists have directed themselves specifically to the problem of how to relate experiential and information-processing conceptions of imagery. Neisser (1969) refers to the fact that self-report measures of vividness of imagery frequently correlate poorly or zero with performance measures on tasks involving spatial information processing (see, for example, Sheehan and Neisser, 1969). He regards this as 'paradoxical'. The finding is only paradoxical, of course, if we expect self-report data to reflect awareness of functionally significant processes. An approach which could handle Neisser's paradox easily, without recourse to rejecting introspective data as 'unreliable', is that of Singer (1966). In explanation of daydream reports, Singer proposes that many internal processes go on continually, whether or not we are aware of them. Conscious attention may be given to these processes or else to external (perceptual) channels. On Singer's model individuals could differ with respect to their awareness of internal processes, including those experienced as imagery. There is no reason to suppose a correlation between those who are most aware of their internal visual information processing, and the efficiency of those processes in solving problems, etc. This 'partial awareness' hypothesis does nothing to enhance the value of introspective data in explaining behaviour.

The main problem which has arisen in the study of imagery is the use of *covert* mentalistic assumptions. That is to say imagery is apparently defined 'operationally', but the interpretation of data is actually determined by phenomenological conceptions. That this may arise from the implicit assumptions of the author, as well as from misinterpretation of introspective data, has been argued most strongly and cogently by Pylyshyn (1973). The kind of work which Pylyshyn criticizes is typified by the approach of Paivio (1971) and his co-authors to the role of imagery in verbal learning. Paivio's theory proposes a dual coding mechanism for memory, one code being verbal and the other visual in nature. In support of the functional role of imagery, Paivio cites evidence based on a number of different converging operations; for example, the effect of instructions to image upon performance, or demonstration that material more evocative of images is easier to learn.

Pylyshyn (1973) makes a powerful criticism of this sort of evidence.

Although imagery is defined operationally, each different converging operation defines a different theoretical construct of *image*.

> The identity of these various constructs (image 1 = image 2 = ...) does not, however, follow from any of the operational definitions nor from the results of the experiments . . . . The unity of these constructs, and consequently the coherence of the notion of imagery, rests on a metatheoretical assumption. This assumption in turn, rests on the persuasiveness of subjective experience and the ordinary informal meaning of the word *image*.

Against this the imagery researcher may claim that a perfectly proper process of construct validation is being employed; thus 'it is legitimate for a scientific enterprise in a formative period to be engaged in research on a construct whose definition has not yet been precisely formulated' (Kosslyn and Pomerantz, 1977).

Inspection of Pylyshyn's other criticisms of imagery reveals that he is an anti-mentalistic cognitive psychologist. He does not deny the reality of mental experience but doubts the value of phenomenal reports in revealing functional processes. One point he makes is that information cannot be stored as images in the form of unprocessed mental photographs; there would be far too many and no possible means of organizing access to them. He argues that the nature of recalled imagery is *conceptual* and that they must therefore be constructed from information stored in a more abstract form. He thus argues that we should base our theories on these abstract representations and regard the presence of imagery as epiphenomenal; i.e., not the functional process itself, but a by-product. Although his interest in internal representation clearly makes Pylyshyn a cognitive psychologist, his critique of mentalism is strikingly similar to that of modern behaviourists (see Skinner, 1972).

Pylyshyn also attacks the 'picture in the head' metaphor of imagery as being conceptually dangerous: the analogy might be false, for example, in regarding the 'picture' as a stimulus to be processed, instead of the end-product of perceptual processing which he claims it must be. In a systematic attempt to refute Pylyshyn's criticisms, Kosslyn and Pomerantz (1977), with reference to his criticism of the picture metaphor say, 'We agree with Pylyshyn that this approach is untenable, but fail to see what is gained by attacking such a strawman. No serious student of imagery holds this view.' Notwithstanding this denial, various comments of Kosslyn and Pomeranz give the impression that they do indeed regard images and entities to be seen and inter-preted by the mind's eye. Thus, 'If images are sensory patterns that have been partially processed and stored, the question of how know-ledge can be derived from imagery is quite similar to the question of how knowledge is derived from ongoing sensory activity.' To take another example, 'Many of the operators . . . that are used in analysing percepts are also applied to images.'

Their treatment of the problem of introspective data is equally unsatisfactory. If Pylyshyn's notion that experienced imagery is epiphenomenal is correct, then considerable doubt must attach to the value of such data. Not only is the subject's reported experience not a description of the functional process itself, but there is no reason to suppose that the same experience will accompany the same process in different individuals. Further problems arise from the question of whether subjects are able to describe their mental experience in clear and consistent terms.

Kosslyn and Pomerantz ignore most of these problems and state that introspective reports may be used as 'corroborative' evidence. Thus they say,

> Introspections are not adequate in and of themselves to attest to the functional role of imagery in cognition. However, they are one source of evidence which, when taken together with behavioural performance data, can assist in demonstrating that images have genuine functions in cognition.

This kind of vague statement is most unhelpful: unless we know exactly what information introspective evidence is giving us *independently* of other measures in the situation, it is useless. The use of introspections as corroborative evidence is dangerous for a particular reason, emphasized in recent papers by Wason and Evans (1975) and Nisbett and Wilson (1977). The nature of this problem will be elaborated later. First, we look at a specific research field in which imagery has been evoked as an explanatory construct.

Transitive inference

A field of research in which the issue of imagery as a functional process has been recently debated, concerns reasoning with transitive relationships. Transitive inference arises when objects can be *ordered* on some dimension such as tall-short, good-bad, hot-cold. For example, if we are told that John is taller than Bill and that Jim is shorter than Bill, we may infer that John is taller than Jim. Such problems are also known as linear syllogisms or three-term series problems. Considerable controversy has been focussed on whether or not an 'imagery strategy' is employed in solving this sort of problem. This approach, initiated by De Soto *et al.* (1965), and developed by Huttenlocher (1968), postulates that subjects construct a vertical spatial array in which the objects are placed. Thus, in the problem given earlier, a subject might construct an array with 'tall' at the top and 'short' at the bottom. On reading the first premise he would place John above Bill in his mental array; on reading the second premise he would place Jim below Bill. An inference about the relationship between John and Jim can then be made by inspecting their relative positions in the array; John is above Jim and therefore taller.

The imagery theory can generate predictions about problem difficulty by making certain additional postulates: for example, that it is easier to reason from top to bottom of the array than vice versa, and that it is easier to reason inward from an end item than to reason outwards from a middle item. However, problem difficulty can also be predicted by an alternative linguistic theory proposed by Clark (1969), which resulted in a lively controversy between Clark and Huttenlocher. Those who have reviewed this controversy have tended to conclude that a satisfactory discrimination between the two theories cannot be made on the basis of their predictions as assessed by errors and response latencies (Johnson-Laird, 1972; Shaver *et al.*, 1975).

The imagery case does not, however, rest on this kind of evidence alone. A large number of different kinds of evidence have been adduced to show that visual imagery is involved:

1 Introspective reports indicate that 'imagery' accompanies problem-solving on these tasks (e.g., Huttenlocher, 1968; Quinton and Fellows, 1976; Shaver *et al.*, 1975).

2 Manipulation of actual spatial materials by children produces parallel data to adults' reasoning with propositions (e.g., Huttenlocher *et al.*, 1970).

3 The spatial arrangement of the elements of a linear syllogism, when written down by a subject, corresponds to that predicted to occur in the imaginal array (e.g., De Soto *et al.*, 1965; Jones, 1970).

4 Performance on transitive inference problems deteriorates when

the subject reads the problem rather than listens to it (Shaver *et al.*, 1975). This evidence is based upon Brooks's (1968) converging operation.

5   Facilitation of reasoning behaviour occurs on imagery-provoking materials (Shaver *et al.*, 1975). This evidence is based on one of Paivio's (1971) converging operations employed in memory research.

6   Correlations of reasoning performance with spatial test scores has been claimed (Shaver *et al.*, 1975).

7   Subjects instructed in the use of an imagery strategy show improved performances (Shaver *et al.*, 1975).

The imagery theorist would claim that taken together all these different pieces of evidence accumulate overwhelming evidence for the theory. We should, however, recall Pylyshyn's caution with respect to linking different operational definitions by metatheoretical assumptions. In view of this, it is worth examining each piece of evidence on its merits in order to see whether imagery is, in fact, acting usefully as an explanatory construct. We have already alluded to the danger of regarding introspection as corroborative evidence. When a theory is constructed from inspection of such reports as in Huttenlocher (1968), they certainly cannot be claimed as independent evidence of it. Furthermore, an extraordinary misuse of such data occurs in the Shaver *et al.* (1975) paper. They asked subjects to report the 'strategy' they used in solving the problems, which they classified as visual-spatial and so on. They then correlated reported strategy, not with reasoning performance, but with the subjects' report of 'which mode of presentation . . . seemed most difficult'. What on earth could a correlation of one subjective report with another prove? Quinton and Fellows (1976), who do correlate reported strategy with performance, nevertheless impute a quite unjustified *causal* relationship. For a critique of this paper see Evans (1976) and, for a reply, Fellows (1976).

Leaving aside the introspective evidence as highly dubious, we now turn our attention to the other claims. Huttenlocher's evidence of parallel performance in spatial manipulation tasks does not even furnish evidence of spatial processing, let alone visual imagery. Since the sentences have to be understood in either task, Clark's (1969) linguistic theory would predict parallel problem difficulty in any case.

The use of converging operations, derived from Paivio and Brooks, appear in the paper of Shaver *et al.* (1975). This paper has a number of flaws, however, one of which has already been mentioned. Shaver *et al.* make much of the fact that significant *main effects* of visual *v.* auditory presentation, and the imagery-provoking nature of the materials occur in the predicted directions. Brooks (1968), from whom they derive this technique, makes it quite clear that it is only *interactions* which can demonstrate imagery. For example, visual presentation may cause more difficulty than auditory presentation for any number of reasons. The crucial point in the Shaver study was to show that any interference caused by visual presentation would be greater for problems likely to evoke an imagery strategy. This interaction, although in the predicted direction, is not statistically significant in their study. To make matters worse, a recent study by Phillips and Christie (1977) has cast doubt on Brooks's original conclusions and hence the validity of converging operations based on input modality.

In a second experiment, Shaver *et al.* instructed one group of subjects with an imagery strategy and found superior performance to that obtained by a non-instructed group. The evidence this provides for the imagery hypothesis is not so much weak as non-existent. There is no control for the effect of instructions with *any* strategy, with its inevitable additional contact with the subject and the better understanding of the problems which may result. Nor is there any evidence that the instructed subjects used imagery apart from introspection. This evidence is particularly worthless here since the subject is likely to give a verbalization which is biased by the instructions given at the outset.

A recent experiment in my own department attempted to rectify these faults (Evans and Rollason, unpublished). In our experiment, one group of subjects were instructed with an imagery strategy and another with a strategy based on Hunter's (1957) theory of transitive reasoning. Neither type of instruction facilitated performance compared with a control group. Furthermore, there was absolutely no evidence that instructions to image interacted with the imagery-provoking nature of the materials. Although Shaver *et al.* manipulated this latter variable also, they strangely report no data on it. Finally, Shaver *et al.*'s evidence of correlation of performance with spatial test scores could result from any common factor of ability, including the old familiar IQ.

The one source of evidence which we have not yet discussed is the spatial arrangement that occurs when subjects write down the objects of the problem. This evidence is interesting, but has nothing whatever to do with visual imagery. To equate spatial information processing with visualization is quite unnecessary. Such an assumption would lead, for example, to the quite erroneous conclusion that a chess master's ability to analyse the positions 'in the head' required visual imagery. Jones (1970) has shown that the spatial arrangements which occur correlate with one of Clark's (1969) linguistic principles. Since Clark's theory does indeed fail to specify the process by which information in different premises is combined (as Huttenlocher suggests), Jones's results suggest a useful combination of elements of both theories could be made.

Shaver *et al.* (1975) conclude their paper as follows: 'Clark's "only firm conclusion" that "it has not been demonstrated that the use of spatial imagery differentially affects the solution of three-term series problems" appears to be incorrect'. My conclusion to this section in turn contradicts theirs. There does not appear to be any good evidence that visual imagery is either a necessary or useful explanatory construct for transitive inference. Clark's quoted conclusion still holds. The conclusion that we should rather draw from this review is that Pylyshyn's analysis of the danger and futility of pursuing a mentalistic notion of imagery has been amply demonstrated in this field. We now turn our attention to a different field of research into deductive reasoning, which has managed to develop its own introspective difficulties, without any assistance from the concept of imagery.

Propositional reasoning

Like imagery, the study of reasoning with verbal statements or propositions has its roots in ancient philosophy. It is from philosophy that we derive various systems of formal logic, which tell us how conclusions may validly be deduced from assumptions. Many philosophers believed that in proposing the rules of logic they were actually describing the laws of human thought, an idea which has returned to fashion in psychology following a paper by Henle (1962). For a critical appraisal of this view, and a detailed review of the usefulness of formal logic in explaining human reasoning, the reader is referred to a previous article (Evans, 1978). The present section will focus selectively on research with a particular reasoning problem which has raised questions relevant to the main issue under consideration in this chapter.

The problem was devised by Wason (1966) and has become known as the Wason selection task or four-card problem. In one form of the problem the subject is told that a set of cards have each got a triangle on one side and a circle on the other. The figures are either red or blue in colour. He is then shown four such cards lying on a table. The visible symbols on the upward facing sides are: red triangle, blue triangle, red circle and blue circle. The subject is then given a rule which applies to the four cards and may be true or false:

IF THERE IS A RED TRIANGLE ON ONE SIDE OF THE CARD, THEN THERE IS A BLUE CIRCLE ON THE OTHER SIDE OF THE CARD.

The subject's problem is to select those cards and *only* those cards which must be turned over in order to find out whether the rule is true or false. Most commonly subjects choose only the red triangle, or else the red triangle and the blue circle. Neither selection is logically correct: the solution is the red triangle and the *red* circle. The reason is that only a red circle on the back of the red triangle could disprove the rule. Only by choosing those cards could a potentially falsifying combination be discovered. Wason (1966) interpreted the errors of failing to select the red circle, and incorrectly choosing the blue circle as reflecting a *verification bias*. Subjects, he supposed, were attempting to find a verifying combination of red triangle and blue circle, rather than attempting to find the falsifying combination as is logically required.

Since the selection task is presented with a variety of different materials, it is convenient to represent it in general terms. The rule presented is of the form *If p then q*, and the cards presented are *p*, *not p*, *q* and *not q* (for example, *not q* is the red circle in the above example). In these terms the correct selection is *p* and *not q*, and the common erroneous selections *p* alone and *p* and *q*.

In early experiments (see Wason and Johnson-Laird, 1972) the pattern of error was found to be highly stable and indifferent to variations in task presentation. Experiments were designed which introduced 'therapeutic' procedures in an attempt to improve performance, particularly with respect to *not q* selections (Wason, 1969; Wason and Johnson-Laird, 1970). As a result, a new pattern of responding emerged. Some subjects adopted *not q*, but retained *q*, thus choosing overall *p*, *q* and *not q*. The therapy administered consisted of forcing the subject to consider the consequences of turning over each card, and thus realizing that turning *not q* could lead to falsification of the rule. The interesting result was that although all subjects gave verbal recognition of this, a substantial number refused to alter their original selections. In the Wason and Johnson-Laird (1970) study verbal protocols were recorded, which led the authors to distinguish a *selection* process underlying performance on the main task from an *evaluation* process induced by the therapy. They comment that 'the selection and evaluation processes may either interact, or pass one another by . . . . Such processes conflict in some individuals but evidently not in others'. We will return to these ideas later.

Johnson-Laird and Wason (1970) produced a formal information processing model in which they proposed that subjects are in one of three states of insight: 'no insight' when they attempted to verify and not to falsify the rule; 'partial insight' where they attempted to do both; and 'complete insight' where they attempted only falsification. The response associated with each level of insight was p or p and q ('no insight'), p, q *and not* q ('partial insight') and p *and not* q ('complete insight'). As formulated, the model appears to be circular, since the states of insight can only be deduced from the responses which they 'underlie'. In an attempt to solve this problem Goodwin and Wason (1972) asked subjects to give a verbal justification for selecting or failing to select each card. As presented the justifications revealed the level of insight specified in the model to accompany a given selection. Thus, a subject choosing p and q might justify his choice of p on the grounds that a q on the back would prove the rule true. A subject choosing p and *not* q, however, would justify his choice of p by saying that if there were *not* a q on the back then the rule would be false.

There are two flaws in Goodwin and Wason's evidence. Firstly, it is not a truly independent test of the model since Johnson-Laird and Wason (1970) had studied many verbal protocols *before* they constructed the model. Second, the evidence for the model rests on the mentalistic assumption that the subject is in fact reporting the thought process which mediated his selections. Doubt was cast on this latter assumption by the discovery of evidence that a quite different factor could explain selections on Wason's task.

On a different reasoning problem I had discovered a phenomenon which I called 'matching bias' (Evans, 1972). Suppose that we have a set of cards which have a letter on one side and a number on the other. I propose a rule to apply to such cards:

IF THE LETTER IS A *T* THEN THE NUMBER IS NOT A *4*.

You are required to name a combination of a letter and a number which in conjunction would violate or falsify this rule. Almost all subjects set this problem correctly specify the T and 4. In a different problem the rule might be:

IF THE LETTER IS NOT A *T* THEN THE NUMBER IS A *4*.

To be logically constant subjects should say that a letter other than T with a number other than 4 (e.g., M3) would falsify this rule: both problems are solved by making the first part of the rule true, and the second part false. In fact most subjects say T and 4 on the second problem as well, showing a bias to match the values named in the rules, irrespective of the logical effect of such choices. On the selection task the common erroneous choices of *p* and *q* might, then, be due to matching bias, since these are the matching choices. Matching bias and verification bias can only be separated in Wason's selection task by manipulating the presence and absence of negative components. For example, on the rule *If not p then not q*, the verifying choices are *not p* and *not q*, both of which mismatch. The crucial experiment, conducted by Evans and Lynch (1973), showed highly significant evidence of matching bias on the selection task, and no evidence of verification bias.

The apparent conflict between the Goodwin and Wason and Evans and Lynch results was resolved by some joint research carried out by Wason and myself. In one experiment subjects were given the selection task with the rules *If p then q* and *If p then not q* and asked to justify their selections (Wason and Evans, 1975). On the former, affirmative rule the matching response *p* and *q* is incorrect, but on the second, negative rule it leads to the logically correct choices. Most subjects matched on both rules. In addition, subjects invariably gave a verbal justification consistent with their behaviour. Since subjects each did both problems an interesting paradox arose. Wason and Evans (1975) give examples of protocols in which the subjects who are given the negative rule first, give the selection *p* and *q* and justify their responses with apparent 'complete insight'. The same subjects subsequently given the affirmative rule again gave *p* and *q* (now incorrect) with typical 'no insight' protocols. Since any reasonable definition of 'insight' (e.g., Wertheimer, 1961), requires *transfer* to problems of similar structure, it is hard to accept that the first protocol reflected a genuine insight. The obvious alternative is that the protocol is a *rationalization*, constructed *post hoc* to fit the behaviour and the instructions. In a second experiment (Evans and Wason, 1976), it was shown that subjects will happily justify any common selection pattern if it is presented to them as the 'correct' answer.

Wason and Evans (1975) go on to propose a dual-process theory of reasoning. It is proposed that a non-verbal (Type 1) process principally determines selections, and a verbal (Type 2) process underlies the introspective report. In the discussion of this paper the theory is applied to various previously puzzling findings in the literature. For example, the selection and evaluation process in the Wason and Johnson-Laird (1970) paper would correspond to our Type 1 and Type 2 processes. In Wason's '246' problem (see Wason and Johnson-Laird, 1972) a characteristic finding is that subjects continue to test an erroneous hypothesis despite being told that their verbal statement of this hypothesis is incorrect. They do this by successive verbal reformulations of the hypothesis which are semantically equivalent. In this situation, as well as those of Wason and Johnson-Laird (1970) and Wason and Evans (1975), the Type 1 process appears to dominate the actual reasoning *behaviour*, while the Type 2 process attempts to provide the subject with a *post hoc* justification or explanation of his behaviour. For further discussion of the original theory see Wason (1978).

In retrospect, the original statement of the dual-process theory seems somewhat deficient. First of all, the Type 2 process was described as 'conscious' and the Type 1 process as 'unconscious' without proper definition of those terms. Verbal and non-verbal now seems more appropriate to me. Second, the processes were seen as operating in alternation rather than parallel. However, since reasoning data has been analysed into two components, one *logical* and the other *non-logical* in nature (see Evans, 1978) it is tempting to associate these with Type 2 and Type 1 processes respectively. Clearly this assumption entails the Type 2 process exerting some control over the reasoning behaviour as well as the verbalization. Furthermore, the formal model fitted to these two components by Evans (1977) implies underlying processes that operate in parallel, and 'compete' for control of the response.

If Type 1 and Type 2 processes are assumed to operate in parallel, this leads to interesting speculation as to their origin. One possible idea is that Type 1 processes reflect primarily right-hemisphere activity and Type 2 processes left-hemisphere activity. This notion is consistent with recent work on hemispheric specialization in cognition (see Cohen, 1977) with respect to the verbal/non-verbal distinction. There is no direct evidence for this hypothesis as yet, and only one small-scale study suggesting the existence of hemispheric effects on these kinds of reasoning task (Golding *et al.*, 1974). At the time of writing, a large program of research into the psychological nature of the Type 1 and Type 2 process has just been initiated in my own department. It would, however, be premature to draw conclusions from the preliminary results available.

The story told in this section of work on a particular reasoning problem illustrates well the problems of confusing experiential and information-processing approaches to thinking, and the consequent misuse of introspective data. This contributed to the formulation of an incorrect reasoning model by Johnson-Laird and Wason (1970), and led to the faulty claim of supportive evidence by Goodwin and Wason (1972). This point is made with the benefit of hindsight, of course, and I am the first to concede the interesting nature of the research generated by Wason and Johnson-Laird's efforts. We must, however, learn from the conceptual errors made. It is now time to summarize and consider general implications.

Overview and new directions

The issue which has been the main focus of this chapter is that of the role of phenomenological data in cognitive approaches to thinking. This is, of course, an issue of general importance in cognitive psychology (see Claxton's introduction to this volume). The justification for this focus in a book on New Directions is that it is a problem causing concern and confusion in current work, as I hope the previous sections have demonstrated, and that the problem must be resolved to permit of useful progress in this field. To summarize the material considered, we note that cognitive psychologists may either be completely anti-mentalistic such as Pylyshyn, or place partial reliance on introspective data, such as Kosslyn. I contend that, quite apart from the theoretical arguments reviewed, the Kosslyn type of position is strongly undermined by the Wason and Evans findings.

Although Kosslyn does not specify the conditions under which he expects introspective reports to be useful, it seems that he and like minds accept them if they achieve three criteria: clarity of expression, confident assertion by the subject, and consistency with the behaviour observed. In the experiments which I ran with Wason all three criteria were met on protocols that were nevertheless apparent rationalizations. Thus Kosslyn's notion of introspections as useful corroborative data is unsound. Fortunately, considering their importance in the argument, the reasoning experiments detailed above are by no means the only evidence for this view. A recent survey of a large range of evidence in both social and cognitive psychology by Nisbett and Wilson (1977) led to essentially similar conclusions. They conclude that introspective reports do not indicate awareness of underlying causal processes, and that introspective reports consist of cause-effect type *theories* which the subject constructs in an attempt to explain his own behaviour.

The work reviewed leads, then, to the conclusion that mentalistic thinking has undesirable effects on theory construction and testing in psychology in two ways: (a) by leading us into false analogies, and to a misplaced faith in the unity of theoretical constructs such as imagery; and (b) by inviting a misinterpretation of verbal reports as descriptions of an underlying process. One question asked at the outset was whether or not the study of mental experience was a legitimate part of cognitive psychology. Perhaps the answer should be negative, since the safest course seems to be to regard it as epiphenomenal. Verbal protocol analysis, stripped of mentalistic assumption, is, however, most certainly an essential part of cognitive psychology. Many problem-solving and other important cognitive processes are output in verbal form; to ignore such data would be absurd.

I should like to consider briefly the implications of our conclusions for other fields of cognitive psychology. Although studies of thinking have been especially subject to mentalistic explanations, they are by no means confined to this area; indeed, Pylyshyn's critique of mental imagery was based largely on its application to the study of memory. Nor is thinking the only area in which introspective reports are considered admissible, particularly in the kind of 'corroborative' role advocated by Kosslyn. The attitude of Norman (1976) in introducing a book on memory, is typical of many:

> There is a difference between the level of our understanding
> derived from careful experimentation and that derived from
> careless introspection. One is precise and detailed . . . . The other is
> vague and imprecise . . . . That the two results do concern the same
> processes should be satisfying . . . It would be peculiar if our

careful study of thought processes led to results that were at odds with all of our intuitions.

Norman's words typify the attitude of many cognitive psychologists – introspective reports are imprecise and unreliable but do nevertheless relate to the processes controlling behaviour in the experiments. In view of the evidence discussed here it is not too 'peculiar' that our intuition is wrong. The well-established need for cognitive consistency may determine rationalization because (a) we need a rational account of our own behaviour; (b) we wish to please the experimenter who evidently regards introspection as feasible; and (c) we wish to preserve the illusion that we are in control of our own behaviour. The danger of the Norman-type attitude is that when experimental evidence is lacking or hard to interpret introspective reports tend to be accepted. A good example relates to the use of mnemonic strategies in memory; Luria's (1968) fascinating individual case study is, for example, based almost entirely on introspection.

It is necessary for our purposes to distinguish two kinds of verbal report: the *phenomenal report* and the *reported strategy*. The first type arises frequently in the study of perception and I have no quarrel with it. If we wish to know what a person experiences, for example in observing a visual illusion, there is no reason why we should not ask him, nor why he should not tell us. It is the reported strategy which arises frequently in studies of memory, as well as thinking, about which we are concerned.

Although it may be unkind to knock a fellow-contributor, a recent example may be found in Hitch and Baddeley (1976), who completely reinterpret the results of one experiment in the light of a rehearsal strategy reported by their subjects. Furthermore, no details are given of the method of questioning subjects, scoring of answers, and so on. To be fair to the authors, they were accepting a strategy which was in conflict with their predicted explanation of the results. (For the theoretical context of this research see Hitch, Chapter 5.) However, the view taken here is that the subject asked to introspect may be engaging in a similar exercise to the experimenter: constructing a theory to fit his behaviour. Therefore, what Hitch and Baddeley's observation really amounts to is a problem in the experimental design, which permitted of an alternative explanation of the results to that considered at the outset. Had introspective reports not been taken, then other psychologists would have criticized the authors' interpretation on similar grounds. Although in this particular case the introspective report helped to locate a fault in design, there may be many other cases where they have been used to disguise faults by reinforcing the experimenter's expectations. In any event it seems clear to me that many cognitive psychologists do regard introspective reports of 'strategy' as admissible in conjunction with experimental data, without considering the validity of the assumptions underlying this. The answer to the problem lies in designing the experiment sufficiently well that recourse to this form of data is not needed to interpret the results.

I would like to end with some very general speculations on how the study of thinking could and should develop in the future. Notwithstanding the mentalistic problems, the emergence of research interest into imagery in recent years has been vitally important. The reason is that is has served to break down the obsession of cognitive psychologists with the use of language, and thus conceive of ideas in verbal terms. problem in the study of memory as well as thinking (see Claxton's introductory chapter). I cannot help feeling that, important though language is, we heavily overestimate its role in cognition. The reason is, perhaps, that we communicate our ideas and formulate our theories with the use of language, and thus conveive of ideas in verbal terms. However, there are many types of thought which may be entirely non-verbal (e.g., chess playing) and the organization of such thought may be quite different.

In general I would like to see development of the idea of different *modes* of thinking operating in parallel: they may, for example, be linguistic, visual or abstract in nature. The imagery work advances this notion, although I am inclined to agree with Pylyshyn's criticisms of the picture analogy. The questions of whether or not cognitive processes operate in parallel or through one central executive, is, however, controversial in cognitive psychology at present (see, for example, the chapters by Allport and Hitch in this volume).

In future research we must be open to new theoretical and methodological ideas. I myself feel that mathematical models may have a lot to offer and have made a modest contribution in that direction (Evans, 1977). It seems a great shame to me that technical ignorance and prejudice have led to isolation of the mathematical modellers. Whilst a number of mathematical models have tended to trivialize the psychological nature of the problems studied, this need not necessarily happen. In any case the sanctity of the flow-charted alternatives, whether or not tied to Artificial Intelligence programs, seems to be based more on blind faith than proven usefulness.

On the methodological side – interpretation of protocols apart – we have real problems. Having rejected the old approach to 'verbal learning' due to its obsession with the psychology of nonsense syllables, cognitive psychologists have fallen into similar traps. The field is littered with paradigm-bound researchers unable to see out. As one who has consistently fallen into this trap myself, I could probably offer as good an explanation (i.e. *post hoc* rationalization) as anyone else. It seems that we adopt a Newell and Simon type heuristic of problem reduction, and then get stuck in a loop. In order to solve a problem like how do people see, think or remember, we set ourselves the sub-problem of explaining behaviour within a particular experimental situation. This problem is so much easier than the original one that it tends to become the final goal, with the original intention conveniently forgotten. The optimistic view is that we will learn to better our ways. Unless we do, progress will be very slow indeed.

References

Brooks, L. R. (1968), 'Spatial and verbal components of the act of recall', *Canadian Journal of Psychology*, *22*, pp. 249-68.

Byrne, R. (1977), 'Planning meals: problem solving on a real data base', *Cognition*, *5*, pp. 287-332.

Clark, H. H. (1969), 'Linguistic processes in deductive reasoning', *Psychological Review*, *79*, pp. 387-404.

Cohen, G. (1977), *The Psychology of Cognition*, Academic Press: London.

De Soto, C. B., London, M. and Handel, S. (1965), 'Social reasoning and spatial paralogic', *Journal of Personality and Social Psychology*, *2*, pp. 513-21.

Duncker, K. (1945), 'On problem solving', *Psychological Monographs, 58*, no. 270.

Evans, J. St B. T. (1972), 'Interpretation and matching bias in a reasoning task', *Quarterly Journal of Experimental Psychology*, *24*, pp. 193-9.

Evans, J. St B. T. (1976), 'A critical note on Quinton and Fellows' observation of reasoning strategies', *British Journal of Psychology*, *67*, pp. 517-18.

Evans, J. St B. T. (1977), 'Toward a statistical theory of reasoning', *Quarterly Journal of Experimental Psychology*, *29*, pp. 621-35.

Evans, J. St B. T. (1978), 'The psychology of deductive reasoning', in A. Burton and J. Radford (eds), *Thinking in Perspective,* Methuen: Lonon.

Evans, J. St B. T. and Lynch, J. S. (1973), 'Matching bias in the selection task', *British Journal of Psychology*, *64*, pp. 391-7.

Evans, J. St B. T. and Wason, P. C. (1976), 'Rationalization in a reasoning task', *British Journal of Psychology*, *67*, pp. 479-86.

Fellows, B. J. (1976), 'The role of introspection in problem solving research: a reply to Evans', *British Journal of Psychology*, *67*, pp. 519-20.

Galton, F. (1883), *Inquiries into Human Faculty and its Development*, Macmillan: London.

Golding, E. Reich, S. and Wason, P. C. (1974), 'Inter-hemispheric differences in problem solving', *Perception*, *3*, pp. 321-35.

Goodwin, R. Q. and Wason, P. C. (1972), 'Degrees of insight', *British Journal of Psychology*, *63*, pp. 205-12.

Henle, M. (1962), 'On the relation between logic and thinking', *Psychological Review*, *69*, pp. 336-78.

Hitch, G. J. and Baddeley, A. D. (1976), 'Verbal reasoning and working memory', *Quarterly Journal of Experimental Psychology*, *28*, pp. 603-21.

Humphrey, C. (1951), *Thinking: an introduction to its experimental psychology*, Methuen: London.

Hunter, I. M. L. (1957), 'The solving of three-term series problems', *British Journal of Psychology*, *68*, pp. 155-64.

Huttenlocher, J. (1968), 'Constructing spatial images: a strategy in reasoning', *Psychological Review*, *75*, pp. 550-60.

Huttenlocher, J., Higgins, E. T., Milligan, L. and Kaufman, B. (1970), 'The mystery of the "negative equative" construction', *Journal of Verbal Learning and Verbal Behavior*, *9*, pp. 334-41.

Johnson-Laird, P. N. (1972), 'The three-term series problem', *Cognition*, *1*, pp. 57-82.

Johnson-Laird, P. N. and Wason, P. C. (1970), 'A theoretical analysis of insight into a reasoning task', *Cognitive Psychology*, *1*, pp. 134-8.

Johnson-Laird, P. N. and Wason, P. C. (1977), *Thinking: Readings in Cognitive Science*, Cambridge University Press.

Jones, S. (1970), 'Visual and verbal processes in problem solving', *Cognitive Psychology*, *1*, pp. 201-14.

Kosslyn, S. M. and Pomerantz, J. R. (1977), 'Imagery, propositions and the form of internal representations', *Cognitive Psychology*, *9*, pp. 52-76.

Kubie, L. S. (1958), *Neurotic Distortions of the Creative Process*, University of Kansas Press.

Luria, A. R. (1968), *The Mind of a Mnemonist* (L. Salataroff, trans.), Basic Books: New York.

Mandler, J. M. and Mandler, G. (1964), *Thinking: from Associationist to Gestalt*, Wiley: New York.

Neisser, U. (1963), 'The multiplicity of thought', *British Journal of Psychology*, *54*, pp. 1-14.

Neisser, U. (1969), 'Visual imagery as process and experience', paper read to the British Psychological Society, London.

Newell, A. and Simon, H. A. (1963), 'GPS, a program that simulates human thought', in E. A. Feigenbaum and J. Feldman (eds), *Computers and Thought*, McGraw Hill: New York.

Newell, A. and Simon, H. A. (1972), *Human Problem Solving*, Prentice-Hall: Englewood Cliffs, N. J.

Nisbett, R. E. and Wilson, T. D. (1977), 'Telling more than one can know: verbal reports on mental processes', *Psychological Review*, *84*, pp. 231-59.

Norman, D. A. (1976), *Memory and Attention*, 2nd edn, Wiley: New York.

Paivio, A. (1971), *Imagery and Verbal Processes*, Holt, Rinehart and Winston: New York.

Perky, C. W. (1910), 'An experimental study of imagination', *American Journal of Psychology*, *21*, pp. 422-52.

Phillips, W. A. and Christie, D. F. M. (1977), 'Interference with visualization', *Quarterly Journal of Experimental Psychology*, *29*, pp. 637-65.

Pylyshyn, Z. W. (1973), 'What the mind's eye tells the mind's brain: a critique of mental imagery', *Psychological Bulletin*, *80*, pp. 1-24.

Quinton, G. and Fellows, B. J. (1976), '"Perceptual" strategies in the solving of three term series problems', *British Journal of Psychology*, *66*, pp. 69-78.

Reeves, J. W. (1965), *Thinking about Thinking*, Secker & Warburg: London.

Reitman, W. R., Grove, N. B. and Shroup, R. G. (1964), 'Argus: an information processing model of thinking', *Behavioural Science*, *9*, pp. 270-81.

Richardson, A. (1977), 'The meaning and measurement of visual imagery', *British Journal of Psychology*, *68*, pp. 29-43.

Segal, S. J. (1971), (ed.), *Imagery: Current Cognitive Approaches*, Academic Press: New York.

Shaver, P., Pierson, L. and Lang, S. (1975), 'Converging evidence for the functional significance of imagery in problem solving', *Cognition*, *3*, pp. 359-75.

Sheehan, P. W. and Neisser, U. (1969), 'Some variables affecting the vividness of imagery in recall', *British Journal of Psychology*, *60*, pp. 71-80.

Singer, J. (1966), *Daydreaming*, Random House: New York.

Skinner, B. F. (1972), *Beyond Freedom and Dignity*, Cape: London.

Wason, P. C. (1966), 'Reasoning', in B. M. Foss (ed.), *New Horizons in Psychology 1,* Penguin: Harmondsworth.

Wason, P. C. (1969), 'Regression in reasoning?' *British Journal of Psychology*, *60*, pp. 47-80.

Wason, P. C. (1978), 'Hypothesis testing and reasoning', Cognitive Psychology, D303, Block 4, Unit 25, Open University Press: Milton Keynes.

Wason, P. C. and Evans, J. St B. T. (1975), 'Dual processes in reasoning?', *Cognition*, *3*, pp. 141-54.

Wason, P. C. and Johnson-Laird, P. N. (1970), 'A conflict between selecting and evaluating information in a reasoning task', *British Journal of Psychology*, *61*, pp. 509-15.

Wason, P. C. and Johnson-Laird, P. N. (1972), *Psychology of Reasoning: Structure and Content*, Batsford: London.

Watson, J. B. (1914), *Behaviour: an Introduction to Comparative Psychology*, Holt, Rinehart & Winston: New York.

Wertheimer, M. (1961), *Productive Thinking*, Tavistock: London.

9 Cross-cultural perspectives on cognition

H. Valerie Curran

Introduction

Are there cultural differences in cognitive processes? Today, we are little nearer to answering this apparently simple question than we were at the turn of the century when the Cambridge expedition set off for the Torres Strait to carry out the first cross-cultural experiment: an investigation of the visual acuity of 'savages'.

Many studies, on most aspects of cognition, have been conducted in the years in between, and we have accumulated a mass of information on how different cultural groups perform on standard and not-so-standard western experiments. We know, for example, that adults from different cultures show differential susceptibility to classic visual illusions (Segall *et al.*, 1966). Or that, given a Piagetian volume conservation task, Wolof children in Senegal are apt to think that the experimenter has 'magically' changed the amounts of water by pouring it from one beaker into another (Greenfield, 1966). Or again, that verbal reasoning by non-literate Kpelle (Liberia) depends on the 'truthfulness' of the information they are given to reason with (Cole *et al.*, 1971; Scribner, 1977).

Certainly, these kinds of result are often interesting in their own right. But what is the ultimate aim of cross-cultural studies? Is it only to document cultural differences and similarities in cognitive functioning? Or is it more than that? 'Cross-cultural psychology is like virtue', said Frijda and Jahoda (1966), 'everybody is in favour of it, but there are widely differing views as to what it is or ought to be.' And nearly a decade later, 'Cross-cultural psychology, like many other adolescents, is suffering from an identity crisis' (Brislin *et al.*, 1975).

The identity issue arises when cross-cultural psychology is treated, as it often has been, as separate from other areas of psychology, as if studying 'other people' involved fundamentally different issues and problems from studying 'people like us'. On the contrary, in fact, the main issues are the same and the major problems are common to any area of comparative research, be it across age-groups, species, socio-economic classes, cultures, or even across experimental treatments.

'Main-line' psychology has been slow to realize the fertility of studies which cut across cultural boundaries. This chapter looks at what cross-cultural studies can contribute to cognitive psychology as a whole, and how far that potential has been fulfilled. It will not be concerned with any one 'area' of cognition. Cross-cultural studies have spanned the chapter heading boundaries of perception, memory, problem-solving, etc. and whole books could be written on each. Rather, our theme is how different cultural factors may influence those processes.

On returning to our original question – are there cultural differences in cognitive processes? – we shall find that although a century of debate has yielded few clear answers, it has led to a reappraisal both of our concepts of 'culture' and of 'cognition'. Instead of asking whether different cultural groups 'have' certain ways of thinking, the question is now about the contexts in which those thought processes are applied.

The role of cross-cultural studies

Generality

The first role of cross-cultural studies is seen when we ask how *general* are our theories and concepts of human cognition? This question has become one of cognitive psychology's major contemporary headaches: do principles of cognition based on laboratory situations have any implications for cognitive functioning in other, wider contexts? The generality issue forms the main basis of the current demand for cognitive psychology to have 'ecological validity'. Although there is no clear consensus about what ecological validity is, it is most often used to mean the generalizability of (laboratory-based) principles of cognition to everyday, 'real-world' cognitive functioning. The behaviour of subjects processing unusual information (like nonsense syllables) for extraordinary purposes (like learning paired-associates) in laboratory conditions is clearly not a sufficient basis on which to build a general psychological theory. Few would disagree with this fact, but as yet fewer have succeeded in doing anything about it. The problem broadens when we consider not only the tasks, stimuli and situations on which we base our studies but also the subjects we use.

Consider for a moment how far physics would have developed if Newton's law of gravity applied only to ripe, English apples, or if Archimedes' principle held only in Greek baths. The analogy is not so far-fetched. As is widely acknowledged, most experiments on human cognition are carried out on convenient subjects such as university students, who are clearly an unrepresentative sample of humans. Most of our theories and concepts of cognition are in turn based on the problem-solving strategies of those very same subjects. To what extent, then, can we generalize to 'other people's' cognitive processes? Ignoring this question may well restrict our conversation to English apples and prevent our ever discovering gravity.

General principles of human cognition must, by definition, apply more broadly than the particular subject population on which they were originally tested. This does not mean that we should only focus on ways in which people are the same; any truly general theory should be able to predict differences as well as universals in cognitive functioning. One obvious way in which to test the range and limits of our theories is to test them on other people who are, at least super-ficially, very different from western students, by working in diverse cultures.

Culture and cognition

The second and most widely acknowledged role of cross-cultural studies is to relate cognition with culture and to describe the nature of their interaction. But is this not also an ultimate aim of psychology?

Most psychologists would agree that cognition, by its very nature, concerns how past knowledge is brought to bear on interpreting and acting upon current experience. The importance of the exact form of that 'current experience' has been realized, as we noted, in the demand for ecological validity. Clearly, the 'past knowledge' part of the system is equally important. How current experience is interpreted will depend on the kind of knowledge that is brought to bear on it. By selecting our subjects on convenience grounds we inevitably restrict the range of past experiences that they bring.

Most of us would again agree that adult cognitive processes have developed through organism-environment interaction. It follows from this that the environment plays a key role in influencing adult cognition. By allowing variation in the environments of the people we study, cross-cultural research can investigate what role the environment does play. In other words, cross-cultural studies of cognition are ecological in the literal sense of 'ecology': the study of the relations between living organisms and their environment.

What we have called 'main-line' psychology is dependent on cultural information about subjects at every level of research. Clearly, there is no more a culture-free man than there can be a culture-free test. Researchers rely on cultural knowledge of their subjects when designing and interpreting experiments so that they know, for example, how instructions would be interpreted and what reinforcements are required to engage their co-operation. Experimenters know these things implicitly because they share their subject's cultural experiences. Only when they move outside their own particular culture does this dependence on cultural information become explicit.

Psychology seems to run the risk of creating a 'psychological man' along the same lines as the classic 'economic man'. Economic man, as a model for economic theory, makes ideal, rational decisions whatever situation he is faced with. Similarly, psychological man is an idealized subject who processes information in ideal ways. He maximally trades off speed and accuracy, makes logical errors, holds seven or so bits in short term memory, and allows no non-rational processes to affect his performance. By concentrating on how certain highly selected groups of people process unusual stimuli in unusual situations, we are prone to mistaking the problem-solving strategies of psychological man for universal laws of human cognition. Psychological man may or may not prove a useful model for psychological theory. We shall never know until we test him out by introducing some significant variations into both the situations we present him with and the knowledge he brings to bear on them.

Cultures as 'natural' laboratories

Once we agree on the importance of investigating the effects of environmental factors on cognitive processes, then a major attraction of cross-cultural studies is how cultures can often function as natural laboratories. This can happen in two ways. One uses *cross*-cultural variation to examine the effects of factors like language, physical environment or subsistence modes. Sometimes it may be crucial to a theory to use this kind of variation. A notable case in point is Rosch's (1977) research on linguistic relativity, where testing her hypothesis required populations whose languages varied in the numbers of colours they coded.

The second way uses *intra*-cultural variation in factors which do not vary substantially in the west. Many traditional societies in certain parts of the world are presently undergoing rapid social change. Technological innovations have been introduced in some parts but not others; formal education is available for some people but not all; nutritional programmes are being carried out only in limited areas. Such 'transitional state' societies allow comparisons to be made to assess the effects of such factors as schooling, literacy, urbanization and nutritional levels on cognitive functioning. Clearly, such comparisons are unobtainable in the west, at least as a rule. In this way then, cross-cultural studies can expand the *range* of variables we can investigate.

On understanding culture: logic and magic

Despite the importance of cross-cultural studies to the development of a general psychology, it is not surprising that until very recently main-line cognitive psychology has paid little attention to the area. Indeed, the history of cross-cultural psychology is so unpromising that one writer recently denied that it really had one (Warren, 1977).

Early studies were enmeshed in value-laden concepts of 'savages' whose 'primitive' societies were seen to reflect their primitive mentalities. Their thought processes were considered to be magical, irrational and concrete, in contrast with the scientific, rational and abstract thought of western man. Evidence for magical thought, for example, was seen in primitive belief systems which stressed the power of unobservable elements like witches, gods and spirits in causing observable events. But as early writers (e.g., Boas, 1911) pointed out, it is in fact illogical to make inferences about thought *processes* from the *content* of beliefs. Bizarre conclusions can follow quite logically from bizarre premises.

Misapplication of Darwinian concepts led to 'savage thought' being seen as somehow childlike and immature. The notion that 'ontogeny recapitulates phylogeny' implied that adults in primitive societies could be seen to be at the same level of mental development as young children reared in western societies.

Misconceptions about savage thought were paralleled by misconceptions about 'civilized thought'. Western man was not as rational and scientific as he liked to think. There are many examples of his magical thinking, not only in superstitions (cf. Malinowski, 1954) but also in the everyday way in which causes are attributed to events (cf. Shweder, 1977). Modern western medicine provides a striking instance of magical thinking in its use of electro-convulsive therapy as a treatment for depression, as Johnson-Laird and Wason (1977) point out. The basis of the treatment was that epileptics appeared less likely to suffer from schizophrenia than non-epileptics, and so it seemed a good idea to induce epileptic-like seizures in schizophrenics. In fact, it was found that ECT had more marked therapeutic effects on depression, for which it continues to be used, although no one knows whether these effects are due to a current being passed through the brain or simply to the patient's and doctor's faith in the treatment. The logic of this medical touch of magic is clearly no more sound than that of Zande attempts to cure epilepsy by eating the burnt skull of a red bush monkey (Evans-Pritchard, 1937).

In the 1940s and 1950s, the influx of psychometricians bearing intelligence tests across Africa only added to the chaos of cross-cultural research. And the situation was not improved later by the experimentalists who made global comparisons of the performance of culture X with culture Y on some particular task. These 'direct confrontation' approaches, as Serpell (1976), aptly calls them, attempted to relate performance differences to differences in the two cultures. Any such two-group design, as Campbell (1961) complained, is virtually uninterpretable. To show, for instance, that Maku hunter-gatherers in the Amazon rain forest do not classify geometric figures in as many ways as English undergraduates tells us nothing about the relation between culture and cognition. Not only are there all kinds of extra-experimental factors to consider (the task is clearly not equivalent for the two groups); but also, the list of differences between the cultures of Maku and undergraduates would be so enormous that it would be impossible to relate specific cultural differences to differences in performance. So, if almost everything about two groups differs, it is just anecdotal to show that they also differ in some aspect of cognitive functioning.

The crux of the problem is that to investigate the relation between culture and cognition we need to understand *both* parts of the system. Only then can we hypothesize about how they might interact. On the one hand, then, we are dependent on our psychological understanding of cognitive processes. On the other, we require a detailed knowledge of culture.

The recognition of our need for knowledge about culture has made anthropology an increasingly important influence on cross-cultural research. By looking at culture as if it was a single, independent variable, psychologists have grossly oversimplified the issues involved. Cultures are complex, interdependent networks of organizations which have evolved over time through reciprocal adaptation between man and his social and physical environment. They are dynamic systems, not static structures. Few societies today exist in total isolation, and most of those studied by psychologists have been influenced to a greater or lesser degree by western culture.

Anthropological accounts of cultures (ethnographies) provide an essential context in which to carry out cross-cultural studies. Ethnographies are detailed descriptions of societies: their social, political and economic organization and functioning, their religion and mythology. Their main data source is the day-by-day behaviour of people living in the society. Later in this chapter we shall look at the influence of anthropology, especially on the work of Michael Cole and his associates (Cole *et al.*, 1971; Cole and Scribner, 1974), who have conducted an extensive programme of research among the Kpelle and Vai people of Liberia. Cole's research is essentially *intra*-cultural and is concerned with the effects of schooling and literacy on cognitive development and adult cognition. The next section in contrast looks at another kind of 'natural' laboratory approach which is *cross*-cultural and is concerned with linguistic effects on thought processes.

Cultures, concepts and words

In many ways, language seems an obvious candidate for linking culture and cognition. Language is a primary medium through which culture is transmitted, and the world's languages show considerable variation in structure, both syntactically and lexically. The Yoruba language labels only three colours; the language of Lesu Islanders has a dozen or so words for 'pig'; LoDagaa speakers have only one term to code both 'day' and 'market'. There are many similar examples of how languages differ in the words they have to refer to the world. But what do such lexical differences mean?

It is widely documented in anthropological texts that the elaboration of the vocabulary reflects the particular interests and preoccupations of the society concerned. The more culturally meaningful events, objects or experiences, the more elaborate their associated vocabularies. So, for example, pigs for Lesu Islanders are a central cultural concern, in part because pigs constitute their major source of protein. For the LoDagaa, the incidence of markets is more important than 'days' as such, and even the 'week' for them is a six-day revolution of the main markets in the area (Goody and Watt, 1963). Clearly, words are not only tools for thought but also tools for communicating with others. The words in any language will then come to reflect the communication needs of speakers of that language.

From their very different point of view, psychologists have not been concerned with why languages vary in structure but with what effects those variations have on individual thought processes. In attempting to find direct relationships between language structure and thought processes, psychologists and linguists treated language in *isolation* from other aspects of culture. So, for instance, instead of trying to understand the importance of pigs in Lesu Island culture, they looked for direct consequences of differences in vocabulary for differences in individual cognition: Do English speakers, with only a very few words for different kinds of pig, not *perceive* the differences in pigs that Lesu Islanders perceive? Can Yoruba speakers only *discriminate* three colours? Do the LoDagaa not *know* the difference between a day and a market?

That lexical differences between languages reflect differences in the perceptual and conceptual distinctions made by speakers of those languages was expressed in Whorf's (1956) famous linguistic relativity hypothesis. Benjamin Lee Whorf, ethnographer, linguist and insurance claims investigator, argued that language embodies our view of the universe:

> We dissect nature along lines laid down by our native languages.
> The categories and types that we isolate from the world of
> phenomena we do not find there because they stare every observer

in the face; on the contrary, the world is presented in a
kaleidoscopic flux of impressions which has to be organized by our
minds – and this means largely by the linguistic systems in our
minds (1956 p. 213).

Linguistic relativity thus asserts that speakers of different languages
will have different conceptions of, and experiences in, the world. In its
strongest form, we are each intellectually imprisoned by the language
we speak (Lloyd, 1972).

However, as it is generally possible to translate, at least approximately, from one language to another, there is no need to accept this
view of language as a conceptual straitjacket. Whorf's own ability
to translate Eskimo words for snow into English phrases is evidence
that lack of words does not directly imply a corresponding lack of
conceptual distinctions.

In fact, as Hockett (1954) pointed out, the differences between
language are not so much what *can* be said in them all. Yoruba
speakers, with only three colour terms, can express many colour
distinctions by referring to the colours of standard objects. And asked
to differentiate pigs, English speakers use many distinguishing
adjectives. Rather, languages differ in terms of what it is relatively
easy to say in them, in the sense that, for instance, it is 'easier' to say
the English word 'green' than the Yoruba phrase 'colour of plants'.

Does the ease with which distinctions can be expressed linguistically
have any effect on thought? Most studies of linguistic relativity have been
based on the 'weakest' form of Whorf's hypothesis (see Miller and
McNeill, 1969), whereby one language rather than another may make it
easier to remember certain categories of events. And most of that work
has concentrated on recognition memory for colours.

For several reasons, colour appeared an ideal domain for translating Whorf's conjectures into an empirically testable hypothesis. First,
anthropological reports indicated a large variation in the numbers of
colours coded in different languages. Second, normal people can
distinguish between literally thousands of colours and therefore the
division of the colour space into a few labelled areas appeared quite
arbitrary. Third, as a physical continuum of light waves, colour could
be measured independently of both linguistic and cognitive factors.

Brown and Lenneberg (1954) carried out a classic experiment
demonstrating linguistic effects on memory. Their experiment was in
two parts. They started by indexing the 'codability' of colours by

asking one group of subjects to name the colours in an array of plastic chips. 'Codability' was a compound measure of the length of the name, the speed of naming and the consensus about the name. A second group of subjects were then given a recognition task with those same colours. Brown and Lenneberg found that the more codable a colour, the more accurately it was recognized from the array of chips. Moreover, the longer the retention interval, the greater the positive correlation between recognition accuracy and codability.

This relation, however, was subsequently not found to hold with all arrays of colours (Burnam and Clark, 1955; Lenneberg, 1961). More important though, is the general problem with interpreting correlational results: showing that codability correlates with recognition accuracy does not tell us that one causes the other. There could always be a third factor which causes both.

This possibility was not tested for some years. The two anthropologists, Berlin and Kay (1969) challenged the assumption that the division of the colour space was arbitrary. They took as their starting point the reported diversity of colour terms, but claimed that in fact there was only a limited number of *basic* colour words in any language. 'Basic' excluded terms referring to objects (e.g., white but not ivory) or qualified (e.g., blue but not dark blue). On such criteria, they argued that no language contained more than eleven basic colours: three achromatics (in English, black, grey and white) and eight chromatics (green, blue, pink, red, yellow, brown, orange and purple).

Eleanor Rosch (formerly Heider) suggested that those basic or 'focal' colours were perceptually more salient than other, non-focal colours (Heider, 1972). Further, she proposed that Brown and Lenneberg's apparent linguistic relativity effect was in fact due to colour salience. Rather than recognition accuracy being directly related to codability, she argued that colour salience was the factor underlying both.

If codability was related to salience, then the same colours would be the most codable in any language. Specifically, focal colours would be more codable than non-focal colours across all languages. To test this hypothesis, Heider (1972) asked 23 students whose first language was not English to name (in their native language) the colours in an array. She confirmed her hypothesis: focal colours were given shorter names and named faster than non-focal colours in all 23 diverse languages represented.

Having shown that salience related to codability, Rosch's hypothesis needed a second test for confirmation. If memory for colours was a direct result of salience rather than codability, then focal colours should be more memorizable than non-focal colours – even when a language did *not* code those colours. It was at this point that Rosch needed a culture whose language, unlike English, did not code all the focal colours. The Dani of Indonesian New Guinea have only two colour terms, translatable roughly as dark and light. Using a task very similar to the original Brown and Lenneberg study, Heider (1972) again confirmed her hypothesis. Dani, like a second sample of North Americans, recognized focal colours more accurately than non-focal ones. In a later study, Rosch went on to give further support to her conclusions by showing that Dani also learned names for focal colours faster than names for other colours (for details, see Rosch, 1977).

As Rosch (1975) points out in retrospect:

It would appear that the colour space, far from being a domain well suited to the study of the effects of language on thought, is a prime example of the influence of underlying perceptual-cognitive factors on the formation and reference of linguistic categories (1975 p. 183).

For the colour domain then, there seems to be quite the *opposite* of Whorf's linguistic relativity principle in operation: coding of colour terms depends on perceptual and cognitive factors.

Why should some colours be more perceptually salient than others? Rosch suggests that the apparent universality of colour salience implies that there could be a physiological basis. As yet, there is no physiological support for this notion. A physiological explanation of colour salience based on Hering's opponent channel model of colour perception has been advanced by McDaniel (1972). Hering's theory, however, does not account for four of the basic colours (pink, orange, brown and purple). An alternative physiological explanation has been proposed by Bornstein (1975), who argues that there are racial differences in colour perception which, he suggests, are due to differential retinal adaptations to ultra-violet sunlight, altitude and dietary factors. Bornstein, however, only discusses six 'primary' colours, and his hypothesized racial differences in retinal pigmentation await detailed empirical support. (For a critical review of physiological and cultural explanations of colour coding, see Lloyd 1977.)

It is unlikely that any physiological correlates of focal colours *will* be found until we can arrive at a clearer definition of 'focal'. Specification of focal colours as all those given Berlin and Kay's basic names may well turn out to be misleading. There are considerable problems with Berlin and Kay's linguistic analyses and research methods, especially their use of bilingual informants and subjects (cf. Hickerson, 1971). Some focal colours may be shown to be more focal than others. In fact, it could be argued that a more meaningful definition of focal would be the *minimum* (as opposed to the maximum) number of colours given basic names in any language.

Further, if colour coding is a result of universal colour salience, we are still left with one major question: why do some languages code only two focal colours when others code them all? The answer to this question clearly cannot lie in the relation of language to individual thought processes. Rather, we must look to the role of language within its broader cultural context and to its relationship with society as a whole.

Levi-Strauss (1966) argues that societies only name things which serve some practical or symbolic purpose for them. For example, if a plant has no function within a particular culture, it is not necessary to talk about it other than to say, perhaps, that it is a weed which 'has no function'. So Eskimos have several terms for the English word 'snow' because it is important in their daily lives (and not ours) to discriminate different types of snow. And the enormous variety of Hananoo (Philippines) words for rice similarly reflects their cultural preoccupation with rice as the staple food. In traditional societies, where interests and occupations are less diversified than in the western world, it seems reasonable to suppose that words are coded in terms of the discriminations that it is necessary to make *and* communicate within each particular culture.

In technological societies, the greater division of labour and interests within cultures requires increasingly elaborate vocabularies to cope with increasingly specialized fields. Correspondingly, this specialization results in smaller and smaller proportions of the population having access to certain areas of the vocabulary. Thus physicists, for instance, have many more terms for discriminating colours than non-artists. Or, going back to the colour domain, artists have access to many more terms for discriminating colours than non-artists.

There may, however, be cases where colour distinctions are universally used. One example might be the description of the sky, the colour of which is important for judging the time of day and weather conditions. And colours may have *symbolic* functions in all societies, like the widespread use of the black/white contrast to signify death/life, impure/pure, profane/sacred (cf. Sahlins, 1976). Another example might be descriptions of people. In English, one might refer to blue or brown eyes, redheads, blondes, or brunettes. Obviously such terms would be virtually useless for discriminating Chinese, African or Asian people. When Curran* asked twenty eight-year-old Yoruba-English bilinguals (Nigeria) to describe themselves 'so that they could be spotted in their classrooms' by someone who had not seen them before, their physical descriptions (as opposed to comments on clothing) only included three colour terms. Although the children were fully conversant with the many English colour words, the only three English terms used corresponded to the only three colour terms coded in Yoruba. It would be interesting to examine the actual use of colour terms in societies which coded varied numbers of colours to substantiate this discrimination-function concept of coding.

We begin with the notion of linguistic relativity, whereby the language we speak imposes upon us our way of thinking about the world. At present, there is not only no empirical support for Whorf's hypothesis, but also it seems that in some cases the reverse of it is nearer the truth. As Rosch has shown for categories of geometric form and human emotion, as well as for colour categories, perceptual cognitive factors can have some effect in determining linguistic coding.

In the final analysis, though, the *effects* of linguistic categories cannot be considered as *separate* from the effects of factors which caused those categories to be labelled rather than others in the first place. Language is an integral part of culture. One of the central problems with the Whorfian hypothesis was that it treated language in isolation from its cultural context, and by so doing, ignored the communicative functions of linguistic codes. A more reasonable hypothesis is that what is coded in any language depends on what discriminations one is required to make and communicate within that culture. The relation of language to thought can then only be considered in terms of the relation of both to the whole culture.

We turn now to a very different approach to the relation between culture and cognition, which takes not language but formal

---

*'Portrait in colour: the use of colour terms in physical descriptions by Yoruba-English bilinguals' (in preparation).

education, literacy and urbanization as its central variables. This research is *intra-*, rather than *cross-*cultural, and uses as its 'natural' laboratories traditional societies undergoing rapid cultural change.

Changing cultures, changing thoughts

The vast majority of subjects in psychological experiments in the west share a great deal in common. Even if not undergraduates, they have invariably attended school for ten years or so, are able to read and write and are influenced on a broader level by western technological developments, such as the mass media. All these factors – formal education, literacy, technology – have a profound effect on the organizing and functioning of a society. One only has to think back in western history to what might be called 'magical thinking' about witches, devils, blood-letting and so on to realize the social impact of technological explosions.

But do such changes in society affect individual thought processes? Do they influence how we think and not just what we think about? To take two examples, literacy, by reducing the dependency on oral transmission of information, might consequently relieve the dependency on memory and affect the acquisition of different mnemonic strategies. And schools claim to be directly concerned with promoting cognitive development and with the acquisition of skills such as literacy and numeracy, so would we think differently if we had never entered a classroom? Vygotsky (1978) and Luria (1976) maintained that, just as the tools of labour change over history, so do the tools of thought; and just as new tools of labour give rise to new social structures, so do new tools of thought give rise to new mental structures.

We obviously cannot do the perfect experiment on these issues and go back into history to study cognition over the centuries. Instead, researchers have taken advantage of societies undergoing rapid cultural change and which have, in a sense, speeded up those historical changes. The rapid industrialization of many traditional societies in the Third World has created 'transitional states' where only part of the population is literate; where formal schooling is available to some but not all children; where technological innovations have yet to have global effects.

As formal schooling is generally the precursor to literacy, studies have been divided rather arbitrarily according to the age of their subjects: developmental studies take schooling as the major factor, whereas studies of adults have mainly focussed on literacy.

Scribner and Cole (1973) emphasized three main differences between the formal education offered by schools and the informal education of everyday life: (i) schools take learning out of the context in which it is used; (ii) schools put more emphasis on *what* is being learned than *who* is doing the learning and teaching – by contrast, informal education stresses the social aspects of learning; (iii) language (both written and spoken) is the primary mode of transmission in schools, whereas much of informal education involves non-verbal (e.g., observational) learning.

How do these differences in learning environments affect cognitive development? What are the cognitive consequences of literacy? We cannot review all the relevant research on these issues in the space available here, but three interesting findings will serve to illustrate. First, although schooled and non-schooled groups are not always found to differ in how they *perform* a task, they often differ in how they *explain* their responses (e.g., Greenfield *et al.*, 1966; Cole *et al.*, 1971; Scribner, 1974 and Jonathan Evans's chapter in this book). Non-schooled groups often explain their task strategies without referring to the task itself (e.g., 'God helped me'; 'I watched your [experimenter's] eyes'. Second, Cole *et al.* (1971) imply that non-schooled subjects tend to treat each instance of a related set of problems as a separate sub-problem and show little evidence of 'learning to learn'. Similarly, in an ingenious study, Greenfield and Childs (1974) found some evidence of ungeneralized learning of patterns among young Zinacantecan weavers. Third, unschooled children and non-literate adults are found to show what Scribner (1977) calls an 'empirical bias' in verbal problem-solving. That is, the way they solve problems like syllogisms is dependent on whether the statements they are given to reason with are subjectively considered to be true or false. Luria (1971) reports similar results from his 1930 studies in the Uzbekistan in Central Asia.

What do these results tell us about the effects of schooling on cognitive development? There are two main problems in attempting to make any general statements from these kinds of finding. First, where a large number of results are available, findings are far from consistent. For example, in reviewing cross-cultural Piagetian studies, Ashton (1975) quotes cases where schooling has had an apparently negative effect on the development of concrete operational thought. Clearly, there are schools and schools, and results may depend on the particular kind and quality of schooling obtainable. A rural African village school with one teacher and one class for children of all ages often has little in common with the local English primary school. Pollnac and Jahn (1976), in fact, reported significant differences in the free recall performance of children from ostensibly similar, neighbouring schools in Uganda.

Second, a more fundamental problem with schooling comparisons is that schooling probably never occurs as an isolated change in a society. The introduction of state education often follows the introduction of new roads and the host of social changes which that entails. Even when samples are obtained from the same village where some children go to school and others not, it is very unlikely that these groups have been allocated at random. Fahrmeier (1975) found that although there were significant differences between schooled and non-schooled groups of Hausa children on a variety of tasks, the differences were constant throughout his 6- to 13-year-old age groups. The schooled groups were performing at a higher level when they started school at six, and it appeared that the same gap was simply maintained over the years. Fahrmeier implies that the children who attended school were more 'motivated' in going to school in the first place. Other factors could also be involved. Parents may actually select their 'brighter' children for schooling, keeping the others behind as co-workers, or it may be the more education-oriented parents who send most of their children to school.

To show a relation between schooling and cognitive development clearly does not tell us *how* one affects the other. Schools, like cultures, are complex systems which should not be oversimplified or isolated from their broader cultural context. Similar problems arise when we consider other cultural variables. Literacy, schooling, urbanization and nutritional levels generally co-vary. What they all add up to on a global level is 'westernization': a move from traditional organizations of society towards a western value system with its emphasis on education, urban economy and the like. And what studies almost always show across the spectrum of cognitive research is that the more people in other cultures have had the same kind of experiences as westerners – the more 'westernized' they are – then the more they perform like westerners on western experiments.

On interpreting group differences

The deficit approach

Such results were easily fitted into the logic of what has become known as the 'deficit interpretation' (Cole and Bruner, 1971). Within this framework, differences in cognitive performance are attributed not simply to differences in cultural influences but to a *lack* of some aspect of experience of one group as compared with the other. In effect, cultural experiences are viewed not as different but on a scale ranging from 'deficient' to 'enriched'. Literacy (Goody and Watt, 1963), formal education (Bruner, Olver and Greenfield, 1966) and 'acculturation' (Doob, 1961) are all claimed to give people new intellectual tools and new ways of thinking. In consequence, the 'deprived' groups who 'lack' those experiences are seen as similarly 'lacking' in those ways of thinking.

The same type of interpretive framework was used in the west to explain class and ethnic differences in school achievement (e.g., Bereiter and Engelmann, 1966). Minority ethnic group and working-class children were seen to underachieve at school because they had linguistic and cognitive deficits. These deficits were created by a lack of certain cultural experiences in early childhood as compared with middle-class white children. Factors invoked ranged from linguistic interaction with adults, to the absence of father figures, to the number of books in the home.

A similar approach is seen in the notions of 'arrested' or 'levelled off' development implicit in many cross-cultural studies by the Piagetian school (e.g., Piaget, 1966; Dasen, 1972a). Although this research has generally found that children in very diverse societies, from Geneva to rural Senegal, go through the same stages of cognitive development in the same sequence, the rate of development is found to vary considerably. So much so that in many non-technological societies, adult thinking does not proceed beyond – if indeed it attains – the level of concrete operations (Dasen, 1972a).

Many sound arguments have been advanced against the logic of the deficit approach (e.g., Labov, 1969; Cole and Bruner, 1971). A main objection is clearly that differences only become deficits when one has a norm or standard against which the performance of different groups is assessed. The choice of such a norm as the performance of North American middle-class whites on an ontogenetic scale made in Geneva comprises a simple value judgment. People in non-technological societies could easily reverse the argument and claim that western society is 'deficient' in training rhythm and dance, complex hunting skills (cf. Blurton-Jones and Konner, 1976), altered states of consciousness (cf. Price-Williams, 1975), story-telling, ritual and so on. The very term 'acculturation' used to describe traditional people's increasing contact with western technology implies that the change is a positive one, a taking in of elements of other cultures. However, that 'taking in' also involves a 'losing out' of elements of the traditional culture.

The ethnocentrism of the deficit approach has disturbing consequences when its educational implications are drawn out. Having 'diagnosed' a deficit in some aspect of experience, it is argued that by adding the 'missing elements' one can compensate for the deficit. In this vein, it is asserted that researchers should aim to identify the crucial experiences for the development of cognitive processes: 'so that modifications could be introduced in the physical, social or educational environments of these children which would help them achieve the same level of conceptual development as is found in children from western societies' (De Lemos, 1974, p. 380). For example, DeLacey (1970), on finding that the performance levels of Aborigine children on classification tasks increased with their degree of 'European contact' (meaning interaction with white Australians) goes on to suggest that: 'the interests of optimal cognitive development of Aboriginal children would best be served by ensuring that they should in the future be reared near or even integrated with substantial European settlements' (p. 365). Deficits and compensations are thus structured within an imperialistic research ethic which presupposes that 'other people's' goals are, or should be, the same as westerners' goals.

Criticizing the deficit approach for its implicit values clearly does not dismiss the empirical findings of deficit research. But it is precisely on an empirical level that the limitations of the deficit framework are revealed. Essentially, the problem is that a subject's failure to perform in certain ways on one experiment has been found to be ungeneralizable (i) to performance on slightly varied versions of that same experiment, (ii) to performance on other, related cognitive tasks, and (iii) to performance outside the experimental situation. It is worth considering these findings in some detail because they are results that must be accounted for by any alternative interpretive framework.

By way of illustration, take a finding which has produced some debate in the literature: the failure of certain young Aborigine adults to make conservation responses in experimental situations (e.g., Dasen, 1972a, 1972b). How do we interpret this result? Within a classic Piagetian framework, one would classify these people as non-conservers and perhaps imply that they had not reached the level of concrete operations. But, as Cole (1975, p. 170) asks:

> Are we to believe that Aborigine adults will store water in tall thin cans in order to 'have more water'; do they think they lose water when they pour it from a bucket into a barrel? I am tempted to believe that they would have disappeared long ago were this the case.

On a social level, Aborigines living in semi-arid conditions clearly have a need to conserve in the sense of 'taking care' of their water supply, and this may or may not have anything to do with their responses on a conservation task.

Dasen (1977) retorts (citing De Lemos) that even in a more natural situation, Aborigine women were non-conservers. On being offered a choice of (a) two measures of sugar from a large container or (b) one measure from a tall, thin container, eight out of twelve women chose (b), the one with less sugar but a higher level. Ignoring the small number of subjects tested, it is likely that many westerners classified as conservers would also be fooled by appearances. Indeed, the 'conservation trick' is basic to many western packaging and marketing techniques (there are too many chocolates in *our* half pound bag to fit into *your* half pound box).

The first point then, in interpreting results is that when one looks outside the laboratory at subjects' everyday behaviour, one may find that they are happily doing things which they appeared unable to do in the experimental situation. The anthropologist, whose main source of data about the people he studies is their everyday behaviour, is naturally suspicious of psychologists' claims about people 'not having' certain ways of reasoning or thinking. From his point of view, man adapts and adapts to his social and physical environment. He is thus sceptical of experimental findings that people living in semi-arid conditions cannot conserve, or even that they fail to achieve formal operational thought when most traditional societies require an understanding of complex symbolic systems (e.g., through myth and ritual) and participation in subtle verbal exchanges (e.g., through riddles, proverbs and stories).

Not only does the concept of an adult non-conserver go against anthropological sense, but also the significance of responses on conservation experiments has been questioned from within psychology. For western children, conservation has generally been taken as a landmark in cognitive development signifying the attainment of concrete operational thought. But in other societies this does not necessarily seem to be the case. In a series of studies of Papuan, Zambian and Yugoslav children, Heron found no relation between conservation responses and either school achievement or performance on other cognitive tasks (Heron, 1971; Heron and Dowel, 1973, 1974). These results have led Heron (1974) to propose that conservation is quite divorced from other cognitive activities.

Even within the experimental situation itself, the significance of conservation responses is a debated issue. Even slight variations in the materials and procedures used often produce substantial changes in subjects' behaviour. What is being conserved, who is manipulating the materials, the subject's familiarity with the task and substances, the form of the perceptual cues available: all these factors have been shown to be crucial in conservation experiments (Greenfield *et al.*, 1966; Price-Williams *et al.*, 1969; Dasen, 1972a).

One is left with the conclusion that conservation responses are situation-dependent and may have little, if any, meaning outside the experimental setting, either in terms of everyday behaviour or performance on other cognitive tasks.

We have taken conservation responses as one example to illustrate the problems of interpreting results which show people's 'inability' to perform in certain ways. Exactly the same issues arise for results in many other areas which demonstrate an apparent failure to perform. The problem with deficits is thus that they appear to come and go depending on where we look for them. After a long and ingenious series of studies with Kpelle children and adults, Cole *et al.* (1971, p. 233) came to the conclusion that: 'cultural differences in cognition reside more in the situations to which particular cognitive processes are applied than in the existence of a process in one cultural group and its absence in another'. At every point in their research (which spanned categorization and conceptual processes, free recall, problem-solving and verbal reasoning), whenever they had demonstrated their subjects' failure to use a particular process in one situation, they went on to show their use of that same process in another situation.

Cole's studies of free recall can be used to illustrate the importance of situational factors for Kpelle performance. His initial studies used a classic free recall paradigm: subjects were presented with twenty words belonging to four familiar categories and asked to recall them over a series of five trials. Compared with western subjects, three aspects of the performance of non-literate Kpelle adults were remarkable: (a) relatively few (9-11) items were recalled; (b) there was little increase in recall levels over trials; (c) there was little or no evidence of any semantic organization of the items. Certain standard experimental manipulations, such as offering incentives or presenting objects rather than words, made little difference to their performance.

When the same stimulus items were embedded in folk stories, when subjects classified the items before recalling them, or when extraordinary cueing procedures were used (like presenting the items over chairs), Kpelle recall was higher, showed greater improvement over trials and higher levels of semantic organization. The situational variations which elicited particular processes were not always obviously relatable to cultural factors (such as the efficiency of cueing recall with chairs). However, Cole *et al.* maintain that such variations do have significance in terms of everyday activities and that, in general, the more culturally familiar and relevant the situation, the more logical and analytical their subjects' response to it.

Situational determinants of cognition

These kinds of result accord with the common-sense notion that people will be good at doing things that they are used to doing, and not so good at doing unfamiliar things. Non-literate rice farmers will obviously be more adept at classifying types of rice than at sorting geometric figures (as Irwin and McLaughlin (1970) showed), just as North American students do not match Kpelle when it comes to sorting vine and forest leaves (as Cole *et al.* showed). One expects a butcher to be more adept at classifying cuts of meat than a carpenter, who in his turn will be more proficient when it comes to wood. Research strategies which ask 'How well can *they* do *our* tricks?'

(Wober, 1969) before looking at how well they can do their *own* tricks are apt to lead to unjustified assertions of incompetence.

We seem to have reached the position of a dog chasing his own tail. On the one hand, we find that the more 'acculturated' (meaning westernized) people become, the more they perform like westerners on western experiments. On the other hand, the closer to their experiences our experiments become, the more we find non-westerners using the same kinds and range of cognitive processes as westerners.

In general, such findings question the whole concept of using particular experiments to 'diagnose' whether or not people 'have' certain cognitive processes. Once we admit that cognitive functioning is dependent on situations, we can no longer infer that someone does not 'have' a certain way of thinking simply because he did not use it to perform an experimental task. It can always be argued that he would have used it given another situation

Several authors have expressed this distinction between 'having' a particular process and 'using' it to perform a task in terms of Chomsky's concepts of 'competence' and 'performance' (Labov, 1969; Flavell and Wohlwill, 1969; Cole and Bruner, 1971; Scribner, 1974; Dasen, 1977). According to this distinction, it is asserted that a person's performance does not always reflect his underlying competence. So what a person does not do should not be taken as indicative of what he cannot do. We can only infer his linguistic and cognitive competences when they are expressed in his actual performance. We cannot, however, infer any lack of competence from a lack of performance, as the competence may require another situation in which to be expressed. As there are an infinite number of possible situations, it becomes theoretically impossible to ever show a lack of competence. In fact, according to this distinction, one has to assume competence because it can never be shown to be absent.

On conceptualizing situations

This still leaves us with the problem of explaining cultural differences in performance while taking into account the situational determinants of cognitive functioning. We have therefore returned to what we referred to initially as cognitive psychology's major contemporary headache: there is no interpretive framework, let alone theory, which accounts for situational variables (see Claxton's opening chapter).

This particular headache, which Cole and Bruner (1971) point out has long been a shadow issue in psychology, has become a focus in developmental research as well as cross-culturally. For example, Fodor (1976) argues that, contrary to Piaget's theory, a child's thinking does not develop in logical power. Rather, there is a progressive extension of the sorts of *content* to which specific computational processes can be applied. Development is seen as a decontextualization of cognitive processes, not as a logical growth in the intellect. In fact, Piaget himself has stated that formal operational thought (for westerners) may be contextualized within certain fields of expertise, so that propositional logic may be applied in some situations but not others. Use of standard experiments which emphasize mathematical and physical concepts may thus fail to elicit formal operational strategies from many adults. Piaget (1972) therefore proposes that people should be tested in a field which is relevant to their career and interests.

These arguments have very clear implications for cultural differences. If cognitive development is, at least in part, an extension of the situations which elicit certain cognitive processes, then it will closely depend on the kinds of situation which the child encounters. Those situations will vary both across and within cultures. Therefore cognitive processes will be contextualized within different areas of expertise and elicited by different circumstances for different cultural groups. A child who is attending school has different kinds of experiences from one who spends that time doing other things. And different forms of symbolization (from spoken language to written words to music) will also change the contexts to which different processes are applied. Note, however, that this contextualization is simply in different areas. There is a danger with this formulation that 'deficits' may again be invoked in terms of cognitive processes as relatively context-bound versus context-free (cf. Bernstein, 1970).

How can we account for the contextual determinants of cognition? From a cross-cultural perspective, Cole and Scribner (1974) have put forward a conceptual framework in terms of (a) situations themselves, and (b) the dynamic, functional aspects of cognitive processes.

Cole and Scribner argue that once we admit the situation-dependent nature of cognitive processes, we have to have a 'theory of situations'. As they admit, we are a long way from achieving this. For a start, there is still confusion as to what situations actually are. Some have attempted to make the problem manageable by using situation synonymously with 'experimental treatment'. Even considering the experimental situation alone, this clearly avoids the main issues. Experiments involve all the complex social factors of experimenters and subjects communicating with each other, and not just the 'treatment' of the latter by the former.

Is it possible to describe situations at all? One could conceivably describe them in terms of external stimulus variables. And perhaps one could imagine a kind of 'grammar' of situations which would be capable of generating the infinite number of possible combinations of situational variables in terms of physical parameters. The main point, however, is this: would such an account or even theory of situations get us any nearer to explaining the problems of cognition in context? I don't think so.

Imagine a fairly simple situation: one person in a mud hut with a snake. The situation may be described physically in terms of the parameters of the hut, the position of the snake, the viewpoint of the person, and so on. Now imagine that in this situation the person was an Amazonian Indian. He would see the situation in certain ways, focussing on certain aspects of it and not others. But, whatever the situation represented to him, it would be quite different for a three-year-old child, Tarzan, or a zoologist specializing in snakes. And for each of them, the situation would be different again according to whether someone had asked them to kill the snake, to describe its anatomy or to charm it with pipe music.

The point is simply that we cannot represent situations independently of the person who is perceiving them or what that person's aims are. The situation of two people can never be identical: it can only look the same to a third observer. What is important about situations is how they are interpreted in terms of a person's current personal goals. And that will depend not just on the cognitive processes which he can employ, but on his whole system of personal constructs (Kelly, 1955).

Cognitive processes cannot be represented independently of the situations in which they are used or the purposes to which they are put. By the same argument, situations cannot be represented independently of the person who is perceiving them or his aims in them. A 'theory of situations' would not begin to help explain the situational determinants of cognitive functioning.

Functional cognitive systems

The second aspect of Cole and Scribner's framework emphasizes the purposes and functions of cognitive processes. Cognitive processes are not just ways of representing the world. We mostly represent the world in order to do something about it. Or as Neisser (1976) succinctly puts it: 'Perception and cognition are usually not just operations in the head, but transactions in the world.'

As a basis for discussing the purposefulness of cognition, Cole and Scribner have used the Vygotsky-Luria concept of higher mental processes as being complex, organized, functional systems (Vygotsky, 1978; Luria, 1966). These functional systems consist of components which are represented in different areas of the brain. The components are combined in various ways depending on the particular task at hand. Luria stresses that neither the components nor the functional relations into which they enter are present at birth, but are formed during the child's development. So developmental changes will take place not only in basic component processes but also in the inter-functional relations of those processes. And all these changes will be closely dependent on the child's social/cultural experiences.

It is not exactly clear what Cole and Scribner mean by 'component processes' nor how literally they take Luria's account of them. One example they give is categorization, which can be a component process of remembering, although obviously there is no indication that there is a single categorization area in the brain. Despite the considerable ambiguities in their account, the theme of functional systems may prove to be a useful one. A similar theme was emphasized long ago by Bartlett (1932) when he complained of 'faculty psychology' whereby mental processes are studied in isolation from each other without regard to their inter-dependencies and inter-relationships.

The functional systems approach is hardly a theory, but as a way of approaching experimental results it does have appeal in comparative research, if not more generally. It does not resolve the problem of the situation-dependent nature of cognition, although it does assume that how components are organized to meet particular goals will depend on situational factors. As applied cross-culturally, Cole and Scribner stress that we are unlikely to find cultural differences in basic component processes. Instead:

If cultural differences are assumed to be reflected in the way functional systems are organized for various purposes, then a double line of research becomes important: the first is to uncover the culturally determined experimental factors that give rise to different dominant functional systems . . . the second is to determine which situational features – content domain, task requirements – call out which functional organisations (1974 p. 194).

Alan Allport's chapter *Patterns and Actions* looks at how the idea of functional systems can be tightened and elaborated.

Experiments in context

Once we conceptualize cognitive processes in terms of their functional organizations and situational determinants, Cole (1975) argues that experiments are insufficient for making inferences about cultural differences in cognition. Instead he calls for 'an ethnographic psychology of cognition', whereby ethnographic techniques of observation in the field are combined with psychological techniques of experimentation in controlled conditions.

Cole sees two ways in which this combination of techniques and data might be utilized. First, ethnographic data can be used to 'check' experimental results so that when laboratory findings go against what is observed in everyday situations, those findings are questioned. Second, ethnographic data can be used in designing experiments so that they can be based on analogies to everyday problem-solving activities.

In effect, what Cole is suggesting is a very direct way of determining the ecological validity of experimental studies: observing what goes on in the 'real world' as well as what happens in laboratories. Clearly, if we want ecological validity, we will have to look further than the laboratory to find it. This does not, however, mean abandoning experiments but rather an interplay between laboratory and field methods.

Cognitive psychologists are reluctant to work outside the laboratory because natural behaviour is uncontrollable and hard to interpret. Cole *et al.* (1971) provide a clear illustration of these problems in their own research on Kpelle problem-solving and verbal reasoning. Moving on from classic, Aristotelian syllogisms, they tried to use some very different kinds of data obtained from observing behaviour in traditional games and in Kpelle law courts. Treated as isolated data, both the games and the law court discussions proved too complex and ambiguous to interpret. The point that Cole stresses is that field data should not be treated as if it were a substitute for experimental results but as a basis for devising experiments.

There is actually nothing new in this approach, although it is one which psychologists have been slow to exploit. Ethologists, for example, long gave up any hope of understanding animal behaviour on the basis of laboratory studies alone. A rat in a Skinner box does not behave like a rat in the wild, and pigeons pecking coloured keys seem a far cry from pigeons navigating in races. Ethologists have successfully combined field studies of wild animals with laboratory studies for many years now. Even closer to home, studies in child socialization and language acquisition are increasingly using this approach, especially now that video-recording has made possible more sophisticated observational techniques.

Moreover, there is no need to stop at just an ethnographic approach to cognition. If we look to ethology for our methodological lessons, we find there are several stages between the two extremes of laboratory experiments and field observation. Both experimental and observational techniques can be used in both field and laboratory situations. Ethology has found its richest data base is obtained from using several combinations (cf. Blurton-Jones, 1972).

Natural behaviour is ambiguous; but by basing experiments on observed behaviour, by using parallels of everyday problem-solving activities in laboratory studies, we can progressively reduce those ambiguities and analyse the sequences and combinations of processes involved. Perhaps more importantly, by comparing observational and experimental data obtained in various situations, we can increasingly clarify what are the crucial differences between situations for differences in cognitive functioning. It follows from functional systems approach that the crucial contextual cues for different functional systems will vary not only culturally but also developmentally.

All this will undoubtedly increase the complexities, as well as broaden the range, of experimentation. But this in turn will pay off in greater relevance and generalizability. And as yet, there is no viable alternative.

Conclusions: their thoughts and our psychology

This chapter began by arguing that cross-cultural studies were necessary to the development of a general science of cognition. It should be clear that their contribution to date has been strictly limited. The investigation of cultural differences and universals relies on existing theories of cognition. So far, the search for universals has found more about the problems with our understanding of cognitive processes than about any cultural variations in them. If deficits exist on any side, they are in our theories rather than the people we study.

Theoretical deficits derive from attempts to represent cognitive processes in a vacuum, independently of the situations in which they are used or the purposes to which they are put. Generalizing from laboratory studies to everyday cognition presents a crucial problem for the whole of cognitive psychology. In cross-cultural studies, the problem is simply more obvious because the gap between laboratory and field, between problem-solving in experiments and everyday behaviour, is so much wider. But just as, on the one hand, the study of culture and cognition has highlighted shortcomings in our concepts of cognition, so also, on the other hand, it has highlighted shortcomings in our understanding of culture.

Rosch's research provides a clear example of how cultural variation can be used to create natural laboratory conditions for testing theories. Her studies used cross-cultural variation in language categories to test a very specific hypothesis about linguistic effects on memory for colours. The methodological and interpretive problems involved in this kind of research are minimal compared with most intra-cultural studies which have looked for global effects of particular environmental factors. Questions phrased in terms of the *effects* of Variable X (schooling, literacy, ecology, language, urbanization, malnutrition, etc.) *on* cognitive development or *on* adult thought processes have produced ambiguous findings. It is unlikely that we will find any general effects of Variable X, both because that variable itself is so complex and because it will interact with many of the others. Such studies will continue to produce ambiguous findings until the interdependencies and complexities of those variables are clarified, both conceptually and empirically. Only then can we begin to draw up explicit hypotheses about about how they might affect cognition.

We can now see that our original question – are there cultural differences in cognitive processes? – is not so simple as it seemed.

Studies which have tackled this question by direct confrontation have produced no clear answers. There is no evidence to date that cultural groups vary in their repertoires of cognitive processes. Rather, cultural differences have been shown to reside in the contexts in which particular processes are combined into functional systems. Questions about whether different cultural groups 'have' certain ways of thinking and reasoning have now been replaced by questions about the contexts in which those thought processes are applied.

To understand the situational determinants of cognition, it was argued that what we do not want is a theory of situations. Rather, we need to emphasize the purposefulness of cognition and investigate not only cognitive processes in isolation but also their functional inter-relationships. One line which might be developed profitably for this is the concept of functional systems.

Empirically, a context-sensitive approach means that laboratory experiments alone may be insufficient for making inferences about cultural differences in cognitive processes. This is clearly the case when observations of everyday behaviour conflict with conclusions from experiments.

But it is not enough merely to demonstrate that a group who does not use particular cognitive processes in situation A does use them in situation B. Although such studies have drawn attention to the whole issue of cognition in context, simply documenting what people do and do not do in a multitude of situations can only produce a mass of unrelated data. We have to stipulate precisely what differences in those situations are crucial. So, to go back to the conservation example, if a group does not conserve in the classic situation but does conserve in situation A, what differences in those situations are causing the differences in behaviour? This question first involves delineating the possible contextual factors which differ between the two situations (e.g., format of questioning, comprehension of particular words, types of perceptual cues). On that basis, one can then go on to identify which ones are crucial by controlling varying combinations of factors in situations B, C, D, and so on. The number of alternative situations examined could be reduced by the careful use of observational, as well as experimental, techniques.

The functional systems approach combined with varied data sources has several clear repercussions for both developmental and main-line psychology. If we are to do more than pay lip-service to the demand for ecological validity, then it has precisely the same advantages for research within the west as it has for cross-cultural studies. It has a very direct application to developmental studies where the issues about the contextualization of cognitive processes parallel those in cross-cultural research. But its potential implications go beyond comparative studies. Experimenters in the west generally have an *implicit* ethnography: they know their subjects' experiences and activities mostly because they share them (as with undergraduates) or have controlled them (as with rats). What is needed is to make this ethnography explicit by going outside the laboratory and collecting objective field data.

This in turn will entail a greater emphasis on cognitive functioning. It will also require a greater concern with the generality of theory, both across situations and across different groups of people. This means phrasing hypotheses so that implications can be drawn out for not only main-line but also developmental and cross-cultural research. As Rosch (1977) stresses, any truly general theory should have implications for all these fields. In turn, it is important that researchers should base their studies on theory and not simply on their associated experimental procedures. One of the frequent criticisms of cross-cultural Piagetian research is that people have too often followed Piaget's procedures rather than his theory. Certainly, the greater co-operation of researchers across the spectrum of cognitive psychology should prove profitable in itself.

It is appropriate to finish on a reflexive note and put western psychology itself within its own cultural context. The concepts of cognitive psychology reflect western cultural values: emphasizing rational thought, 'going beyond the information given', trading off speed and accuracy, cognition as divorced from any social or affective context. The major theory positing universal stages in intellectual development is almost totally concerned with *logical* abilities. A pertinent contrast is seen in how Baganda villagers in Wober's (1974) study conceptualized 'intelligence': spiritual, careful and friendly.

The very questions we ask about human cognition are enmeshed in our own cultural traditions. Consider an often quoted piece from Bertrand Russell (1927):

Animals studied by Americans rush about frantically with an incredible display of hustle and pep, and at last achieve the desired result by chance. Animals observed by Germans sit still and think, and at last evolve the solution out of their inner consciousness.

The obvious point is not that there are cultural differences between American and German *rats,* but that working in different traditions, American and German *psychologists* were posing their animals different problems.

Similarly today, despite the increasing availability of translated non-western research, much of it is ignored within the west simply because it is not investigating the same issues. Chinese studies, for example, within the Maoist theory of human conflict (cf. You-Yuh, 1976) or Russian research emphasizing the social and historical origins of higher mental processes (cf. Cole and Maltzman, 1969; Luria, 1976) remain outside our frame of reference precisely because they are asking different questions. This is not to call for a study in cross-cultural 'psychologist-ology', but simply to point out that an awareness of our own cultural assumptions, values and goals is necessary before we can export our theories to foreign lands.

Acknowledgments

For helpful comments on a first draft of this chapter, the author thanks Guy Claxton, Esther Goody, Paul Jorion, Elena Lieven, Barbara Lloyd, Mike Pickering and Howard Reid. She is also grateful to the Trustees of the Susan Isaac's Research Fund for financial support.

References

Ashton, P. T. (1975), 'Cross-cultural Piagetian research: an experimental perspective', *Harvard Educational Review*, 45, pp. 475-506.
Bartlett, F. C. (1932), *Remembering*, Cambridge University Press.
Bereiter, C. and Engelmann, S. (1966), *Teaching Disadvantaged Children in the Pre-school*, Prentice-Hall: Englewood Cliffs, N. J.
Berlin, B. and Kay, P. (1969), *Basic Color Terms: Their Universality and Evolution*, University of Chicago Press.
Bernstein, B. (1970), 'Social class, language and socialization', in P. P. Giglioli (ed.), *Language and Social Context*, Penguin: Harmondsworth.
Blurton-Jones, N. (1972), 'Characteristics of ethological studies of human behaviour', in N. Blurton- Jones (ed.), *Ethological Studies of Child Behaviour*, Cambridge University Press.
Blurton-Jones, N. and Konner, M. J. (1976), '!Kung knowledge of animal behaviour', in R. B. Lee and I. Devore (eds), *Kalahari Hunter Gatherers: Studies of the !Kung San and their Neighbors*, Harvard University Press.

Boas, F. (1911), *The Mind of Primitive Man*, republished: Free Press: New York, 1965.

Bornstein, M. H. (1975), 'The influence of visual perception on culture', *American Anthropologist, 77*, pp. 774-98.

Brislin, R. W., Bochner, S. and Lonner, W. J. (eds) (1975), *Cross-cultural Perspectives on Learning*, Halstead Press: New York.

Brown, R. and Lenneberg, E. H. (1954), 'A study in language and cognition', *Journal of Abnormal and Social Psychology, 49*, pp. 454-62.

Bruner, J. S., Olver, R. R. and Greenfield, P. M. (1966), *Studies in Cognitive Growth*, Wiley: New York.

Burnham, R. W. and Clark, J. R. (1955), 'A test of hue memory', *Journal of Applied Psychology, 39*, pp. 164-72.

Campbell, D. T. (1961), 'The mutual methodological relevance of anthropology and psychology', in F. L. K. Hsu (ed.), *Psychological Anthropology*, Dorsey Press: Homewood, Ill.

Cole, M. (1975), 'An ethnographic psychology of cognition', in R. W. Brislin, S. Bochner and W. J. Lonner (eds), *Cross-cultural Perspectives on Learning*, Halstead Press: New York.

Cole, M. and Bruner, J. S. (1971), 'Cultural differences and inferences about psychological processes', *American Psychologist, 26*, pp. 867-76.

Cole, M., Gay, J., Glick, J. and Sharp, D. W. (1971), *The Cultural Context of Learning and Thinking*, Basic Books: New York.

Cole, M. and Maltzman, I. (1969), *A Handbook of Contemporary Soviet Psychology*, Basic Books: New York.

Cole, M. and Scribner, S. (1974), *Culture and Thought: a Psychological Introduction*, Wiley: New York.

Dasan, P. R. (1972a), 'Cross-cultural Piagetian research: a summary', *Journal of Cross-Cultural Psychology, 3*, pp. 23-39.

Dasen, P. R. (1972b), 'The development of conservation in Aboriginal children: a replication', *International Journal of Psychology, 7*, pp. 75-86.

Dasen, P. R. (1977), 'Are cognitive processes universal? A contribution to cross-cultural Piagetian psychology', in N. Warren (ed.), *Studies in Cross-Cultural Psychology*, Academic Press: New York.

De Lacey, P. R. (1970), 'A cross-cultural study of classificatory ability in Australia', *Journal of Cross-Cultural Psychology, 1*, pp. 293-304.

De Lemos, M. M. (1974), 'The development of spatial concepts in Zulu children', in J. W. Berry and P. R. Dasen (eds), *Culture and Cognition: Readings in Cross-Cultural Psychology*, Methuen: London.

Doob, L. (1961), *Communication in Africa: A Search for Boundaries*, Yale University Press.

Evans-Pritchard, E. E. (1937), *Witchcraft, Oracles and Magic among the Azande*, Clarendon: Oxford.

Fahrmeier, E. D. (1975), 'The effect of school attendance on intellectual development in Northern Nigeria', Child Development, 46, pp. 281-5.

Flavell, J. H. and Wohlwill, J. F. (1969), 'Formal and functional aspects of cognitive development', in D. Elkind and J. H. Flavell (eds), *Studies in Cognitive Development*, Oxford University Press: New York.

Fodor, J. A. (1976), *The Language of Thought*, Harvester Press: Hassocks, Sussex.

Frijda, N. and Jahoda, G. (1966), 'On the scope and methods of cross-cultural research', *International Journal of Psychology, 1*, pp. 29-54.

Goody, J. and Watt, I. (1963), 'The consequences of literacy', *Comparative Studies in Society and History*, vol. 5, pp. 304-45.

Greenfield, P. M. (1966), 'On culture and conservation', in J. S. Bruner, R. R. Oliver and P. M. Greenfield, *Studies in Cognitive Growth*, Wiley: New York.

Greenfield, P. M. and Childs, C. (1974), 'Weaving, color terms and pattern representation: cultural influence and cognitive development among the Zinacantecos of Southern Mexico', in J. L. M. Dawson and W. J. Lonner (eds), *Readings in Cross-Cultural Psychology*, University of Hong Kong Press.

Greenfield, P. M., Reich, L. C. and Olver, R. R. (1966), 'On culture and equivalence, II', in J. S. Bruner, R. R. Olver and P. M. Greenfield, *Studies in Cognitive Growth*, Wiley: New York.

Heider, E. R. (1972), 'Universals in colour naming and memory', *Journal of Experimental Psychology, 93*, pp. 10-20.

Heron, A. (1971), 'Concrete operations, "g" and achievement in Zambian children', *Journal of Cross-Cultural Psychology, 2*, pp. 325-36.

Heron, A. (1974), 'Cultural determinants of concrete operational behaviour', in J. L. M. Dawson and W. J. Lonner (eds), *Readings in Cross-Cultural Psychology*, University of Hong Kong Press.

Heron, A. and Dowel, W. (1973), 'Weight conservation and matrix-solving ability in Papuan children', *Journal of Cross-Cultural Psychology, 4*, pp. 207-19.

Heron, A. and Dowel, W. (1974), 'The questionable unity of the concrete operations stage', *International Journal of Psychology, 9*, pp. 1-9.

Hickerson, N. P. (1971), Review of 'Basic colour terms: their universality and evolution', *International Journal of American Linguistics, 37*, pp. 257-70.

Hockett, C. F. (1954), 'Chinese versus English: an exploration of the Whorfian thesis', in H. Hoijer (ed.), *Language in Culture*, University of Chicago Press.

Irwin, M. H. and McLaughlin, D. H. (1970), 'Ability and preference in category sorting by Mano school children and adults', *Journal of Social Psychology, 82*, pp. 15-24.

Johnson-Laird, P. N. and Wason, P. C. (1977), *Thinking: Readings in Cognitive Science*, Cambridge University Press.

Kelly, G. (1955), *The Psychology of Personal Constructs*, Norton: New York.

Labov, W. (1969), 'The logic of nonstandard English', *Georgetown Monographs on Language and Linguistics, 22*, pp. 1-31.

Lenneberg, E. H. (1961), 'Colour naming, colour recognition, colour discrimination: a reappraisal', *Perceptual and Motor Skills, 12*, pp. 375-92.

Levi-Strauss, C. (1966), *The Savage Mind*, University of Chicago Press.

Lloyd, B. B. (1972), *Perception and Cognition: a Cross-Cultural Perspective*, Penguin: Harmondsworth.

Lloyd, B. B. (1977), 'Culture and colour coding', in G. Vesey (ed.), *Communication and Understanding*, Harvester Press: Hassocks, Sussex.

Luria, A. R. (1966), *Higher Cortical Functions in Man*, Basic Books: New York.

Luria, A. R. (1971), 'Towards the problem of the historical nature of psychological processes', *International Journal of Psychology*, 6, pp. 259-72.

Luria, A. R. (1976), *Cognitive Development, its Cultural and Social Foundations*, Harvard University Press.

McDaniel, C. K. (1972), 'Hue perception and hue naming', unpublished A. B. Honors thesis, Harvard College.

Malinowski, B. (1954), *Magic, Science and Religion*, Doubleday: New York.

Miller, G. A. and McNeill, D. (1969), 'Psycholinguistics', in G. Lindsey and E. Aronson (eds), *Handbook of Social Psychology*, vol. 3, Addison-Wesley: Reading, Massachusetts.

Neisser, U. (1976), *Cognition and Reality*, Freeman: San Francisco.

Piaget, J. (1966), 'Nécessité et signification des recherches comparatives en psychologie génétique', *International Journal of Psychology*, 1, pp. 3-13.

Piaget, J. (1972), 'Intellectual evolution from adolescence to adulthood', *Human Development*, 15, pp. 1-12.

Pollnac, R. B. and Jahn, G. (1976), 'Culture and memory revisited: an example from Buganda', *Journal of Cross-Cultural Psychology*, 7, pp. 73-85.

Price-Williams, D. R. (1975), 'Primitive mentality – civilized style', in R. W. Brislin, S. Bochner and W. J. Lonner (eds), *Cross-cultural Perspectives on Learning*, Halstead Press: New York.

Price-Williams, D. R., Gordon, W. and Ramirez, M. (1969), 'Skill and conservation: a study of pottery making children', *Developmental Psychology*, 1, 769.

Rosch, E. (1975), 'Universals and culture specifics in human categorization', in R. W. Brislin, S. Bochner and W. J. Lonner (eds), *Cross-Cultural Perspectives on Learning*, Halstead Press: New York.

Rosch, E. (1977), 'Human categorization', in N. Warren (ed.), *Studies in Cross-Cultural Psychology*, Academic Press: New York.

Russell, B. (1927), *An Outline of Philosophy*, Allen & Unwin: London.

Sahlins, M. (1976), 'Colours and cultures', *Semiotica*, 16, pp. 1-22.

Scribner, S. (1974), 'Developmental aspects of categorized recall in a West African society', *Cognitive Psychology*, 6, pp. 475-94.

Scribner, S. (1977), 'Modes of thinking and ways of speaking: culture and logic reconsidered', in R. O. Freedle (ed.), *Discourse Production and Comprehension*, Lawrence Erlbaum: Hillsdale, N. J.

Scribner, S. and Cole, M. (1973), 'Cognitive consequences of formal and informal education', *Science*, 182, pp. 553-9.

Segall, M., Campbell, D. and Herskovits, M. (1966), *The Influence of Culture on Visual Perception*, Bobbs-Merrill: Indianapolis.

Serpell, R. (1976), *Culture's Influence on Behaviour*, Methuen: London.

Shweder, R. A. (1977), 'Likeness and likelihood in everyday thought: magical thinking in everyday judgments about personality', *Current Anthropology*, 18, pp. 637-58.

Vygotsky, L. S. (1978), *Mind in Society: the Development of Higher Psychological Processes*, Harvard University Press.

Warren, N. (1977), *Studies in Cross-Cultural Psychology*, Academic Press: New York.

Whorf, B. L. (1956), *Language, Thought and Reality*, Wiley: New York.

Wober, M. (1969), 'Distinguishing centri-cultural from cross-cultural tests and research', *Perceptual and Motor Skills, 28*, p. 488.

Wober, M. (1974), 'Towards an understanding of the Kiganda concept of intelligence', in J. W. Berry and P. R. Dasen (eds), *Culture and Cognition: Readings in Cross-Cultural Psychology*, Methuen: London.

You-Yuh, K. (1976), 'China', in V. S. Sexton and H. K. Misiak (eds), *Psychology around the World*, Brooks Cole: Belmont, California.

Index

Action, 33, 53, 188-9; communicative, 236; control of, 28; domains of, 141, 143, 145; modes of, 40; planning, 77-9; styles of, 269; system, 144; *see also* metaphor
Adams, J.A., 86, 90-2, 95
Allport, D.A., 184
alpha-gamma coactivation, 70
Anderson, J.R., 207-13, 219, 220, 230
Anderson, R.C., 207, 210, 213
aphasia, conduction, 50
apraxias, 49
arithmetical calculation, 138, 180-2
articulation, 93; articulatory suppression, 167-9, 179-81
artificial intelligence, 29, 30, 31, 36, 52, 54, 101, 275-6, 297; *see also* computer
assimilation, 54
associationist philosophy, 276
associations: conceptual, 220-1; contextual, 218-20, 222; serial, 220-1
Atkinson, R.C., 158, 186, 222-3
attention, 44, 54, 112, 122, 147; divided, 39, 41, 146; selective, 114; unattended stimuli, 47, 129; working memory and, 184-5

Baddeley, A.D., 54, 56, 157, 162, 167, 177, 179, 212, 230
Barber, P.J., 97
behaviourism, 65-6, 277; radical, 26
Berlin, B., 311
Bever, T., 240-2
Black, M., 256
blindsight, 46
Bobrow, D.G., 117-21
Boies, S.J., 134

bottleneck, 114-5, 137, 142
Bower, G.H., 207-9, 219-20, 225
Bransford, J.D., 208-9, 213
Broadbent, D.E., 114, 169, 184, 223
Brooks, L.R., 281, 287
Brown, R., 308
Bruner, J.S., 201, 316

calling-patterns, 18, 20, 34, 37, 43, 51, 128, 185; conflict between, 129
cell assemblies, 28, 204
Chernikoff, R., 88
Chomsky, N., 239, 321
Clark, E.V., 174, 177
Clark, H.H., 10, 174, 177, 244, 249, 253, 285-6
Claxton, G.L., 155
cognition, situational determinants of, 320, 328
Cole, M., 306, 314, 316, 318-20, 322, 325
Collins, A.M., 1-18, 212-13
colour salience, 310
compatibility, 135; ideo-motor, 45, 136; spatial, 45; S – R, 44; *see also* ideo-motor hypothesis
computer, 27; simulation, 30; *see also* artificial intelligence
conceptualization, 15
consciousness, 48, 112, 113, 161
conservation experiments, 318
content-free processes, 10-14, 211; *see also* processing
content-specific processes, 201; *see also* interference, data-specific; processing
control structure, 54
corollary discharge, 82
Craik, F.I.M., 160, 211

335

cross-cultural studies, 187, 300
cue: overload, 43; strength, 44
cultural differences, 300, 327; deficit
    interpretation of, 316-17; in literacy,
    313, 327; in schooling, 313-15, 327

Dasen, P.R., 316, 318
deafferentation, 87
decision tables, 245
declarative knowledge, 200, 229-30
déjà vu, 224
demons: action, 41, 42; cognitive, 28, 32;
    goal, 43
depth of processing, 160, 211-12
dichotic listening, 126, 131, 133; *see also*
    simultaneous, monitoring
dictionary units, 28, 33
disorders of writing, 50
dissociation of function, 49
Dixon, N.F., 72

ecological validity, 19, 157, 189, 301-2
effort, 116, 118
elaboration, 209, 211
encoding specificity, 226, 228
epiphenomena, 283, 294
episodic memory, 200, 230
error, 5; absent-minded, 34; recovery
    from, 138
ethnographic psychology, 325
Evans, J.StB.T., 287, 290-3
execution phase, 245; *see also* translation
experiential knowledge, 16, 231-2

feedback, 73; augmented, 79; extrinsic,
    79; interoceptive, 80; intrinsic, 80;
    kinaesthetic, 84-9; as knowledge of
    results, 80-7; loop, 67
feedforward, 73
flow-charts, 30
Fodor, J., 240-2, 322
frames, 210
Franks, J.J., 208, 213
Fromkin, V., 176
functional cognitive systems, 324, 328

Galanter, E., 42, 65, 77
general-purpose, limited-capacity,
    central processor, 22, 50, 55, 56, 112,
    121, 142; central executive, 168-72,
    182; password hypothesis, 115; *see also*
    working memory
Golgi tendon organs, 70

grammar: transformational, 238-40
Greenfield, P.M., 300, 314
Greenwald, A.G., 75-6, 82, 135
Greer, K., 72
Groen, G.J., 181-2

Hebb, D.O., 28, 204, 223
hemispheric specialization, 292
Henle, M., 255
Henry, F.M., 75, 77
Hewitt, C., 42
Hitch, G.J., 162, 167, 177, 180
homunculus, 37, 57, 113, 124
Huttenlocher, J., 285-6

ideo-motor hypothesis, 75
imagery, 276, 280-1, 294; as memory aid,
    225; picture metaphor, 283-4; in
    transitive inference, 285-8
inference: linguistic theory of, 285-8; *see
    also* reasoning
information processing, 26, 31, 51; and
    imagery, 281; unconscious, 46-8; *see
    also* thinking
information theory, 27
interference, 116, 119, 130; data-specific,
    139; dual-task, 118, 169-71; structural,
    117
introspection, 26, 275-6; protocol
    analysis, 278-9, 294; rationalization,
    291-2, 297; reports, 280, 285, 294-7
item, 11

Jarvella, R.J., 174
Johnson-Laird, P.N., 31, 244, 250, 252,
    261, 278, 289-90, 305
joint receptors, 71
Juola, J., 222-3

Kahneman, D., 116-21, 128, 143, 169
Kay, P., 311
kinaesthetic receptors, 72
Kleiman, G.M., 179
Kosslyn, S., 283-4, 293

language: and colour coding, 308-12; and
    thought, 306
Lashley, K.S., 87, 88, 176
learning, 9, 22, 230; as
    decontextualization, 20; verbal, 206,
    224, 282, 297
Legge, D., 97-8
Lenneberg, E., 308-9

Levi-Strauss, C., 311
limited capacity, 28, 31, 51, 113, 114, 122-3, 134, 142, 147; data-specific limitations, 38-9, 55, 141, 145; function-specific limitations, 144, 148; *see also* resource
limits: attentional, 125; performance, 125; psychology of, 4-5; *see also* limited capacity
linguistic relativity, 307-9, 312
Lloyd, B.B., 308
localization of function, 48
Lockhart, R.S., 211, 160
logogens, 28
Lucy, P., 249, 253
Luria, A.R., 313, 324

McCarrell, N.S., 257, 259, 260, 263
McLeod, P.D., 135, 170
MacNeilage, P.F., 102
man-as-scientist, 18
Marcel, A.J., 47
Memory, 2, 12, 32, 197, 294-5; associative metaphor, 198-205; content-addressible, 38; integrative metaphor, 198-205; network models, 17; span, 51, 166-9, 171, 176; storage metaphor, 214-16
'memory-drum' model, 75
mental experience, 275, 277, 279-83; *see also* introspection; thinking
mentalism, 279, 293
metamemory, 198; recognition as, 223-4
metaphor, 252-65; as communicative action, 252; comprehension of, 253; computer as, 13; as contextual-anomaly, 258; for Mind, 16; psychological approaches, 257-65; traditional theories of, 253-7; *see also* action; computer
Miller, G.A., 42, 65, 77, 244, 252, 261
mnemonics, 225-6
Moray, N., 127
Morton, J., 33, 175, 184, 221, 223
motivation, 39-40; GOAL, 39, 43
motoneurons, 69
motor control, 53, 65; heterarchical, 76-7; hierarchical, 76; inflow, closed-loop theories of, 87; outflow, open-loop theories of, 87
motor equivalence, 92
motor programme, 84
Murdock, B.B., 217-18
muscle spindles, 69

natural laboratories, 303
Neisser, U., 29, 115, 148, 157, 277, 279, 282, 324
neuropsychology, 49
Newell, A., 3, 31, 34, 42, 182, 186, 229, 277-8
Nickerson, R., 32
Norman, D.A., 115, 117-21, 162, 169, 294

Occurrence information, 216; contextual associations, 218-20, 222; strength, 216-18, 222
organization: adaptive, 237; modular, 32, 33
Ortony, A., 207, 213, 258-61, 263

Paivio, A., 282
pandemonium, 28, 30
Parkman, J.M., 181-2
pattern perception, 37; motor theories of, 99; speech, 101, 173-5; working memory and, 183-4
Perky phenomenon, 281-2
personal world, 249; inter-personal world, 250; intra-personal world, 250
phoneme monitoring, 174-5
phonemic coding, 159-61, 166
Piaget, J., 316, 322
Pomerantz, J.R., 283-4
Posner, M.I., 134
practice, 8-9
Pribram, K., 42, 65, 77
primary memory, 5, 162; *see also* working memory
problem-solving, 181-2, 187-8, 278, 281; gestalt approach, 278
procedural knowledge, 200, 229-30
procedural theory, 262; *see also* semantics; translation
processing: automatic *vs* controlled, 121-4, 143; content-dependent, 32, 41; content-specific, 51; data-limited, 118-19; distributed, 33, 41, 52, 124; resource-limited, 118-19
production systems, 18, 21, 34, 36, 53, 182, 188; productions, 34, 127
proprioceptors, 72
psychological refractory period, 128, 133-6
Pylyshyn, Z.W., 279, 282-4, 293

Quillian, M.R., 1-18, 212-13

reaction time, 4-8; kinaesthetic 88
reading, 49, 129, 139, 178-80
reasoning and inference: dual process theory of, 292-3; logical and non-logical, 292; mathematical models, 296; propositional, 288-93; transitive, 19, 284-8; *see also* thinking
rehearsal, 160, 165,'172, 175
relaxed cognition, 6
resource, 120; general, 118, 120; specific, 118, 120
retrieval: as decomposition, 227; free recall, 158-68, 177; as recruitment, 203, 205, 229; as search-and-decision, 203, 215
Rogers, E.E., 75, 77
Rosch, E.H., 304, 309-10, 312, 327, 329

Schema, 247; model of action, 91; theory of metaphor, 257-61
Schmidt, R.A., 90-2
Schneider, W., 122-4, 128, 129
Scribner, S., 306, 314, 322
Segal, S.J., 281
Selfridge, O., 28
semantic memory, 6, 27, 200, 212-14, 220, 230
semantic processing, 242-4
semantics: procedural, 245
sentences: as associative structures, 202, 206-10; as gestalts, 202, 206-10
shadowing, 175, 179; *see also* attention, selective; simultaneous monitoring
Shallice, T., 144, 177
Shaver, P., 286-8
Shiffrin, R.M., 122-4, 126, 128, 129, 158, 172, 186
short-term memory, 27, 50, 54, 122, 154; short-term visual memory, 172; *see also* working memory
Simon, H.A., 34, 40, 42, 182, 186, 228-9, 277-8
simultaneous: monitoring, 125, 126, 131; targets, 127; tasks, 121, 140-1, 169-71
skill acquisition, 97
skilled transcription tasks, 136; abacus, 138; piano playing, 136; typing, 140
space-co-ordinate system, 93; egocentric, 94
speech production, 175-7
Sternberg, S., 77
stories, 265-70, 210-11

strategies, 6, 201, 209
Stroop phenomenon, 130, 145
subjects in psychological experiments, 7-8
subliminal stimuli, 72
symbolic activity, cycles of, 251
systems, 14; *see also* action

tacit processing, 11-12; *see also* thinking, unconscious
Taylor, F.V., 88
thinking: as information processing, 277, 279, 282, 293; as mental experience, 275, 279-80, 293; parallel processes, 292, 296; unconscious, 276, 292; *see also* reasoning; tacit processing
Thompson, D.M., 226
timekeeper, 96
TOTE unit, 42, 44, 67-70, 87
transcortical reflex, 89
transition network, 247; semantic, 247; text, 268
translation: forward and backward scanning, 266; phase, 245; procedural, 245; translation-execution strategy, 250, 253
Treisman, A., 28, 33, 131, 133, 175
Tulving, E., 43, 200, 201, 211, 226, 229, 230
Turvey, M., 92, 98, 102
Tversky, A., 263

Verbrugge, R.R., 257, 259, 260, 263
Visual search, 121, 128
Vygotsky, L., 313, 324

Warrington, E., 177
Wason, P.C., 249, 278, 288, 290-3, 305
Wason selection task, 288-93; information processing model, 290, 293; matching bias, 290; 'therapeutic' procedures, 289; verification bias, 289, 291
Waugh, N.C., 162
Whorf, B.L., 307, 312
word-meanings, 201; effect of context on, 207-8; as fuzzy sets, 36, 202, 204; as netlets, 201
working memory, 34, 53, 57, 154, 162, 173; articulatory subsystem, 166-8, 175-81; input register, 162-6, 174-5, 177-9; *see also* short-term memory; primary memory